solutions@syngress.com

With more than 1,500,000 copies of our MCSE, MCSD, CompTIA, and Cisco study guides in print, we continue to look for ways we can better serve the information needs of our readers. One way we do that is by listening.

Readers like yourself have been telling us they want an Internet-based service that would extend and enhance the value of our books. Based on reader feedback and our own strategic plan, we have created a Web site that we hope will exceed your expectations.

Solutions@syngress.com is an interactive treasure trove of useful information focusing on our book topics and related technologies. The site offers the following features:

- One-year warranty against content obsolescence due to vendor product upgrades. You can access online updates for any affected chapters.
- "Ask the Author" customer query forms that enable you to post questions to our authors and editors.
- Exclusive monthly mailings in which our experts provide answers to reader queries and clear explanations of complex material.
- Regularly updated links to sites specially selected by our editors for readers desiring additional reliable information on key topics.

Best of all, the book you're now holding is your key to this amazing site. Just go to **www.syngress.com/solutions**, and keep this book handy when you register to verify your purchase.

Thank you for giving us the opportunity to serve your needs. And be sure to let us know if there's anything else we can do to help you get the maximum value from your investment. We're listening.

www.syngress.com/solutions

SYNGRESS®

SYNGRESS®

1 YEAR UPGRADE
BUYER PROTECTION PLAN

Check Point
NG

Next
Generation
Security
Administration

Drew Simonis CISSP, CCSE

Corey S. Pincock CISSP, CCSA

Daniel Kligerman CCSE

Doug Maxwell CCSI

Cherie Amon CCSI, Technical Editor

Allen Keele CCSI, Technical Reviewer

KEY	SERIAL NUMBER
001	L9F8TM93QD
002	AFG5Y4MPE4
003	VMER634RTN
004	SGD34BAS6Y
005	8Q5TYU6NVH
006	NFG477JEM4
007	BK7VFTR46T
008	2PMK9965MR
009	83N5C6YDAS
010	GT6YDR46FC

PUBLISHED BY
Syngress Publishing, Inc.
800 Hingham Street
Rockland, MA 02370

Check Point Next Generation Security Administration

Printed in the United States of America

1 2 3 4 5 6 7 8 9 0

ISBN: 1-928994-74-1

Technical Editor: Cherie Amon
Technical Reviewer: Allen Keele
Acquisitions Editor: Jonathan E. Babcock
Indexer: Nara Wood

Cover Designer: Michael Kavish
Page Layout and Art by: Shannon Tozier
Copy Editor: Janet Zunkel

Distributed by Publishers Group West in the United States and Jaguar Book Group in Canada.

Acknowledgments

We would like to acknowledge the following people for their kindness and support in making this book possible.

Ralph Troupe, Rhonda St. John, and the team at Callisma for their invaluable insight into the challenges of designing, deploying and supporting world-class enterprise networks.

Karen Cross, Lance Tilford, Meaghan Cunningham, Kim Wylie, Harry Kirchner, Kevin Votel, Kent Anderson, Frida Yara, Bill Getz, Jon Mayes, John Mesjak, Peg O'Donnell, Sandra Patterson, Betty Redmond, Roy Remer, Ron Shapiro, Patricia Kelly, Andrea Tetrick, Jennifer Pascal, Doug Reil, and David Dahl of Publishers Group West for sharing their incredible marketing experience and expertise.

Jacquie Shanahan and AnnHelen Lindeholm of Elsevier Science for making certain that our vision remains worldwide in scope.

Annabel Dent and Paul Barry of Harcourt Australia for all their help.

David Buckland, Wendi Wong, Marie Chieng, Lucy Chong, Leslie Lim, Audrey Gan, and Joseph Chan of Transquest Publishers for the enthusiasm with which they receive our books.

Kwon Sung June at Acorn Publishing for his support.

Ethan Atkin at Cranbury International for his help in expanding the Syngress program.

Jackie Gross, Gayle Voycey, Alexia Penny, Anik Robitaille, Craig Siddall, Darlene Morrow, Iolanda Miller, Jane Mackay, and Marie Skelly at Jackie Gross & Associates for all their help and enthusiasm representing our product in Canada.

Lois Fraser, Connie McMenemy, Shannon Russell and the rest of the great folks at Jaguar Book Group for their help with distribution of Syngress books in Canada.

Contributors

Drew Simonis (CISSP, CCNA, SCSA, SCNA, CCSA, CCSE, IBM CS) is a Senior Security Engineer with the RL Phillips Group, LLC, where he provides senior level security consulting to the United States Navy, working on large enterprise networks. Drew is a security generalist, with a strong background in system administration, Internet application development, intrusion detection and prevention, and penetration testing. He is a co-author of *Hack Proofing Your Web Applications* (Syngress Publishing, ISBN: 1-928994-31-8) and *Hack Proofing Sun Solaris 8* (Syngress, ISBN: 1-928994-44-X). Drew's background includes various consulting positions with Fiderus, serving as a Security Architect with AT&T and as a Technical Team Lead with IBM. Drew has a bachelor's degree from the University of South Florida and is also a member of American MENSA. He lives in Suffolk, Virginia with his wife, Kym and daughters, Cailyn and Delany. He would like to pay special thanks to Travis Corson and Ron Ostrenga for helping him break into the industry.

Daniel Kligerman (CCSA, CCSE, Extreme Networks GSE, LE) is a Consulting Analyst with TELUS. As a member of TELUS Enterprise Solutions Inc., he specializes in routing, switching, load balancing, and network security in an Internet hosting environment. A University of Toronto graduate, Daniel holds an honors bachelor of science degree in computer science, statistics, and English. Daniel currently resides in Toronto, Canada, and would like to thank Robert, Anne, Lorne, and Merita for their support.

Corey S. Pincock (CISSP, MCSE, GSEC, MCDBA, CCSA, CCNA) is the Senior Information Security Architect for CastleGarde in Tampa, Florida. As an expert in the information security aspects of Graham-Leach-Bliley and HIPAA, Corey consults with financial and healthcare organizations on a national level to implement information security programs that include policy development, risk assessments, security infrastructure design, implementation, training, and monitoring. Other specialties include firewall assessments and audits, Windows 2000, and cryptography. Corey's background includes positions as a Network Administrator for CommerceQuest, Systems Engineer for MicroAge, and Senior Instructor for Certified Tech Trainers. Corey holds a bachelor's degree from the University of Washington and is a member of ISSA. Corey lives in Tampa, Florida with his wife and two daughters. He would like to thank his wife, Shelly for encouraging him to be his best, and Allen Keele of Certified Tech Trainers.

Dan "Effugas" Kaminsky (CISSP) worked for two years at Cisco Systems designing security infrastructure for large-scale network monitoring systems. Dan has delivered presentations at several major industry conferences including Linuxworld, DEF CON, and the Black Hat Briefings, and he also contributes actively to OpenSSH, one of the more significant cryptographic systems in use today. Dan founded the cross-disciplinary DoxPara Research (www.doxpara.com) in 1997, seeking to integrate psychological and technological theory to create more effective systems for non-ideal but very real environments in the field. He is based in Silicon Valley, presently studying Operation and Management of Information Systems at Santa Clara University in California. Dan is also a co-author of the best-selling *Hack Proofing Your Network* (Syngress Publishing, ISBN: 1-928994-70-9).

Jeff Vince (CCSA, CCSE) is a security consultant in Waterloo, Ontario where he specializes in secure network architecture and firewall configuration for medium- to large-scale network installations. His specialties focus on security products ranging from anti-virus software to intrusion detection and enterprise security management software running on the Microsoft Windows and Linux platforms. In addition to normal client consulting work, Jeff has—as part of a team of security professionals—performed successful attack and penetration tests on networks owned by companies ranging from major financial institutions and broadband service providers to smaller software development companies. Working as both an outsider trying to break in and as a security manager responsible for securing corporate assets has given Jeff a unique perspective on network security. Applying this dual vision of security has allowed him to help clients build network infrastructure that provides the high availability and security required in today's Internet environment.

Doug Maxwell (CCSI) is a Senior Network Engineer with Activis, Ltd. in East Hartford, Connecticut. He currently works as a third-tier engineer in the technical support division, and is a certified Check Point instructor. His specialties include Unix network security and firewall network integration. Doug holds a bachelor of science degree in computer science from the University of Massachusetts at Amherst, and is a member of the Association for Computing Machinery (ACM), USENIX, and SAGE, the System Administrator's Guild. He happily resides in Ellington, Connecticut with his wife and 1-year-old son.

Simon Desmeules (CCSE, ISS, MCSE+I, CNA) is an independent security perimeter specialist. He currently provides architectural design, technical consulting, and tactical emergency support for perimeter security technologies for several Fortune 1000 companies in Canada and the United States. Simon's background includes positions as a Firewall / Intrusion Security Specialist for a pioneer of Canadian Security, Maxon Services, and their Managed Security clients. He is an active member of the FW-1, ISS & Snort mailing lists where he discovers new problems and consults with fellow security specialists.

Technical Editor

Cherie Amon (CCSA, CCSE, CCSI) is a Senior Network Security Engineer and Security Instructor for Integralis. She is a Check Point Certified Security Instructor and has been installing, configuring, and supporting Check Point products since 1997. Cherie teaches the Check Point courses at the Integralis Authorized Training Center (ATC) in East Hartford, Connecticut, which is the only Check Point ATC in the state. Prior to working at Integralis, she held a position at IBM supporting the IBM Global Dialer, which is now the ATT Global Dialer. Cherie lives in Tampa, Florida and attended college at the University of South Florida in Tampa, where she is now pursuing a math degree. She would like to thank her husband, Kyle Amon, and father, Jerry Earnest, for leading her in the direction of computers and technology.

Technical Reviewer

Allen Keele is an author and lecturer and holds over 20 technical accreditations including CISSP, SCNP, CCSE+, CCSI, CCNP, CCDA, NSA, NVGA, MCSE, CCEA, CCI, and PSE. Allen holds a business degree in risk management from the University of Georgia, and has provided advanced technical and security training throughout the United States and Western Europe since 1998. He currently leads Certified Tech Trainers, Inc. to provide comprehensive InfoSec training throughout the United States and Europe for Check Point (CCSE/CCSE/CCSE+) and Security Certified Program (SCNP/SCNA) accreditation.

Contents

Chapter 2 Installing and Configuring VPN-1/FireWall-1 Next Generation   41

Configuring & Implementing...

Fetching Licenses

If you have saved your license(s) to a file with a .lic extension (e.g. licenses.lic), then you could alternatively use the "Fetch from File..." button that would enable you to browse your file system for the file. Once you've located the *.lic file, select **Open**, and the license details will be imported into the Licenses configuration window.

Chapter 3 Using the Graphical Interface   141

View Selection

Chapter 4 Creating a Security Policy   191

Management High Availability

When performing a manual synchronization, you have two modes of behavior to select from.

■ Synchronize Configuration Files Only If this is selected, only the database and configuration files will be synchronized between Management Modules.

■ Synchronize Fetch, Install and Configuration files This mode also synchronizes the Fetch and Install files, allowing the interaction with a standby management server.

Chapter 5 Applying Network Address Translation

Chapter 6 Authenticating Users   255

User Access

To configure user authentication, create a new rule in your rule base, right-click on the Source section, and choose Add User Access.

OPSEC Applications

■ There are three types of OPSEC Server applications: CVP, UFP and AMON.

■ OPSEC Client applications, as a general rule, either send data to or pull data from VPN-1/Firewall-1 and generally do not effect the control process directly as servers do.

■ ELA allows third party applications to send log data to the VPN-1/FireWall-1 log database for consolidation and alerting functions

■ LEA provides a method for applications to extract, historically or in real time, log data from the central log database

■ SAM provides a conduit for IDS devices to signal and make changes to the current Security Policy, such as blocking traffic from a specific host

■ The OMI provides support for legacy applications that need to access the VPN-1/FireWall-1 object database

Configuring NG for Performance

There are a number of things that you can do when initially configuring FireWall-1 NG so that it provides optimum performance for your environment.

- Use hosts files on management servers and remote enforcement modules.

- Disable decryption on accept.

- Modify logging Global Properties.

Chapter 9 Tracking and Alerts   393

Alert Context Menu

When you create a new rule, or wish to modify an existing rule, simply right-click on the Action column, and you'll see a Context menu.

Chapter 10 Configuring Virtual
Private Networks   **415**

Chapter 11 Securing Remote Clients   451

Installing and Configuring a Policy Server

- Install the Policy Server from the Check Point NG CD-ROM.

- Enable the Policy Server as an installed product in your firewall object.

- Set the user group to use with the Policy Server in the Authentication tab of your firewall object.

Chapter 12 Advanced Configurations   479

You can selectively weed out protocols that are hogging too many resources when compared to the necessity of their HA condition by editing the $FWIDR/lib/user.def file and inserting a line like this:

//Dont sync the web!

In this Appendix, we will make a slight departure from focusing on securing your network using Check Point products, and instead focus on the theories and methodologies behind spoofing attacks. To successfully secure your systems, you must understand the motives and the means of those who intend to launch a malicious attack against your network. In this Appendix Dan "Effugas" Kaminsky, world-renowned cryptography expert and frequent speaker at the Black Hat Briefings and DEF CON, provides invaluable insight to the inner workings of a spoof attack. Look for the Syngress icon in the margin to find utilities and code samples, which are available for download from www.syngress.com/solutions.

Foreword

We live in an ever shrinking world. Thanks to the growing ubiquity of the Internet, we can keep in closer touch with more people than at any other time in the history of civilization. We can transact business with someone on the other side of the globe with the same ease that we can chat with our neighbor. What was just a decade ago considered a miracle of technology has become commonplace. These conveniences have not, however, come free of charge.

Although the world is shrinking, we can't revert to the behavior of the proverbial small town. I'm sure we've all heard about places where everyone knows their neighbor, and no one locks their doors. Unfortunately, for those of us involved in network security, we are not in that place. To do our jobs well, we must assume that we live in a paranoid, dysfunctional city. We don't know all of our neighbors, but we do know that many of them are out to get us. We not only have to lock our doors, we have to weld them shut and put bars on our windows. We don't want anyone coming in unless we say so, and we want to watch them very closely while they are inside.

Check Point has supplied us with a solution to our digital dilemma. Their excellent VPN-1/FireWall-1 security product can go a long way towards soothing the fears associated with connecting your little neck of the woods to the rest of the world. In its latest incarnation, the market leading VPN-1/FireWall-1 eschews a version number for the term "Next Generation." The moniker fits rather nicely, as there are many improvements over previous versions. These improvements include support for the new Advanced Encryption Standard (AES), the successor to DES, a new, feature rich GUI, and increased ease of configuration.

The goal of this book is to instruct you. We want you to be able to take this book right to your desk and implement a solid security solution utilizing Check Point VPN-1/FireWall-1. We haven't made any assumptions about your previous experience; so don't be afraid if you haven't worked with the product before. Each chapter in this book builds on the previous ones, so that reading the book cover to cover will give you comprehensive coverage of the topic matter, but each chapter can also stand on its own. What this means is that you can turn right to a particular topic and use that chapter as a reference to get the desired results in the fastest time possible.

We will begin by introducing you to the Check Point Next Generation Suite of products in Chapter 1. You will learn about the various components available in NG and how they communicate using the Secure Virtual Network (SVN) foundation. NG utilizes an internal certificate authority on the primary management station, which generates, distributes, and authenticates certificates using Secure Internal Communication (SIC). You'll get your first glimpse of the Security Dashboard and the Visual Policy Editor. We will explain the VPN-1/FireWall-1 architecture, describing how it inspects packets, and we'll touch on performance and scalability.

In Chapter 2 we will start by preparing you to install the VPN-1/FireWall-1 product. We will discuss licenses, securing a firewall host, networking, and DNS. Once prepared, we will walk you through the software installation on a Windows, Solaris, and Nokia platform step-by-step. This chapter should prove to be an invaluable resource for those of you who must install the product, whether installing NG in a standalone or a distributed environment.

Once the product is installed and your basic configuration is finished, you'll need to utilize the management GUIs. Chapter 3 will familiarize you with each of the VPN-1/FireWall-1 GUI clients: Policy Editor, Log Viewer, System Status and SecureUpdate. We will explain how to login and use each interface, as well as detail a long list of objects that need to be defined before you can begin creating a security policy. These will be the building blocks for your rules.

Before you can start creating your security policy in the FireWall-1 Rule Base, you will need to have an enterprise-wide information security policy that includes an Executive Security Policy accompanied by standards, guidelines, and procedures for implementing and maintaining an information security program. Chapter 4 starts out by guiding you in this process. Once the policy is down on paper, then you can begin translating those written words into an enforceable Security Policy within the FireWall-1 NG Policy Editor. The rest of the chapter is focused on utilizing the Check Point Policy Editor. Starting with an empty policy, we will give you the tools necessary to create and maintain a security rule base.

Next, we go into Network Address Translation (NAT) in detail in Chapter 5. NAT is an important piece to the network puzzle, which allows organizations to use private addresses inside their firewall and preserve their public addresses outside.

Previous versions of FireWall-1 always used server side NAT, which required administrators to configure host routes in the operating system to push traffic through a given interface before NAT occurred. Next Generation provides you with the ability to configure NAT to happen on the client side, which means that you no longer need to add a route for the connection to work. You can also configure the system so that ARP is performed automatically. We will cover this, as well as go into detail about hide vs. static NAT and manual vs. automatic NAT.

Chapter 6 provides you with the tools needed to configure and administer users in VPN-1/FireWall-1. We will discuss different types of username/password authentication schemes available and how to implement them (such as FireWall-1 password, RADIUS, etc). We walk you through configuring User Auth, Client Auth and Session Auth in the rule base and discuss the pros and cons to using each of these authentication methods. Finally, we will go over LDAP authentication and configuring your firewall to manage and authenticate LDAP users.

Next Chapter 7 takes you into Check Point's Open Security standard (OPSEC), supported applications, and content security. If you want to use virus scanning software with your firewall, use a content filtering device like WebSense to filter websites based on category, or utilize reporting tools, then this chapter is for you. We will examine the content security options you can use with the FireWall-1 Security Servers without the need for a third party application as well.

Chapter 8 is dedicated to managing policies and logs. In this chapter we will give you some important administration tools to maintain your Check Point VPN-1/ FireWall-1 NG system. We will discuss topics such as switching your logs and maintaining security policies in the Policy Editor, making backups of important firewall files, and performance tuning that you can easily follow. We will also provide you with some troubleshooting tools that can help you to diagnose performance problems on the system.

We get into configuring various logging and alerting options in Chapter 9. You can enable tracking in many places within the Policy Editor GUI in rules, under user properties, in the policy global properties, etc. We will define an alert and describe the different alerting mechanisms within NG.

Chapter 10 takes us into the world of Virtual Private Networks. We will first provide some background and give you a tutorial on encryption and the various encryption schemes and algorithms utilized in Check Point VPN-1. We will then talk about gateway-to-gateway VPNs, as well as SecuRemote VPNs, and walk you though configurations for each.

Chapter 11 ties in well with Chapter 10 by securing your remote clients utilizing Check Point's Policy Server, Desktop Security options, and SecureClient software. SecureClient is the same as SecuRemote, with the addition of personal firewall capabilities. The Desktop Security tab in the Policy Editor is used to create a Granular Security Policy for remote user's desktops. We will also provide information on the SecureClient Packaging Tool, and take you on a step-by-step procedure for creating a customized SecuRemote/SecureClient package.

Chapter 12 deals with Advanced Configurations. In this chapter we will discuss Single Entry Point (SEP) and Multiple Entry Point (MEP) VPN designs, and go through these configurations in VPN-1/FireWall-1. We'll setup the Check Point High Availability module and discuss other high availability options such as routing and VRRP on the Nokia platform as well as hardware devices such as the Foundry ServerIron XL content switch.

Appendix A presents readers with a useful netmask cheat sheet that readers will find helpful when working with network addresses and subnet masks. In Appendix B we will make a slight departure from focusing on securing your network using Check Point products, and instead focus on the theories and methodologies behind *spoofing attacks*. To successfully secure your systems, you must understand the motives and the means of those who intend to launch a malicious attack against your network. In this Appendix Dan "Effugas" Kaminsky, world-renowned cryptography expert and frequent speaker at the Black Hat Briefings and DEF CON, provides invaluable insight to the inner workings of a spoof attack.

Working on this book has been an enjoyable experience. I think that you will find it to be a powerful resource for anyone interested in using the Check Point VPN-1/FireWall-1 product. My hope is that you get as much out of reading this book as the authors and I got out of writing it for you.

—*Cherie Amon, Technical Editor and Contributor*
  Check Point Certified Security Professional: CCSA, CCSE, CCSI
  Senior Network Security Engineer/Security Instructor, Activis/Integralis

—*Drew Simonis, Contributing Author*
  Check Point Certified Security Professional: CCSA, CCSE
  Senior Security Engineer, RL Phillips Group, LLC

Chapter 1

Introduction to Check Point Next Generation

Solutions in this chapter:

- Introducing the Check Point Next Generation Suite of Products

- Understanding VPN-1/FireWall-1 SVN Components

- Looking at Firewall Technology

☑ Summary

☑ Solutions Fast Track

☑ Frequently Asked Questions

Introduction

The Check Point Next Generation suite of products provides the tools necessary for easy development and deployment of enterprise security solutions. Check Point VPN-1/FireWall-1 has been beating out its competitors for years, and the Next Generation software continues to improve the look, feel, and ease of use of this software. Most notably, there is a new security dashboard that gives security administrators a more detailed view of the Security Policy and management objects in one window. The user interface is easy to comprehend and provides optimal functionality all in one place.

With the Next Generation software, you can manage multiple firewalls from a central management server, and can now centrally manage licenses and software upgrades with the SecureUpdate application. Other useful tools in the Next Generation suite include LDAP account management, SecuRemote VPNs, bandwidth usage services, DNS/DHCP services, reporting, logging, and high availability configurations.

In this chapter we will introduce you to each of these tools, and discuss the various components of VPN-1/FireWall-1 in a little more detail. You will learn the difference between proxy firewalls, packet filtering firewalls, and the technology that Check Point Next Generation uses, called Stateful Inspection. You will become familiar with the inspection engine, which is the nuts and bolts of the software, and learn how it analyzes traffic going through the firewall.

Introducing the Check Point Next Generation Suite of Products

It seems that the Internet moves a little further into the network everyday, and along with it comes new network security and management challenges. A few years ago, when I first started working with firewalls, it was easy to define and visualize a network into simple security zones: "trusted" for anything behind the firewall and "un-trusted" for anything in front of it. Security at that time seemed easy: stick a firewall where the internal network met the Internet, maybe add a De-Militarized Zone (DMZ) for the Web and e-mail servers, and call it a day. Now, however, with new Internet applications, Extranets, and VPNs becoming common, I find the un-trusted network creeping through into the DMZ and even right into what I used to call the trusted network. To address the security needs of this new network, we need not only secure scaleable firewall technology but also the tools to provide Quality of Service (QoS), network management, and to log and report on the usage and health of the network infrastructure.

The Check Point Next Generation (NG) Suite is composed of several different products bundled to create a complete enterprise security solution. The combination of these specialized tools allows the NG suite to address the major security and network management challenges facing today's security managers. Rather than look at network security solely from the firewall or Virtual Private Network (VPN) solution, Check Point set out with its Secure Virtual Network (SVN) architecture, to encompass all areas of Enterprise security into a single, easy-to-use product offering. Until recently, many enterprise security managers believed that simply firewalling their network at the Internet connection provided all the security they needed. In today's network world we have Intra- and Extranet connections to secure, not to mention remote dial and VPN access to worry about. The SVN architecture looks at the entire enterprise network, encompassing not only Local Area Network (LAN) and Wide Area Network (WAN) connections, but extending right down to the individual VPN connected user. This new enterprise level view of security defines a complete, scalable, and secure architecture that requires the integration of several products to achieve.

The Next Generation (NG) product suite is designed to fill the security and management needs of the SVN architecture. Using VPN-1/FireWall-1 to firewall between networks and provide a robust endpoint for VPN traffic addressed most companies' primary security needs. Having secured the front door, SecuRemote was added to the NG suite as a desktop application to enable easy VPN setup. Secure Client was designed to build on to the functionality of SecuRemote by enabling Security Managers to set and enforce a desktop Security Policy for desktop machines connecting to the VPN service. Having addressed the firewall and user VPN capabilities most companies are looking for, NG turned to address the user management problems identified by the SVN. Two products were added to the suite to enable security managers to easily manage users and accounts. The Account Management component was added to manage user accounts stored on LDAP servers, and the UserAuthority (UA) was introduced to make authentication information acquired by VPN-1/FireWall-1 available to other applications. To help manage the IP network, two more tools where added to the NG suite. Meta IP allows easy management of DNS and DHCP servers, while FloodGate-1 provides the Quality of Service (QoS) management needed for VPN and Internet networks. Finally, to provide detailed security and usage reports from not only the NG suite of products, but also from supported third-party applications, Check Point added the Reporting Module tool. By combining all eight of these tools into a single suite, NG provides network and security managers with the security and management tools needed in today's enterprise networks in one integrated, scaleable package.

To tie all these products together into an easy-to-manage solution, NG includes a new Security Dashboard that incorporates the best features of the Policy Editor with additional object display windows and the optional Visual Policy Editor. The Security Dashboard, shown in Figure 1.1, not only provides a single point of access for managing the entire NG suite, but also shows how the different products integrate together allowing configuration information to be moved and shared between applications quickly and easily.

Figure 1.1 NG Security Dashboard

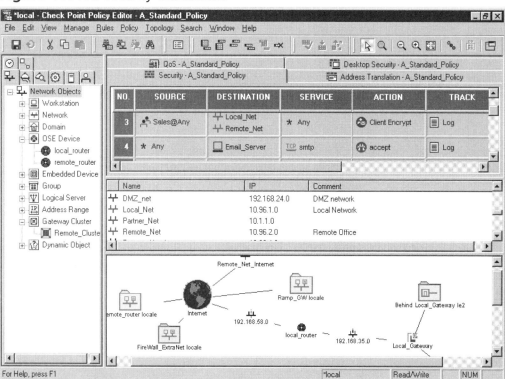

VPN-1/FireWall-1

At the cornerstone of the NG Suite, and what most of us think about when someone mentions the Check Point name, is VPN-1/FireWall-1. The VPN-1 and FireWall-1 products are designed to prevent unauthorized access to or from the networks connected to the firewall, based on the rules defined by the security manager. VPN-1/FireWall-1 uses a set of rules to create a Security Policy. This policy is loaded into the inspection engine component of the firewall and is applied to all traffic that crosses the firewall's network interfaces.

Although it's common to think of VPN-1 and FireWall-1 as a single product, and although many people use the term FireWall-1 (FW-1) to refer to both products, they have very different functions. FireWall-1 provides the data filtering, logging, and access control as expected of any firewall gateway. VPN-1 integrates tightly into FireWall-1 to add virtual private networking tools alongside the firewall. Combining VPN-1 with FireWall-1 has allowed Check Point to provide firewall and VPN products that not only leverage each other's strengths, but that also function together seamlessly and are managed through a single management application. Tying VPN-1 and FireWall-1 together enables you to build VPN gateways into your firewall rather than having to maintain two separate machines to provide firewall and VPN services. This can simplify the network complexity and Security Policy required, allowing for easier management and reducing the possibility of configuration errors.

Although VPN-1 provides all the tools you need to support site-to-site VPNs, and has even improved support for easy set-up with third-party firewall products, there is still the issue of individual user-to-site VPN connections. To ensure that VPN-1 could provide the level of encryption, security, and control required when used with user-to-site VPNs, Check Point has updated the SecuRemote and Secure Client software packages. By integrating SecuRemote and Secure Client so tightly with VPN-1, Check Point has not only provided you with the tools you need to secure your user-to-site VPN, but has also ensured their continued dominance in the VPN market space.

Check Point provides, in the NG suite, the tools required to manage VPN-1/FireWall-1 in a distributed environment, allowing security managers to define and enforce a single Security Policy across the entire enterprise. By building FireWall-1 on a distributed model, Check Point has designed a product that functions equally well as a stand-alone single gateway product, as it does in large multiple firewall gateway networks. This distributed nature allows multiple VPN-1 and FireWall-1 gateways to be managed from a single management station, simplifying not only Security Policy definition, but also logging functions since the logs from all gateways are available from a centralized server.

Managing NG products has been simplified by the creation of the Security Dashboard. This new application took the best features of the Policy Editor from FireWall-1 4.1 (CP2000) and added new tools to simplify firewall and other product management. New drag-and-drop lists and the Visual Policy Editor not only speed up the rule creation process, but also provide an easy-to-understand visual look at your Security Policy, hopefully reducing security holes caused by errors in the policy. To further enhance the manageability of VPN-1/FireWall-1 in a distributed environment, several new tools were added to the NG suite. SecureUpdate enables security managers to maintain the newest product code levels not only on FireWall-1 products but also on Open Platform for Security (OPSEC) certified products from a centralized location. To ensure that communication between firewall enforcement points, the management station, and the management client is reliable, Check Point uses the Secure Internal Communication (SIC) function to encrypt and validate traffic between modules.

Designing & Planning…

What is OPSEC?

Although the NG suite contains many products to help you secure your network, no one vendor can account for every security challenge you may face. Whether it's load balancing network hardware or two factor authentication software, there will almost always be a requirement to use additional, third-party applications to achieve the level of security and robustness you need. Using OPSEC certified solutions will guarantee central management, interoperability, and ease of use by ensuring the security products you implement will work together.

Check Point's Open Platform for Security Partner Alliance program allows Check Point to extend their security suite well beyond what any one company can offer, by certifying hardware and software solutions from third-party vendors in the security enforcement, network management and reporting, performance, and high availability, as well as eBusiness markets.

To become OPSEC certified, applications are tested to ensure compliance with the defined OPSEC standards as well as the SVN architecture. This ensures that solutions you invest in today will operate and integrate with legacy OPSEC applications as well as new applications as they come to market. With the support of over 300 vendors, finding OPSEC security solutions for even your most unique issues, while ensuring compatibility in your environment, is fast and easy. For more information, including a list of certified partners, head to www.checkpoint.com/opsec.

Although, on the surface, VPN-1/FireWall-1 NG just looks like an update to version 4.1, when you dig in a little deeper you find that although the core FireWall-1 technology of Stateful Inspection is still the heart of the system, new tools and updated applications work together to provide an updated, complete security solution. VPN-1/FireWall-1 NG provides the security tools that enterprises are looking for with the ease of manageability that security managers need. Over the next few pages we'll examine the additional products that enable FireWall-1 NG to be a complete security solution before we dive into the heart of FireWall-1, pointing out the technology and features that have made Check Point the market leader in Internet and VPN gateway solutions.

Account Management (LDAP)

One of the many features that distinguishes VPN-1 and FireWall-1 from the competition is the ability to easily authenticate users at the gateway. Whether it's as simple as verifying a user's access to surf the Internet or as sensitive as authenticating VPN connections, managing user accounts quickly becomes a big part of managing your enterprise Security Policy. To help make user management easier, Check Point provides the Account Management application. Account Management allows one or more OPSEC compliant Lightweight Directory Access Protocol (LDAP) servers to provide user identification and security information to FireWall-1. Once enabled, FireWall-1 can use information stored on the defined servers to enforce rules within the Security Policy.

The Account Management module also contains a specialized GUI that can be used to manage user accounts and define user level access. Users and privileges defined with the Account Manager are then available not only to FireWall-1 but also to any other application that is able to query the LDAP database. Although the Account Management GUI can be started independently, launching the GUI from within VPN-1/FireWall-1 enables security administrators to manage both the Security Policy and user account properties from a single application. When used as an integrated component in the NG Security Dashboard, the Account Management tool is available as a tab on the Objects List, allowing you to manage user accounts stored in LDAP directories as easily as users defined in the local FireWall-1 user database.

To ensure that sensitive user information is not collected or tampered with in transit, Secure Sockets Layer (SSL) communications can be enabled between the Account Management machine and the LDAP server. SSL can also be enabled between the LDAP server and the firewall module, ensuring that sensitive information such as user encryption schemes or account passwords are always protected.

SecuRemote/Secure Client

As part of the VPN-1 solution, Check Point developed the SecuRemote application to provide the VPN end point on client machines. Designed for the Microsoft 32-bit Windows and Apple Macintosh operating systems, SecuRemote provides the authentication and encryption services required to support simple desktop-to-firewall VPNs. SecuRemote can not only be used to encrypt traffic from Internet-based clients, but also for LAN and WAN users who deal with sensitive information. By encrypting all data between the users desktop and the VPN-1 Gateway, you can be sure that information transferred has not been read or modified in transit.

The explosion in affordable home broadband cable modem and Digital Subscriber Line (DSL) access revealed the need to secure these "always on" VPN connected users that lead to the Secure Client product. Secure Client is an extension to the SecuRemote software, along with the standard encryption and authentication services; it also provides powerful client-side security and additional management functions. The Secure Client application contains "personal firewall" software that can be centrally managed by the VPN-1 security manager and uses the same proven stateful inspection technology found in VPN-1/FireWall-1. To ensure that the client machine cannot be configured in a way that would circumvent the Security Policy set by the security manager, VPN-1 will use a set of Secure Configuration Verification (SCV) checks to ensure that the desired security level is in place. The SCV checks can be as simple as setting the Security Policy enforced at the client, right down to ensuring that the newest version of your chosen virus scanning software is installed. Coupled with the encryption and authentication services found in SecuRemote, Secure Client provides the security tools needed to build a secure VPN tunnel between individual desktop hosts and the VPN-1 gateway. This enables you to, in effect, extend the enterprise network to include the client PC, whether that machine is LAN connected in the next office, or a mobile user working via an Internet connection.

To make user setup easier, VPN-1 Secure Client enables you to build custom install packages with all the connection options pre-defined. This reduces the setup complexity for the end user, which ultimately results in fewer support calls to your helpdesk. Secure Client also includes centrally managed Security Policy update software to ensure that VPN clients are always up-to-date with the newest code level and policy settings.

Secure Client and SecuRemote support the industry standard encryption algorithms, including 256 bit Rijndael Advanced Encryption Standard (AES) as well as 168-bit Triple Data Encryption Standard (3DES) and all the way down to 40-bit single DES, to ensure compatibility with whatever application you have in mind. Add flexible user authentication including everything from token-based two factor mechanisms through x.509 Digital Certificates, down to OS or FireWall-1 stored passwords, and you have a VPN solution that can be easily integrated into almost any environment.

To keep your users connected and working, both SecuRemote and Secure Client support Multiple Entry Point (MEP) VPN-1 Gateway configurations. This allows the SecuRemote or Secure Client software to be aware of more than one gateway for an internal network destination. Should one path or gateway become unavailable for any reason, the connection will be attempted through another VPN-1 gateway, if defined. This provides not only for redundancy to maintain high availability statistics on your VPN solution, but can also allow you to spread the network and firewall load out to reduce latency.

Reporting Module

Although the built-in Log Viewer is perfect for most day-to-day log file examination, the FireWall-1 suite has, until NG, lacked a good tool to produce "state of the network" and diagnostic graphs. The Reporting Module fills this need to produce summary, as well as detailed reports from the log data. To provide the best view possible of your network, you can create reports with the detail level you specify not only from log data generated from traffic intercepted by Check Point products, but also from the logs of other OPSEC applications.

Using the Reporting Module to create reports from your logs enables you to check the security and performance of your network, firewalls, and Security Policy at a glance. Generating network traffic reports can help you ensure that you dedicate your bandwidth budget dollars where needed and reduce spending on services that are under-utilized. The network traffic reports also enable you to see trends in network usage, which, with a little luck, will allow you to increase capacity proactively rather than have to scramble when network users start to complain of slow access.

Generating reports of dropped or rejected session attempts can turn up suspicious traffic you may not otherwise have noticed. This may enable you to see "low and slow" port scans that take days or weeks to complete, in an effort to be stealthy or to see that one of your servers is acting funny. I once worked with a company whose Web server had been "rooted" or taken over by an unauthorized user. The server administrator had not noticed the server malfunctioning or failing in any way, but the firewall logs showed dropped packets from attempted connections to hosts on the Internet and to the firewall's own interface (presumably from a host scan to identify other machines in the DMZ) from the Web servers' network address. Seeing this dropped traffic alerted the administrator to a problem since anyone authorized to work on the Web server would have known that they'd not have any network access from its console and would normally not attempt these connections. Situations like this are hard to see from even the filtered log data with the firewall Log Viewer since, instead of filtering for something specific, what you really want to see is everything from a high level to be able to spot odd behavior that is easy to achieve by generating overview reports.

One of the best reasons to use this tool, aside from trending usage of your network and security resources, is what I've always called the "pretty picture effect." Especially when trying to increase bandwidth budgets or lobbying to double some of your infrastructure and enable load balancing, a picture is definitely worth more than a thousand words. You can try to explain to the budget managers that your Internet connection is running at capacity and will soon become a bottleneck with no results, but pull out six months' worth of bandwidth graphs that show a steady increase in bandwidth usage that is now approaching the limit, and things may start moving. To help automate this trending and history creation of your Security Policy enforcement and network health reports can be scheduled to automatically generate. This allows you to have the most current reports waiting in your e-mail inbox every Monday at 8:00 a.m. if you like, or have the reports saved in HTML format that is easy to share via an internal Web site.

The Reporting Module is made up of two components, the Consolidation Policy Editor and the Reporting Tool. The Consolidation Policy Editor is integrated into the Security Dashboard and can be viewed from the **View | Products | Log Consolidator** menu. The Consolidation Policy Editor enables you to set the level of detail recorded into the log database as well as to summarize log entries into meaningful connection data. For example, rather than log every session that is established with the Web server, you can consolidate this information and log it every 10 minutes. You can create consolidation rules for an individual Web server or for the entire farm, enabling you to trend and report the data in whatever format is most useful in your environment. Since the Report Module logs are stored onto a separate log server (or at least separate application database on the same server, if you so choose) the original raw log data is still stored in the source device's logs. Using FireWall-1 as an example, you could see the individual sessions allowed through to your Web server in the FireWall-1 logs, and see the summarized data in the Report Server database. Another advantage of this architecture is the ability to consolidate and correlate the logs from all your supported OPSEC applications; this enables you to create reports that show the interaction of devices and give a more complete picture of your environment.

The second half of the Reporting Module is the Report Tool, which is used to actually mine data from the report database and create the final output. Built on the same model as FireWall-1, the Report Tool can be run as a separate client to the report server from another PC. The Report Tool contains many default reports that can be used out of the box or customized as needed. As well, you can create your own reports from scratch, enabling you to see as much or as little data from only the devices and servers that you need to see.

Check Point High Availability (CPHA)

With Virtual Private Network connections being used for more critical day-to-day network operations, and with more businesses selling online though e-commerce sites 24 hours a day, 7 days a week, keeping firewall and VPN services always up and online is becoming increasingly important. Aside from the lost productivity from a service outage, businesses also have to consider customer confidence. Even the shortest outage may be all it takes to lose a potential customer to a competitor. The Check Point High Availability Module enables you to create highly available VPN-1 and FireWall-1 services to help keep your infrastructure online and running 24x7.

The High Availability module enables you to create clusters of VPN-1/FireWall-1 machines, providing seamless fail-over for critical services and network connections. By tightly integrating into VPN-1/FireWall-1, the CPHA module allows one or more of the cluster machines to fail without impacting the users' ability to connect and maintain established sessions with your servers. By keeping state information synchronized between the individual machines in the cluster, when a failure occurs, another machine is able to seamlessly take over the sessions that had been using the now-failed gateway. Since users never see the fail-over, any file transfers or VPN sessions continue as normal, without the need to restart or re-authenticate.

Aside from protecting against hardware or operating system failures, creating high availability clusters can also be useful for performing routine maintenance such as backups, disk checks, or upgrades that may require a machine to be taken offline or rebooted. In the always-on, always-connected world of the Internet, there no longer exists a good time to take services offline for maintenance, and many companies are turning to clusters and redundancy to keep their availability statistics as close to 100-percent uptime as possible. In addition to creating highly available VPN and Internet gateways, you can also create Management Station clusters, so that logging and Security Policy creation and maintenance can continue as normal in the event that the primary Management Station is unavailable. This enables you to geographically separate additional gateways and management stations, if needed, to provide for disaster recover and offsite maintenance of your security infrastructure.

Once a previously down server is back online, either from being repaired or from finishing its maintenance programs, the cluster will automatically return the machine to active duty without administrator intervention. This means that if your servers are configured to automatically reboot after a failure, and the reboot successfully repairs the problem so that the server returns to the cluster, the only evidence of the failure may be in the logs.

UserAuthority

The UserAuthority module provides authentication services to VPN-1/FireWall-1 and other third-party applications. By extending the user account and group information from multiple sources, such as VPN-1/FireWall-1, Windows NT, or LDAP servers to the firewall and other eBusiness applications, the UA module reduces the need to maintain multiple user information databases for application authentication services. This provides not only reduced complexity for the users by being able to use the same account information for multiple applications, but also simplifies development of new applications by providing the necessary authentication procedures.

The UserAuthority module can be used to enable a single sign-on solution for multiple applications. Many companies have seen increased support calls and user dissatisfaction from the need for users to authenticate themselves to multiple systems and applications, often with different credentials each time. The UA module allows authentication services and information to be shared between applications so that users only need to provide authentication credentials once, per session, to be able to use multiple applications. To enable this, the authorization information is captured by the UserAuthority module and is made available to all trusted UserAuthority enabled applications.

FloodGate-1

FloodGate-1 enables you to improve performance of your IP networks by assigning and controlling Quality of Service (QoS) priority to traffic passing through the VPN-1/FireWall-1 gateway. Like FireWall-1, FloodGate-1 is policy based on and managed from the Policy Editor. This integration with VPN-1/FireWall-1 is what allows FloodGate-1 to outperform other QoS solutions. For example, by working with VPN-1, FloodGate-1 can manage VPN traffic with finer control than other QoS products because it can manage data before it is encrypted and assign weighting to different types of VPN data, whereas other applications can only see and manage the entire encrypted data stream as one. Being built into VPN-1/FireWall-1 also allows the same objects and user definitions to be used in the QoS policy as in the Security Policy.

To control QoS, FloodGate-1 enables you to set a weighting on individual types of traffic. The weighting for each rule is relative to that of the other active rules in the database. For example, if data is applied to a rule that has a weight of 10 and, when combined, all the rules with open connections have a total weight of 90, then the data gets 10 percent of the available bandwidth dedicated to it. However, if the rule has a weight of 10 and the rules with open connections have a total weight of only 10, then the data receives 50 percent of the available bandwidth. This allows QoS to be applied dynamically, maximizing use of the available bandwidth, and ensuring that no class of traffic is starved completely even under heavy load. Figure 1.2 shows a FloodGate-1 policy loaded into the Policy Editor in the same fashion as the Security or Network Address Translation (NAT) policy.

Figure 1.2 Floodgate-1 Policy

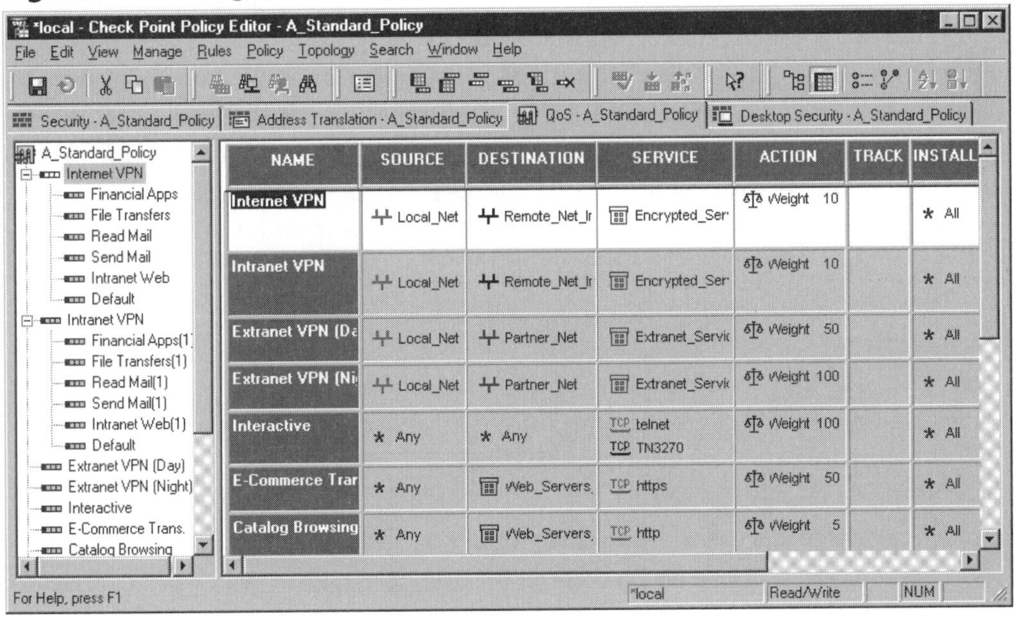

QoS performance can be monitored from the Traffic Monitor NG application and can be selected to show all rules and networks, or can be customized to only show VPN or specific application traffic. Since Floodgate-1 integrates with VPN-1/FireWall-1, general QoS overview statistics are available from the System Status viewer. This enables you to check the health and effectiveness of your QoS policy by looking at the current number of connections as well as pending byte and packet information. Since Floodgate-1 integrates so tightly into FireWall-1, data logged by your QoS policy (if enabled) is stored in the normal VPN-1/FireWall-1 logs, enabling you to correlate your policy actions with QoS information with the standard log viewing tools.

Meta IP

As your network grows larger and more complex, Internet Protocol (IP) addressing and name resolution services can become time consuming and often difficult to manage. Not only are Dynamic Host Configuration Protocol (DHCP) and Domain Name System (DNS) services important to keep your network running smoothly, but they may also be a large part of your overall network security architecture. We often write security rules by creating groups of IP addresses or defining entire networks as objects, and grant access to services based on a client machine's membership in one of these IP address ranges. For example, it is common to allow all user workstation machines to be used to browse the Internet, but restrict operators from browsing when logged onto a server. This is a good practice if you're concerned that someone may inadvertently download and execute a virus or another malicious code on a server where it could do more damage than it would if just run on a workstation. This raises the issue of keeping the workstations out of the server IP network space and ensuring that the servers are not configured with "workstation" addresses. To help you address this problem, Check Point designed Meta IP to provide you with the ability to securely manage DHCP and DNS services on your network.

The centrally managed DHCP and DNS servers provided by Meta IP can interoperate with any existing standards-based service, making integration into your network easy as well as providing the framework necessary to scale up as your network expands. These features not only help you to manage the IP address and namespace on your network, but also can help you reduce support costs by managing related services from a central location. The built-in analysis tools help you manage the often-complex server configuration files and enable you to periodically check all files for errors and corruption, either interactively or as an automated, scheduled task.

High availability has been built right into the Meta IP DNS and DHCP servers to help ensure that the IP address management services stay up and service clients 24 hours a day. The DNS servers support the primary/secondary configuration that we're all used to, but DHCP Check Point has something unique. The Meta IP DHCP service supports a one-to-one fail-over module as well as a many-to-one model that will enable you to have a single centrally located server provide backup for any number of severs in a distributed network, reducing the hardware and support costs of maintaining service availability.

To protect the IP address and name service database and configuration from being tampered with or corrupted, Meta IP servers can use Transactional Signatures (TSIG) to digitally sign and verify the configuration update and replication information they send and receive. This ensures that only services with the appropriate TSIG keys can modify the DHCP scope or DNS zone information.

Arguably the most exciting feature of Meta IP is the ability to provide what Check Point calls the SecureDHCP service. By integrating with VPN-1/FireWall-1 and the User Authority, Meta IP's DHCP service enables you to authenticate users to a Windows domain or to the FireWall-1 user database before being issued a useable IP address. To accomplish this, the client machine is first given a non-routable IP address that provides them with sufficient connectivity to authenticate. Once authenticated, the user's workstation is issued a new address that allows the user to work normally. This not only increases the security of your network by allowing only authenticated users access to network services, but also improves user accountability, by showing users that all network access can be logged, if needed, back to their username. This can be particularly useful if your company needs to enforce an "acceptable use" policy for accessing LAN or Internet resources.

Understanding VPN-1/FireWall-1 SVN Components

Now that you've seen the major components of the NG suite of products, you've likely noticed an underlying theme develop. Everything in the NG suite seems to integrate into, requires, or works best in combination with VPN-1/FireWall-1. Although some of the NG suite products can operate alone, parts of Meta IP, for example, the product's true power and full feature set, is only available when used in conjunction with VPN-1/FireWall-1. Over the next few pages, we'll look at the individual components of FireWall-1 itself, and examine how these individual components combine to provide the network security and management tools required to satisfy the Secure Virtual Network specifications.

The GUI, Management, and VPN/Firewall modules make up the core of VPN-1/FireWall-1. These three modules can reside on a single computer or be built on separate, distributed machines depending on the size and specific needs of your network. The Management module provides a centralized point to manage and log data from a single or multiple network security enforcement point. The Graphical User Interface (GUI) provides an easy-to-use interface for the Management Module, simplifying configuration and maintenance. Since the GUI and Management modules are what you interact with most when working with VPN-1/FireWall-1, we'll explore them before looking at the VPN/Firewall Module that does the actual traffic inspection a little later in the chapter.

VPN-1/FireWall-1 Management Module

At the center of the FireWall-1 architecture is the Management Module. The Management Module is most commonly configured using the GUI Client and resides on the Management Server. The Management Module not only stores the Security Policy but also is responsible for maintaining the logs, user databases, and the various network objects used in the Security Policy. The Management Module moves the logging and policy maintenance functions away from the core inspection module. This allows a single management server to service multiple enforcement points, and allows VPN/Firewall modules to perform better by not having to maintain and sort the log files. The Management Module also checks that the Security Policy is defined correctly and compiled into the format that the inspection module needs. The Management Module also expands the Security Policy beyond just Check Point VPN-1/FireWall-1 devices by enabling you to define and push out an Access Control List (ACL) to any number of supported third-party devices.

Although the Management Module can be deployed on the same physical machine as the GUI clients and even on the VPN/Firewall module, the true benefit of separating the management aspect from the GUI configuration and enforcement point really shows in a larger, distributed environment.

Central Management of VPN-1/FireWall-1 Modules

The Management Module leverages the Client/Server architecture to enable you to manage an entire enterprise from a single Management Server. This configuration provides performance, scalability, and centralized control of your security environment from a single supported platform that could, if needed, be duplicated and made into a highly available service. Figure 1.3 shows a typical distributed configuration of a single Management Server maintaining multiple FireWall-1 and VPN-1 enforcement points.

Figure 1.3 Distributed Client/Server Architecture

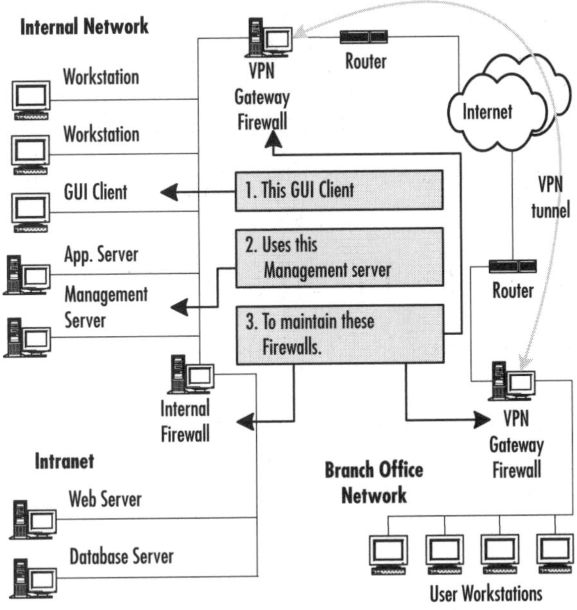

The key point to notice in the above network example is that the Management Server can be accessed from a workstation that is running the management GUI and that a single server can manage multiple firewalls. If desired, the Management Server could be used to manage the ACLs on the routers and other supported network equipment. This enables you to, from a GUI client running on your desktop workstation, create and maintain a single Security Policy, stored on a centralized Management Server and enforced on any number enforcement points. The enforcement points can be Check Point Firewall or VPN modules running on any supported Operating System or purchased preinstalled onto network appliances, as well as a number of routers, switches, and other network devices from different vendors. This allows a single centrally managed Security Policy to define and enforce the basic security needs of your entire enterprise.

Designing & Planning…

Choosing Your OS

VPN-1 and FireWall-1 can be purchased pre-installed on a hardware appliance or as a software application available for a variety of commercial Operating Systems. If you choose to go the software application route, you need to first decide which of the supported Operating Systems to install on. The Management GUI is supported on all Microsoft 32-bit Operating Systems as well as Sun Solaris SPARC. The Management Server and firewall enforcement modules can be installed on any of the following:

- Windows 2000 with or without Service Pack 1
- Windows NT 4.0 with Service Pack 4 or greater
- Sun Solaris 8
- Sun Solaris 7
- RedHat Linux 6.2, 7.0 and 7.2

Choosing the platform that is right for your company has more to do with your ability to support the OS than with actual security. When you choose your OS, you need to consider what your company is best able to maintain, and troubleshoot if problems arise. We've all heard that OS X is more secure than OS Y (insert your favorites for X and Y), but when it comes to the Firewall configuration, mistakes can lead to security problems faster than OS vulnerabilities. By working with the OS you're most comfortable with, you reduce the chances of making configuration mistakes, which generally outweigh any perceived benefit from running on a "more secure" platform. In my experience, a skilled administrator can make any supported OS just as secure as any other, and after VPN-1/FireWall-1 is installed, it will take care of securing the machine.

Furthermore, many companies "harden" the OS before installing the firewall by uninstalling or locking down unneeded services and restricting user and application access to the firewall just to be extra cautious. This type of configuration requires an in-depth knowledge of the OS that is hard to get if the firewall is running on a "one of" OS in your enterprise.

Secure Internal Communication (SIC)

We all know that anytime data is in transit over our networks that it is vulnerable. Sensitive network data could be recorded, in order to reconstruct the session later, or it could even be modified or corrupted while in transit using standard man in the middle tactics. For most network data, this isn't much of a concern since the risk of loss or corruption is low, or the data is simply not worth the effort involved to secure it (such as users browsing the Internet). However, when working with firewall configuration and logs, the risk is much higher, and trusting the configuration and logs from your firewall is paramount to securing your network. To address this issue, Check Point developed the Secure Internal Communication (SIC) module.

SIC is used to encrypt the data passed between modules and applications, such as information passed between the GUI client, Management Server and Firewall module for policy downloads and sending log data, as well as for a variety of other communication between devices that work with VPN-1/ FireWall-1. For example, SIC can be used between the firewall module and a Content Vectoring Protocol (CVP) server or a Log Export API (LEA) application, in addition to various other OPSEC products and components.

SIC provides three basic functions that enable you to trust communication between supported devices, most notable between your Management Server and enforcement points. Along with the encryption that you'd expect between devices or modules, SIC also ensures that communication is proceeding only with the host intended by authenticating that host. When running on the server side of the Client/Server model, SIC checks that the client has been granted access to the function or procedure that it is trying to execute even after the peer has successfully authenticated. By authenticating its peers, applying access control, and encrypting traffic, the SIC module ensures that communication between components is accurate and private.

NG SIC is certificate based and makes use of the Management Server as a party that all hosts trust. The Management Server hosts the internal Certificate Authority (CA) that is used to issue new certificates, as well as maintains the Certificate Revocation List (CRL). The internal CA is also used to service certificate pull requests generally issued by third-party OPSEC applications. This again shows off the central nature of the Management Server and makes another argument for running the Management Server on a separate machine, even though it can be hosted with the firewall module, so as to remove this extra functionality and overhead from your Security Policy enforcement point.

SecureUpdate

SecureUpdate is an application, included with the Management Module, that enables you to maintain and upgrade software and licenses for Check Point and OPSEC applications from a central server. For example, SecureUpdate can be used to install a new service pack or feature pack onto your VPN-1/FireWall-1 NG installation as well as push out updated license information when you need to renew expired licenses or if you license additional features.

SecureUpdate enables you to track Operating System and application versions from all of your Check Point modules as well as supported OPSEC applications. Figure 1.4 shows a typical SecureUpdate window displaying Operating System, service pack, and IP address information for all the modules currently defined to the Management Server.

Figure 1.4 SecureUpdate Products Tab

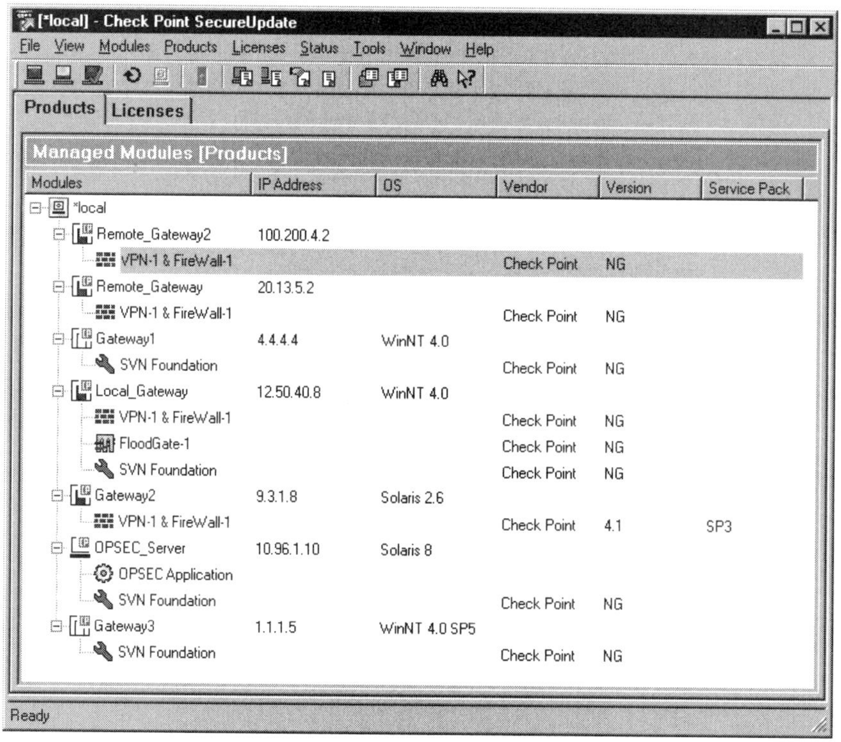

The licenses tab of SecureUpdate allows you to see the installed license details for all your firewalls and supported OPSEC applications in one convenient location. Aside from showing you the features currently licensed on all your gateways, SecureUpdate could also be used to upgrade those licenses remotely. This feature is extremely useful if you need to change the external IP address and, therefore, to update the license for a remote gateway since, with SecureUpdate, you can change the license properties without the need to reinstall the license, which might otherwise require you to be at the gateway's console. Most commonly, the license tab is used to install new licenses for modules whose existing license is about to expire or when upgrading licensed features, such as adding encryption or adding Secure Client licenses to an existing gateway.

SecureXL

SecureXL is a specification used in conjunction with Check Point's computer and appliance partners to help develop the most fully featured, high-performance firewall devices at varying price points. In general terms, SecureXL is helping Check Point service partners develop the hardware and software required to embed VPN-1and FireWall-1 into devices that meet the requirements of as many applications as possible.

SecureXL aims to provide smaller companies with affordable firewall appliances as well as develop high-end machines with multi-gigabyte throughput for larger networks. To accomplish this, the SecureXL framework is employing the newest technology developments from the microprocessor field as well as Application-Specific Integrated Circuits (ASICs) and board-level encryption to develop high performance VPN-1 gateways. A direct benefit from the SecureXL work is the ability to use low-cost encrypting Network Interface Cards (NICs), built to SecureXL specification, to boost VPN-1 encryption throughput.

In addition to encrypting NIC cards, the SecureXL standard allows vendors to increase device performance by moving firewall functions, such as NAT and anti-spoofing, to specialized hardware for processing. Even core firewall processes like access control and the connection tables can be replicated or moved to dedicated devices for improved performance and scalability. For more information, see the Check Point VPN-1/Firewall-1 performance brief at www.checkpoint.com/products/security/vpn-1_firewall-1_perfdetails.html

The ultimate goal of SecureXL is to develop the security products that enterprise network managers are looking for, at a variety of price points, by using the newest hardware and software technology and customizing the features included. This creates a variety of firewall and VPN solutions that enable you to not only pick the feature set, but in some cases also pick from multiple vendors to ensure that you get the products you need to secure your network, at a price that will fit your budget.

Graphical User Interface

The Graphical User Interface (GUI) is the component of the Management Module that you will interact with the most. The GUI is made up of several tools and modules, designed to help you create and enforce a Security Policy as well as monitor the current and historical state of your security infrastructure. As a FireWall-1 security manager, you will spend most of your time in the two main GUI tools: the Security Dashboard and Log Viewer. These two tools enable you to create the rules that make up your Security Policy and check the effectiveness of those rules in action. The Security Dashboard contains the Policy Editor that will help you to build your Security Policy from objects that you define, as well as to build in definitions. The Log Viewer enables you to sort and process data generated by your Security Policy in action on your network and is explored in detail in chapter 3.

The Security Dashboard GUI is designed to help you create the most accurate policy possible. Working as a network security consultant, I've seen several companies expose themselves to risk, not from a lack of security understanding but from poorly written firewall rules or policy. The graphical rule base of the Policy Editor, combined with the optional components such as the Visual Policy Editor, aim to help you visualize and better understand your network topology and firewall rule base, enabling you to write an effective, enforceable Security Policy.

Security Dashboard

The combination of the Policy Editor, Object tree, Object List, and Visual Policy Editor make up the majority of what Checkpoint calls the Security Dashboard. The Security Dashboard provides you with the tools you need to analyze and manage your company's network security through the creation and maintenance of a Security Policy. The main advantage of the macro-level view provided by the Security Dashboard, is the elimination of having to hunt through menus and other dialogs to find the objects and resources required to efficiently build your Security Policy rules.

The Policy Editor has been designed to help show the relationships between objects better with the use of the Visual Policy editor, as well as generally making the job of building security policies easier by enabling you to drag and drop objects from the Objects Tree, and making detailed object information readily available from the Objects List. Figure 1.5 shows the integration of all these components to create the Security Dashboard.

Figure 1.5 Security Dashboard

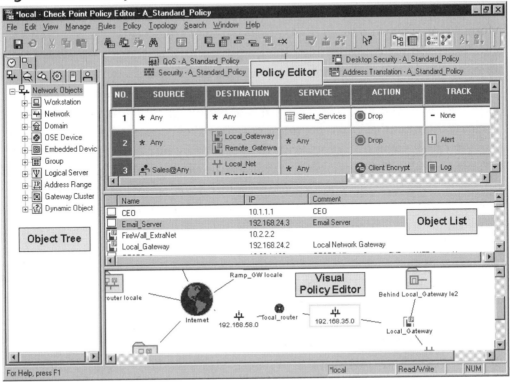

Policy Editor

The easiest way to manage your Security Policy is to use the Policy Editor, although a command-line interface is available. The Policy Editor has seen major improvements from previous versions to provide a user-friendly, GUI-based approach to security rule base creation and management. The Policy Editor has been designed to give a more detailed, visual representation of your Security Policy providing fast, easy, and more accurate rule creation.

Depending on the products licensed, all four VPN-1/FireWall-1 policies are available from the main Policy Editor window. Along with the standard Security and Network Address Translation (NAT) policy tabs, the Quality of Service (QoS) and Desktop Security policies are also available. This all-in-one approach to maintaining all the major policies from a single GUI is a direct result of Checkpoint's Secure Virtual Network (SVN) architecture that attempts to treat network security as an easy-to-manage, end-to-end solution rather than separate, isolated components. The added advantage of managing all four policies together is the reduction in duplicating objects into multiple applications, since the same set of network and user definitions are used in all four policies. The SVN-inspired Policy Editor enables you to maintain the entire network, from the Internet-based, VPN-connected user desktop through Network Address Translation and Quality of Service rules, right up to your Internet gateway Security Policy from a single easy-to-use tool.

Expanding on the distributed nature of FireWall-1, Check Point has developed the Policy Editor to work as a separate product that can be installed on the average workstation machine as part of the normal GUI tools. This enables you to use the Policy editor to work with the Security Policy stored on the Management station from another computer known as a GUI Client. Using this distributed design enables you to manage your firewall security rules, whether you are sitting at the console of the Management Server or working from a GUI Client on the other side of the country.

Object Tree

The Object Tree provides the security administrator with quick access to all the objects that make up the Security Policy. Normally found running down the left side of the Policy Editor window, the Object Tree displays and sorts all the objects defined for use in the Security Policy. To make what you need easier to find, the Object Tree groups available objects into eight tabs: Network Objects, Services, Resources, OPSEC Applications, Servers, Users, Time Objects, and Virtual Links. For more information on how to use each these objects, see Chapter 3, in which we discuss the Policy Editor in detail.

Aside from just categorizing the policy objects to make it easier to find what you're looking for, the Object Tree also speeds up policy building by enabling you to drag and drop objects directly into policy rules rather than opening dialog boxes from the Manage menu.

Object List

The Object List is normally used simultaneously with the Object Tree to show the details of all objects available under the currently selected heading on the Object Tree. The main advantage of the Object List is the ability to see all the objects' important properties in a convenient table format rather than having to open each object's properties panel. Using the Object list will enable you to quickly ensure that you are working with the object you intend; for example, when selecting workstation objects you will be able to compare IP addresses and comments for each object (that is, if you specified a comment of course) rather than just relying on the object names. This is especially handy when your object-naming convention is not completely clear, in that you can quickly verify that you are using the proper objects to build a new rule. As with the Object Tree, you can drag and drop objects from the list directly into new or existing rules.

Visual Policy Editor (VPE)

Check Point designed the Visual Policy Editor (VPE) to help security managers better visualize the network topology contained within the Security Policy. Prior to FW-1 NG (and the VPE beta for FireWall-1 4.x), I often found myself using a white board or scrap of paper to draw network device connections and services to help build and verify the rule base. With the VPE, the whiteboard network diagram has been built right into the Policy Editor, providing not only a visual display of the network built from defined objects, but also allowing you to define new groups and other objects easily right in the visualization.

Along with making it easier to visualize the security rules, the ability to build and keep the network diagram with the Security Policy solves a couple of administration issues. First off, white board or even printed network diagrams, although often necessary for visualizing the network layout, are very difficult to keep secure. When network diagrams contain sensitive information, such as Intrusion Detection System (IDS) locations or other sensitive security device IP address information, it may be important to keep that information secured. Keeping the diagram with the policy ensures only users capable of building the Security Policy have access to the diagram. Secondly, if you have multiple security managers, using the VPE ensures that everyone is working from the same diagram. This can be very important when the primary security manager is unavailable and a secondary operator must finish or troubleshoot a new service installation. As well, this is extremely useful when one or more of your security administrators work off-site or in another office where VPE diagrams may be the most convenient way to share network diagrams.

I think one of the most useful features of the Visual Policy Editor's integration with the Policy Editor is the ability to highlight individual rules from the Policy Editor on the network diagram. This feature is perfect for displaying complex rules to ensure that you've actually created what you expected, as shown in Figure 1.6. To make the visualization easy to read, different colors are used for different actions (accept, drop, encrypt, etc), which can be customized to suit your needs.

Figure 1.6 Visual Policy Editor Showing Rule

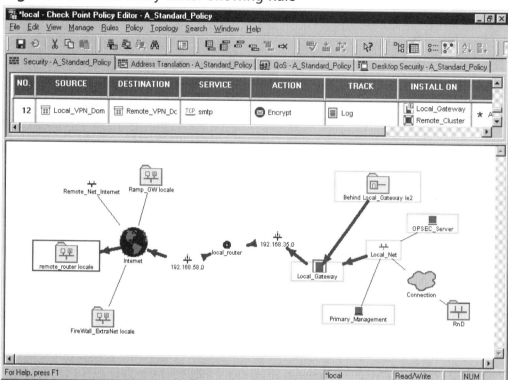

Policy Server

The Policy Server integrates into VPN-1, enabling you to manage the Secure Client software installed on a VPN user's machine from a central location. The Policy Server is responsible for sending Secure Client policy information for the specific Desktop Security settings to load, as well as using Secure Configuration Verification (SVC) to ensure that the Secure Client machine's configuration meets your policy requirements.

In addition to verifying the clients' configuration and sending the Desktop Security policy, the Policy Server is also responsible for handling logs from the Secure Client machines. As a final step of logging into the Policy Server, the Secure Client software will package its local alert logs and send them to the Policy Server. The Policy Server then opens these files and sends each alert log entry to the Management Server to be incorporated into the log database, where it is viewable through the VPN-1/FireWall-1 Log Viewer. This enables you to view alert data from not only VPN-1/FireWall-1 and local OPSEC applications, but also from remote VPN desktops with Secure Client installed.

Desktop Security

The Desktop Security policy is created with the policy editor on the Desktop Security tab. In addition to the actual policy, which is similar to the main Security Policy, operational settings can be modified from the Desktop Security section of the global policy properties. Once defined, the Desktop Security policy is downloaded to your Policy Server, making it available to your Secure Client version 4.1 and NG users when they next log on.

Desktop Security enables you to control the tiny or "personal" firewall built into the Secure Client software package. This enables you to extend the security of your network down to encompass the Internet connected VPN client machines, as specified in the SVN architecture. Part of the Desktop Security policy can also incorporate checking to ensure that a minimum configuration level is maintained on the VPN client machine, by using the SCV module. This enables you to expand the default Desktop Security options to include custom checks that you define, grant, or deny VPN access based on the configuration state of the computer attempting to connect.

Looking at Firewall Technology

The final component of VPN-1/FireWall-1, after having looked at the configuration GUI and Management Server components, is the actual Firewall Module. The Firewall Module provides NAT, access control, logging, content security, as well as user, client, and session authentication services. The Firewall Module contains, among other functions, the Inspection Module that actually makes control decisions, based on the Security Policy, on how to handle traffic attempting to cross between the firewall's network interfaces. VPN-1/FireWall-1 uses a Check Point-patented technology called Stateful Inspection to examine IP data packets, and after applying knowledge of previous communication and the Security Policy, decide on what action to perform on that data.

To understand the benefits of Stateful Inspection to control network traffic, it is necessary to look at the other types of firewall technology available today. In the next few pages we'll examine proxy or Application Gateway and Packet Filtering device technology and compare the advantages and disadvantages with those of Check Point's Stateful Inspection firewall technology.

Proxy Server vs. Packet Filter

When comparing firewall technology, it is necessary to consider the layer of the Open System Interconnection (OSI) reference model where the firewall inspects traffic. Table 1.1 lists the seven layers of the OSI reference model and explains the type of data at each layer. In general terms, firewalls that inspect close to the top of the model have very detailed control over application specific data, whereas firewalls inspecting farther down the model have courser control over many types of traffic. As well, the position of the firewall's control module in the IP stack has an effect on how much of the underlying OS can be exposed to unfiltered traffic.

Table 1.1 OSI Reference Model

OSI Layer	Function
7 - Application Layer	Provides a set of interfaces allowing applications network access
6 - Presentation Layer	Converts application data into a generic format for transmission
5 - Session Layer	Allows two network devices to hold ongoing communication (session)
4 - Transport Layer	Manages the transmission of the data on the network (packet sizes, etc)
3 - Network Layer	Addresses packets by resolving physical addresses from logical names
2 - Data Link Layer	Translates physical frame data into network layer format (NIC drivers)
1 - Physical Layer	Converts bits into signals (NIC and network medium at this layer)

Packet filtering examines data at the Network layer of the OSI model. This allows the packet filter device to apply a user-defined rule base on the source and destination service port and IP address only. Although this is relatively effective and can be made completely transparent to users, it is also often difficult to configure and maintain as your rule set grows. Packet filtering is inexpensive and can be found in many network devices from entry-level routers to enterprise firewall solutions. Packet filtering can offer complete application transparency and greater data throughput performance than application or proxy gateways.

The limitations of the packet filtering method of controlling data stem from the inability to apply rules to data above the network layer. This ignores a large part of the data packet when making a control (pass or drop) decision. In addition to often being difficult to configure and monitor, packet filtering does not provide detailed logging of network data, again because of the lack of knowledge of the packets' contents above layer three and the simplicity of the devices often used. Since the packet filter device cannot keep or use application or session state to make decisions on what to do with specific data packets, and only having a limited ability to manipulate traffic (such as address substitution), it is often considered to have a lower security level than a proxy or Stateful Inspection solution.

Application Gateway (often called proxy) firewalls inspect network data at the very top of the OSI model, the Application layer. This gives the proxy firewall extremely detailed control over the applications' data since packets are fully decoded before a decision to pass or drop the traffic is made. This provides good security, but only for applications that the proxy is aware of, as new applications are introduced new proxy components must be developed.

The main disadvantages of the proxy firewall technology are that the gateway cannot always be made transparent to the users and that the firewall is more vulnerable to Operating System or application security problems and bugs than other technologies, because the firewall sits so high on the IP Stack. Proxies also have problems supporting User Datagram Protocol (UDP), Remote-Procedure Call (RPC), and other common connectionless services and protocols, such as Internet Control Message Protocol (ICMP).

Performance and Scalability

The need to continuously increase the Internet bandwidth available to your network to support new applications and services, as well as the need to segregate other high-speed networks, makes performance and scalability a high priority for any firewall solution. The ability of a solution to fit your current needs and grow as your network grows needs to be considered alongside with the overall feasibility of the solution to fill your security requirement.

Although a proxy firewall can provide good security, scaling up to new applications is not always easy. Each application or protocol (such as HTTP or FTP) needs to have its own application gateway; this makes controlling new applications difficult and sometimes impossible. The performance or data throughput of a proxy solution is often lower than other options since data must be decoded all the way up to the Application layer before a control decision can be made.

Packet filters, on the other hand, often scale up to large installations easily. This is partially due to the fact that the packet-filtering firewall is often built into network routers and switches and, as such, can operate at or near network line speed. This makes packet filtering scale up with growth very easily since most networks already use routers; it's just a matter or purchasing devices capable of filtering, installing them where needed, and creating some rules. Even when built as an application running on a server, from the performance side, the packet filtering firewall is inspecting at a lower layer of the OSI model, meaning less processing overhead is introduced, and greater throughput can be achieved. It's for these reasons that packet filtering is often used at the edges, or borders, of the network to reduce the volume of traffic before passing it to a firewall that can provide better security. It's easiest to think of this implementation as a kind of course filter applied to the data stream; once you've reduced the volume of noise, you can use a more secure firewall, which may or may not perform at a lower rate, to provide fine control over the network data.

FireWall-1's Inspection Engine

FireWall-1's Inspection Engine inspects all data inbound and outbound on all of the firewall's network interfaces. By inserting into the TCP/IP stack between the Data Link and Network layer, the Inspection Engine is running at the lowest level of the OSI model accessible by software, since the Data Link layer is actually the Network Interface Card driver and the Network layer is the first layer of the IP protocol stack.

With FireWall-1 inspecting data at the lowest point possible, it is possible to keep state and context information from the top five layers of the OSI model that can be used when making control decisions. To obtain this state information, the Inspection engine examines the source and destination service port and IP address fields from the data packets as well as other application information. This data is then used to determine what action to take based on the Security Policy. Figure 1.7 shows an overview of the firewall's position during a typical session between a client and server as well as an overview of how data flows through the Inspection module.

The Stateful Inspection technology maintains two types of state information. Communication-derived state is information that is gained from previous communication. For example, the Inspection Engine will note an outgoing FTP PORT command and will allow the incoming FTP data session to pass through to the client even though the data session on TCP port 20 is completely separate from the control session between a client and server on TCP port 21. Application-derived state is information saved by FireWall-1 from other applications, such as a user-authenticating to the firewall to be allowed HTTP access, and can also be allowed HTTPS access if both rules in the Security Policy require the same type of authentication.

Figure 1.7 FireWall-1 Data Flow and Inspection Engine detail

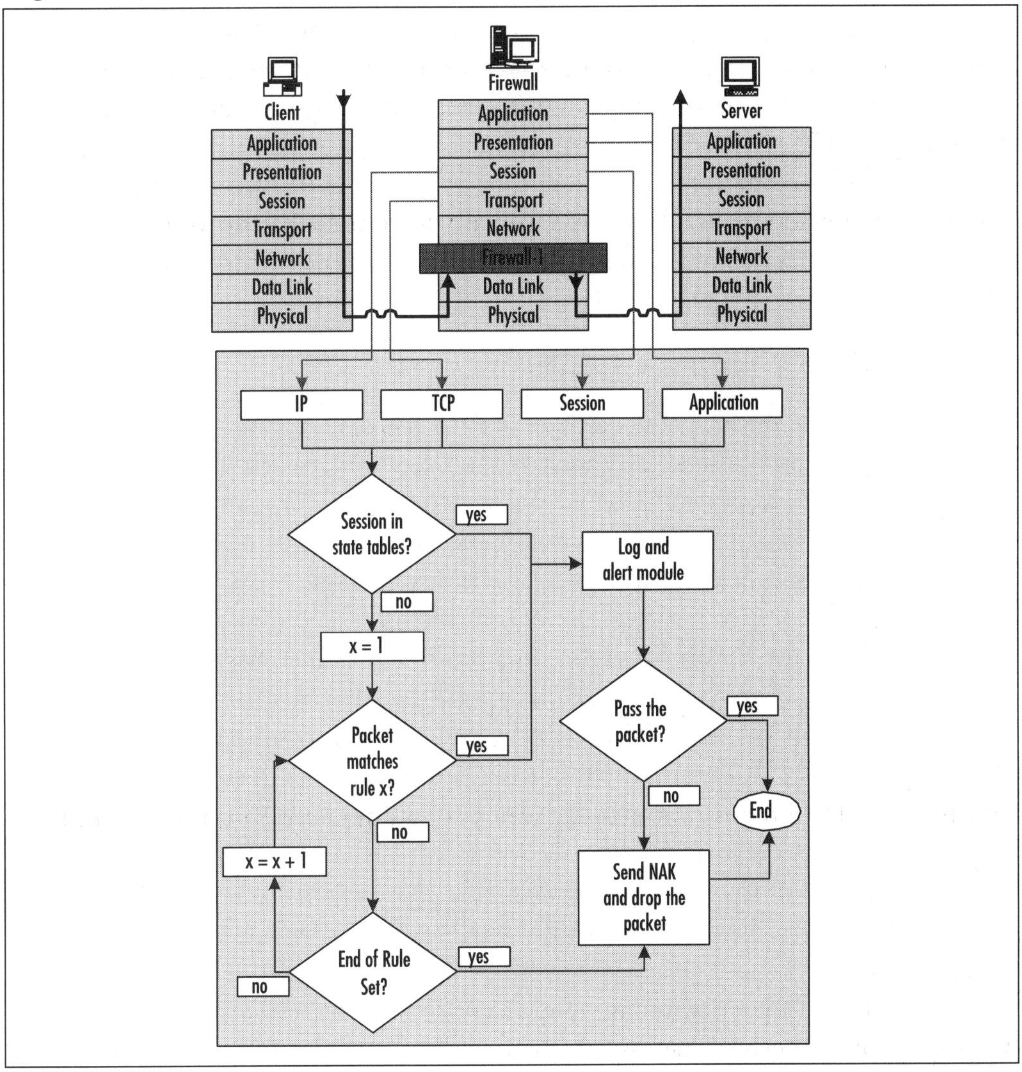

Collecting state and context information allows FireWall-1 to not only track TCP sessions, but also connectionless protocols such as UDP or RPC. Consider a standard DNS query; if the query were done with TCP, tracking the response

would be easy, since it would be part of the established connection between the client and the server. However, DNS queries are always done with UDP, usually on port 53 (TCP port 53 being used for DNS zone transfers); this complicates allowing the DNS response to pass through the firewall since it's not part of an existing connection. A packet-filtering device would have to allow defined (or all) hosts to send UDP port 53 data to the client at anytime, regardless of whether or not a request was made, since no application tracking can be done. In contrast, by keeping state information, FireWall-1 will be expecting a DNS response from a specific server after recording that the client had made a request, which was permitted by the Security Policy, into the state tables. To make this work, FireWall-1 allows data on UDP port 53 from the server back to the client that made the request, but this "open port" is only held open until a user-configurable timeout has expired, and then it will be closed again. This ensures that a request must go out from the client before any data from the server will be accepted, and that if no response is received, the port will not be held in an open state.

Performance and Scalability

Controlling traffic using Stateful Inspection is very efficient and introduces minimal load to the firewall and very little latency to the network data stream. This is partly because the Inspection Engine is inserted into the Operating System kernel, allowing it to control data quickly and efficiently, but also because of the use of state tables to help make control decisions. As Figure 1.6 shows, incoming data packets are compared to information in the state tables before evaluating the rules in the Security Policy. Since the state tables are kept in kernel memory, access to them is considerably faster than checking the rule base rule by rule, which allows traffic to be handled faster. To help increase performance of the Security Policy, try to keep frequently used rules near the top of the rule base; this will help to ensure that the minimum number of rules will need to be evaluated before making a control decision.

Adding Encryption or logging with the account option will add a noticeable amount of overhead to your firewall. Performance is always traded for additional functionality, but purchasing or upgrading to a faster hardware platform will help to relieve most performance problems if your network grows beyond what your existing firewall was built to serve. For firewalls doing a lot of encryption, consider using a multiple CPU machine or adding a hardware encryption accelerator to handle some of the load.

Taking advantage of the VPN-1/FireWall-1 distributed design helps not only with scalability, but also with performance issues. As your network grows, you can add additional firewalls, either in a clustered load-balancing configuration or as stand-alone enforcement points, to spread different functions to separate gateways. For example, I've seen medium-sized organizations use one firewall for outbound user traffic, such as HTTP and FTP access, as well as protecting an Intranet segment, and a second firewall to provide inbound services, such as access to the corporate Web servers, for internal and external (Internet) users, and a third machine to serve as a VPN gateway for employees and business partners. Since a single Management Server can manage multiple firewalls, scaling up to new growth and application demands by adding another firewall, when a simple hardware upgrade won't meet the performance requirement, can be done quickly and easily without significantly increasing your management overhead.

Summary

The Check Point NG suite of products provides a combination of market-leading tools and applications aimed to meet the basic security needs of the entire enterprise. By using the SVN architecture to step back and view security, not only from the firewall or stand-alone VPN connected user, but also from an end-to-end solution perspective, has allowed Check Point to bring together the tools you need to secure your data assets.

VPN-1/FireWall-1 is the cornerstone of the NG suite, providing network security and VPN capabilities, as well as serving as the foundation for many of the other NG products. To complete the VPN capabilities of VPN-1, SecuRemote and Secure Client were included in the NG suite. SecuRemote provides a mechanism to authenticate users and encrypt data between the user's desktop and the VPN-1 gateway, while Secure Client adds a personal firewall to the user's computer that can be managed from the Policy Server integrated into VPN-1. This effectively enables you to expand the perimeter of your network to encompass and secure even Internet-connected VPN users.

Although VPN-1/FireWall-1 meets the basic security need of providing gateway protection and a secure VPN endpoint, additional products have been added to the NG suite to address other security challenges identified in the SVN architecture. Since efficient network management so often becomes a big part of network security, Check Point developed Meta IP to provide and manage DNS and DHCP services and introduce new features to these crucial services such as Secure DHCP. To help you make efficient use of your limited bandwidth, FloodGate-1 enables you to prioritize network traffic and provide QoS on data passing through your gateways, ensuring timely delivery of high priority data, such as traffic to your Web site, or of time-sensitive application data like streaming video.

Managing and sharing user account and authorization information is critical to ensuring that legitimate users get access to the resources they need while blocking access to unauthorized parties. Proper authentication mechanisms can also increase user satisfaction by not forcing multiple, often redundant, logons. Two tools were added to the NG suite to help manage user credentials and authorization information. The Account Management module allows LDAP-stored user accounts and associated information to be easily created and maintained alongside the Security Policy that uses them. To help share user authorization information between OPSEC applications, the User Authority module was developed, allowing other applications access to the user privilege information already gathered by VPN-1/FireWall-1.

Finally, the Reporting Module and tools for real-time status monitoring were added to help you keep track of how your security infrastructure is performing. By monitoring and trending your network usage, the monitoring and reporting tools aim to help you not only spot security problems or attempted violations and suspicious activity, but also can enable you to proactively monitor network traffic levels, allowing you to plan for growth or reduction of provided services.

After looking at the entire NG suite, we focused in on the VPN-1/FireWall-1 module, looking at how the three major components of FireWall-1 work together in a distributed or stand-alone environment. The GUI client enables you to remotely manage the Security Policy and provides the main interface for most NG products. The GUI is comprised of several modules and tools including the Visual Policy Editor and object lists that help you maintain your network policies. These tools help you easily create and visualize your network security rules, reducing the chances for configuration errors caused by oversight or confusion when creating and updating the rule base.

The GUI client is the tool you use to create the Security Policy that is stored on the Management Server. The Management Server's Management Module not only stores the Security Policy used by FireWall-1-based devices but can also create and distribute ACLs for OPSEC-certified network devices such as routers and switches. The Management Module is also responsible for keeping the logs from all VPN-1/FireWall-1 enforcement modules and from Secure Client machines. Network traffic between the GUI, Management Server, and Firewall module is encrypted using SIC to ensure that an unauthorized third party cannot read or modify sensitive data while in transit.

After being compiled into the appropriate format, the Security Policy is pushed from the Management Server to the Firewall Inspection Module to be enforced. To understand how the Inspection Module makes control decisions for data attempting to pass through the firewall, it is necessary to understand the technology Check Point calls Stateful Inspection. By comparing the pros and cons of Proxy firewalls that provide excellent application control with limited scalability, and Packet Filters that scale well but can't provide in depth application control, to Check Point's Stateful Inspection, you should have a basic understanding of how the FireWall-1 Inspection engine works, and why Stateful Inspection simplifies security management while increasing overall security with application awareness.

Although network security application vendors would like to produce a single product or suite that could storm the market by providing all the security tools any organization will need, the fact is, it's just not possible. Although Check Point VPN-1/FireWall-1 and the NG suite will cover the basic security needs of most enterprises, there will always be small gaps where third-party applications are needed. To help you ensure that you can leverage your existing investment and provide easy integration with your Check Point security infrastructure, OPSEC was created to certify that the third-party products you require will work well with VPN-1/FireWall-1 and other OPSEC applications.

Combining the proven, market-leading NG versions of VPN-1 and FireWall-1 with the NG Suite of products as well as with Check Point OPSEC partner applications enables you to build and manage the highly available, secure network infrastructure needed to support today's eBusiness models and to scale up to future growth in enterprise network security.

Solutions Fast Track

Introducing the Check Point Next Generation Suite of Products

- ☑ FireWall-1 is the cornerstone of the NG suite providing data filtering, logging, and authentication in stand-alone, distributed, and high-availability clustered gateway models.

- ☑ VPN-1 builds onto the features of FireWall-1 adding encryption and VPN support.

- ☑ The LDAP Account Management module can run as a separate application or be integrated into the Security Dashboard, enabling you to manage LDAP database-stored user accounts easily.

- ☑ SecuRemote is used with VPN-1 and creates the client or user end of the VPN tunnel, providing the authentication and encryption needed to establish and maintain the VPN connection.

- ☑ Secure Client adds a personal firewall to the SecuRemote feature set. This small firewall installed onto the user's computer enables you to centrally control the security settings of VPN connected desktops. In addition to the firewall capabilities, Secure Client can send its logs to the central Management Server, once connected.

☑ The Reporting Module helps you trend and analyze your network by using predefined or customized report criteria to generate data traffic statistics and reports.

☑ The Check Point High Availability module helps you to create clusters of firewalls to reduce service downtime by providing seamless fail-over from one gateway to another.

☑ FloodGate-1 has been integrated into VPN-1/FireWall-1 to provide Quality of Service prioritization of network traffic as it passes through the gateway.

☑ Meta IP provides you with secure, scalable solutions for DNS and DHCP server management. As well as providing standards-based servers, Meta IP provides additional tools such as Secure DHCP that you use to authenticate your users before giving their machine a fully functional IP address.

☑ The User Authority module extends the user-authorization information acquired by VPN-1/FireWall-1 to trusted third-party applications. This can help reduce multiple logons and reduce development time for new applications.

Understanding VPN-1/FireWall-1 SVN Components

☑ The VPN-1/FireWall-1 Management Module resides on the Management Server, and not only stores and pushes out the Security Policy to the enforcement points, but is also responsible for storing all the objects and definitions used in the policy. Logs from Check Point enforcement modules, including Secure Client, are stored in the log database hosted by the Management Server.

☑ The Management Module is at the heart of the distributed model for firewall deployment, allowing for centralized logging and easy security management even for environments with several firewalls.

☑ The GUI client is used to manage and configure the options and policies stored on the Management Server. The GUI is made up of a number of tools and components combined into a Security Dashboard that allows for easy, visual configuration of the Security, NAT, QoS, and Desktop Security polices.

☑ The Firewall Module contains the Inspection Engine that uses a compiled version of the Security Policy to control traffic attempting to pass between the firewall's interfaces.

☑ The SIC module ensures that communication between GUI clients, Management Servers, and the Inspection Engine is secure to prevent modification or copying of data in transit.

Looking at Firewall Technology

☑ Proxy or Application Gateway firewalls provide in-depth control of a single application, allowing for very detailed filtering. However, this makes scaling to new applications difficult and can reduce performance of the firewall.

☑ Packet Filters offer great performance and affordability because this type of firewall is often built-in routers or similar network devices. Since Packet Filtering firewalls are unaware of the application layer, granular control is not possible.

☑ VPN-1/FireWall-1 uses a Check Point Patented technology called Stateful Inspection to control IP network data.

☑ Stateful Inspection is able to make control decisions based on information from the top five layers of the OSI model, providing granular control and application awareness.

☑ By tracking communications data, throughput performance is increased by leveraging the ability to determine continuations of previously accepted sessions versus new connection attempts that need to be applied to the rule set.

Frequently Asked Questions

The following Frequently Asked Questions, answered by the authors of this book, are designed to both measure your understanding of the concepts presented in this chapter and to assist you with real-life implementation of these concepts. To have your questions about this chapter answered by the author, browse to **www.syngress.com/solutions** and click on the **"Ask the Author"** form.

Q: What is this "Fingerprint" I see when first connecting to the Management server?

A: In order to verify that you are connecting to the intended Management station (rather than an imposter) FW-1 uses a Fingerprint phrase. To ensure that secure communication between the GUI client and Management Server is set up properly, be sure that you have the server's fingerprint to verify before initiating the first connection to a new server.

Q: What happened to the "Apply gateway rules to interface direction" property?

A: In previous versions of FireWall-1 you could specify, in the policy properties, the data direction (inbound, outbound, or eitherbound) in which the security policy would be applied on the Firewall's interfaces. In VPN-1/FireWall-1 NG, Check Point has removed this option and the security policy rules are now applied inbound and outbound on all interfaces. Aside from not being needed in the new version of the Inspection Engine, removing this option is likely for the best since few people actually understood how it worked or why it was needed.

Q: How are the rules in the Security Policy applied to incoming data?

A: The Security Policy rules are applied from top to bottom. Data for which no rule applies will be dropped after falling to the bottom of the Security Policy. Data dropped in this fashion is not logged, which is why a "drop all" rule is used with source: any, destination: any, service: any and track set to log is normally written at the bottom of the rule base.

Q: VPN-1/FireWall-1 just looks like an application running on my server; how does it protect the underlying Operating System from attack?

A: The FireWall-1 Inspection Engine is inserted into the Operating System's Kernel just above layer two of the OSI model. Since layer two is actually the firewall's Network Interface Card driver, this means that data must pass through the firewall Security Policy before being allowed to move onto the Operating Systems' IP stack. Therefore, the underlying OS is never exposed to raw, unfiltered network data.

Q: How does the Inspection Engine handle fragmented packets?

A: When you look at fragmented packets individually, most of the information needed to make a control decision is in the first packet. However, FireWall-1 needs the entire assembled packet for a couple of reasons. First, the data section of the packet is most likely to be fragmented since it's at the end of the packet and is the largest section. Depending on the rules in your policy, this data may need to be inspected in its entirety to make a control decision. Second, the second and subsequent fragments only contain the remainder of the original packet (usually the data portion), not another copy of the full packet headers, which may also be needed to make the control decision. Without reassembling the packet, it may not be possible to apply it to the security policy since information about source and destination ports would be missing. To get around this, FireWall-1 will completely reassemble a packet before applying it to the Security Policy. To prevent a Denial of Service (DOS) attack caused by a high volume of incomplete packet fragments, a timer is used when the first fragment arrives. If the timer expires before the complete packet is reassembled, the fragments are discarded. Once a packet is reassembled and a control decision is made to pass the packet on, the original fragments are released in the same fragmented condition and order as they arrived in, to the destination.

Q: Can I get a copy of VPN-1/Firewall-1 for evaluation?

A: To request an evaluation package with the software, documentation, and licenses required to fully test VPN-1/Firewall-1 in your network, head to www.checkpoint.com/getsecure.html.

## Chapter 2

Installing and Configuring VPN-1/ FireWall-1 Next Generation

Solutions in this chapter:

- **Before You Begin**

- **Installing Check Point VPN-1/FireWall-1 NG on Windows**

- **Uninstalling Check Point VPN-1/FireWall-1 NG on Windows**

- **Installing Check Point VPN-1/FireWall-1 NG on Solaris**

- **Uninstalling Check Point VPN-1/FireWall-1 NG on Solaris**

- **Installing Check Point VPN-1/FireWall-1 NG on Nokia**

- ☑ **Summary**

- ☑ **Solutions Fast Track**

- ☑ **Frequently Asked Questions**

Introduction

This chapter is written to familiarize you with the installation and configuration options available in the Check Point Next Generation Enterprise Suite of Products. Specifically, we will be installing and configuring VPN-1/FireWall-1 NG on the Windows, Solaris, and Nokia Platforms. The installation process is pretty straightforward. We will focus on installing a Management Module and Enforcement Module on each platform, and will point out the subtle differences you will encounter if you choose to install these components in a distributed environment instead. After installing and configuring each platform, we will walk you through the uninstall process so you will know what you need to do in case you need to remove the software from your system as well.

Prior to starting the installation procedure of VPN-1/FireWall-1 NG, there are several steps that you should take to prepare the system and get ready for the installation screens you will be presented with. Most systems are not secure out-of-the-box, and we will help you to secure the host computer before you turn it into a firewall. We will also advise you on some good techniques you can use when preparing for your firewall installation. The information in this chapter is built on top of five years' experience installing, configuring, and supporting the Check Point VPN-1/FireWall-1 product.

Before You Begin

In this section we hope to prepare you to install the Next Generation product. There are several things that you need to consider prior to installing a firewall. We will discuss each step so that you understand its importance, and guide you in your endeavor to secure your network. The list of minimum system requirements as defined by Check Point is outlined in Table 2.1. You will need to ensure that your hardware meets these requirements at the very least. You can find these online at http://www.checkpoint.com/products/security/firewall-1_sysreq.html.

Table 2.1 Minimum System Requirements

System Requirement	Primary Management & Enforcement Module	GUI Clients (Policy Editor, Log Viewer, etc)
Operating Systems	Microsoft Win2k Server and Advanced Server SP0 and SP1 Windows NT 4.0 SP6a	Microsoft Win2k Windows 98/ME Windows NT 4.0 SP4, SP5 and SP6a

Continued

Table 2.1 Continued

System Requirement	Primary Management & Enforcement Module	GUI Clients (Policy Editor, Log Viewer, etc)
	Sun Solaris 7 (32-bit mode only)* Sun Solaris 8 (32- or 64-bit mode)** RedHat Linux 6.2, 7.0 and 7.2	Sun Solaris SPARC
Disk Space	40 MB	40 MB
CPU	300+ MHz	No minimum specified
Memory	128 MB	32 MB
Network Interfaces	ATM, Ethernet, Fast Ethernet, Gigabit Ethernet, FDDI, Token Ring	Any supported by the operating system.
Media	CD-ROM	CD-ROM

You must have patch 106327 on Solaris 2.7

**You must have patches 108434 and 108435 on Solaris 2.8*

Solaris patches can be obtained from http://sunsolve.sun.com.

Tools & Traps…

Solaris 32-bit vs. 64-bit

To check whether your Solaris machine is in 32- or 64-bit mode, use the following commands:

    isainfo –b
    isainfo –vk

To change from 64- to 32-bit mode in Solaris 2.7 or 2.8, perform the following actions:

1. Enter EEPROM mode using the STOP-A keyboard combo.
2. Type **setenv boot-file kernel/unix** and press <RETURN>.

Continued

> 3. Reboot.
>
> 4. If the machine has difficulty booting, user the "set-defaults" command to return to 64-bit mode.
>
> To change from 32- to 64-bit mode, do the following:
>
> 1. Enter EEPROM mode using the STOP-A keyboard combo.
>
> 2. Type **setenv boot-file /platform/sun4u/kernel/sparcv9/unix.**
>
> 3. Reboot.

Performance of your firewall will rely on the hardware you choose. It is highly recommended that you increase your hardware requirements above the minimum listed in Table 2.1 in real-world environments. Keep in mind that your management station will be handling logs from each module it controls, so you will want to ensure that you have adequate disk space, memory, and CPU to handle these connections. Before you start your installation, make sure that you complete the items listed below:

- Get your licenses.

- Secure the Host.

- Configure routing and test network interface cards.

- Enable IP forwarding.

- Configure DNS.

- Prepare for Check Point Installation and Configuration Screens.

Obtaining Licenses

Check Point licenses have changed (again) with the Next Generation release. In order to obtain a license, you can either get them through your Check Point Value Added Reseller (VAR) or use the Check Point User Center to license your products at http://usercenter.checkpoint.com (see Figure 2.1). You have two options when it comes to licensing your firewall modules. You can either have them tied to their individual IP addresses (external interface recommended) as was the way with previous versions, or you can tie them all to the management station's IP address. These licenses are called either *local* or *central* respectively. All licenses are maintained on the management console, and administrators can add or remove licenses using the SecureUpdate management tool.

Figure 2.1 Check Point's User Center

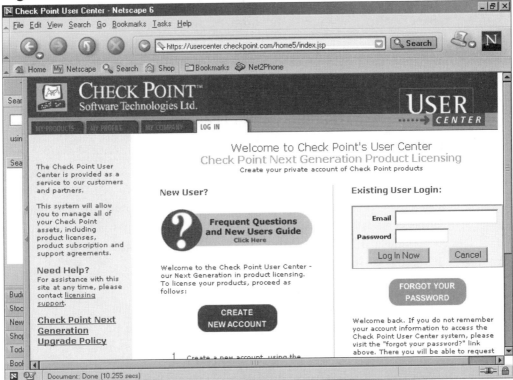

The management module itself must have a local license based on its own IP address. The nice thing about using central licenses for the enforcement modules is that you can change their IP addresses without needing to replace the license, and you can easily move a license from one module to another.

It is always best to obtain your licenses before you install the firewall software. The program will ask you for your license details during the install procedure. If you cannot obtain your permanent license prior to the install, then you should ask for an evaluation license. Check Point's eval licenses have full functionality for all VPN-1/FireWall-1 features. They are usually valid for one month, and the product is not crippled in any way while running on eval.

Securing the Host

With any firewall installation it is important to consider the security of the host computer on which you are installing the firewall software. There are some guidelines available on the Internet for securing the various operating systems. Below is a list of URLs to some good guides:

- **WinNT** http://support.checkpoint.com/kb/docs/public/os/winnt/pdf/Securing_NT.pdf

- **WinNT** http://www.enteract.com/~lspitz/nt.html

- **Solaris** http://support.checkpoint.com/kb/docs/public/os/solaris/pdf/strip-sunserver.pdf

- **Solaris** http://www.enteract.com/~lspitz/armoring2.html

- **Linux** http://www.enteract.com/~lspitz/linux.html

Lance Spitzner also has several great papers at http://www.enteract.com/~lspitz/, which you might want to check out.

You should start out by installing the base operating system without any bells or whistles, and then apply any necessary OS patches. You should not install any additional Internet servers on your firewall host either. For example, you do not want to have IIS or an FTP server running on your firewall since these services could be vulnerable to attack.

Disabling Services

Probably the most important step in any of these guides is the process of disabling services on the firewall host. Almost any OS installation enables various services out-of-the-box, which are not needed for the operation of a firewall. Your firewall should have as few services running as possible. If you are installing on a Windows machine, you should disable NETBEUI or any other non-IP protocols. The kernel processes of the NG product do not inspect traffic on non-IP protocols, so your NETBEUI and IPX traffic would not be protected, therefore it should not be installed on the firewall.

Configuring & Implementing…

Nokia Services Disabled

By default, the Nokia hardware platform comes with a hardened FreeBSD operating system out-of-the-box. There is nothing that needs to be done to secure a Nokia platform prior to installing the NG product when starting with a default install.

If you are installing the firewall on a Unix system, the most common method of disabling services is through the /etc/inetd.conf file. This file tells the system which services/protocols are enabled, and therefore which ports the system will be listening to. Illustration 2.1 shows the beginning of a typical inetd.conf file as installed in Solaris 2.7. As you can see, there are several services running that do not need to be enabled. Pretty much everything in the inetd.conf file can be disabled. If you want to leave ftp or telnet open temporarily, then that is your option.

Illustration 2.1 Example of inetd.conf File

```
# more inetd.conf
#
#ident  "@(#)inetd.conf 1.33    98/06/02 SMI"   /* SVr4.0 1.5    */
#
#
# Configuration file for inetd(1M).  See inetd.conf(4).
#
# To reconfigure the running inetd process, edit this file, then
# send the inetd process a SIGHUP.
#
# Syntax for socket-based Internet services:
#   <service_name> <socket_type> <proto> <flags> <user> <server_pathname>
<args>
#
# Syntax for TLI-based Internet services:
#
#   <service_name> tli <proto> <flags> <user> <server_pathname> <args>
#
# Ftp and telnet are standard Internet services.
#
ftp     stream  tcp    nowait  root    /usr/sbin/in.ftpd          in.ftpd
telnet  stream  tcp    nowait  root    /usr/sbin/in.telnetd
in.telnetd
#
# Tnamed serves the obsolete IEN-116 name server protocol.
```

Continued

Illustration 2.1 Continued

```
#
#
name      dgram    udp      wait      root     /usr/sbin/in.tnamed
in.tnamed
#
# Shell, login, exec, comsat and talk are BSD protocols.
#
shell     stream   tcp      nowait    root     /usr/sbin/in.rshd        in.rshd
login     stream   tcp      nowait    root     /usr/sbin/in.rlogind
in.rlogind
exec      stream   tcp      nowait    root     /usr/sbin/in.rexecd
in.rexecd
comsat    dgram    udp      wait      root     /usr/sbin/in.comsat
in.comsat
talk      dgram    udp      wait      root     /usr/sbin/in.talkd       in.talkd
```

To disable services in this file, simply edit it, and insert a pound sign or hash mark in front of the line that you wish to disable. When completed, send a HUP signal to the inetd process running on the system as shown in Illustration 2.2.

Illustration 2.2 SIGHUP to inetd Process

```
# ps -ef | grep inet
    root    229     1   0    Nov 06 ?           0:00 /usr/sbin/inetd -s
# kill -HUP 229
```

You can verify that the processes are no longer listening on the system by running the `netstat -an` command. Because there are fewer services running on the firewall, the system is more secure. You can think of each of those listening ports as holes into your operating system. Although the firewall software will protect the operating system from direct attack if you have the security policy defined properly, it is better to stay on the safe side and reduce the number of possible ingresses.

Routing and Network Interfaces

I recommend that before you install the Check Point product, first configure and test the networks that the firewall will be communicating on. When you install VPN-1/FireWall-1, the product binds to the interface adapters, and even begins configuring the firewall at this early stage. Regardless of the platform you are installing on, I recommend that you configure the first interface on your firewall as the external interface, and that this IP address resolves to the name of the host computer in the hosts files. On Windows systems, that means the external IP address of the enforcement firewall should go on the network interface that is displayed first in the interface pull-down list under the IP Address tab of the Microsoft TCP/IP Properties window. If this is not defined properly, then several problems may occur with SIC and VPN configurations.

Prior to installation, configure your firewall interfaces with the correct IP addresses and subnet masks. See the Netmask Cheat Sheet available in Appendix A for a quick method of discerning subnet boundaries. Ideally you can plug your system into a test network so that you are not putting your unprotected system on the live network before installing the firewall software. It is always best to install a firewall in an isolated environment so that it cannot be compromised before it has been protected. You will want to test routing and IP forwarding first. Check Point VPN-1/FireWall-1 NG will control IP forwarding once it is installed, but you must first enable it in the OS and test that your network adapters and routing is functioning properly. Just imagine if you didn't perform this test before installing the software, and then found that you had a faulty Network Interface Card (NIC). It would have saved you a lot of blood, sweat, and tears if you had determined this first.

Configuring & Implementing…

Windows Default Gateway

When you are configuring your interfaces on a Windows system, be sure that you only configure one interface with a gateway. This is a common mistake since each interface gives you the option of filling in a gateway, but you should never have more than one default gateway configured on your firewall.

Next, make sure you understand the WAN connections that will be coming into your firewall, and configure routing accordingly. You may decide to set up a dynamic routing protocol on your firewall to maintain its routing table, or you may decide that static routes are the way to go. If you add a route on a Windows system, then you should provide the −p switch so that the route will still be there after a reboot. This switch permanently adds the route into the system registry. For example, the following command will route the 10.1.1.0/24 network to the next hop router of 10.2.2.1 on a WinNT system:

```
route add -p 10.1.1.0 mask 255.255.255.0 10.2.2.1
```

In Solaris, you need to set up your route statements in a file that will be run at startup. I typically use the /etc/rc2.d directory. The file name will need to begin with a capital S for the system to run it (e.g. S99local), and you should set the file modes to allow execution. The same route command above can be written in Solaris as follows:

```
route add 10.1.1.0 -netmask 255.255.255.0 10.2.2.1
```

If your firewall will be on the boarder of your network, connecting your LANs and WANs to the Internet, then you will need to ensure that default routes are configured throughout on all your workstations and routers so that they are routed to the next hop closest to the Internet. It may prove helpful if you create a network diagram that shows how your network looks prior to having a firewall, and another to show the network after the firewall is in place. This will help you to visualize what connections will be changing so that you can prepare accordingly.

Enabling IP Forwarding

To test your routing and interfaces you must enable IP forwarding in your OS. To do this on WinNT, you go to your **TCP/IP properties** window and select **Enable IP Forwarding** from the **Routing tab** as shown in Figure 2.2. To enable IP forwarding in Win2k, you must edit the registry as outlined in Microsoft's KB article Q230082 as follows:

1. Open the registry by running "regedt32.exe."

2. Find the following registry key: HKEY_LOCAL_MACHINE\ SYSTEM\CurrentControlSet\Services\Tcpip\Parameters

3. Add the following value to this key:

   ■   Value Name: IPEnableRouter

- Value type: REG_DWORD

- Value Data: 1

Figure 2.2 Enable IP Forwarding in WinNT 4.0

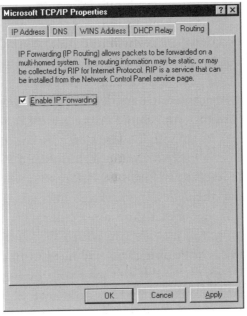

In Solaris, IP forwarding is usually enabled by default. You can switch it off and on with the following command: ndd –set /dev/ip ip_forwarding 1. The settings for this command are as follows:

- 0 disables IP forwarding

- 1 enables IP forwarding

Configuring DNS

Since it is suggested to install your firewall while it is not plugged into any untrusted networks, it will be best to start with DNS disabled on the firewall. If you have DNS enabled and the system cannot reach its name servers, then the system may become sluggish and system performance will be affected. It is important that once you do configure DNS that you configure it properly. The firewall should be able to resolve its own external IP address to the name of the host computer. This could be set up in advance by creating an A record in your domain for the firewall, and you should enter it into the firewall's hosts file. In

Unix, this file is located in /etc/hosts, and in Windows it is located in c:\winnt\ system32\drivers\etc\hosts. The Nokia platform also needs to have the host name associated with its external IP address, and this is done through the "Host Address Assignment" link found under the System Configuration heading in the Voyager GUI. You can use this interface to configure host entries instead of editing a host's file.

You should also include IP addresses in the host's file that your firewall may communicate with frequently, like a management server and/or enforcement module. Policy installation performance can be increased on a management server by having all network objects (which are defined in the next chapter) resolvable.

Another DNS record that you should create is a PTR record for your fire-wall's external IP address or any other address(es) that you will be using for Network Address Translation (NAT). Some Web sites and FTP servers require that you have a reverse resolvable IP address before they will grant you or your users access to download their files. If you have obtained a block of IP addresses from your ISP, then chances are that they control the PTR records for your addresses. Sometimes they will provide you with a Web site where you can administer these yourself. Other times, you will need to find the right person who can make the changes for you. If you have your own ASN, then you can set up your own in-addr.arpa domain and create your own PTR records.

Preparing for VPN-1/FireWall-1 NG

During the install process, you will be asked which components you want to install and then you will need to be prepared to fill in the configuration screens at the end of the installation procedure. The Check Point Next Generation CD gives you the following options for installation:

- **Server/Gateway Components** Choose this option if you wish to install one or more of the following components from the Next Generation Suite:

  - **VPN-1 & FireWall-1** This includes FireWall-1 Management module and enforcement point software along with the VPN-1 encryption component.

  - **FloodGate-1** Provides an integrated Quality of Service (QoS) solution for VPN-1/FireWall-1.

  - **Meta IP** Integrated IP Management with DNS and DHCP servers.

- **Management Clients** The Graphical User Interface for Check Point including the Policy Editor, Log Viewer, and System Status GUI.

- **UserAuthority** A user-authentication tool that integrates with FireWall-1, FloodGate-1, and other ebusiness applications.

- **VPN-1 SecureClient Policy Server** Allows an enforcement module to install Granular Desktop Policies on mobile users' SecureClient personal firewalls.

- **Reporting Module** An integrated Reporting tool that can generate reports, graphs, and pie charts to display information obtained from the VPN-1/FireWall-1 logs.

- **Real Time Monitor** Allows an organization to monitor their VPN connections, Internet connections, etc.

- **Mobile/Desktop Components (Windows Only)** If you just want to install client software on your mobile users or desktops in the office as described below, then choose this option.

  - **VPN-1 SecuRemote** Client Encryption software loaded on your mobile clients

  - **VPN-1 SecureClient** Client Encryption software with Desktop Security (personal firewall) features.

  - **Session Authentication Agent** This agent is installed on desktop computers where your users will need to authenticate with Session Authentication.

If you are installing from files, be sure that you download and install the Check Point SVN Foundation first. This package is the base of the entire Check Point Next Generation software suite as its name suggests. It's this program that allows the easy integration of all other NG components. The only VPN-1/FireWall-1 applications that don't rely on the SVN Foundation are the Management Clients.

The next important question that the installation process will ask you (if you are installing a management server on your firewall) is whether you want to enable backward compatibility. If you choose *not* to install backward compatibility, then you will only be able to manage other NG modules. If you do choose to install backward compatibility, then you will be able to manage NG, 4.1, and 4.0 modules from this management station.

The default folder installation in Windows is c:\winnt\fw1\ng and Check Point installs files on Solaris in /opt and /var/opt. Make sure that you have partitioned your disk properly to accept the default installation folder, or be prepared to give a custom location for the installation (Windows only). If you don't accept the defaults, you should verify that the install program configures the firewall's environment variables properly.

Configuring & Implementing...

FireWall-1 Environment Variables

You will see the use of the $FWDIR environment variable throughout this book. It is the nature of an environment variable to contain some value (similar to a variable used to represent a number in algebra). The $FWDIR variable contains the value of your firewall's installation directory, and it is configured upon install. If you install on Windows, this variable is set to c:\winnt\fw1\ng. In Solaris the $FWDIR environment variable is set to /opt/CPfw1-50.

There is also a $CPDIR variable, which contains the installation directory of the CPShared (SVN) components. In Windows, the $CPDIR variable is set to C:\Program Files\CheckPoint\CPShared\5.0, and in Solaris it is set to /opt/CPshared/5.0.

So, whenever you see these terms used, $FWDIR or $CPDIR, then just substitute the appropriate directory for your firewall installation in their place. On a Unix system, you can type "echo $FWDIR" to see the value of the variable, or type "set" to see a list of all environment variables and their associated values. To be technically accurate, we should probably use %FWDIR% when talking about the Windows environment, but we are going to stick to the Unix method of describing variables in this book.

The VPN-1/FireWall-1 component options are as follows:

- **Enterprise Primary Management** To install a Management server only, which will be acting in a primary capacity.

- **Enterprise Secondary Management** To install a Management server only, which will be acting in a backup capacity.

- **Enforcement Module & Primary Management (Default)** To install both a Primary Management Module and VPN-1/FireWall-1 Enforcement Module.

- **Enforcement Module** To install an Enforcement Module only, the management server will be installed on a separate host.

The Management Client options are as follows:

- **Policy Editor** Used to connect to your management server to configure your Rule Base, Network Address Translation, FloodGate-1 QoS policy, and SecureClient Desktop Security Policies.

- **Log Viewer** Used to view your VPN-1/FireWall-1 security logs, accounting logs, and audit logs on the management server.

- **System Status** Used to view the status of your remote enforcement points connected to your management server.

- **SecureClient Packaging Tool** Used to create custom packages for SecuRemote/SecureClient mobile users.

- **Traffic Monitoring** Used to monitor an interface, QoS rule, or virtual link in real time. The display is in the form of a line or bar graph.

- **SecureUpdate** Used for managing licenses and doing remote software updates of your remote enforcement points connected to your management server.

- **Reporting Tool** Used to generate reports with graphs and pie charts from the data in the VPN-1/FireWall-1 logs.

After the Check Point installation wizard copies files, it will run through a number of configuration screens. These will be identical if you are installing a Management Module with or without an Enforcement Module with the exception of the SNMP option in Solaris, which is only configured if you are installing an Enforcement module. The screens that you can prepare for in advance are the following:

- **Licenses** You should read the section on Licenses above, if you need help getting licenses. You will fill in the following fields:

  - **Host/IP Address** The IP address associated with this license or "eval."

  - **Expiration Date** The date that the license expires, which may be "never."

- **SKU/Features** These are the features that this license will enable (e.g. Management or 3DES)

- **String/Signature Key** The license string provided by Check Point to validate the license. This key will be unique for each license and IP Address.

- **Administrators** You will need to configure at least one administrator during install. See below for more on adding Administrators.

  - **Administrator Name** Choose a login name for your admin. This field is case sensitive.

  - **Password** Choose a good alphanumeric password. It must be at least four characters long.

  - **Confirm Password** Repeat the same password entered above.

- **GUI Clients** These are the IP addresses of the Management Clients that your administrators will use when connecting to this Management Module. You may need to configure static IP addresses for your admins. You may add as many GUI clients as you'd like or you may enter none; it's up to you. See below for your GUI Client options.

- **SNMP extension (Unix only)** If you wish to utilize external network management tools such as HP OpenView, then you can install the Check Point FireWall-1 SNMP daemon. With the daemon installed and activated, you will be able to query the firewall status. You could use a network management tool to monitor the firewall's health and generate alerts based on certain criteria.

- **Group Permissions (Unix only)** If you choose to set group permissions on your VPN-1/FireWall-1 installation on Solaris, then enter the group name at this prompt (from /etc/group). If you do not want to set group permissions, then only root will be able to execute all FireWall-1 commands. You might want to set group permissions so that you can enable a number of firewall operators to execute FireWall-1 commands without having to grant them super-user privileges to the system.

Administrators

It is best to use individual admin usernames instead of a generic username like fwadmin. The problem with using a generic login ID is that you cannot properly audit the activities of the firewall administrators. It may be important for you to know who installed the last security policy when you are troubleshooting a problem. This becomes more and more important when there are several people administering a firewall system. The fields that you need to fill in follow:

- **Administrator Name** Choose a login name for your admin. This field is case sensitive.

- **Password** Choose a good alphanumeric password. It must be at least four characters long.

NOTE

If you are installing just an Enforcement Module, then you will not have any administrators or GUI clients to configure.

There is a section labeled Permissions that enables you to define the access level you will require on an individual basis for each administrator. If you select **Read/Write All** or **Read Only All**, then your admin will have access to all the available GUI client features with the ability to either make changes and updates or view the configuration and logs (perhaps for troubleshooting purposes) accordingly. You may also choose to customize their access so that they may be able to update some things and not others. To do this, select **Customized** and configure each of these options:

- **SecureUpdate** This GUI tool enables you to manage licenses and update remote modules.

- **Objects Database** This tool is used to create new objects to be used in the Security Policy Rule Bases. Objects will be covered in the next chapter.

- **Check Point Users Database** This tool is used to manage users for firewall authentication purposes.

- **LDAP Users Database** This tool is used to manage LDAP users.

- **Security Policy** This tool is used to create and manage Rule Bases using the Policy Editor GUI.

- **Monitoring** This option enables access to the Log Viewer, System Status, and Traffic Monitoring GUI clients.

GUI Clients

When you enter GUI Clients, you type their hostname or IP address into the Remote hostname: field, and then add them to the list of clients allowed to connect to your Management Module. You are allowed to use wildcards as follows:

- **Any** If you type in the word "Any," this will allow anyone to connect without restriction (not recommended).

- **Asterisks** You may use asterisks in the hostname, e.g. 10.10.20.* means any host in the 10.10.20.0/24 network, or *.domainname.com means any hostname within the domainname.com domain.

- **Ranges** You may use a dash (-) to represent a range of IP addresses, e.g. 1.1.1.3-1.1.1.7 means the 5 hosts including 1.1.1.3 and 1.1.1.7 and every one in between.

- **DNS or WINS resolvable hostnames**

I would recommend staying away from using hostnames or domain names, however, since it requires DNS to be configured and working on the firewall. Using IP addresses are the best method since it doesn't rely on resolving, and will continue to work even if you cannot reach your name servers from the firewall.

Upgrading from a Previous Version

Although I will be walking you through a fresh install of NG in this chapter, some of you may be interested in upgrading from your existing versions of FireWall-1. You can install or upgrade to NG from version 4.0 or 4.1, and it can manage v4.x firewalls if you choose the Backward Compatibility option during the install. Although NG utilizes Secure Internal Communication (SIC) for other NG modules, it can also use the `fw putkey` command to communicate with previous versions of the product. FireWall-1 NG is not compatible with versions earlier than 4.0.

It's very important that you upgrade your management console prior to upgrading any of your firewall enforcement modules to NG. A 4.1 management station cannot control an NG module. When you do upgrade your enforcement points, you will need to edit their workstation objects in the Policy Editor, and change their version to NG before you will be able to push or fetch a policy.

Read the release notes before you begin. This is very important since there is a list of limitations in the NG release notes that you will need to consider ahead of time. Some of these include, but are not limited to, your resources, VPNs, and external interface settings. NG does not support more than one resource in a rule. If you have rules configured with multiple resources, then NG will copy this rule into the new format with only one resource, and will not create new rules for the others. NG does not support Manual IPSec or SKIP VPNs any longer. If you have these types of VPNs in your rule base before the upgrade, then they will be converted to IKE VPNs without notification during the upgrade to NG. If you have a limited license on your VPN-1/FireWall-1 v4.x firewall, your $FWDIR\conf\ external.if settings will not be preserved during the upgrade. You will need to define your firewall's external interface in the workstation properties window under the **Topology** tab after the upgrade. You may also need to run the confmerge command to manually merge your objects.C file with the new objects in NG. These things and more are laid out for you in the product release notes.

I would also highly recommend that you have a back-out plan in place if your upgrade to NG does not go as smoothly as planned. Check Point recommends upgrading on a new piece of hardware; that way you will minimize downtime as well. If you do it this way, remember that you may need to redo SIC or putkeys, and your Internet router or any routers directly connected to the firewall may need to have their ARP cache cleared after putting the new hardware in place.

Last but certainly not least, make sure that you have a backup of the entire system prior to an upgrade. It is especially important to save the $FWDIR/conf directory and any files that may have been edited from $FWDIR/state (like local.arp in Windows), $FWDIR/database, and $FWDIR/lib (for files like base.def and table.def that may have been modified).

Installing Check Point VPN-1/FireWall-1 NG on Windows

Finally, all of your hard work at preparing for the firewall installation is about to pay off. This section will be dedicated to installing the Check Point VPN-1/FireWall-1 NG on Windows. Hopefully you have read the previous section "Before you Begin" and are prepared to start with the Check Point software installation. If you did not read the "Before you Begin" section above, then I suggest that you go back to the beginning of this chapter and read this section before you continue.

Although I will be walking you through a standalone installation, I will point out the different options you would make if you wanted to install the firewall on Windows in a distributed environment. In other words, you will be installing the Management and Enforcement Modules as well as the GUI all on one machine; however, you could install each piece on separate machines (and use different operating systems) if that is what your network design calls for. The distributed installation is not much different, and my goal is that you will feel just as comfortable with that process after reading this section as well.

Installing from CD

Now I'm going to walk you through the Check Point VPN-1/FireWall-1 installation on Windows using the Check Point Next Generation CD. You can obtain a copy of this CD from Check Point by going to www.checkpoint.com/getsecure .html and requesting an evaluation of the software. If you have a login setup with Check Point, then you can download the software and updates from Check Point here: www.checkpoint.com/techsupport/downloadsng/ngfp1.html.

The following screenshots will be taken from a new install via CD to a Windows 2000 Professional server. If you are installing on Windows NT, the procedure is the same.

1. Insert the Check Point Next Generation CD into the CDROM drive on your firewall system. The Check Point NG Welcome Screen appears (Figure 2.3). If the Welcome screen does not appear after inserting the

CD, then you may start it manually from the CD's wrappers\windows folder by running demo32.exe. From this screen you may choose to read the important information regarding evaluation licenses, purchased products, and the contents of the CD.

Figure 2.3 Welcome Screen

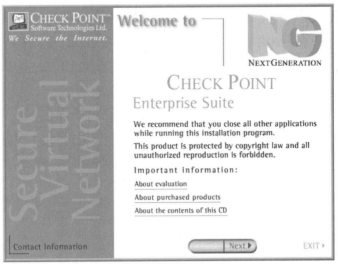

2. If you are ready to continue the installation, then select **Next** to start the Installation Wizard. You will be presented with the License Agreement as illustrated in Figure 2.4.

Figure 2.4 License Agreement

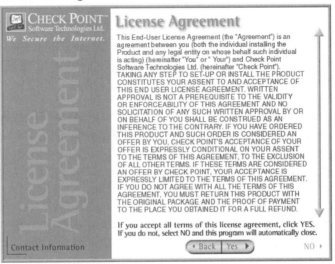

3. You must accept the license agreement in order to continue with installation. Select **Yes** when you are ready to continue. Otherwise, select **No** to exit the installation wizard.

4. The next screen, displayed in Figure 2.5, provides you with the Product Menu so that you can choose which Check Point products you want to install. You have two choices:

- **Server/Gateway Components (Default)** Choose this option if you wish to install one or more of the following components from the Next Generation Suite:

  - **VPN-1 & FireWall-1** This includes FireWall-1 Management module and enforcement point software along with the VPN-1 encryption component.

  - **FloodGate-1** Provides an integrated Quality of Service (QoS) solution for VPN-1/FireWall-1.

  - **Meta IP** Integrated IP Management with DNS and DHCP servers.

  - **Management Clients** The Graphical User Interface for Check Point including the Policy Editor, Log Viewer, and System Status GUI.

  - **UserAuthority** A user-authentication tool that integrates with FireWall-1, FloodGate-1, and other ebusiness applications.

  - **VPN-1 SecureClient Policy Server** Allows an enforcement module to install Granular Desktop Policies on mobile users' SecureClient personal firewalls.

  - **Reporting Module** An integrated Reporting tool that can generate reports, graphs, and pie charts to display information obtained from the VPN-1/FireWall-1 logs.

  - **Real Time Monitor** Allows an organization to monitor their VPN connections, Internet connections, etc.

- **Mobile/Desktop Components** If you just want to install client software on your mobile users or desktops in the office as described below, then choose this option.

  - **VPN-1 SecuRemote** Client Encryption software loaded on your mobile clients.

- **VPN-1 SecureClient** Client Encryption software with Desktop Security (personal firewall) features.

- **Session Authentication Agent** This agent is installed on desktop computers where your users will need to authenticate with Session Authentication.

Figure 2.5 Product Menu

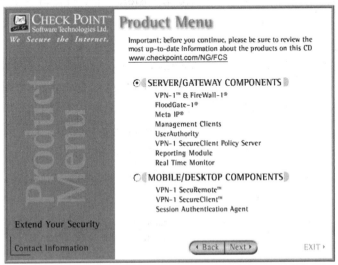

5. Make sure that Server/Gateway Components is selected, and click on **Next.**

NOTE

During the installation process, use the **Back** button at any time to move to the previous screen, use the **Next** button to advance to the next screen, use the **Exit** option to exit at any time, and use the elevator buttons along the side of the page to scroll up and down.

---

6. The next screen that comes up is the Server/Gateway Components (see Figure 2.6), which provides you with the various options for which individual Check Point components you wish to install. We will select **VPN-1 & FireWall-1** and **Management Clients** to install the Management and Enforcement modules as well as the Graphical User

Interface. If you place your mouse pointer over each item, you will see a detailed description displayed on the right–hand side.

Figure 2.6 Server/Gateway Components

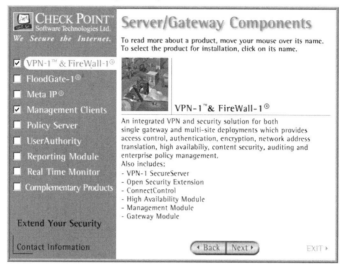

NOTE

If you wish to install the Management Module only, your selections here will be the same. If you wish to install the Enforcement Module only, then you will only select VPN-1 & FireWall-1.

---

7. Click on **Next** when you are ready to begin the install process.

8. The Check Point Installation Wizard will start the InstallShield Wizard program to begin the installation based on the options you've chosen thus far. Figure 2.7 illustrates the screen that you should see next. Select **Next** when you are ready to continue. The InstallShield Wizard will start installing the Check Point SVN Foundation. You should note that this is the first piece that is always installed on a Next Generation system. It will also be the last piece if you uninstall. A progress window will pop up as shown in Figure 2.8. You should see the window displayed in Figure 2.9 when the SVN installation is complete.

Figure 2.7 Selected Products

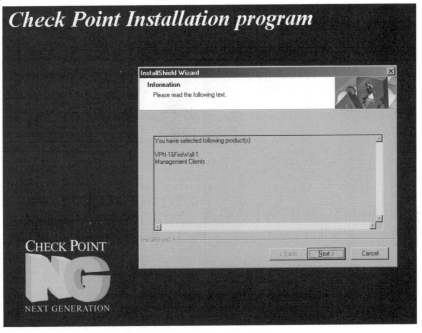

Figure 2.8 Progress Window

Figure 2.9 VPN-1 & FireWall-1 Installation

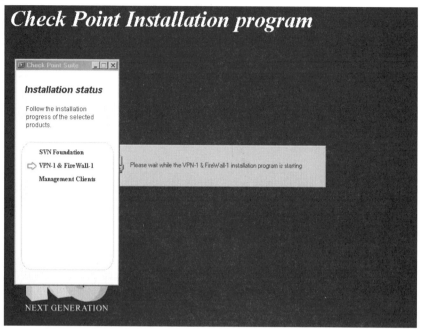

9. Immediately after this screen, another window will pop up asking you for the specific components of VPN-1/FireWall-1 that you wish to install. This screen listing your options is displayed in Figure 2.10. You will be given the options shown below. Select **Enforcement Module & Primary Management** as shown in Figure 2.10, and click **Next**.

    ▪ **Enterprise Primary Management** To install a Management server only that will be acting in a primary capacity.

    ▪ **Enterprise Secondary Management** To install a Management server only that will be acting in a backup capacity.

    ▪ **Enforcement Module & Primary Management (Default)** To install both a Primary Management server and VPN-1/FireWall-1 Enforcement Module.

    ▪ **Enforcement Module** To install an Enforcement Module only, the Management server will be installed on separate hardware.

Figure 2.10 VPN-1 & FireWall-1 Product Specification

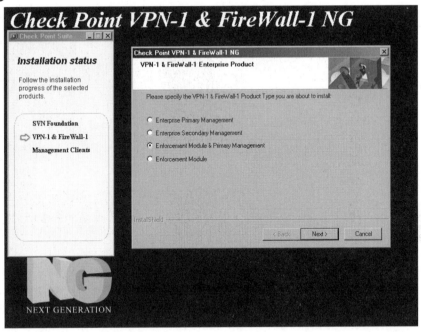

NOTE

If you wish to install the Management Module only, select **Enterprise Primary Management** and then click on **Next**. If you wish to install the Enforcement Module only, then select **Enforcement Module** and click on **Next**.

10. The next screen (Figure 2.11) gives you the option of installing with or without backward compatibility. If you choose to install without backward compatibility, then you will only be able to manage NG enforcement modules, and you will not be able to manage VPN-1/FireWall-1 v4.0 nor v4.1 firewalls from this management station. Choosing to install with backward compatibility support will enable you to manage these older versions of the product. Since we will not be managing any older versions of the product with this management server, choose the default option to **Install without backward compatibility**, and then click on **Next**.

Figure 2.11 Backward Compatibility Screen

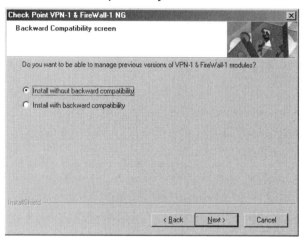

11. Next, Check Point will ask you where you want to install the product files. The default folder location in Windows is c:\winnt\fw1\ng. If you wish to install to a different folder, then choose **Browse**; otherwise, select **Next** to accept the default location and continue. Whatever value you choose for the firewall's installation directory will be the value of the $FWDIR environment variable, which will be used throughout this book when referencing this directory. This is the last screen before VPN-1/FireWall-1 files are copied to your hard drive (Figure 2.12). Now the system copies files and installs the software. You should see a screen similar to the one in Figure 2.13 as the install program shows you its progress. You may click on the **Cancel** button on the bottom right-hand side of this screen if you wish to stop the installation at this point.

12. Once the system is finished copying files, you may see some messages pop up such as "Installing FireWall-1 kernel," "Installing FireWall-1 Service," "Setting Permissions" (NTFS only), and "Register product add-ons…." These windows appear whenever you are installing an Enforcement Module. The installation wizard will then give you a final popup window from VPN-1/FireWall-1 explaining that the installation will complete upon reboot as shown in Figure 2.14. Click on **OK**.

Figure 2.12 Choose Destination Location

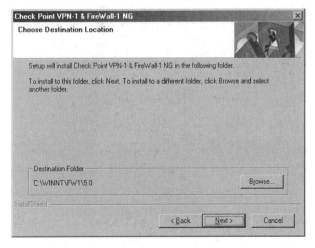

Figure 2.13 Copying Files

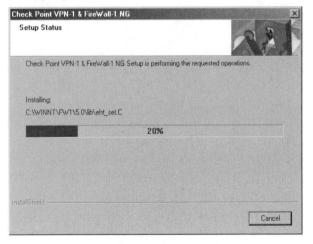

Figure 2.14 Setup Information

13. The system will not reboot after you select **OK**. Instead, it will begin installing the Check Point Management Clients. You will see a window like the one in Figure 2.15 asking if you wish to install the Management Clients in the default folder C:\Program Files\CheckPoint\Management Clients. You can either accept the default or click on "Browse..." to choose a new target for the files. Accept the default folder location and click on **Next** to continue.

Figure 2.15 Management Client Location

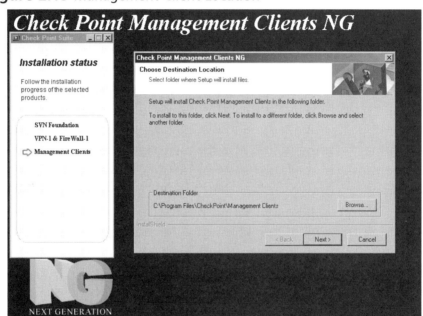

14. Now you will need to choose which of the Management Clients you want to install. Figure 2.16 displays the window you will see with your available options, which are as follows:

- **Policy Editor** Used to configure your Rule Base, Network Address Translation, FloodGate-1 QoS policy, and SecureClient Desktop Security Policies.

- **Log Viewer** Used to view your VPN-1/FireWall-1 security logs, accounting logs, and audit logs.

- **System Status** Used to view the status of your remote enforcement points connected to your management server.

■ **SecureClient Packaging Tool** Used to create custom packages for SecuRemote/SecureClient mobile users.

■ **Traffic Monitoring** Used to monitor an interface, QoS rule, or virtual link in real time. The display is in the form of a line or bar graph.

■ **SecureUpdate** Used for managing licenses and doing remote software updates of your remote enforcement points connected to your management server.

■ **Reporting Tool** Used to generate reports with graphs and pie charts from the data in the VPN-1/FireWall-1 logs.

Figure 2.16 Select Management Clients to Install

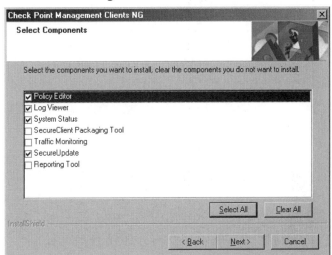

Accept the default values, Policy Editor, Log Viewer, System Status, and SecureUpdate, and click on **Next**. This is the last screen before the Check Point installation wizard begins copying files to your system (Figure 2.17).

15. When the system is done copying files, the installation process is nearly complete. You can now click on any of the icons in the Check Point Management Clients folder. You can also open the Management Clients by going to **Start | Programs | Check Point Management Clients**. Click on **OK** to finish the installation (Figure 2.18) and begin the configuration process.

Figure 2.17 Management Clients Copying Files

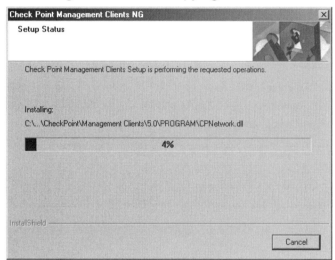

Figure 2.18 Setup Complete

Configuring Check Point VPN-1/FireWall-1 NG on Windows

Once the system is done copying files during the install procedure, it will begin to go through the configuration screens. If you read the first section of this chapter, then you should be prepared to configure the firewall. After this initial configuration, you can always come back to any of these screens by opening the **Check Point Configuration NG** window via **Start | Programs | Check Point Management Clients | Check Point Configuration NG**.

The initial configuration will take you through the following screens:

- Licenses

- Administrators

- GUI Clients

- Certificate Authority Configuration

Licenses

You should have obtained all of your licenses before you get to this step. If you didn't, don't worry. There is even a link to the Check Point User Center, where you can get your licenses, right in the Licenses window. If you need help with your license, read the first part of this chapter titled "Before you Begin." If you don't have any permanent licenses to install at this time, you can always request an evaluation license from either Check Point or your Check Point reseller.

Since you have installed a Primary Management Module, you should be installing a local license that was registered with the local Management station's IP address. Follow this step-by-step procedure for adding your license(s).

1. Click on **Add** as shown in the Licenses configuration window in Figure 2.19.

Figure 2.19 Licenses

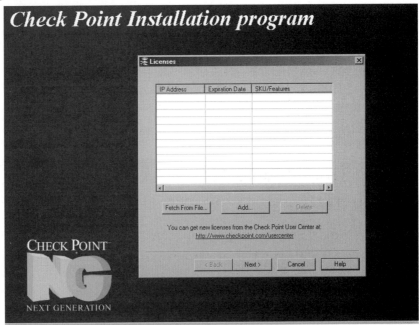

2. Once you click on **Add,** you will see a window pop-up like the one illustrated in Figure 2.20. In this window you can either select **Paste License** or enter the license details into the appropriate fields. The figure below shows the following license installed: cplic putlic eval 01Mar2002 aoMJFd63k-pLdmKQMwZ-aELBqjeVX-pJxZJJCAy

CPMP-EVAL-1-3DES-NG CK-CP. In addition you will see the following fields:

- **IP Address** The IP address associated with this license or "eval."

- **Expiration Date** The date that the license expires, which may be "never."

- **SKU/Features** These are the features that this license will enable (e.g. Management or 3DES).

- **Signature Key** The license string provided by Check Point to validate the license. This key will be unique for each license and IP Address.

Enter your license details in the Add License window, and click on **Calculate** to verify that the information you entered is correct. Match the Validation Code that you receive in this cell to the Validation Code on the license obtained from the Check Point User Center. You can also copy the entire 'cplic putlic' command into your clipboard, and then click the **Paste License** button at the top of the screen to fill in all the fields. Click **OK** to continue, and if you entered everything correctly you should see the license entered into the main Licenses window (Figure 2.21).

Figure 2.20 Adding a License

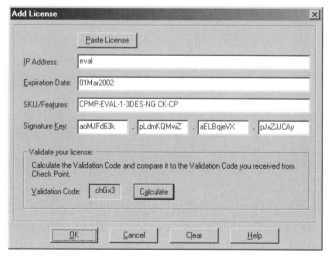

Figure 2.21 License Added Successfully

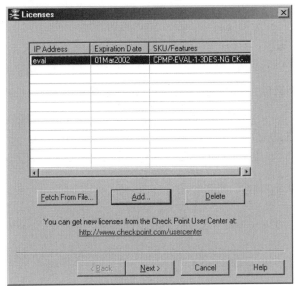

NOTE

The license configuration window will be displayed whether you are installing just the Management or the Enforcement Module in a distributed install as well.

---

3. Click on **Next** to continue. The next screen deals with the Check Point configuration of the Management module.

Configuring & Implementing...

Fetching Licenses

If you have saved your license(s) to a file with a .lic extension (e.g. licenses.lic), then you could alternatively use the "Fetch from File..." button that would enable you to browse your file system for the file. Once you've located the *.lic file, select **Open**, and the license details will be imported into the Licenses configuration window.

Administrators

After installing your licenses, you will be presented with another configuration window (see Figure 2.22) in which you need to configure your firewall administrators. You will need to define at least one administrator during this time. You can always come back to this window later to add, edit, or delete your admins.

Figure 2.22 Configuring Administrators

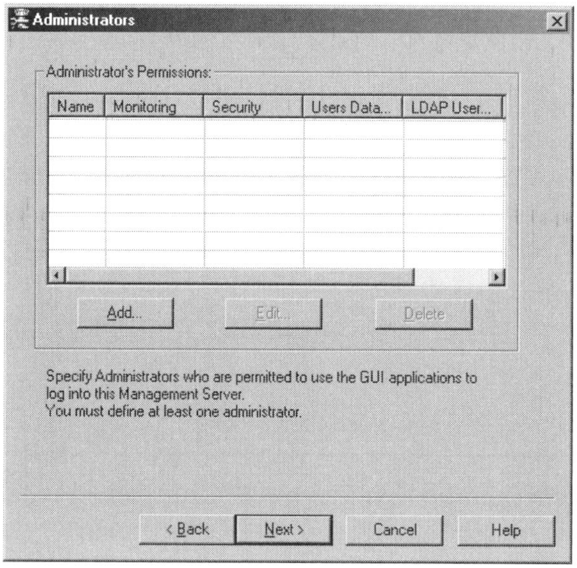

1. The first step to configuring your administrators is to click on **Add...**

2. You will be presented with another window similar to the one in Figure 2.23 where you can define the attributes for one administrator. It is best to use individual admin usernames instead of a generic username like fwadmin. The problem with using a generic login ID is that you cannot properly audit the activities of the firewall administrators. It may be important for you to know who installed the last security policy when you are troubleshooting a problem. This becomes more and more important when there are several people administering a firewall system. The fields that you need to fill in are listed below. Fill in the required fields in the Add Administrator Window and select **Read/Write All** for the permissions. Click on **OK** to finish adding the administrator.

   ▪ **Administrator Name** Choose a login name for your admin. This field is case sensitive.

- **Password** Choose a good alphanumeric password. It must be at least four characters long and is also case sensitive.

- **Confirm Password** Repeat the same password entered above.

Figure 2.23 Adding an Administrator

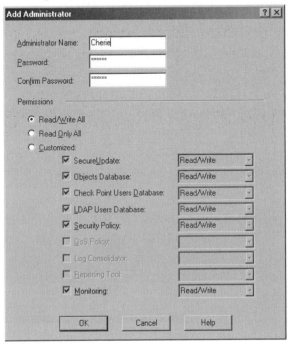

The section labeled Permissions enables you to define the access level that you will require on an individual basis for each administrator. If you select **Read/Write All** or **Read Only All**, then your admin will have access to all the available GUI client features with the ability to either make changes and updates or view the configuration and logs (perhaps for troubleshooting purposes) respectively. You may also choose to customize their access so that they may be able to update some things and not others. To do this, select **Customized** and configure each of these options:

- **SecureUpdate** This GUI tool enables you to manage licenses and update remote modules.

- **Objects Database** This tool is used to create new objects to be used in the Security Policy. Objects will be covered in the next chapter.

- **Check Point Users Database** This tool is used to manage users for firewall authentication purposes.

- **LDAP Users Database** This tool is used to manage LDAP users.

- **Security Policy** This tool is used to create and manage a rule base using the Policy Editor GUI.

- **Monitoring** This option enables access to the Log Viewer, System Status, and Traffic Monitoring GUI clients.

3. When you finish adding your administrator, you will be brought back to the main Administrators configuration window. Your administrator should now be listed in the Administrator's Permissions window. From here you may choose to **Add...**, **Edit...**, or **Delete administrators** from this list (see Figure 2.24). When you are done adding your administrators, click on **Next** to continue with the configuration of the Check Point Management Module.

Figure 2.24 Administrators

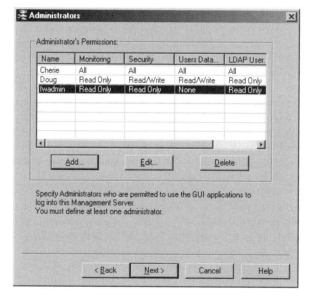

GUI Clients

The Graphical User Interface (GUI) Clients are the Management Clients we installed. These clients could also be installed on as many desktops as you wish, but before they can connect to the management server, you need to enter their IP addresses into the GUI Clients configuration window shown in Figure 2.25.

You can use this feature, for example, if you install the GUI clients on your own workstation to enable you to control the management server from your PC. This will enable you to connect remotely to manage the Security Policy and view your logs and system status. You do not need to configure any clients at all during the install, but if you are already prepared for this step, you may enter as many clients into this window as necessary. This client info will be saved in a file on your firewall under $FWDIR/conf and will be named gui-clients. This file can be edited directly, or you can bring up this GUI Clients window at any time in the future.

Figure 2.25 GUI Clients

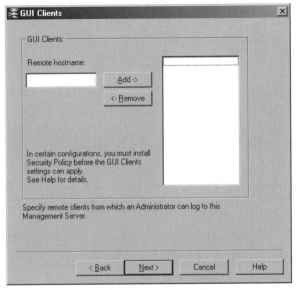

> **NOTE**
>
> If you have installed an Enforcement Module only, then you will not configure GUI clients.

1. For the example installation in this book, we are not going to enter any GUI Clients. Select **Next** to continue on with the Check Point Management Module installation and read the next section. When you enter GUI Clients, you type their hostname or IP address into the

Remote hostname: field, and then click **Add** to insert the clients to the window on the right. You are allowed to use wildcards as follows:

- **Any** If you type in the word "Any," this will allow anyone to connect without restriction (not recommended).

- **Asterisks** You may use asterisks in the hostname, e.g. 10.10.20.★ means any host in the 10.10.20.0/24 network, or ★.domainname.com means any hostname within the domainname.com domain.

- **Ranges** You may use a dash (–) to represent a range of IP addresses, e.g. 1.1.1.3–1.1.1.7 means the 5 hosts including 1.1.1.3 and 1.1.1.7 and every one in between.

- **DNS** or **WINS resolvable hostnames**

Figure 2.26 displays an example of the configured GUI Clients window with various options that you can use for your GUI Client entries. I would recommend staying away from using hostnames or domain names, however, since it requires DNS to be configured and working on the firewall. Using IP addresses are the best method since it doesn't rely on resolving, and will continue to work even if you cannot reach your name servers from the firewall.

Figure 2.26 GUI Clients

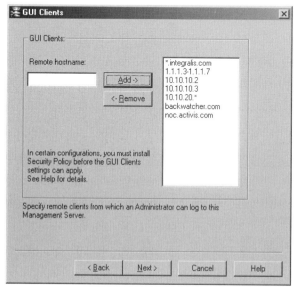

Certificate Authority Initialization

Your Management server will be a Certificate Authority for your firewall enforcement modules, and will use certificates for Secure Internal Communication (SIC). This is the step in the installation process where the Management Server's CA is configured, and a certificate is generated for the server itself.

You will be presented with a Key Hit Session window where you are asked to input random text until you hear a beep. The data you enter will be used to generate the certificate, and it is recommended that you also enter the data at a random pace; some keystrokes may be close together and others could have a longer pause in between them. The more random the data, the more unlikely that the input could be duplicated. If the system determines that the keystrokes are not random enough, it will not take them as input, and will display a bomb icon under Random Characters, but if the input is good, then it will display a yellow light bulb. I personally think this step is fun because you get to pound on the keyboard, and I love the way this sounds when we do this in the classroom.

NOTE

The Key Hit Session screen will also be presented to you if you have installed an Enforcement Module only so that you can generate an internal certificate for SIC.

1. Type random characters at random intervals into the Key Hit Session window until the progress bar is full, and the message "Thank you!" appears at the bottom of the window as seen in Figure 2.27. Click on **Next** to continue with the CA configuration.

2. You will be presented with a window titled Certificate Authority (Figure 2.28). This window simply informs you that the CA is not yet configured and that it will be initialized when you select **Next**. Click **Next** to initialize the Management Module's Certificate Authority. You should receive a message that the initialization completed successfully as shown in Figure 2.29.

3. Click on **OK**.

Figure 2.27 Key Hit Session

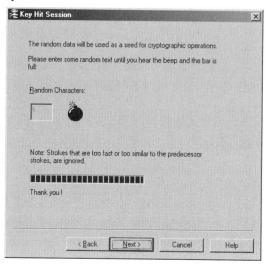

Figure 2.28 Certificate Authority Initialization

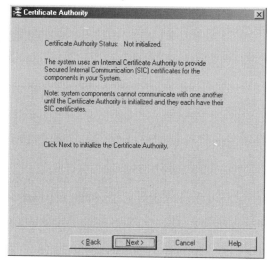

Figure 2.29 CA Initialized Successfully

4. Click on **Finish** from the Fingerprint window shown in Figure 2.30 to exit out of the configuration. This window will be the last one in the set of configuration screens during the install process. This window displays the fingerprint of the Management Server's CA. You will be able to bring this window up again after the installation through the Check Point Configuration NG Tool, which I will show you in the section titled "Getting Back to Configuration." When a GUI client first connects to the Management Server, it will be asked to verify the fingerprint to ensure that they are connecting to the right machine. After that, the client software will compare the Management server's fingerprints at each connect. If the fingerprints do not match, then the client will be warned and asked if they wish to continue. The fingerprint could be exported to a file also, which the GUI Clients would have access to.

Figure 2.30 Management Server Fingerprint

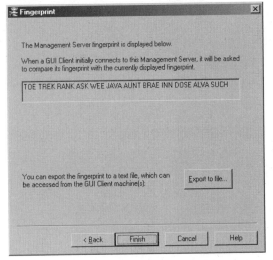

Installation Complete

Congratulations. You have now successfully installed and configured a Check Point VPN-1/FireWall-1 firewall on a Windows system. All you need to do now is navigate your way out of the Check Point Installation program and reboot your computer. Check Point will thank you for using their SVN Integrated installation suite (see Figure 2.31) and ask you if you wish to reboot now or reboot later (Figure 2.32).

Figure 2.31 NG Configuration Complete

Figure 2.32 Reboot Computer

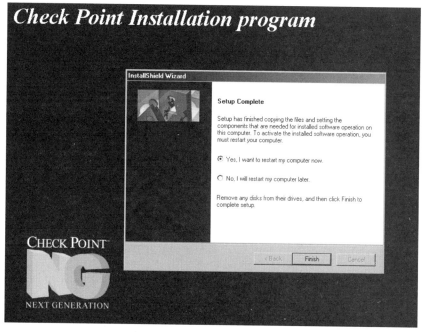

1. To finish the installation process, click **OK**.

2. From the InstallShield Wizard dialog box illustrated in Figure 2.32, choose **Yes, I want to restart my computer now** and click on **Finish**. Your computer will be shut down and restarted.

Getting Back to Configuration

Now that installation is complete, you may need to get back into the Configuration screens that you ran through at the end of the install. You can add, modify, or delete any of the previous configuration settings by running the Check Point Configuration NG GUI.

1. Select **Start | Programs | Check Point Management Clients | Check Point Configuration NG**. This will bring up the Configuration Tool displayed in Figure 2.33. As you can see, all of the configuration options that we went through during the initial install are available through the various tabs at the top of the Configuration Tool window, and there may be a couple of others as well. The tabs you can configure from this tool are listed below.

   - Licenses

   - Administrators

   - GUI Clients

   - PKCS#11 Token—Used to configure an add-on card, like a VPN accelerator card, for example.

   - Key Hit Session

   - Fingerprint

   Each of the options in Figure 2.33 is described in detail above, so I won't go into them again here. If you are just reading the chapter at this point, jump to the top of this section "Configuring the Management Module" to get a walk through of each of these screens and your options.

2. When done making changes to your firewall configuration, click on **OK** to exit the tool.

Figure 2.33 Check Point Configuration Tool

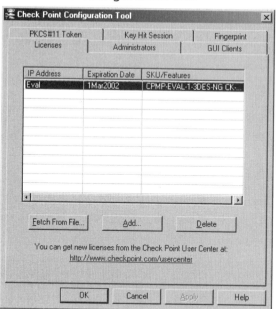

NOTE

If you had installed the Primary Management Module only, then the tabs on the Configuration Tool NG will be exactly the same as in Figure 2.33 without the tab for PKCS#11 Token.

If you installed an Enforcement Module Only, then the Configuration Tool screens will be a little different (see Figure 2.34). The two new tabs are as follows:

- **Secure Internal Communication** Enables you to initialize an Enforcement module for communication. You must enter the same password here as you enter in the Policy Editor GUI (Figure 2.35).

- **High Availability** Lets you enable this Enforcement module to participate in a Check Point High Availability (CPHA) configuration with one or more other Enforcement modules. This tab, illustrated in Figure 2.36, will not show up in your installation since you cannot have a management module installed on an enforcement module in a CPHA cluster.

Figure 2.34 Enforcement Module Configuration Tool

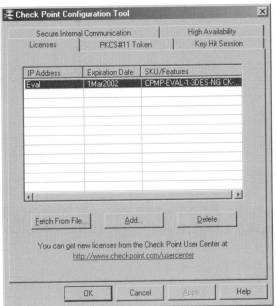

Figure 2.35 Secure Internal Communication

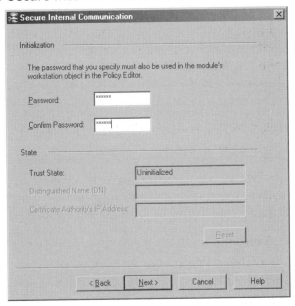

Figure 2.36 High Availability

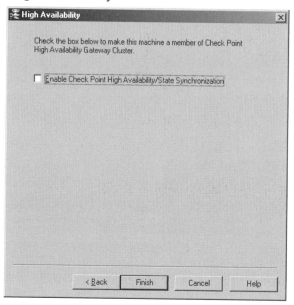

Uninstalling Check Point VPN-1/FireWall-1 NG on Windows

When you uninstall VPN-1/FireWall-1, it is recommended that you make a full system backup before you begin. If you only need to back up the firewall configuration, then you should make a backup of the $FWDIR directory and all of its subdirectories. The default $FWDIR directory in Windows is c:\winnt\fw1\ng.

> **WARNING**
>
> When you remove the Check Point VPN-1/FireWall-1 software on your system, you will lose all configuration data. The uninstall process deletes all the files and directories associated with this package.

Uninstalling VPN-1 & FireWall-1

When you uninstall the firewall, you should remove the Check Point installed components from the Add/Remove Programs in your system's Control Panel. The components should be removed in the following order:

1. Check Point VPN-1 & FireWall-1 NG

2. Check Point SVN Foundation NG

You can remove the Management Clients package at any time, but the order in which you remove these two packages is important.

Follow the steps below to completely uninstall all Check Point products from your Windows platform.

1. Exit all GUI Client windows that you may have open.

2. Open your Control Panel by going to **Start | Settings | Control Panel**.

3. Click on the **Add/Remove Programs** icon. If you are on Windows 2000, you should see a window similar to the window displayed in Figure 2.37. Now you should select **Check Point VPN-1 & FireWall-1 NG** and click on **Change/Remove** to uninstall this program.

Figure 2.37 Add/Remove Check Point VPN-1/FireWall-1 NG

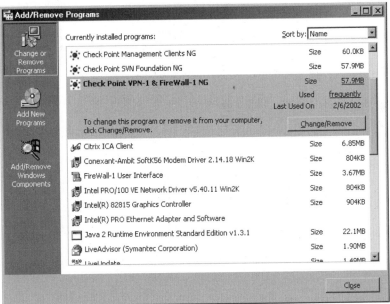

4. You will receive a message asking if you are sure that you want to remove this program as seen in Figure 2.38. Click on **OK** to continue and remove the VPN-1/FireWall-1 components.

Figure 2.38 Confirm Program Removal

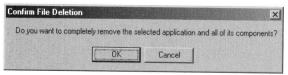

5. You will receive a Question/Warning message from Check Point (see Figure 2.39) asking if it is O.K. to continue with the uninstall of your Primary Management Server. Click **Yes** to continue. This is your last chance to change your mind. After you have confirmed that you really do wish to remove the Management server VPN-1/FireWall-1 component, the uninstall process will then stop any running Check Point services before starting to remove files. You will see the message displayed in Figure 2.40.

Figure 2.39 Check Point Warning

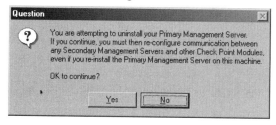

Figure 2.40 Stopping Services

6. Next, you will see a window pop up, which will show you the progress of the uninstall process (Figure 2.41). Select **Yes, I want to restart my computer now** and click on **Finish** to reboot your computer (Figure 2.42).

Figure 2.41 Removing VPN-1/FireWall-1 Files

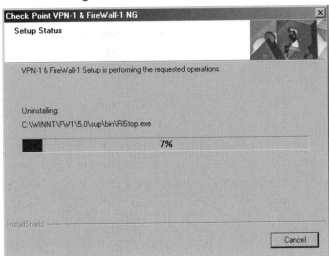

Figure 2.42 VPN-1/FireWall-1 Uninstall Complete

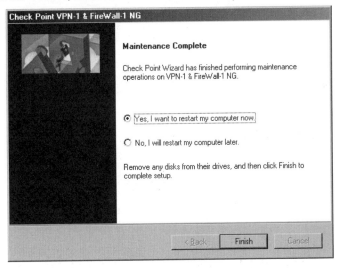

Uninstalling SVN Foundation

You have already uninstalled the VPN-1/FireWall-1 software, but now you must remove the SVN Foundation. This should always be removed after all other Check Point components, which are built on top of this foundation. If you had installed FloodGate-1 or the Policy Server, for example, these should be removed prior to removing the SVN program files.

1. Log into your computer

2. Choose **Start | Settings | Control Panel**.

3. Click on the **Add/Remove Programs** Icon. You should see a window similar to the one illustrated in Figure 2.43. Select **Check Point SVN Foundation NG** and click on **Change/Remove** to completely remove the SVN Foundation from your system.

Figure 2.43 Add/Remove Check Point SVN Foundation NG

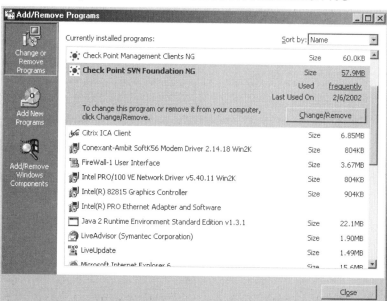

4. Click **OK** to confirm the removal of the selected application (see Figure 2.44). The InstallShield Wizard will then start up and begin uninstalling the SVN Foundation.

5. Click on **Finish** when you receive the message **Maintenance Complete** as illustrated in Figure 2.44. You may be prompted to reboot instead. If so, select **Yes, I want to restart my computer now** and click on **Finish** to reboot your computer. Once the machine reboots, log in again and open the control panel to remove the GUI Clients, which is your next step.

Figure 2.44 SVN Foundation Maintenance Complete

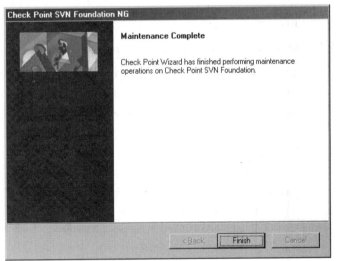

Uninstalling Management Clients

The management clients do not really depend on the SVN foundation installation; therefore, you could really remove them at any time without any difficulty.

1. Go back to the **Add/Remove Programs** window after removing the SVN Foundation, and you should see a screen similar to that in Figure 2.45. Highlight **Check Point Management Clients NG** and click on **Change/Remove** to complete uninstall all of the NG Management clients (e.g. Policy Editor, Log Viewer, etc).

2. Choose to uninstall the GUI Clients.

3. Click **OK** when you see the Maintenance finished window displayed in Figure 2.46.

4. Click **Close** to exit the Control Panel, and you are done uninstalling all Check Point components.

Figure 2.45 Add/Remove Management Clients NG

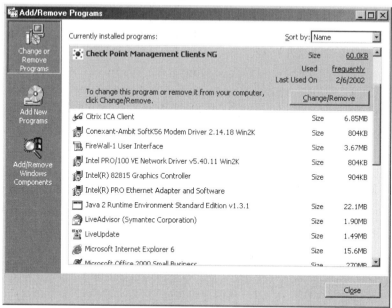

Figure 2.46 Maintenance Finished

Installing Check Point VPN-1/FireWall-1 NG on Solaris

Finally all of your hard work at preparing for the firewall installation is about to pay off. This section will be dedicated to installing the Check Point VPN-1/ FireWall-1 NG on Solaris. Hopefully you have read the first section of this chapter "Before you Begin" and are prepared to start with the Check Point software installation. If you did not read the "Before you Begin" section above, then I suggest that you go back to the beginning of this chapter and read this section before you continue.

Although I will be walking you through a standalone installation, I will point out the different options you would make if you wanted to install the firewall on

Solaris in a distributed environment. In other words, you will be installing the Management and Enforcement Modules as well as the GUI all on one machine; however, you could install each piece on separate machines (and use different operating systems) if that is what your network design calls for. The distributed installation is not much different, and my goal is that you will feel just as comfortable with that process after reading this section as well. I am going to take the approach that you are already familiar with the Unix operating system, and know how to navigate the file system and list directories within Solaris.

If you are installing on Solaris 2.7, then you need to ensure that you are in 32-bit mode and that you have patch 106327 applied before you start. If you are installing on Solaris 2.8, you can install in either 32- or 64-bit modes, and you must have patches 108434 and 108435 applied before you start installing VPN-1/FireWall-1 NG. Solaris patches can be obtained from http://sunsolve.sun.com. Are you ready?

Installing from CD

Now I'm going to walk you through the Check Point VPN-1/FireWall-1 installation on Solaris using the Check Point Next Generation CD. You can obtain a copy of this CD from Check Point by going to www.checkpoint.com/getsecure .html and requesting an evaluation of the software. If you have a login setup with Check Point, then you can download the software and updates from Check Point here www.checkpoint.com/techsupport/downloadsng/ngfp1.html.

The following screenshots will be taken from a new install via CD to a Solaris 2.7 (32-bit mode) system. If you are installing on other versions of Solaris, the procedure is the same.

1. Insert the Check Point Next Generation CD into your computer's CDROM drive. If you have the automount daemon running on your Solaris system, then the drive will be mounted automatically. If not, then mount the CDROM drive.

    The syntax for mounting the CDROM drive is below. You will need to determine which disk to mount before you type this command. Replace the Xs below with the appropriate drive numbers for your system.

    ```
    mount -o ro -F hsfs <device> <mount point>
    ```

2. Move into the CDROM mount point directory by typing **cd /cdrom/ cpsuite_ng_hf1** and press <RETURN>. The directory name that you

are using may be different depending on the version of the CD that you have. For this install, you are using the Check Point NG HotFix1 CD. There is a file in this directory titled ReadmeUnix.txt, which explains the contents of the CD and how to begin the install process.

Configuring & Implementing...

Installing Packages

If you have downloaded the packages to install on Solaris, you must first unzip and untar them to a temporary directory. Once the files are extracted, use 'pkgadd –d <directory>' to install the Check Point VPN-1/FireWall-1 packages. Problems have been known to occur if these temporary directories are several subdirectories away from the root of the file system. It would be best to extract these packages to /opt or directly to / instead of burying them too far down in the file system hierarchy. If you are in the same directory as the package, then type **"pkgadd –d ."** to begin the installation.

You must install the SVN Foundation package prior to installing any other modules on your system. Make sure you download this package, too, if you want to install VPN-1/FireWall-1. You can install Management Clients without the SVN Foundation.

3. When you are ready to start with the installation, type **./UnixInstallScript** <RETURN> to initiate the Check Point installation wizard (see Figure 2.47). If you are in the Common Desktop Environment (CDE) then you can also use a file manager and double-click on **UnixInstallScript** file to begin.

   After you press <RETURN>, you will be presented with Check Point's welcome screen.

NOTE

If you are installing Check Point NG on Linux, you use the same UnixInstallScript to begin the install process.

Figure 2.47 UnixInstallScript

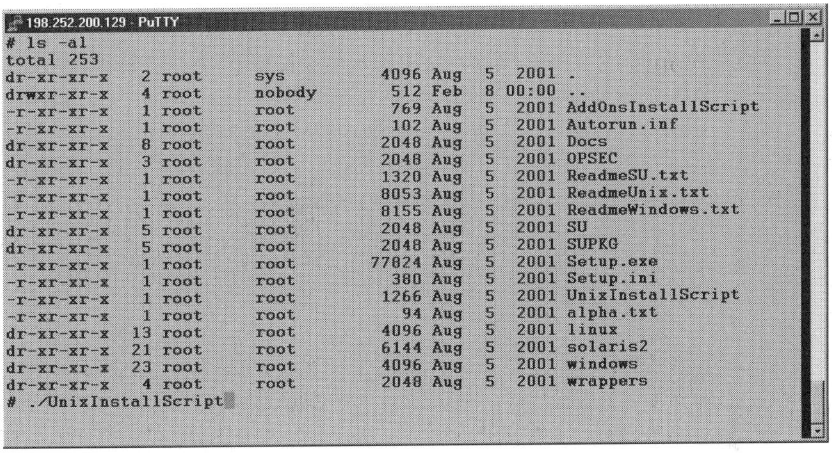

NOTE

While running the UnixInstallScript, keep your eye at the bottom of the screen to see your navigation options. You will enter the letter associated with the menu item to perform the requested action. For example, to exit the system, you see E – exit at the bottom of the screen. Simply press **e** to exit and end the installation at any time.

---

4. From the Welcome Screen (Figure 2.48) you have the options listed below to continue. Type **n** to advance to the next screen.

- **V – Evaluation Product** Informational page on running this software on an evaluation license.

- **U – Purchased Product** Informational page on installing this software if it is a purchased product.

- **N – Next** Proceed to the next screen.

- **H – Help** To get help with navigating the installation screens.

- **E – Exit** To quit the installation and exit.

It makes no difference to the installation process if you are installing a purchased product or if you are installing for evaluation purposes. The software installation is exactly the same; the only thing that is different is the license you apply during configuration. You can always apply a permanent license to a system installed on evaluation at any time to turn it into a production firewall.

Figure 2.48 Welcome to Check Point NG

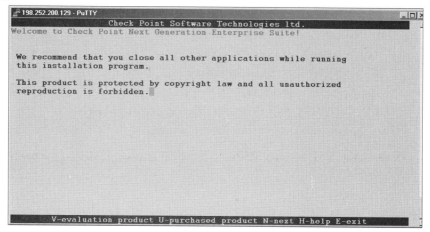

5. You will see a message at the top of the screen that says, "Checking the OS Version" and then you will receive the license agreement as shown in Figure 2.49. Press the **space bar** until you reach the end of the agreement. When you reach the end, the program will prompt you to indicate whether you accept the terms in the license agreement, "Do you accept all the terms of this license agreement (y/n) ?" Enter **y** and press <RETURN>.

Figure 2.49 License Agreement

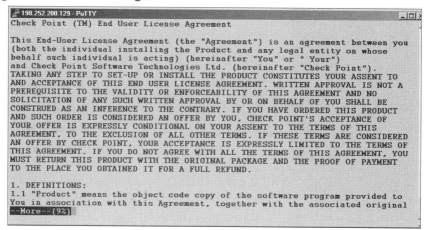

6. You should now be presented with a screen while the system installs the SVN Foundation. This may take a couple of minutes. This screen reads as follows, "Please wait while installing Check Point SVN Foundation…." Once the SVN install is complete, you will need to select the products that you want to install from this CD (Figure 2.50). Your options are explained below. Type in the numbers of the packages you wish to select in this window. Type the number again to unselect it. If you enter **r** for Review, then you will get a new screen in which you can select a product by entering its number, and then pressing **r** again to get a description of the product. You're going to type **1** and then **4** to select **VPN-1 & FireWall-1** and **Management Clients** respectively, then enter **n** to advance to the next screen.

- **VPN-1 & FireWall-1** This includes FireWall-1 Management module and enforcement point software along with the VPN-1 encryption component.

- **FloodGate-1** Provides an integrated Quality of Service (QoS) solution for VPN-1/FireWall-1.

- **Meta IP** Integrated IP Management with DNS and DHCP servers.

- **Management Clients** The Graphical User Interface for Check Point including the Policy Editor, Log Viewer, and System Status GUI. Using the Management Clients on Solaris requires a Motif license and you may need to tweak your environment to get them to run, but you can connect with as many remote Windows GUI Clients to a Solaris management server as you wish without any additional license.

- **UserAuthority** A user-authentication tool that integrates with FireWall-1, FloodGate-1, and other ebusiness applications.

- **VPN-1 SecureClient Policy Server** Allows an enforcement module to install Granular Desktop Policies on mobile users' SecureClient personal firewalls.

- **Reporting Module** An integrated Reporting tool that can generate reports, graphs, and pie charts to display information obtained from the VPN-1/FireWall-1 logs.

- **Real Time Monitor** Allows an organization to monitor their V' connections, Internet connections, etc.

Figure 2.50 Select Products to Install

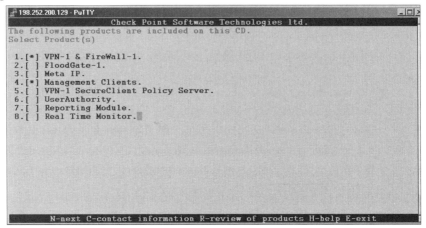

NOTE

If you are installing the Enforcement Module only, then select **VPN-1 & FireWall-1**.

7. Next you will need to select the type of firewall installation you want on this server. You must select one of these options. Enter the option number to select, and enter a different option number to unselect. Select one of the options as shown in Figure 2.51. Enter **1** to select **Enterprise Primary Management and Enforcement Module**, and then press **n** to continue.

- **Enterprise Primary Management and Enforcement Module** To install both a Primary Management server and VPN-1/FireWall-1 Enforcement Module.

- **Enforcement Module** To install an Enforcement Module only, the Management server will be installed on separate hardware.

- **Enterprise Primary Management** To install a Management server only that will be acting in a primary capacity.

- **Enterprise Secondary Management** To install a Management server only that will be acting in a backup capacity.

Figure 2.51 Choose the Type of Installation

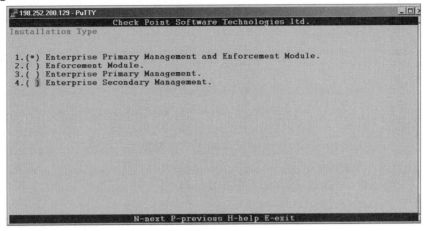

8. If you are installing a Management Module, you will be asked if you want to install with or without backward compatibility as in Figure 2.52. If you select **No,** then you will only be able to manage other NG modules with this management server. If you select **Yes,** then you will be able to manage version 4.0, 4.1 and NG modules with this management server. Enter **2** for No and press **n** to continue.

Figure 2.52 Backward Compatibility

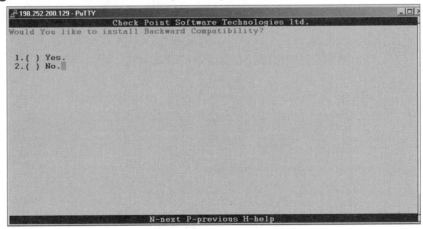

NOTE

If you are installing an Enforcement module only, then you will not configure backward compatibility.

9. On the next screen illustrated in Figure 2.53 press **n** to continue. This will be the last screen where you can exit the configuration before the install script will start copying files. While the install script is installing the package and copying files, you will see a screen similar to the one in Figure 2.54. The installation could take a few minutes. Next, the firewall will install the VPN-1/FireWall-1 kernel module and begin the configuration process.

Figure 2.53 Validation Screen

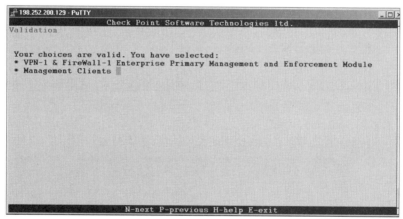

Figure 2.54 Installation Progress

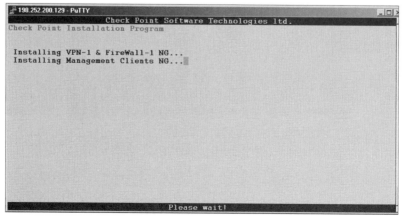

Configuring Check Point VPN-1/FireWall-1 NG on Solaris

Once the system is done copying files during the install procedure, it will begin to go through the configuration screens as shown in Figure 2.55. If you read the first section of this chapter, then you should be prepared to configure the firewall. After this initial configuration, you can always come back to any of these screens by running 'cpconfig' from the root shell. I recommend that you go through all of these screens during the install without canceling; you can always go back in to change your initial configuration settings.

Figure 2.55 Welcome to Check Point

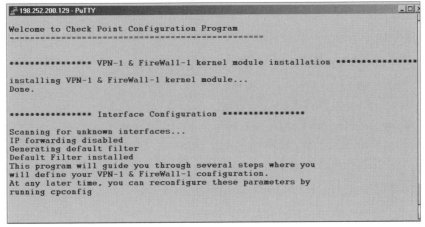

The initial configuration will take you through the following screens:

- Licenses
- Administrators
- GUI Clients
- SNMP Extension
- Group Permissions
- Certificate Authority Configuration

Licenses

You should have obtained all of your licenses before you get to this step. If you need help getting your license, read the first part of this chapter titled "Before you Begin." If you don't have any permanent licenses to install at this time, you can always request an evaluation license from either Check Point or your Check Point reseller.

> **NOTE**
>
> The license configuration option will be displayed regardless of which modules you have installed.

Since you have installed a Primary Management Module, you should be installing a local license that was registered with the local Management station's IP address. Follow this step-by-step procedure for adding your license(s). You can see the license configuration input and output outlined in Illustration 2.3.

1. When prompted to add licenses, enter **y** for yes and press <RETURN>.

2. Enter **M** to add the license manually and press <RETURN>. Now you will be prompted for each field of the license. The illustration below shows the following license installed: cplic putlic eval 01Mar2002 aoMJFd63k-pLdmKQMwZ-aELBqjeVX-pJxZJJCAy CPMP-EVAL-1-3DES-NG CK-CP

    ■ **Host** The IP address or hostid associated with this license or the word "eval."

    ■ **Date** The date that the license expires, which may be "never."

    ■ **String** The license string provided by Check Point to validate the license. This key will be unique for each license and IP Address/Host.

    ■ **Features** These are the features which this license will enable (e.g. Management and/or 3DES).

    As you can see in Illustration 2.3, you also have the option of choosing **f** for [F]etch from file. If you select this option, the configuration will prompt you to enter the file name of the file.

3. Enter the values for Host, Date, String, and Features pressing <RETURN> after each entry.

Illustration 2.3 Configuring Licenses

```
Configuring Licenses...

=======================

The following licenses are installed on this host:


Host             Expiration Features



Do you want to add licenses (y/n) [n] ? y


Do you want to add licenses [M]anually or [F]etch from file?: M
Host:eval
Date:01Mar2002
String:aoMJFd63k-pLdmKQMwZ-aELBqjeVX-pJxZJJCAy
             Features:CPMP-EVAL-1-3DES-NG CK-CP
```

Administrators

If you have installed a Management Module, then as soon as you enter a license into the configuration program, it will move on to the next setting, which will be to add an administrator. You must define at least one administrator at this time. You can always come back later to add, edit, or delete your administrators. Illustration 2.4 illustrates the steps involved to add your administrator.

NOTE

If you have installed an Enforcement Module only, then you will not configure Administrators.

It is best to use individual admin usernames instead of a generic username like fwadmin. The problem with using a generic login ID is that you cannot properly audit the activities of the firewall administrators. It may be important for you to know who installed the last security policy when you are troubleshooting a problem. This becomes more and more important when there are several people administering a firewall system. The fields that you need to fill in follow:

- **Administrator Name** Choose a login name for your admin. This field is case sensitive.

- **Password** Choose a good alphanumeric password. It must be at least four characters long and is also case sensitive.

- **Verify Password** Repeat the same password entered above.

- **Permissions for all Management Clients** (Read/[W]rite All, [R]ead Only All, [C]ustomized)

Illustration 2.4 Adding an Administrator

```
Configuring Administrators...

============================

No VPN-1 & FireWall-1 Administrators are currently

defined for this Management Station.

Administrator name: Cherie

Password:

Verify Password:

Permissions for all Management Clients (Read/[W]rite All, [R]ead Only

All, [C]ustomized) w


Administrator Cherie was added successfully and has

Read/Write permission to all management clients


                Add another one (y/n) [n] ? n
```

To do this, follow these steps:

1. Enter the login ID for your Administrator and press <RETURN>. I use "Cherie" in this example.

2. Enter the password for Cherie and press <RETURN>.

3. Confirm the password entered in step 2 and press <RETURN>.

4. Enter **w** for Read/Write All to give administrator Cherie full permissions to access and make changes to all Management Clients.

Setting permissions enables you to define the access level that you will require on an individual basis for each administrator. If you select **Read/[W]rite All** or **[R]ead Only All,** then your admin will have access to all the available

GUI client features with the ability to either make changes and updates or to view the configuration and logs (perhaps for troubleshooting purposes) respectively. You may also choose to customize their access so that they may be able to update some things and not others. To do this, select **Customized** and configure each of these options (see Illustration 2.5):

- **SecureUpdate** This GUI tool enables you to manage licenses and update remote modules.
- **Monitoring** This option enables access to the Log Viewer, System Status, and Traffic Monitoring GUI clients.

Illustration 2.5 Setting Customized Permissions

```
Permissions for all Management Clients (Read/[W]rite All, [R]ead Only
All, [C]ustomized) c
        Permission for SecureUpdate (Read/[W]rite, [R]ead Only, [N]one)
w

        Permission for Monitoring (Read/[W]rite, [R]ead Only, [N]one) w

Administrator Doug was added successfully and has
Read/Write permission for SecureUpdate
                Read/Write permission for Monitoring
```

GUI Clients

The Graphical User Interface (GUI) Clients are the Management Clients you installed. These clients could also be installed on as many desktops as you wish, but before they can connect to the management server, you need to enter their IP addresses into the GUI Clients configuration (Illustration 2.6). You can use this feature, for example, if you install the GUI clients on your own workstation to enable you to control the management server from your PC. This will enable you to connect remotely to manage the Security Policy and view your logs and system status. You do not need to configure any clients at all during the install, but if you are already prepared for this step, you may enter as many clients into this window as necessary. This client info will be saved in a file on your firewall under $FWDIR/conf and will be named gui-clients. This file can be edited directly, or you can bring up this GUI Clients window at any time in the future by running cpconfig.

1. Press **c** to [C]reate a new list of GUI Clients.

2. Type in a GUI client IP address and press <RETURN>.

3. Repeat step two for each GUI client you want to add to the list.

4. Enter <CTRL-D> to complete the list.

5. Verify that the list is correct, enter **y** for yes and press <RETURN> to continue.

Illustration 2.6 Configuring GUI Clients

```
Configuring GUI clients...

============================

GUI clients are trusted hosts from which

Administrators are allowed to log on to this Management Station

using Windows/X-Motif GUI.


Do you want to [C]reate a new list, [A]dd or [D]elete one?: c

Please enter the list hosts that will be GUI clients.

Enter hostname or IP address, one per line, terminating with CTRL-D or
your EOF
              character.
```

NOTE

If you have installed an Enforcement Module only, then you will not con-figure GUI Clients.

You can either choose to [C]reate a new GUI Clients list, [A]dd a GUI client to the list or [D]elete a GUI client from the list. As you enter GUI Clients into this configuration, you type their hostname or IP address, one per line, pressing <RETURN> at the end of each. When you are done editing the client list, press CTRL-D to send an End Of File (EOF) control character to the program to continue. You are allowed to use wildcards as follows:

- **Any** If you type in the word "Any," this will allow anyone to connect without restriction (not recommended).

- **Asterisks** You may use asterisks in the hostname, e.g. 10.10.20.* means any host in the 10.10.20.0/24 network, or *.domainname.com means any hostname within the domainname.com domain.

- **Ranges** You may use a dash (-) to represent a range of IP addresses, e.g. 1.1.1.3-1.1.1.7 means the 5 hosts including 1.1.1.3 and 1.1.1.7 and every one in between.

- **DNS or WINS resolvable hostnames**

Illustration 2.7 displays an example of the configured GUI Clients window with various options that you can use for your GUI Client entries. I would recommend staying away from using hostnames or domain names, however, since it requires DNS to be configured and working on the firewall. Using IP addresses is the best method since it doesn't rely on resolving, and will continue to work even if you cannot reach your name servers from the firewall.

Illustration 2.7 GUI Client Wildcards

```
Please enter the list hosts that will be GUI clients.
Enter hostname or IP address, one per line, terminating with CTRL-D or
your EOF
character.
*.integralis.com
1.1.1.3-1.1.1.7
10.10.10.2
10.10.10.3
10.10.20.*
backwatcher.com
noc.activis.com
              Is this correct (y/n) [y] ? y
```

SNMP Extension

If you wish to utilize external network management tools such as HP OpenView, then you can install the Check Point FireWall-1 SNMP daemon. With the daemon installed and activated, you will be able to query the firewall status. You could use a network management tool to monitor the firewall's health and to generate alerts based on certain criteria. The MIB files are located in $CPDIR/lib/snmp. If you will not be utilizing SNMP, then you should not enable it at this time. You can always come back and activate it by running cpconfig in the future. Enter **y** to activate the SNMP daemon as shown in Illustration 2.8.

Illustration 2.8 Configuring SNMP

```
Configuring SNMP Extension...

==============================

The SNMP daemon enables VPN-1 & FireWall-1 module

to export its status to external network management tools.

            Would you like to activate VPN-1 & FireWall-1 SNMP daemon ?
(y/n) [n] ? y
```

Group Permission

During configuration, you will be prompted to configure groups on your VPN-1/FireWall-1 module as shown in Figure 2.56. You can choose to either hit <RETURN> to accept the default setting of no group permissions, or you can enter the name of a group (defined in the file /etc/group) that you would like to have set on the Check Point directories. You might want to set group permissions so that you can enable a number of firewall operators to execute FireWall-1 commands without having to grant them super-user privileges to the system. Only one user should have super-user privileges on a Unix system, and that is the root account. Press <RETURN> to set no group permissions. Press <RETURN> again to accept this configuration option as okay.

Figure 2.56 Setting Group Permissions

```
198.252.200.129 - PuTTY                                          _|□|×
Configuring SNMP Extension...
=================================
The SNMP daemon enables VPN-1 & FireWall-1 module
to export its status to external network management tools.
Would you like to activate VPN-1 & FireWall-1 SNMP daemon ? (y/n) [n] ? y


Configuring Groups...
=======================
VPN-1 & FireWall-1 access and execution permissions
---------------------------------------------------
Usually, a VPN-1 & FireWall-1 module is given group permission
for access and execution.
You may now name such a group or instruct the installation
procedure to give no group permissions to the VPN-1 & FireWall-1 module.
In the latter case, only the Super-User will
be able to access and execute the VPN-1 & FireWall-1 module.

Please specify group name [<RET> for no group permissions]:

No group permissions will be granted. Is this ok (y/n) [y] ?

Setting Group Permissions... Done.
```

Certificate Authority Initialization

Your Management server will be a Certificate Authority for your firewall enforcement modules, and will use certificates for Secure Internal Communication (SIC). This is the step in the installation process where the Management Server's CA is configured, and a certificate is generated for the server and its components.

You will be presented with the Key Hit Session configuration option where you are asked to input random text until you hear a beep. The data you enter will be used to generate the certificate, and it is recommended that you also enter the data at a random pace; some keystrokes may be close together and others could have a longer pause in between them. The more random the data, the more unlikely that the input could be duplicated. If the system determines that the keystrokes are not random enough, it will not take them as input, and will display an asterisk to the right of the progression bar.

NOTE

The Key Hit Session screen will also be presented to you if you have installed an Enforcement Module, only so that you can generate an internal certificate for SIC.

1. Type random characters at random intervals into the Key Hit Session window until the progress bar is full, and the message "Thank you" appears at the bottom of the window as seen in Figure 2.57.

Figure 2.57 Random Pool

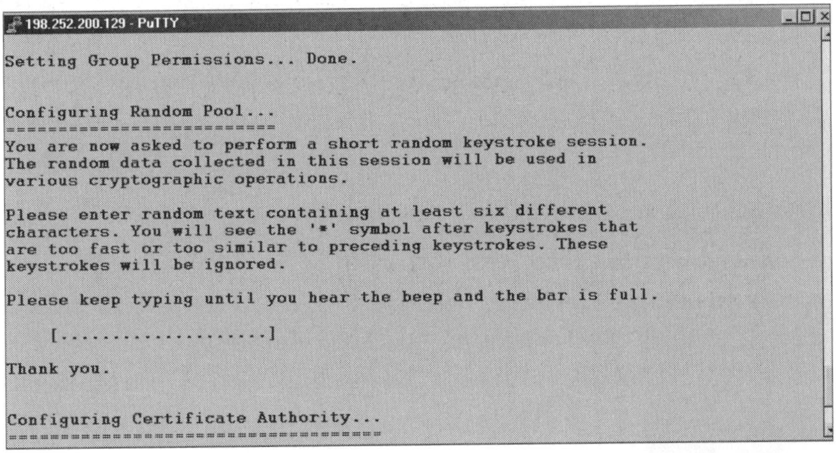

2. The next step is to initialize the internal Certificate Authority for SIC. It may take a minute for the CA to initialize. Figure 2.58 displays the messages you will receive on the console while configuring the CA. Press <RETURN> to initialize the Certificate Authority.

Figure 2.58 Configuring Certificate Authority

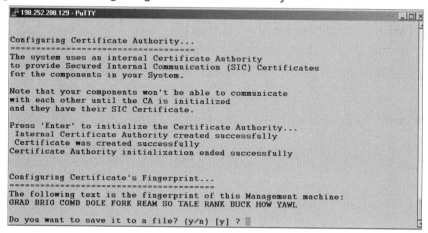

3. Once the CA is initialized successfully, you will be presented with the fingerprint of the Management server. This fingerprint is unique to your CA and the certificate on your server. The first time your GUI Clients connect to the Management server, they will receive the fingerprint so that they can match it to the string listed here and verify that they are connecting to the correct manager. After the first connection, every time the clients connect to the management server, the fingerprint is verified. If the fingerprints don't match, a warning message will be displayed, and the administrator can decide whether or not to continue with the connection. Type **y** and press <RETURN> to save the fingerprint to a file.

4. Enter the filename and press <RETURN>. The file will be saved in $CPDIR/conf.

Installation Complete

The configuration program ends, and you may see a few messages on the screen, such as "generating GUI-clients INSPECT code," as the system finishes up the installation of the VPN-1/FireWall-1 package. Finally, you will receive the following question, "Would You like to reboot the machine [y/n]:" (shown in Figure 2.59). If you select not to reboot, then you will exit the installation and go back to a shell prompt. If you choose to reboot, then the system will be restarted.

WARNING

If you are connected to this firewall remotely, then you will not have access after rebooting. The firewall loads a policy named defaultfilter, which will prevent all access after an install.

---

1. Enter **n** for no and press <RETURN>.

Figure 2.59 Installation Complete

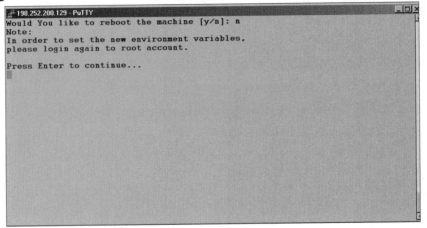

2. Press <RETURN> again to exit the installation script.

Once you press <RETURN> or Enter, you will be put back to the shell. The last message you received on the console was concerning new environment variables. Let's address these environment variables for a minute. The firewall will create a .profile in root's home directory, which runs the Check Point environment script located here /opt/CPshared/ 5.0/tmp/.CPprofile.sh (for bourne shell) and .CPprofile.csh (for c shell). This script sets your Check Point variables such as $FWDIR and $CPDIR among others. See Figure 2.60 for a list of environment variables that are set on my install machine. Without setting these variables, various firewall commands will fail. For example, if I log in to the system as my standard user and then type 'su' to root instead of 'su −', I will maintain my standard user's environment; then when I try to run 'fw unload localhost' to unload the defaultfilter, for example, I'll receive the following error message: "ld.so.1: /etc/fw/bin/fw: fatal: libkeydb.so: open failed: No such file or directory Killed."

Figure 2.60 Environment Variables

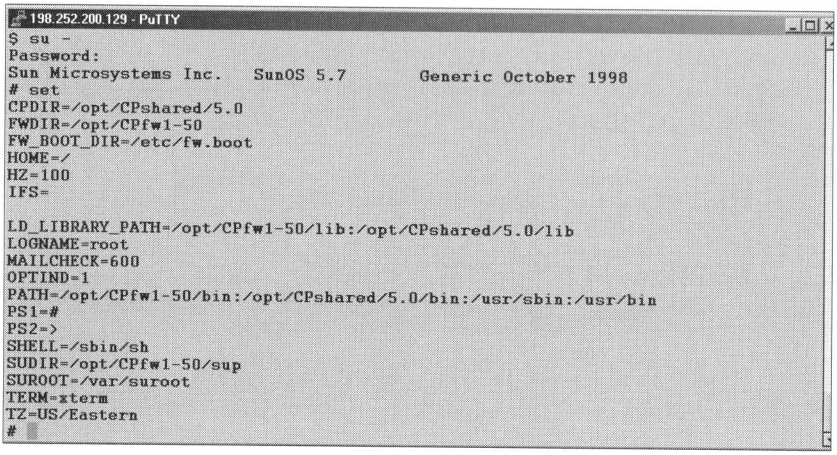

```
198.252.200.129 - PuTTY
$ su -
Password:
Sun Microsystems Inc.    SunOS 5.7      Generic October 1998
# set
CPDIR=/opt/CPshared/5.0
FWDIR=/opt/CPfw1-50
FW_BOOT_DIR=/etc/fw.boot
HOME=/
HZ=100
IFS=

LD_LIBRARY_PATH=/opt/CPfw1-50/lib:/opt/CPshared/5.0/lib
LOGNAME=root
MAILCHECK=600
OPTIND=1
PATH=/opt/CPfw1-50/bin:/opt/CPshared/5.0/bin:/usr/sbin:/usr/bin
PS1=#
PS2=>
SHELL=/sbin/sh
SUDIR=/opt/CPfw1-50/sup
SUROOT=/var/suroot
TERM=xterm
TZ=US/Eastern
#
```

3. When you are ready to restart the server, type **sync; sync; reboot** and press <RETURN>.

Configuring & Implementing…

Unload defaultfilter Script

If you are doing a remote upgrade or install, then you may run into trouble when you reboot at the end of the installation. Before a security policy is loaded, the system will install a default policy, called default-filter, which will block all access to the VPN-1/FireWall-1 host computer. You can log in to the console and verify that the filter is loaded with the 'fw stat' command:

```
# fw stat

HOST        POLICY        DATE

localhost defaultfilter  8Feb2002 16:51:48 :   [>hme1] [<hme1]
```

Continued

If you have access to the console, then log in as root and unload the filter with the following command:

```
# fw unload localhost
Uninstalling Security Policy from all.all@NGtest
Done.
```

If you do not have access to the console, then you could write a shell script to unload the filter and enable it in cron. Here's a sample unload.sh script that I've used for v4.1 firewalls:

```
#!/bin/sh

/etc/fw/bin/fw unload localhost
```

Unfortunately, this isn't enough in NG. The various environment variables in the $CPDIR/tmp/.CPprofile.sh need to be defined. So, easy enough, just copy the contents of the .CPprofile.sh file into the middle of the unload.sh script above. Even before you reboot, you can test that the script works.

1. To enter the script in cron, first verify that you have enabled execute permissions on the file:

   ```
   chmod +x unload.sh
   ```

2. Then set your EDITOR environment variable to vi:

   ```
   EDITOR=vi; export EDITOR
   ```

3. Then edit cron with the following command:

   ```
   crontab -e
   ```

4. Finally, enter the following line into your crontab file:

   ```
   0,5,10,15,20,25,30,35,40,45,50,55 * * * *
   /usr/local/bin/unload.sh > /dev/null 2>&1
   ```

This command tells the system to run the unload.sh script every five minutes and redirect all output to /dev/null.

Now you can safely reboot the system and log back into it within a five-minute period from the time it is booted. Don't forget to remove (or at least comment out) the crontab entry once you are back in the firewall.

Getting Back to Configuration

Now that installation is complete, you may need to get back into the Configuration screens that you ran through at the end of the install. You can add, modify, or delete any of the previous configuration settings by running cpconfig.

If you did not log in as root or login and type 'su –' to gain root access, then your Check Point environment variables may not be set, and you could receive the errors displayed in Illustration 2.9.

Illustration 2.9 Possible cpconfig Execution Errors

```
# /opt/CPshared/5.0/bin/cpconfig

You must setenv CPDIR before running this program

# CPDIR=/opt/CPshared/5.0; export CPDIR

# /opt/CPshared/5.0/bin/cpconfig

ld.so.1: /opt/CPshared/5.0/bin/cpconfig_ex: fatal: libcpconfca.so: open
failed:

No such file or directory

            Can not execute cpconfig
```

If this happens to you simply login with 'su –'. The dash is an optional argument to su, which provides you with the environment that you would have, had you logged in directly as root. See Figure 2.61 for the output of cpconfig on Solaris.

Figure 2.61 cpconfig

There are two options listed here that did not come up during the initial installation process. Number 5 configures a PKCS#11 Token, which enables you to install an add-on card such as an accelerator card, and number 7 enables you to configure the automatic start of Check Point modules at boot time.

If you installed an Enforcement Module Only, then the cpconfig screens will be a little different (see Figure 2.62). The two new choices are as follows:

- **Secure Internal Communication** Enables a one-time password that will be used for authentication between this enforcement module and its management server as well as any other remote modules that it might communicate with as shown in Figure 2.62.

Figure 2.62 Secure Internal Communication Configuration

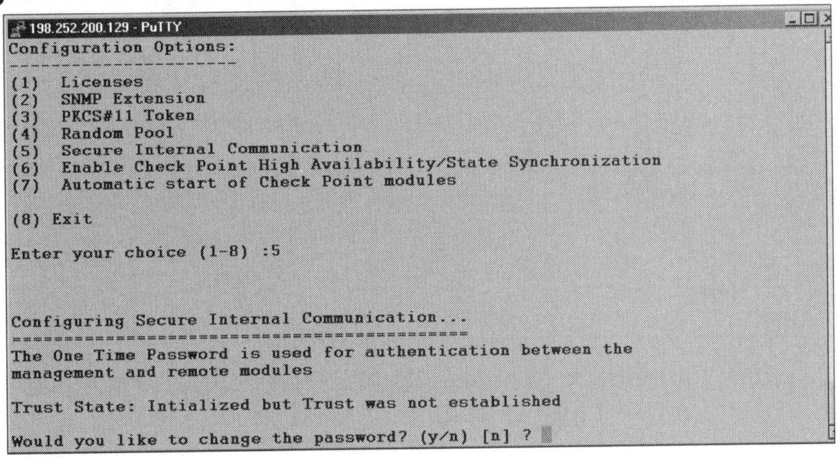

- **High Availability** Allows you to enable this Enforcement module to participate in a Check Point High Availability (CPHA) configuration with one or more other Enforcement modules. This tab will not show up in your installation since you cannot have a management module installed on an enforcement module in a CPHA cluster.

Figure 2.63 illustrates the High Availability option available from the cpconfig menu. If you enable high availability here, then you will need to set up state synchronization between the firewalls that will be participating in the CPHA cluster. This is covered in detail in Chapter 12.

When you uninstall Check Point VPN-1/FireWall-1 NG on Solaris, I recommend that you make a full system backup before you begin. If you only need to back up the firewall configuration, then you should make a backup of /opt/ CP★

and /var/opt/CP* directories. If you are removing a Primary Management Server, then the first time you run pkgrm, the removal will fail. Check Point does this on purpose to ensure that you do not unintentionally delete your Management Module without understanding that you will not be able to restore SIC to its current state after you remove it.

Figure 2.63 High Availability Configuration

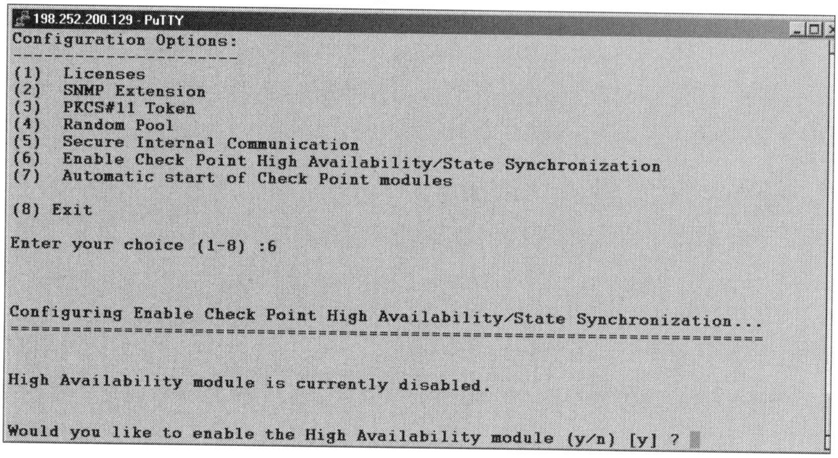

```
198.252.200.129 - PuTTY                                                    _□×
Configuration Options:
----------------------
(1)   Licenses
(2)   SNMP Extension
(3)   PKCS#11 Token
(4)   Random Pool
(5)   Secure Internal Communication
(6)   Enable Check Point High Availability/State Synchronization
(7)   Automatic start of Check Point modules

(8) Exit

Enter your choice (1-8) :6



Configuring Enable Check Point High Availability/State Synchronization...
================================================================================

High Availability module is currently disabled.

Would you like to enable the High Availability module (y/n) [y] ?
```

WARNING

When you remove the Check Point VPN-1/FireWall-1 software on your system, you will lose all configuration data. The uninstall process deletes all files and directories.

Uninstalling VPN-1 & FireWall-1

When you uninstall the firewall, you should remove the Check Point installed packages using the 'pkgrm' program available on your Solaris system. The components should be removed in the following order:

1.   Check Point VPN-1 & FireWall-1 NG

2.   Check Point SVN Foundation NG

You can remove the Management Clients package at any time, but the order in which you remove these two packages is important. Follow the steps below to completely uninstall all Check Point products from your Solaris platform. You may wish to run the command "pkginfo" to see which Check Point packages you have installed before you start. The packages you are going to uninstall are listed in Illustration 2.10.

Illustration 2.10 pkginfo Command

```
# pkginfo | more
application CPclnt-50      Check Point Managment Clients NG
application CPfw1-50       Check Point VPN-1/FireWall-1 NG
            application CPshrd-50      Check Point SVN Foundation
```

1. Exit all GUI Client windows that you may have open.

2. Log in to the firewall and su to root: **su –**

3. Type **pkgrm** <RETURN>. You will see a list of installed packages available for removal as shown in Figure 2.64. In this example, you will choose the Check Point VPN-1/FireWall-1 NG package CPfw1-50, which is number two in the list.

Figure 2.64 Package Removal Choices

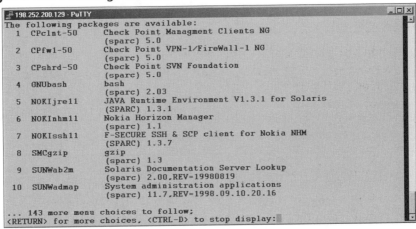

4. Type <CTRL-D>; you will then be presented with the following: Select package(s) you wish to process (or 'all' to process all packages). (default: all) [?,??,q]:

5. Enter **2** and press <RETURN> to uninstall the CPfw1-50 package.

6. Next, the system will ask you if you are sure you want to remove this package, as seen in Illustration 2.11. Enter **y** for yes and press <RETURN>.

Illustration 2.11 CPfw1-50 Package Removal

```
Select package(s) you wish to process (or 'all' to process all
packages). (default: all) [?,??,q]: 2


The following package is currently installed:
   CPfw1-50          Check Point VPN-1/FireWall-1 NG

                     (sparc) 5.0


Do you want to remove this package? y
```

7. Next, the pkgrm program notifies you that the uninstall process will require the use of super-user privileges, and asks you if you want to continue (Illustration 2.12). Enter **y** for yes and press <RETURN>.

Illustration 2.12 Continue with Package Removal

```
## Removing installed package instance <CPfw1-50>


This package contains scripts which will be executed with super-user
permission during the process of removing this package.


Do you want to continue with the removal of this package [y,n,?,q] y
```

8. Next, the package removal will fail. Check Point has done this on purpose so that you can receive the WARNING notification that is displayed in Illustration 2.13. This message informs you that if you uninstall VPN-1/FireWall-1, then you will lose all configured SIC, and you will not be able to restore SIC to its current state by reinstalling the Primary Management Server. Run **pkgrm** again to uninstall the CPfw1-50 package.

Illustration 2.13 Removal Failed

```
## Verifying package dependencies.

## Processing package information.

## Executing preremove script.


There are no packages dependent on VPN-1/FireWall-1 NG installed.


*********************************************************************


                    WARNING:
You are attempting to uninstall your Primary Management Server.r.
If you continue, you must then re-configure communication between
any Secondary Management Servers and other Check Point Modules,
even if you re-install the Primary Management Server on this machine.
Un-installation is aborting, if you still wish to uninstall
VPN-1/FireWall-50 primary management. Please run un-install again.


*********************************************************************


Please disregard the following error message:
pkgrm: ERROR: preremove script did not complete successfully.


Removal of <CPfw1-50> failed.
#
```

9. Enter <CTRL-D>.

10. Enter **2** and press <RETURN> to select the CPfw1-50 package as you did in step 5.

11. Enter **y** for yes and press <RETURN> as you did in step 6.

12. Enter **y** for yes and press <RETURN> as you did in step 7. This time the package removal will be successful. Figures 2.65 and 2.66 show you some of the messages you will see on your console as the package is removed from the system.

Figure 2.65 Uninstall of VPN-1/FireWall-1

```
198.252.200.129 - PuTTY
Do you want to continue with the removal of this package [y,n,?,q] y
## Verifying package dependencies.
## Processing package information.
## Executing preremove script.

There are no packages dependent on VPN-1/FireWall-1 NG installed


*******************************************************************

Proceeding to uninstall VPN-1/FireWall-1 NG Primary Management...

*******************************************************************

## Removing pathnames in class <conf>
/var/opt/CPfw1-50/tmp
/var/opt/CPfw1-50/state
/var/opt/CPfw1-50/log
/var/opt/CPfw1-50/database/lists
/var/opt/CPfw1-50/database
/var/opt/CPfw1-50/conf/vpn.lf
/var/opt/CPfw1-50/conf/vpn.cps
/var/opt/CPfw1-50/conf/ver.txt
/var/opt/CPfw1-50/conf/userdef.C
```

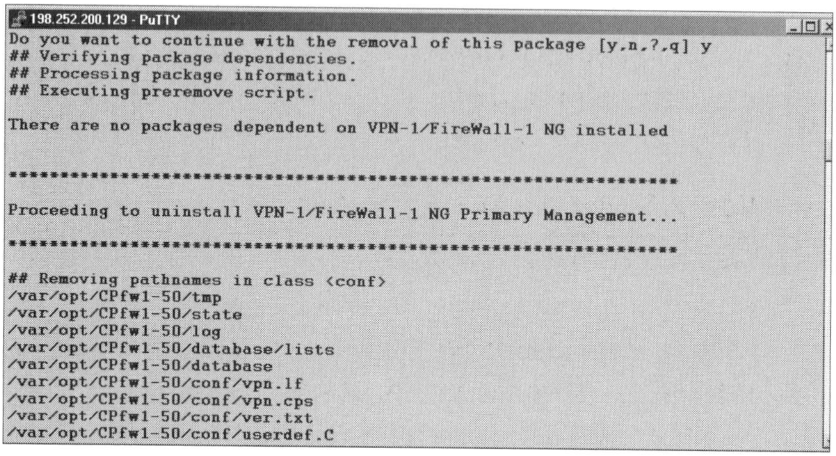

Figure 2.66 Uninstall of VPN-1/FireWall-1 Continued

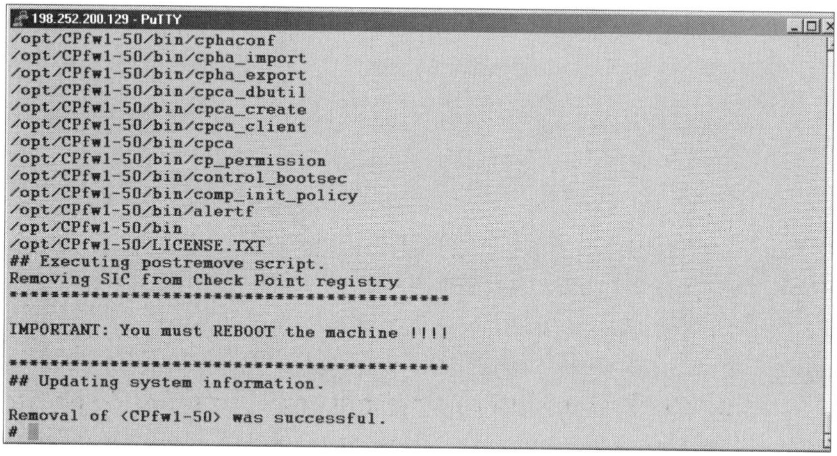

```
198.252.200.129 - PuTTY
/opt/CPfw1-50/bin/cphaconf
/opt/CPfw1-50/bin/cpha_import
/opt/CPfw1-50/bin/cpha_export
/opt/CPfw1-50/bin/cpca_dbutil
/opt/CPfw1-50/bin/cpca_create
/opt/CPfw1-50/bin/cpca_client
/opt/CPfw1-50/bin/cpca
/opt/CPfw1-50/bin/cp_permission
/opt/CPfw1-50/bin/control_bootsec
/opt/CPfw1-50/bin/comp_init_policy
/opt/CPfw1-50/bin/alertf
/opt/CPfw1-50/bin
/opt/CPfw1-50/LICENSE.TXT
## Executing postremove script.
Removing SIC from Check Point registry
***********************************************

IMPORTANT: You must REBOOT the machine !!!!

***********************************************
## Updating system information.

Removal of <CPfw1-50> was successful.
#
```

13. Type **sync; sync; reboot** <RETURN> to reboot the system.

Uninstalling SVN Foundation

You have already uninstalled the VPN-1/FireWall-1 software, but now you must
remove the SVN Foundation. This should always be removed after all other
Check Point components, which are built on top of this foundation (as the name
suggests). If you had installed FloodGate-1 or the Policy Server, for example,
these should also be removed prior to removing the SVN CPshrd-50 package.

1. Once the machine has rebooted, log back into the console.

2. Type **su -** <RETURN> to become the super user (root).

3. Type **pkgrm** <RETURN>. Now your choices to uninstall are the Check Point Management Clients NG and the Check Point SVN Foundation (see Illustration 2.14).

Illustration 2.14 Remove SVN Foundation

```
The following packages are available:
  1  CPclnt-50      Check Point Managment Clients NG

                      (sparc) 5.0

  2  CPshrd-50      Check Point SVN Foundation

                      (sparc) 5.0
```

4. Enter <CTRL-D>.

5. Enter **2** <RETURN> to select the SVN Foundation CPshrd-50 package.

6. When the pkgrm program asks you if you want to remove this program, enter **y** for yes and press <RETURN>.

7. Again, pkgrm will print, "This package contains scripts that will be executed with super-user permission during the process of removing this package. Do you want to continue with the removal of this package [y,n,?,q]." Enter **y** for yes and press <RETURN> to continue.

   See Illustration 2.15 for a complete view of the uninstall process of the Check Point SVN Foundation on Solaris. You do not need to reboot after uninstalling the SVN package.

Illustration 2.15 pkgrm SVN Foundation

```
$ su -
Password:
Sun Microsystems Inc.    SunOS 5.7      Generic October 1998
# pkgrm


The following packages are available:
  1  CPclnt-50      Check Point Managment Clients NG

                      (sparc) 5.0
```

Continued

Illustration 2.15 Continued

```
    2   CPshrd-50        Check Point SVN Foundation
                         (sparc) 5.0
    3   GNUbash          bash
                         (sparc) 2.03
    4   NOKIjre11        JAVA Runtime Environment V1.3.1 for Solaris
                         (SPARC) 1.3.1
    5   NOKInhm11        Nokia Horizon Manager
                         (sparc) 1.1
    6   NOKIssh11        F-SECURE SSH & SCP client for Nokia NHM
                         (SPARC) 1.3.7
    7   SMCgzip          gzip
                         (sparc) 1.3
    8   SUNWab2m         Solaris Documentation Server Lookup
                         (sparc) 2.00,REV=19980819
    9   SUNWadmap        System administration applications
                         (sparc) 11.7,REV=1998.09.10.20.16
   10   SUNWadmc         System administration core libraries
                         (sparc) 11.7,REV=1998.09.10.19.57


... 142 more menu choices to follow;
<RETURN> for more choices, <CTRL-D> to stop display:^D


Select package(s) you wish to process (or 'all' to process
all packages). (default: all) [?,??,q]: 2


The following package is currently installed:
   CPshrd-50         Check Point SVN Foundation
                        (sparc) 5.0


Do you want to remove this package? y


## Removing installed package instance <CPshrd-50>
```

Continued

Illustration 2.15 Continued

```
This package contains scripts thatwhich will be executed with super-user
permission during the process of removing this package.


Do you want to continue with the removal of this package [y,n,?,q] y
## Verifying package dependencies.
## Processing package information.
## Executing preremove script.
There are no packages dependent on Check Point SVN Foundation NG
installed.
rm: /opt/CPshared/5.0/tmp/fg_tmp is a directory
## Removing pathnames in class <conf>
/var/opt/CPshared/registry
/var/opt/CPshared/5.0/conf/sic_policy.conf
/var/opt/CPshared/5.0/conf/os.cps
/var/opt/CPshared/5.0/conf/cp.macro
...
/opt/CPshared/5.0/LICENSE.TXT
/opt/CPshared/5.0/../registry
## Executing postremove script.
## Updating system information.


Removal of <CPshrd-50> was successful.
#
```

Uninstalling Management Clients

The management clients do not really depend on the SVN foundation installation; therefore, you could really remove them at any time without any difficulty.

1. Run **pkgrm** again to remove the Management Clients package.

2. Enter <CTRL-D>.

3. At the prompt, "Select package(s) you wish to process (or 'all' to process all packages). (default: all) [?,??,q]:", enter **1** and press <RETURN> to select the Check Point Management Clients NG package (CPclnt-50).

4. Enter **y** for yes and press <RETURN> when the pkgrm utility asks you, "Do you want to remove this package?"

5. Enter **y** for yes and press <RETURN> when the pkgrm utility presents you with the following prompt, "This package contains scripts that will be executed with super-user permission during the process of removing this package. Do you want to continue with the removal of this package [y,n,?,q]."

The package will be removed. Figure 2.67 illustrates the end of the uninstall process for the Management Clients.

Figure 2.67 Management Clients Package Removal

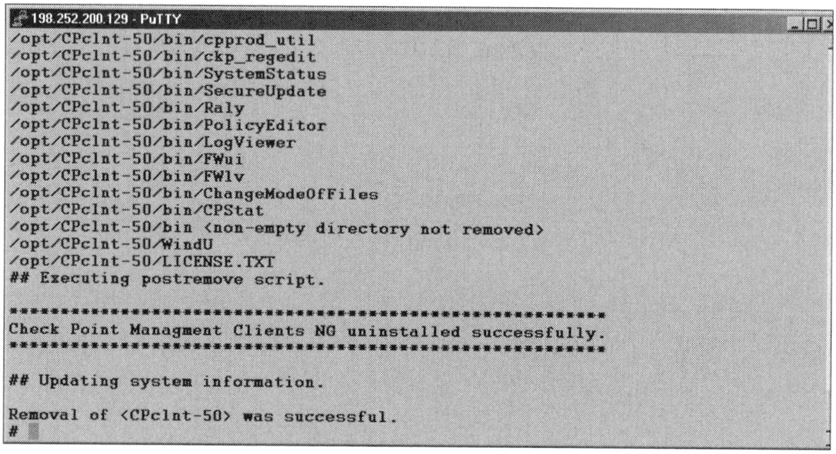

Installing Check Point VPN-1/FireWall-1 NG on Nokia

Check Point's Next Generation Enterprise Suite on the Nokia IPSO appliance is a popular combination. Mike Urban, a Professional Services Engineer at Integralis, explained it best when he said, "Nokia gateways are designed using a hardened UNIX OS specifically tuned for firewall performance and security. As such, they outperform general-purpose OS platforms like Solaris or NT when measuring maximum gateway throughput." Nokia provides a Web front-end, which they call Voyager (see Figure 2.68), for easy package management and system configuration, and they have one of the fasted failover mechanisms utilizing VRRP and Check Point's state synchronization with an average failover time of just four seconds.

The first version of Check Point VPN-1/FireWall-1 NG to run on the Nokia platform is Feature Pack 1. NG FP1 requires Nokia IPSO 3.4.2 for installation. You can either order a Nokia box with Check Point preinstalled, or you can download the installation package from Check Point (with appropriate login ID) and install it yourself. If you need to upgrade your IPSO, you will need to obtain the IPSO image from Nokia support. It may be necessary to upgrade your boot manager prior to upgrading your IPSO image. Please read all release notes prior to installing new packages or images. It is not recommended to upgrade from 4.1 to NG if you have less than 128MB of memory; instead, do a fresh installation.

Figure 2.68 Nokia's Voyager GUI

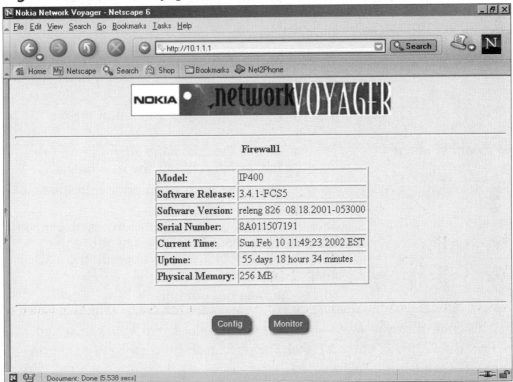

Installing the VPN-1/FireWall-1 NG Package

Since the Nokia appliance is already hardened, there is very little you need to do to prepare it for firewall installation. You must configure and test networking and DNS, set up the Host Address Assignment through the Voyager GUI, and you may need to upgrade your IPSO and boot manager.

Upgrading IPSO Images

I recommend that, if you are on an IPSO version prior to 3.3, you upgrade to 3.3 prior to upgrading to IPSO 3.4.2. You can downgrade from IPSO 3.4.2 to IPSO 3.2.1, 3.3, and 3.3.1 and 3.4. If you are upgrading your IPSO from 3.3 or 3.3.1, then you do not need to upgrade your boot manager prior to installing the new image. The 'newimage' command will automatically upgrade the boot manager on IP300, IP600, IP500, IP100, and IP700 series appliances. You can download the 3.4.2 image from https://support.nokia.com (login required). Once you have the image in /var/admin, you can run newimage to install it. The options for newimage are illustrated in Table 2.2.

Table 2.2 newimage Command Line Arguments

Switch for newimage	Description
-k	Enables you to upgrade the IPSO image and keep all currently active packages so they will be started upon reboot.
-R	Sets the new image to be used upon the next reboot.
-l <path to image>	Tells the newimage command where to find the ipso.tgz file, which contains the new image.
-T	Enables you to perform a test boot with the new image.
-I	Sets the newimage command in interactive mode. Use this if you need to ftp the file or use the CDROM drive (IP440 only) to upgrade the IPSO image.
-b	Forces upgrade of bootmgr.

Assuming that you have the ipso.tgz file downloaded to /var/admin, and your system is on IPSO 3.3 or 3.3.1, then the recommended command to upgrade your IPSO image is as follows:

```
newimage -k -R -l /var/admin
```

After updating the image, reboot your system:

```
sync; sync; reboot
```

Installing VPN-1/FireWall-1 NG

To install the VPN-1/FireWall-1 NG package, you must first install the SVN Foundation and then the VPN-1/FireWall-1 package. You will need to get the software from Check Point or from a Check Point reseller since Nokia does not provide VPN-1/FireWall-1 packages on their support Web site any longer. Follow this step-by-step procedure to install the new package. See Table 2.3 for available arguments to the newpkg command.

Table 2.3 newpkg Command Line Arguments

Switch for newpkg	Description
-i	Installs the package, but does not activate it. Prompts you for media type, new packages and old packages that you wish to install or upgrade.
-s <server>	Specifies the ftp server IP address.
-l <username>	Enter the ftp user name (you don't need to enter a username if you will be using anonymous ftp)
-p <password>	Enter the ftp user's password.
-m <CDROM | AFTP | FTP | LOCAL>	Choose your media type, your options are CDROM, AFTP, FTP or LOCAL
-d	Prints debug messages.
-v	Verbose mode for FTP.
-n <new package>	Enter the full pathname to the new package you are installing.
-o <old package>	Enter the full pathname of the package you are upgrading from.
-S	This sets the newpkg to install the package silently. If you enable silent mode, then you must specify the following arguments: -o, -m, -n and possibly –s and -l, –p if the media type is no LOCAL.
-h	Prints the usage for newpkg (help).

1. Put the following package files in /var/admin. I will be using the NG FP1 packages since they are the most recent, as of this writing.

   ■ **SVN Foundation** cpshared_NG_FP1_0022_1_nokia_packages.tgz

   ■ **VPN-1/FW-1** fw1_NG_FP1_51012_5_nokia_packages.tgz

NOTE

Do not unzip or untar the Nokia packages. When you run the newpkg command, it will do that for you.

---

2. From the /var/admin directory, type **newpkg –i** and press <RETURN>. The newpkg installation program will begin, and will ask you where to install the new package as illustrated in Illustration 2.16.

Illustration 2.16 SVN Foundation Package Installation

```
fwlab1[admin]# newpkg -i


Load new package from the following:

1. Install from CD-ROM.

2. Install from anonymous FTP server.

3. Install from FTP server with user and password.

4. Install from local filesystem.

5. Exit new package installation.


Choose an installation method (1-5):   4


Enter pathname to the packages [ or 'exit' to exit ]: .


Loading Package List


Processing package cpshared_NG_FP1_0022_1_nokia_package.tgz ...

Package Description: Check Point SVN Foundation NG Feature Pack 1 (Sun
Dec 23 19

:05:20 IST 2001 Build 0022)
```

Continued

Illustration 2.16 Continued

```
Would you like to  :


1. Install this as a new package

2. Upgrade from an old package

3. Skip this package

4. Exit new package installation


            Choose (1-4): 1
```

3. Choose the option for local filesystem number **4** and press <RETURN>.

4. When it asks you for the pathname to the package, type a period (**.**) for your current directory (which is /var/admin) and press <RETURN>.

5. The newpkg program will locate any packages located in this directory and begin processing them one by one. The Check Point SVN Foundation NG package will be presented to you. Choose **1** to install this as a new package and press <RETURN>.

   Once the newpkg program has begun, it will process each package in the current directory until it has run through them all. If a package comes up that is already installed, or if you don't want to install it, then choose option 3 to skip the package and continue on with the others. You should reboot your Nokia appliance after each new Check Point package that you install; do not install them all simultaneously.

6. When the installation of SVN is finished, exit the newpkg installation and reboot with the command **sync; sync; reboot**.

7. When the system boots up, log in to Voyager and enable the SVN package.

   - Click on **Manage Installed Packages.**

   - Turn on the new NG SVN package.

   - Click on **Apply** and **Save**.

8. When done in Voyager, type **newpkg –i** once again and press <RETURN> from the /var/admin directory.

9. Choose the option for localfile system number **4** and press <RETURN>.

10. Type a period (.) for your current directory (/var/admin) and press <RETURN>.

11. If you have an earlier version of VPN-1/FireWall-1 installed, then choose to number **2** to upgrade this package from an old package.

12. Choose the package you are upgrading from the available choices.

13. Verify that you want to continue and that the correct packages are being processed by pressing <RETURN>.

14. When the installation is complete, exit the newpkg installation and reboot by typing: **sync; sync; reboot**.

Configuring VPN-1/FireWall-1 NG on Nokia

If VPN-1/FireWall-1 NG is installed on your Nokia appliance, but it hasn't been configured, then you must run cpconfig before attempting to start the new package. If you just received your Nokia fresh from the factory, and NG is installed, then you will still need to run cpconfig before the package will run properly. This is because you must accept the license agreement, choose what components you want to run (Management and/or Enforcement Module), and configure licenses, administrators, GUI Clients, etc. Your configuration options are the same as your options on the Solaris platform. See Figure 2.69 for the output of cpconfig on an NG FP1 Nokia appliance.

Figure 2.69 cpconfig on Nokia

After the NG package is installed on your system, you must run cpconfig to configure the package. Follow these steps to configure and activate your VPN-1/FireWall-1 NG package.

1. Run cpconfig and go through each screen. I recommend that you do not enter CTRL-C at any time during the initial cpconfig configuration screens.

2. When finished with cpconfig, log in to Voyager and enable your NG package (see Figure 2.70).

   ■ Click on **Manage Installed Packages**.

   ■ Turn off the old FireWall-1 package.

   ■ Turn on the new NG FP1 package.

   ■ Click on **Apply** and **Save**.
   The Nokia package management makes it simple to back out of an upgrade. As you can see in Figure 2.70, it is easy to toggle back and forth between installed packages. You can also switch back and forth between IPSO images from Voyager's "Manage IPSO Images" page. After enabling or disabling a package or IPSO image, you must reboot your firewall.

NOTE

Remember to always click **Apply** and then **Save** when making changes in the Voyager GUI. If you don't save your changes, then they will not be retained on a reboot.

---

3. After making changes to the FW-1 packages, then you must reboot the system again. You can either choose to restart the system from the Voyager GUI, or exit Voyager and type **sync; sync; reboot** to restart the box.

Figure 2.70 Managing Installed Packages

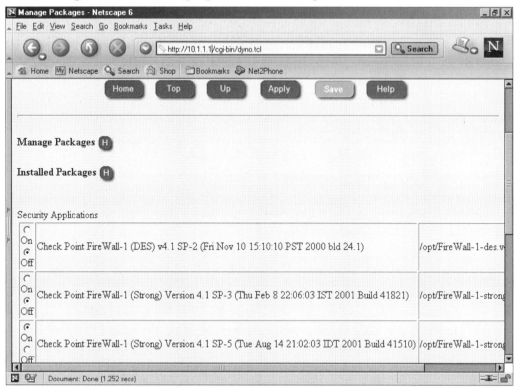

Summary

If you can recall, the beginning of this chapter started out by preparing you to install the Check Point VPN-1/FireWall-1 NG product on a computer. There are several steps you can take to prepare your host computer prior to turning it into a firewall. First, make sure that your hardware meets and exceeds the minimum system requirements provided by Check Point. You will then need to install a base operating system, apply OS patches, configure and test your network interface cards and DNS, enable IP forwarding, disable any unnecessary services, and populate your host's file with at least the external IP address of your firewall, which is configured on the first interface card in your computer.

Next, you will need to prepare for the various Check Point installation screens, you should know in advance which server/gateway components to choose and to be prepared for the initial configuration options by obtaining a license in advance, deciding on admin usernames, passwords, and privileges, and statically assigning IP addresses to your administrator's workstations so that you can add them as GUI clients.

If you are installing the VPN-1/FireWall-1 NG software on a Windows server, then you can start the installation wizard by inserting the CD or running windows\wrapper\demo32.exe. The SVN Foundation will be installed before any other Check Point components. After the installation wizard is done copying files, it will run through the initial configuration screens of Licenses, Administrators, GUI Clients, and then the CA initialization screens. Once the configuration is complete, you will need to reboot your firewall. To run the Configuration Tool again, go to **Start | Programs | Check Point Management Clients | Check Point Configuration NG.**

To uninstall the VPN-1/FireWall-1 NG software from a Windows System, you must uninstall the SVN Foundation last. As the name suggests, this is the base of the VPN-1/FireWall-1 install, and it cannot be removed prior to removing any components that depend on it. After uninstalling VPN-1/FireWall-1 you must reboot.

If you are installing the VPN-1/FireWall-1 NG software on Solaris 2.7 or 2.8, make sure you have the correct patches applied, and that you are in either 32- or 64-bit mode according to the system requirements in Table 2.1 in the beginning of the chapter. To install via CDROM, you will be running the ./UnixInstallScript. If you are installing from files, then you should unzip and untar the package, and then run 'pkgadd –d .' from the directory where the package is located. The SVN Foundation package must be installed prior to installing VPN-1/FireWall-1; the

UnixInstallScript will take care of this for you. After the installation program is done copying files, you will go through the initial configuration screens, which are Licenses, Administrators, GUI Clients, SNMP Extension, Group Permissions, and CA initialization. You can configure the firewall again at any time by running the cpconfig command. After installing VPN-1/FireWall-1, you must reboot.

After rebooting your firewall, a defaultfilter policy will be installed that prohibits all connections to the firewall server. You can unload the defaultfilter with the command 'fw unload localhost.' Keep in mind also that you must su to root with the dash (su -) in order to obtain the right environment variables to run the fw unload and most other FireWall-1 commands, including cpconfig.

To uninstall VPN-1/FireWall-1 on Solaris, use the pkgrm command. The first time you try to remove a Primary Management Server, the uninstall will fail. Simply run pkgrm a second time to successfully remove the package. Reboot your computer after uninstalling the VPN-1/FireWall-1 NG package.

If you are installing the VPN-1/FireWall-1 NG package on a Nokia appliance, then make sure that you are on IPSO 3.4.2 before you begin. Like all the other platforms, you must install the SVN Foundation prior to installing the VPN-1/FireWall-1 package. Also, you should reboot after each new package you install. You can toggle between installed packages in the Voyager GUI under the Manage Installed Packages link. Be sure to click **Apply** and **Save** after making any changes in Voyager. After the Check Point VPN-1/FireWall-1 package is installed, you must run cpconfig in order to finish the installation procedure.

Solutions Fast Track

Before You Begin

- ☑ Your hardware must meet or exceed the minimum system requirements. Your hardware will determine the throughput performance of your firewall.

- ☑ Obtain your VPN-1/FireWall-1 licenses before you start installing the firewall software.

- ☑ You should configure your external IP address on the first interface that comes up on your firewall. This external IP should be configured in your host's file to resolve to the hostname of the computer.

- ☑ IP forwarding must be enabled.

☑ Disable any unnecessary services on your operating system.

☑ Make sure DNS is configured properly, and get a PTR record setup for each NAT address you will be using on your firewall.

☑ Be prepared to answer questions during installation about your Licenses, Administrators, GUI Clients, SNMP Extension, and Group Permissions.

☑ Read the software release notes prior to installing or upgrading.

Installing Check Point VPN-1/FireWall-1 NG on Windows

☑ Begin the installation by inserting the Check Point Next Generation CD.

☑ The SVN Foundation must be installed first.

☑ The default folder installation location for VPN-1/FireWall-1 is c:\winnt\fw1\ng.

☑ You must reboot after installing the VPN-1/FireWall-1 software.

☑ You can configure your firewall Licenses, Administrators, GUI Clients, and CA at any time by choosing **Start | Programs | Check Point Management Clients | Check Point Configuration NG**.

Uninstalling Check Point VPN-1/FireWall-1 NG on Windows

☑ The SVN Foundation must be removed last.

☑ Remove packages from the Control Panel | Add/Remove Programs Icon.

☑ Reboot after uninstalling VPN-1/FireWall-1.

Installing Check Point VPN-1/FireWall-1 NG on Solaris

☑ Begin the installation by inserting the Check Point Next Generation CD and running the ./UnixInstallScript.

☑ If you are installing from files, use the 'pkgadd –d' command.

☑ The SVN Foundation package CPshrd-50 must be installed first.

☑ The initial configuration screens are Licenses, Administrators, GUI Clients, SNMP Extension, Group Permissions, and CA initialization.

☑ You must reboot after installing the VPN-1/FireWall-1 CPfw1-50 package.

☑ After reboot, the firewall will load the defaultfilter, blocking any connection to the firewall. You can unload the filter by typing 'fw unload localhost.'

☑ You must su – to root and run cpconfig to reconfigure the firewall at any time.

Uninstalling Check Point VPN-1/FireWall-1 NG on Solaris

☑ Remove packages with the pkgrm command.

☑ The SVN Foundation CPshrd-50 package must be uninstalled last.

☑ The first time you try to remove a Primary Management Module, the pkgrm will fail. Simply run it again to successfully remove the package.

☑ You must reboot after uninstalling the VPN-1/FireWall-1 CPfw1-50 Package.

Installing Check Point VPN-1/FireWall-1 NG on Nokia

☑ You must be on IPSO 3.4.2 before installing VPN-1/FireWall-1 NG FP1 on a Nokia appliance.

☑ The command newimage is used to install new IPSO images.

☑ The command newpkg is used to install new packages.

☑ The SVN Foundation must be installed first.

☑ Reboot after installing the SVN Foundation package.

☑ Reboot after installing the VPN-1/FireWall-1 package.

☑ After the package is installed, run cpconfig to finish the install process.

☑ Use the Voyager GUI to activate installed packages via the Manage Installed Packages link. Always Apply and Save any change you make in the Voyager GUI.

Frequently Asked Questions

The following Frequently Asked Questions, answered by the authors of this book, are designed to both measure your understanding of the concepts presented in this chapter and to assist you with real-life implementation of these concepts. To have your questions about this chapter answered by the author, browse to **www.syngress.com/solutions** and click on the **"Ask the Author"** form.

Q: If I want to install FloodGate-1 or other add-ons to my firewall, what order should I install the packages?

A: You should install the SVN Foundation first, then VPN-1/FireWall-1 NG, and then FloodGate-1 NG or any other Check Point NG products.

Q: I installed NG FP1 Primary Management Module on a Nokia appliance, but I can't log in with the Check Point NG Management Clients. What am I doing wrong?

A: Your Management Clients must be on the same build as your Management Module. Verify that your IP address is listed in the gui-clients file and upgrade your Management Clients to FP1.

Q: I just upgraded one of my 4.1 firewall modules to NG, and it's not able to fetch a policy. What can I do?

A: Verify that you have changed the module's version to NG in its workstation object, and that you have initialized SIC. You may have to push the policy the first time after an upgrade.

Q: The installation process was running cpconfig for the first time on Solaris, and I received the following message. What's the problem?

```
Installing VPN-1 & Firewall-1 kernel module...devfsadm: driver failed to
attach: fw.
Warning: Driver (fw) successfully added but system failed to attach.
Installation aborted.
```

A: You must boot into 32-bit mode and install the firewall package again.

Q: I keep receiving the error "h_slink: link already exists." Is something wrong?

A: This message is listed in the release notes, which states that it can be safely ignored.

Q: It doesn't seem like my Nokia is forwarding packets. How do I enable IP forwarding on a Nokia?

A: Use the command **ipsofwd on admin** to enable IP forwarding in your Nokia. For help with the ipsofwd command, type **ipsofwd –help** to display the usage.

## Chapter 3

Using the Graphical Interface

Solutions in this chapter:

- **Managing Objects**
- **Adding Rules**
- **Global Properties**
- **SecureUpdate**
- **Log Viewer**
- **System Status**

- ☑ **Summary**
- ☑ **Solutions Fast Track**
- ☑ **Frequently Asked Questions**

Introduction

Once you have the VPN-1/FireWall-1 software installed and configured, then you are ready to log into the graphical user interface and start composing your objects and rule bases. In this chapter I will walk you through all the options you have for creating various objects and show you some of the nice features that you can utilize in the policy editor to manipulate your rules.

I will show you how to access the firewall's implied rules, and explain the global properties that affect every security policy you create. It's important to know why your firewall is allowing pings, if you have not explicitly defined them in your rule base.

After paying a lot of attention to your policy options, I will then show you how to access your firewall logs and system status. The Track options you choose in your policy will affect the outcome of your logs. You may choose to log some rules and not others. I will also describe ways to make certain selections in your Log Viewer so that you can view only logs for a specific source IP address, or logs for a specific user. The Check Point Log Viewer has a really high quality interface, and is easy to understand.

Managing Objects

Managing objects is probably the thing you'll be doing most often as a firewall administrator. Luckily for you, Check Point has made this task much easier than you might think. While there is still a lot of information needed to set the foundation for your rule base, you needn't put forth a great deal of effort to get that information into a useable format.

Your first task is to log into the FireWall-1 GUI management client. On a Windows system, simply start the Policy Editor or your GUI client by double-clicking its icon. On a Unix system such as Solaris or AIX, execute the *fwpolicy* command found in *$FWDIR/bin*. You'll be presented with a login window, as displayed in Figure 3.1. Note that if this is the initial connection from a GUI client, FireWall-1 will present the management server fingerprint. This is used as a security measure to enable you to validate the identity of that management server.

Once you have logged into the GUI, you'll see a lot of information. Don't worry; you can easily customize this default view to show you just what you need. You can also add or subtract from this view as needed. A couple of changes have been made from previous versions of the policy editor. Figure 3.1 shows you the new default view.

Figure 3.1 Policy Editor

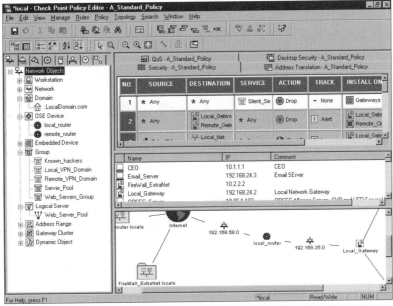

The windowpanes are called (from left moving clockwise) the Objects Tree, Rule Base, Objects List, and Topology Map. You can toggle which one is displayed by selecting **View** from the Policy Editor menu, as displayed in Figure 3.2.

Figure 3.2 View Selection

The Objects Tree gives you a concise and orderly view of the defined objects of each available type. If your boss asks what networks are defined, here's the place that will give you the quickest answer. Next is the rule base. This enables you to instantly sum up the totality of what your firewall is enforcing, but it also enables you to quickly view NAT, QoS,f and Desktop Security rule information. Below the rule base you'll find the Objects List, which presents a little more detail than the Objects Tree about your defined objects.

The final pane in this window is our "belle of the ball," as it were. New in FireWall-1 NG (assuming you've purchased the Visual Policy Editor) is the Topology Map. This gives you a handsome network map showing the interconnections of all your defined objects. Figure 3.3 shows that pane enlarged to full screen.

Figure 3.3 Topology Map

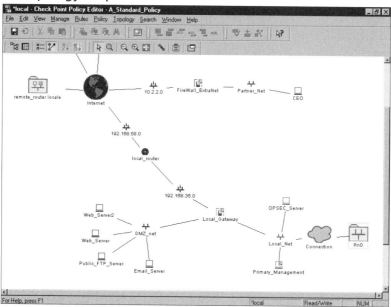

The neat thing is that this map is completely interactive. You can rearrange the placement of the objects and even query them for information, and alter their configuration.

Network Objects

Network objects are, as the name states, simply the objects within your network. An object can be a network range, a group of users, or a single workstation, as examples. Objects can also be groups of other objects, allowing a hierarchical layering and a more concise rule base. Most importantly, you must have properly defined the objects of interest within your network before using them in a FireWall-1 rule.

Network objects can be defined in any of several ways, with the most common method being through the Network Objects Manager, which is shown in Figure 3.4. This GUI window enables you to create, delete, and alter all of the

various types of network entities. To access this screen, select **Manage |
Network Objects** from the Policy Editor GUI.

Figure 3.4 Network Objects Manager

Workstation

The workstation object defines a single computer, and contains many options.
This computer may be a simple workstation, a VPN–1/Firewall–1 system, a third-
party VPN device, a gateway, a host, or any combination of those. This flexibility
comes with a slight increase in complexity. The Workstation properties page contains a great many more options than its counterpart in previous versions of FW-1,
but luckily there is intelligence built in to the window. The branches on the left
become visible as they are needed. A simple workstation will have limited
options, but the choices expand when dealing with Check Point installed products. Table 3.1 defines some of the more common configurations and their displayed options.

Table 3.1 Configuration Matrix

	VPN-1/ FireWall-1	Floodgate-1	Second Management Station	Log Server	UserAuthority Web Plugin
General	X	X	X	X	X
Topology	X	X	X	X	X
NAT	X	X	X	X	X
VPN	X		X		
Authentication	X				X
Management	X	X	X	X	
Advanced	X	X	X	X	X

The General configuration window, as shown in Figure 3.5, enables you to associate a system name and an IP address with this object. If the name is resolvable via something like DNS, then you can use the **Get Address** button to retrieve the IP address, or else you can type it in manually. The comment field is optional. In common with all FireWall-1 objects, you can assign a color to the object. The remaining fields have special meanings when selected, which impact the way VPN-1/FireWall-1 interacts with them.

Figure 3.5 Workstation Properties, General Window

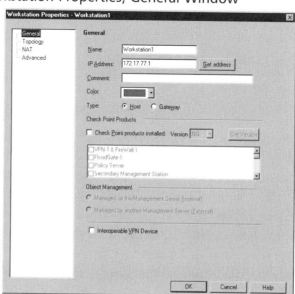

- **Type** Select if this device is a gateway or a host. (Note the caution in the sidebar relating to gateway address specification). If this device is a gateway, then rules selected as installed on gateways will be enforced on this system.

- **Check Point Products** This enables you to identify the workstation device as running Check Point software. If the checkbox is selected, the options in Object Management will become active, as will the **Get Version** button. **Interoperable VPN Device** is an exclusive selection, thus it will become grayed out. Also, the **Management**, **Authentication** and **VPN** branches will become visible, and sub-menus will become available under the **Advanced** branch. Importantly, you will see the **Secure Internal Communication** option, which enables you to establish the link between Check Point installed products. Figure 3.6 illustrates the properties window as displayed when this option is selected.

Figure 3.6 Workstation Properties with Check Point Products Installed

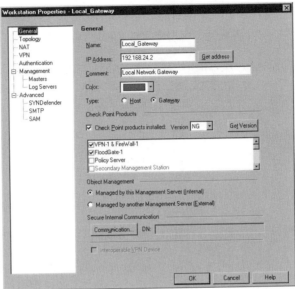

- **Object Management** Here you specify whether the Check Point product specified on the workstation object is internal (managed) or external (not managed) to the management server.

- **Interoperable VPN device** This enables you to denote this object as an interoperable VPN unit. This means that, while no Check Point software is installed on the device, it is still capable of performing IKE encryption for the purpose of establishing a VPN. If this option is checked, you'll have access to the VPN branch of the Workstation Properties. Interoperable VPN devices are only allowed to use IKE encryption, unlike VPN-1/FW-1 VPN setups.

Configuring & Implementing…

What's in a name?

Although the value in the Name field doesn't have to be anything but unique, it is strongly recommended that you use an actual resolvable name. It is also strongly recommended that you include the hostname to address mappings in your systems host files. These files can be found in the following locations:

- For Unix systems, edit the /etc/hosts and /etc/networks files
- For Win32 systems, edit the %SYSTEMDIR%\system32\ drivers\etc\hosts and %SYSTEMDIR%\system32\drivers\ etc\networks

This will ensure the proper function of the Get Address function. Be wary, however, to maintain these files. Hostname and address changes could lead to potential exposure if not properly done.

Also, if the workstation you are defining is a gateway (a multi-homed system that is able to pass traffic between its interfaces), and you are using IKE encryption, be sure to include specify the **outside** address. If you fail to do so, IKE encryption will not function properly!

Network

The network object defines a group of hosts or, more specifically, a network range such as a subnet. When defining individual systems as Workstations becomes too tedious or otherwise untenable, it is quite easy to arrange them with this object type. To create a new Network object, select **New | Network** from the Network Objects management window. This will present you with the panel as shown in Figure 3.7.

The General window allows some simple configuration information to be entered, such as IP address, netmask, and a comment. Note that the portion of the IP address that specifies that the host is ignored. I'm assuming you are already familiar (at least slightly) with IP subnetting. In the example panel, the network is 10.3.4.X, with a 24-bit subnet, producing a mask of 255.255.255.0. In this case, you enter the host portion as a zero. Keep in mind, though, that the host portion might not always be set as zero, and might not always fall on a tidy boundary. For example, you might have a network address of 10.3.4.128, with a subnet of 255.255.255.128. When in doubt, consult your local networking expert.

Figure 3.7 Network Properties—General window

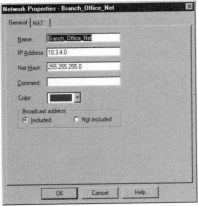

As with all object types, a color can be assigned as well. The last field, **Broadcast address:**, denotes if you desire the broadcast address to be included within the defined network. The broadcast address is defined as the last possible IP within that range.

The NAT panel is the familiar one, which includes the option to establish automatic translation rules. Nothing extraordinary here. NAT will be covered in detail in Chapter 5.

Domain

Another method to group hosts by commonly used techniques is to use the domain object. A machine is determined to be within the domain if a reverse DNS lookup on the machine's IP address yields the proper domain information. Figure 3.8 illustrates this panel, which is accessed by selecting **New | Domain** from the Network Objects management window.

Notice that in the above example the domain name begins with a period. You may be wondering how FW-1 knows what to do with a domain object. When a domain object is used in the rule base as a source or destination, FW-1 will attempt to do a reverse DNS lookup (that is, getting the name for a specified IP) on the appropriate portion of the incoming packet. If the lookup yields the domain information, then you have a match. It is probably obvious that if there is no reverse record, the object will be useless. It is also possible that, through DNS poisoning, this sort of object could lead to a security breach. For these reasons and others, Check Point does not recommend the use of Domain objects in your rule base. If you decide to use them, use them as close to the bottom of the rule base as possible.

Figure 3.8 Domain Properties

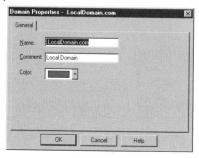

OSE Device

Open Security Extension technology allows FW-1 to manage third-party devices that support these extensions. Most notable among these devices are Cisco routers running IOS version 9 and higher. The number of devices that you may manage depends on your license. The configuration for an OSE compliant device features three windows. To create a new OSE Device, select **New | OSE Device** from the Network Objects management window. Figure 3.9 illustrates the General window.

Figure 3.9 OSE Device—General window

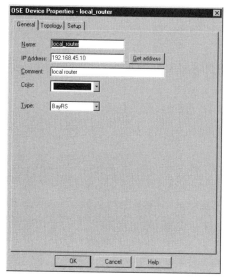

This window enables you to specify some of the basic information about the device, specifically the IP address, name, comment, and device type. The device type may be either of the following:

- BayRS

- Cisco

- 3Com

When a device from this category is managed by the firewall, access control lists are generated based on the security policy and downloaded to them. As with other object types, the **Get address** button will attempt to resolve the specified name to an IP address, saving you that one step.

The topology window is identical to that of its counterpart for the other devices. The main caveat is that at least one interface must be defined (as opposed to, say, a simple workstation) or the ACL entries will not be created successfully. Anti-spoofing and its kin are also defined by editing the interface properties, just as with a workstation. However, there are some additional steps to take, which are accomplished by editing the information on the Setup window.

The Setup window differs depending on the OSE Type specified on the General window. The window as displayed with a Cisco router is displayed in Figure 3.10.

Figure 3.10 Cisco OSE Setup Window

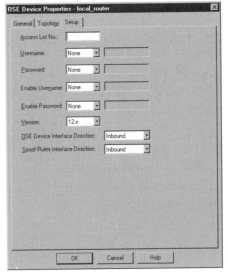

The fields displayed on this window have the following meanings:

- **Access List No.** The number of the ACL that will be applied.

- **Username** This is the exec mode username that will be used for initial access to the device. It, along with the remaining drop-down lists, can be set to None, Known, or Prompt. If set to known, the gray box to the right will become active and allow the entry of a username.

- **Password** Enter the password associated with the exec mode username.

- **Enable Username** The name, if any, of a user with privileged exec access.

- **Enable Password** The password associated with the privileged username.

- **Version** IOS version installed on this router.

- **OSE Device Interface Direction** The direction in which to enforce the security policy. This can be Inbound, Outbound, or Eitherbound.

- **Spoof Rules Interface Direction** The direction in which to enforce anti-spoofing behavior. This can be Inbound, Outbound, or Eitherbound.

The fields for the 3Com and Bay devices are similar in their requirements, and the security policy is enforced in an identical manner.

Embedded Device

An embedded device is defined as a device on which a VPN/FW-1 module or Inspection module is installed. This type of object is restricted to two types (as defined in the **Type** field) with those being Nokia IP5x and Xylan with the supported platforms being Ramp and Xylan.

The configuration is pretty straightforward, with the common rules applying. Define the name, IP address, and an optional comment. Then specify the type, and select **VPN-1 & FireWall-1 installed** if applicable. You must also define your license type. Figure 3.11 illustrates the configuration panel. To open this panel, select **New | Embedded Device**.

Figure 3.11 Embedded Device General Properties

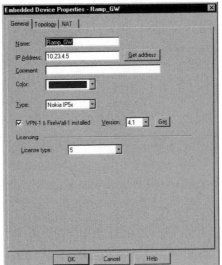

Group

The Group object can be used to manage other objects of dissimilar types. There are three types of groups that you may define within FW-1. To create a new group, select **New | Group** from the Network Objects management window. The group types are as follows:

- Simple Group

- Group with Exclusion

- UAS High Availability group

A simple group is just that. Simple. It is a collection of network devices. The second group type, Group with Exclusion, allows you some granular control over the contents of a group. If you are working in a network with a flat topology, for example, you may be in a situation where there isn't much physical separation within this network. A group of this type enables you to force some structure here. Figure 3.12 illustrates a simple group.

A Group with Exclusion is similar, with the difference being that you specify a major group, defined by Check Point as an "outer group." This will be the group that is included for this definition. You then specify minor, or inner, groups. These will be the groups culled out and excluded from the major group.

Figure 3.12 Group Properties

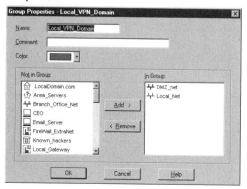

Logical Server

The logical server group (available by selecting **New | Logical Server** from the Network Objects window) enables you to group like servers (FTP, HTTP, SMTP, etc) to be treated as one and used in a sort of resource sharing, or server pooling. Note that this is an optional feature and may not be included within your FireWall-1 installation. Workload is distributed among these servers in a user-configurable manner. Figure 3.13 shows us the configuration options for this object type.

Figure 3.13 Logical Server Properties Window

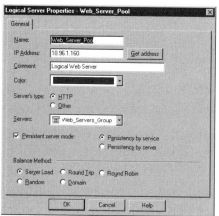

As usual, the name must be entered, and, if resolvable, the **Get address** button can be used to gather the associated IP address. A special note is in order here, specifically regarding the IP you'll select. This address should be that of a non-existent server located on the same network as the destination servers, but can also be that of the FireWall-1 module. Think of this IP as a virtual IP address. It will be used by the clients to connect to the Logical Server group, and therefore cannot belong to any one member of that group.

The **Server's Type** feature really is poorly named. This actually defines the method of load balancing, or even more specifically, the type of algorithm used. The two methods behave very differently. For example, with HTTP selected, only the initial connection will be handled by the logical server address. A redirection is sent to the client informing his or her browser of the new IP (that of the selected destination server), and the remainder of the conversation goes forth without the intervention of the firewall module. If "Other" is selected as the type, dynamic network address translation is performed and the conversation is balanced per connection, with the firewall module constantly involved, unless Persistent Server mode is checked.

The **Servers** section enables you to select the server group that will make up this logical group. If selected, **Persistent server mode** allows some fine-tuning of the balancing mechanism. When enabled, you can enforce connection persistence, meaning you can force packets from an established flow to continue to a single destination. This is very useful for something like an HTTP conversation when using "Other" as the server type. You can select between two modes here, **Persistency by service** and **Persistency by server**. The main difference between the two is that, when the former is selected, only connections to a single server for a single service will have persistency enforced, while in the latter any service on a specific server will be impacted.

The final settings define the type of balancing to be performed. The Balance Method has several possible options.

- **Server Load** FireWall-1 sends a query, using port 18212/UDP, to determine the load of each server. There must consequently be a load-measuring agent on each server to support this method.

- **Round Trip** FireWall-1 sends a simple ICMP ping to each server. The fastest round-trip time is chosen as the preferred server. This lacks somewhat, in that the ping is from the firewall to the server, and may not be optimal from a remote client. (Remember, the servers need not be centrally located to participate in a server group.) Also, a ping doesn't tell you that the HTTP daemon has crashed on the server. As long as the server is up and on the network, regardless of the status of any of its services, traffic will be sent to it. If Round Trip load balancing is configured on a firewall, but the application servers to be balance are behind nested, internal firewalls, then the internal firewalls must allow ICMP through. (This is not desirable normally.)

- **Round Robin** FireWall-1 selects sequentially from a list. This is among the simplest methods, and also uses ICMP to validate application servers.

- **Random** FireWall-1 selects randomly from a list.

- **Domain** FireWall-1 attempts to select the closest server to the client, based on domain naming convention. This method is not recommended.

Address Range

An address range defines a sequential range of IP addresses for inclusion with your rule base. An address range is similar in use to a Network object, with the major difference being that you specify a starting and ending IP address instead of a network number and subnet mask. Figure 3.14 illustrates the General panel for this object type, which is available by selecting **New | Address Range** from the Network Objects management window. As usual, the NAT panel features no special information and is the same as that found on most other object types.

Figure 3.14 Address Range Properties Window

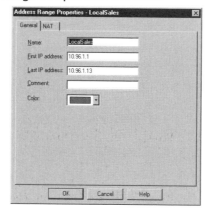

Gateway Cluster

A gateway cluster is a grouping of machines running VPN-1/FireWall-1 that is grouped together as a means of fail over support. Clustering is a complex subject, and configuring it is much more detailed than the majority of other object types. (Detailed coverage of clustering will be discussed in Chapter 12.) First, you have to visit the Global Properties and, under the Gateway High Availability branch, place a checkmark in the setting to enable gateway clusters.

The next step is to create your workstation objects. In order to support clustering, you must have at least three objects, two of which must be firewall modules, and one a manager. The workstation object should be created as normal for a machine with FW-1 installed. It is important that the interfaces are properly defined, as anti-spoofing is required for proper high-availability function. Next, you create a new gateway cluster object. The General panel is illustrated in Figure 3.15. You'll access this panel by selecting **New | Gateway** Cluster from the Network Objects management window.

Figure 3.15 Gateway Cluster—General Panel

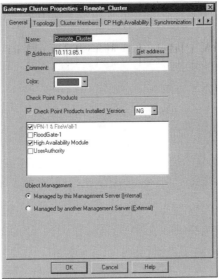

This panel allows the initial configuration for the cluster. The name and IP address are defined here, as are the specific Check Point products that will reside within this cluster. Also, you can specify whether you or another party manage the cluster. You also can specify, on the topology panel, which addresses reside behind this cluster. This is similar to the features on a workstation object's interface properties topology panel.

Dynamic Object

A dynamic object is perhaps the most interesting object type supported on FW-1. It is also one of the most useful in a large enterprise. This object type enables you to define a logical server type, one in which the actual IP address will resolve differently on each FW-1 machine. This enables you to create rules referencing "mail server" and distribute that policy to several different FW-1 machines, all of which will resolve "mail server" as the proper machine within their realm. Neat, huh? Figure 3.16 shows you the basic configuration window, which you can see by selecting **New | Dynamic Object** from the Network Objects management window.

Figure 3.16 Dynamic Object Properties Window

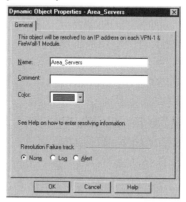

You're probably wondering how this really works. The real key to a dynamic object is the dynamic_objects command. This command is run on the firewall module where the name will be resolved, and enables you to specify the values to which it will resolve. Table 3.2 describes this command and its options.

Table 3.2 Dynamic_Objects Command Options

Option	Explanation
-o <object name>	Specify the object name to work with. This option is often used with operators such as –a to add addresses to an existing object.
-r <address range>	Specifies an address range.
-a <address range>	Add address of <range> to object.
-d <address range>	Deletes addresses from the object.
-l	List all dynamic objects.
-n <object name>	Create a new dynamic object; assuming the VPN-1/FW-1 process has been stopped.
-c	Compare the defined dynamic objects to those defined in the objects.C file.
-do <object name>	Delete the specified object.

Services

The services objects give you a finer level of access control as compared to exclusive use of network entities. With the service object, you can define protocol specific information, like protocol in use (TCP, UDP, etc), and port numbers. FW-1 comes preconfigured with many of the more common services in use today, and further enables you to create custom services based on your unique needs.

To add, modify, or delete services, access the Services window by clicking **Manage | Services**. From here, you will be able to act on the following service types.

TCP

The TCP service object enables you to define a basic TCP service. Figure 3.17 illustrates this service type, using the domain-tcp (DNS) service as an example. To bring up this window, select **New | TCP** from the Services management window.

Figure 3.17 TCP Service Properties

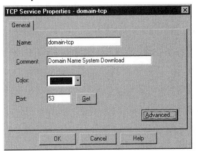

The information for this is very limited (which is nice when you have to define a lot of them!). Besides a name and comment, all you have to enter is the destination port number. This can be a specific port, as in Figure 3.17, a range (e.g. 1024-1028), or a greater-than/less-than definition (e.g. <56). There is also an **Advanced** button, which displays the window as shown in Figure 3.18.

The advanced settings enable you to specify a source port, and allow for the same modifiers as in the General panel's port specification. You can also specify the protocol type, which impacts which security server will provide things like content security for this service. The checkbox marked **Enable for TCP resource**, if checked, enforces screening using a UFP server, mitigating the intervention of a security server. The next item, **Match for 'Any'** allows connections using this service to be matched when a rule is crafted with 'Any' as the service. The **Session Timeout** is a local setting meant to allow override of the global session timeout. The inclusion of the timeout in the GUI is a nice change for FireWall-1 NG. In previous versions, setting a per-service timeout required manual editing of the base.def file, which is obviously a bit more involved.

Figure 3.18 Advanced TCP Service Properties

UDP

The UDP service object enables you to define a basic UDP service. An example of this is the TFTP service. UDP tracking poses a problem for many firewalls, especially circuit level gateways. Since UDP is connectionless, it's generally an all-or-nothing approach to security. Whole port ranges are often opened to allow UDP traffic, which is not a very nice notion. With FireWall-1, a second mechanism has been designed to keep track of a virtual "connection."

The General properties are identical to those for TCP, as seen in Figure 3.17. The Advanced options are slightly different, and are therefore depicted in Figure 3.19.

Figure 3.19 Advanced UDP Service Properties

As with the TCP settings, we are able to specify a source port and a protocol type. Additionally, we have the familiar checkboxes, but this time with slightly different values. These are as follows:

- **Accept Replies** If checked, allows for a bidirectional communication to take place.

- **Accept replies from any port** Allows the server to reply from any port. An example of the need for this is the TFTP service.

- **Match for 'Any'** Allows connections using this service to be matched when a rule is crafted with 'Any' as the service.

RPC

RPC services are usually tricky for a firewall administrator. RPC-based connections do not use a fixed port number, so allowing these types of connections is either an all-or-nothing exercise. Usually, administrators choose to block all RPC connections on their external firewalls, while being far more permissive within their network boundaries.

To alleviate this potential risk, FW-1 transparently tracks RPC ports. Application information is extracted from the packet in order to identify the program used. FW-1 also maintains a cache that maps RPC program numbers to the assigned port numbers. The configuration panel, viewed by selecting **New | RPC** from the Service management window, is as shown in Figure 3.20.

Figure 3.20 RPC Service Properties

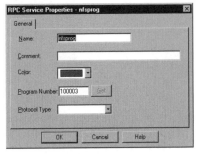

ICMP

ICMP is used for things like network troubleshooting and discovery. Unfortunately, attackers looking to gain information about you also use it. For this reason, many sites decide to block all ICMP traffic. This isn't really necessary, and may cause more problems than it solves. You can, using FireWall-1, pick and choose the specific ICMP types (and even sub types, or "codes") allowed. Table 3.3 details some of the more useful ICMP types, their associated codes, and their meanings, as defined by the IANA (www.iana.org/assignments/icmp–parameters).

Table 3.3 ICMP Codes

ICMP Type	ICMP Code	Explanation
0		Echo (ping) reply
3		Destination unreachable:
	0	-network unreachable
	1	-host unreachable
	2	-protocol unreachable
	3	-port unreachable
	4	Dropped because DF (do not fragment) bit was set, fragmentation needed.
	5	Source routing not allowed or otherwise failed.
4		Slow transmission rate
5		Better network path available:
	0	-for entire network
	1	-for specific host
	2	-for tos and entire network
	3	-for tos and specific host
8		Echo (ping) request
11		Time exceeded for reason:
	0	-TTL reached 0 in transit
	1	-fragment reassembly time exceeded.
12		Bad IP header

Figure 3.21 shows us the configuration panel for an ICMP service. Using the table above, you can see how simple it would be to create services, and thus rules, to allow the beneficial types of ICMP while excluding those that may do you harm.

Figure 3.21 ICMP Service Properties

Other

Often called "user-defined" services, this is a catchall for whatever is missing. Its presence gives you a great deal of flexibility, but requires at least a familiarity with the inspect language. The General panel is similar to that found in its cousin objects, allowing you to define a name, add a comment, and assign a color. It also enables you to define the protocol identifier. This is a very important field, as it is the key to matching against the incoming traffic. Figure 3.22 shows you the General panel for this service type.

Figure 3.22 User-Defined Service Properties—General panel

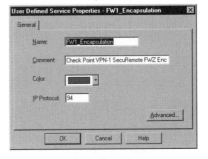

Clicking on the **Advanced** button brings up a screen that allows the entry of the most crucial part of this object, the **Match** field. This field is a snippet of inspect code that will be used to check the incoming packets. It can, therefore, be as complex as you can imagine. This makes the user-defined object a truly powerful tool for the enforcement of very specific requirements.

Group

The group object enables you to combine different protocols. This can be used, for example, to define a service whose individual parts must also be separately defined. Ping is a good example. It consists of an echo request and an echo reply. These can be defined and then combined into a group, and that group used in your rule base. Figure 3.23 displays the configuration window, which is accessed by selecting **New | Group** from the Services management window.

Figure 3.23 Group Properties

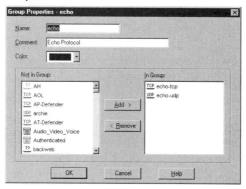

DCE-RPC

This service type works in a similar fashion to the RPC service, in that it tracks DCE-RPC based connections, extracting the information from the packet and creating a virtual session whose information is stored in a local cache. When you define the DCE-RPC service, you will be asked for the UUID for the specific interface as well as the protocol type. Figure 3.24 illustrates this panel.

Figure 3.24 DCE-RPC Properties

Resources

Resource objects are used to configure Content Security on FW-1, and will be covered in greater detail in Chapter 7. Content security includes support for the HTTP, FTP, and SMTP protocols. FW-1 provides this support by using the FW-1 Security Servers. For each connection established through the FW-1 Security Servers, you are able to control access on a granular level according to protocol specific information unique to a specific service. This includes URLs, file names, FTP commands, and so on.

URI

A URI, or Uniform Resource Identifier, defines how to access resources on the Internet. Most of us are familiar with the URI by another name: URL. Which term you use is often a matter of tossing the dice, as there is dispute even among the standards developers as to which is the more proper.

URI for QoS

Another type of URI object is the **URI for QoS**, which is used when defining a rulebase for FloodGate-1. This resource type allows the security administrator to classify certain URIs as part of a QoS policy. This object type is fairly simple to create. You'll need to define a name, comment, and select the color for the object. Additionally, you will need to define a **Search for URL**. This specifies the URL that will trigger a match, and it can be as specific as a complete URL, or as general as *.jpg, which would match any JPEG file.

SMTP

The SMTP resource defines the methods used by the FW-1 to handle incoming or outgoing email. There are many options, including the ability to remove active scripting components, rewriting fields in the envelope (such as to: or from:) or filtering based on content. The configuration of this resource type is similar to that of the URI, including the ability to use a CVP server.

FTP

An FTP resource is defined in order to enforce content security for FTP connections. I like to use this resource to define the verbs or methods that will be allowed through my firewall. For example, if I have an FTP server that is publicly available for downloading, I can back up the system administrator and deny the ability to PUT.

OPSEC Applications

The OPSEC, or Open Platform for Security, object defines for you a means of interacting with a third-party developed security application. These applications add extended functionality to the FW-1 installation. Some examples include virus scanning, content filtering, and intrusion detection. OPSEC allows FW-1 to send its data stream to other applications, and it also allows those applications to send data to the firewall, for example, log entries via the ELA or status via AMON interfaces. This will be covered fully in Chapter 7.

Servers

A server is a host computer running a specific application, or service. The Server object is the representation of that relationship.

Radius

A RADIUS server is used to provide authentication services. While originally used for remote access services, it is also now commonly used for things like routers and firewalls. To define a radius server, select **Manage | Servers** from the policy editor drop-down menu and then select **New | RADIUS**. The configuration appears as in Figure 3.25.

Figure 3.25 RADIUS Server Properties

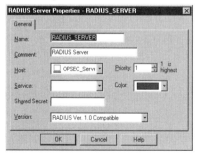

The RADIUS server object is configured in a way that is fairly common with the other server types. After defining the name, adding a comment, and selecting the associated color, you'll need to specify the **Host** that this RADIUS server is running on. You'll also need to assign a **Priority**. The priority is used to determine the preference for an individual server when more than one is available for contact, for example, when the server is assigned to a RADIUS group.

The next step is to define the **Service**, which is the obvious choice of RADIUS. The **Shared Secret** must be entered in order to establish communication between the firewalled object and the RADIUS server. Consequently, it must be the same on both devices. The final step is to select the proper version from the **Version** drop-down menu.

Radius Group

A RADIUS group is used to form a group of RADIUS servers. (You'd never have guessed that one!). These servers are then available for use as a single object, with authentication services being performed by the server with the highest priority (e.g. the lowest number). Unlike most other groups, Server groups such as this may not contain any dissimilar entities.

TACACS

A TACACS (Terminal Access Control Access Control Server) server is another one of your handy access control methods. The definition of this object shares the same generalities of the other server entities, those being name, comment, color, and host. Once these are defined, you have only to specify if the server is running TACACS or a TACACS+, enter a secret key, if necessary, for TACACS+, and select the appropriate **Service** from the drop-down menu. (Note that you won't have to select a service with TACACS+.) This panel is illustrated in Figure 3.26.

Figure 3.26 TACACS Server Properties

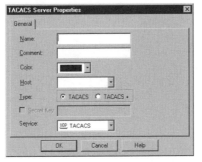

DEFENDER

The Defender server type defines an object running AXENT's Pathways Defender server. This is another authentication method available to you as a FW-1 administrator, and is very easy to incorporate. Besides your four familiar fields of Name, Comment, Color, and Host, you are also able to specify a backup host.

Then all that remains is to enter the **Agent ID**, as defined on the Defender server, and the **Agent Key**, which is used to encrypt the communication with the Defender server, and is also specified in the Defender server's configuration.

LDAP Account Unit

LDAP, or the Lightweight Database Access Protocol, is used for a bevy of purposes. With regards to FW-1, this server object is used for the purposes of user management. A full discussion of the workings of LDAP is beyond the scope of this book (and this author!) but I'll assume if you are configuring an LDAP object, you have access to an existing LDAP server and the necessary information. Figure 3.27 illustrates the **General** panel for LDAP configuration.

Figure 3.27 LDAP Account Unit Properties

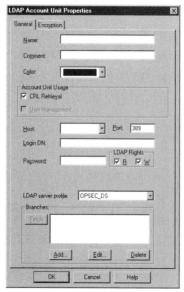

Certificate Authority

We've all heard the buzz about PKI, now here's your chance to jump on the bandwagon. The inclusion of a certificate authority in your security infrastructure enables you to use certificate-based authentication and encryption that eases (or perhaps shifts) the administrative burden of VPN development.

There are three tabs for the Certificate Authority object, with the first being the very simple **General** tab. The associated panel allows the standard configuration information of Name, Comment, and Color, as well as the ability to specify the Certificate Authority via a drop-down menu. You'll have a few choices in this drop-down, with your selection determined by what is available to you. The contents of the second panel depend on the selection in this drop-down box.

The contents of the second panel vary, but generally allow for the importing of a configuration from the PKI server and the importing of the actual certificate. You may also be able to specify the source of the Certificate Revocation List (CRL).

The **Advanced** panel deals with the CRL for this server; specifically, it configures the desire to cache the CRL and when to fetch a new CRL. You can also assign what branches are to be allowed.

SecuRemote DNS

SecuRemote DNS is an internal server type that is used to resolve private addresses to names. SecuRemote DNS replaces the need to create a dnsinfo.C file on the management server's $FWDIR/conf directory. This is a nice change. You will, however, still need to edit *$FWDIR/lib/crypt.def* though, adding the line *#define ENCDNS* to enable SecuRemote users to download this information along with their topology.

Configuration of this server type is fairly straightforward. You have two tabs: **General** and **Domains**. The **General** panel allows the configuration of the Name, Comment, Color, and Host. As usual, the host must have previously been defined as a workstation object.

The **Domains** panel lists the domains that are included for resolution, as well as something called a **Maximum Label Prefix Count**. This count defines the number of prefixes that will be allowed for the specific domain. For example, if the domain is .edu, then troll.gatech.edu has 2 prefixes. If the maximum prefix count were 1, this domain would not resolve.

Internal Users

The ability to define users on the firewall is a nice feature, but it is also rather administratively intensive. The benefit is that you can select specific users as the source for traffic in a rule. The downside is you have to define these users. Fortunately, Check Point has simplified this process somewhat with the ability to define generic user templates. The use of LDAP as an external source of user information is also supported, which greatly decreases the workload redundancy of a firewall administrator. We'll look at the user creation process in detail in Chapter 6.

The first step is to bring up the Users interface. This is accessed by selecting **Manage | Users** from the policy editor menu. This window is used to define and modify users, and also to install the user database to the VPN-1/Firewall-1 systems on which this policy is installed.

Time

Time objects are just that. These objects enable you to schedule events, restrict connections, or simply quantify a time period. For example, you can restrict web browsing not only to specific sites, but also to specific times. There are three possible object types to select from. You can specify a time, a scheduled event, or a group of one or more of these types. To create a new time object, simple select **Manage | Time** from your policy editor window.

The Time object is used to restrict the application of rules to specified times. There are two panels to this object: **General** and **Days.** The General panel allows the standard settings, as well as up to three time ranges. These ranges specify the time spans in which this object would be applicable. The second panel, **Days,** enables you to enforce a finer-grained access control on the time object. We can specify days of a week, or a specific date, or a numbered day in each month. This is a very flexible tool indeed. Figure 3.28 illustrates the **Days** panel.

Figure 3.28 Time Object—Days Panel

Group

A group is formed by the combination of several time object types, and can be used to simplify time-based rules. Instead of using multiple rules, you can create a group of time objects and assign this to a single rule. Creating a time group is similar to the other group types, and consists of assigning a name, comment, and color and then moving time objects from the **Not in Group** list to the **In Group** list.

Scheduled Event

A scheduled event is most often used for administrative purposes, such as scheduling log changes. Configuration is simple, with the only interesting field being the specification of the time at which the event will be triggered. You can also, as with the Time object, schedule the repetition frequency of the object. For example, when you define your Management machine, you have access to the Management branch of the Workstation properties. One of the fields, **Schedule log switch to:**, requires the use of a time object as its option.

Virtual Link

A Virtual Link is a path between two VPN-1/FireWall-1 modules or FloodGate-1 Modules. Virtual Links are defined in the Policy Editor, and can be given Service Level Agreement (SLA) parameters. They can then be monitored using Check Point Traffic Monitoring. To add a new Virtual Link, select **Virtual Links** from the **Manage** menu in the Policy Editor.

There are two panels to be configured. The **General** panel defines the name, etc., for the link, and also enables you to define the endpoints and to optionally activate the link.

The SLA Parameters panel, shown in Figure 3.29, enables you to specify the criteria that will be used to measure the integrity of the link. Thresholds are defined in three directions of traffic. You can specify the Committed Information Rate (CIR) for traffic point A to point B, and the reverse as well. You can also specify a maximum round trip time (RTT) for bidirectional communication, and optionally log the SLA statistics.

Adding Rules

The Policy Editor is the main interface for all your firewall needs. This is where we have been working to add objects, but it is also the interface to define rules. In the next few sections, I'll show briefly how the Policy Editor can be used to put your network objects into play in the form of firewall rules.

Figure 3.29 Virtual Link Properties—SLA Parameters

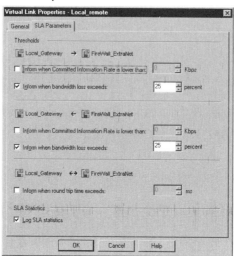

Rules

FW-1, in common with most firewalls, is designed to enforce a set of rules, known as a rule base. This rule base defines the behavior of the firewall, and is configured by you, the firewall administrator. It is dreadfully important that you carefully consider the underlying needs, related to both security and functionality, and make a measured application of both. You'll probably never be able to strike a perfect balance, but the closer you come, the easier your life will be. Fundamentally, there are two models of firewall configuration. The first considers all traffic to be suspect, and only allows what is necessary (blocking all not explicitly allowed). The second model is far more permissive, allowing all traffic that has not proven to be risky (allowing everything except what is explicitly denied). Which model you subscribe to is a decision that must be made at the policy level. Your firewall will be a technical implementation of that policy.

A rule is made up by the combination of source, destination, action, tracking information, enforcement location, enforcement time, and an optional (but highly recommended) time fields. These fields are explained in the next few sections, along with the methods used to create them. We'll cover Rule Base creation in detail in Chapter 4.

Adding Rules

Adding rules in FW-1 is very straightforward. There are a few choices about rule placement you have to decide upon when adding a new rule. When you select **Rules | Add Rule** you'll see a submenu with the following choices.

- **Bottom** After the last rule in the rulebase.

- **Top** Before the first rule in the rulebase.

- **After** After the currently selected rule.

- **Before** Before the currently selected rule.

After you insert the new rule, it will resemble the one shown in Figure 3.30. You will need to configure the specifics of each rule. In each field of the new rule, right-click to enter the necessary information.

Figure 3.30 New Rule

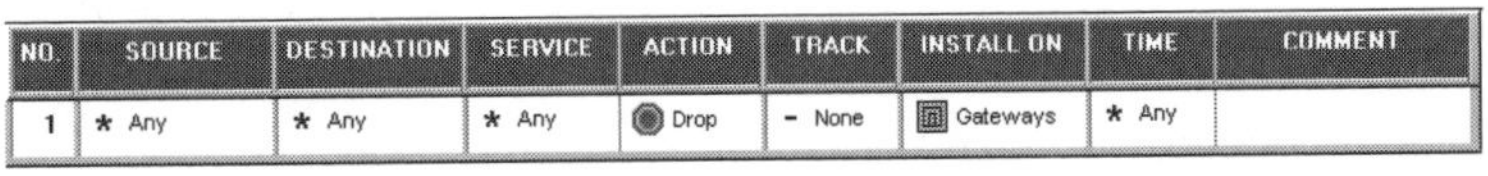

NO.	SOURCE	DESTINATION	SERVICE	ACTION	TRACK	INSTALL ON	TIME	COMMENT
1	★ Any	★ Any	★ Any	⬤ Drop	– None	🖳 Gateways	★ Any	

Source

The source field defines the IP address or hostname that is initiating the data stream. For the sake of your rule base, the source can be any of the properly defined network objects, as well as users or groups of users. When adding a source, you have the choice of adding an object or adding user access. You are not restricted in the number of sources for a rule.

Destination

The destination can be any defined network object. When you right-click in the **Destination** field and select **Add**, you'll see a window similar to that shown in Figure 3.31. Note that a rule can support multiple destinations.

Service

The service field defines the service that must be present in order to generate a match. To add a service, right-click in the **Service** field and select **Add.** You will have the choice of adding a service, or a service with a resource. You can define any number of services for a rule.

Figure 3.31 Add Object

Action

The action is the way that FireWall-1 reacts when a rule is matched. You have a couple of choices when selecting an action, but only one selection is allowed. The available options are the following:

- **Accept** Accept the packet; allow the connection.
- **Reject** Reject the connection and notify the sender of the condition.
- **Drop** Reject the connection, but do not notify the sender.
- **User Authentication** Use User Authentication for this connection.
- **Client Authentication** Use Client Authentication for this connection.
- **Session Authentication** Use Session Authentication for this connection.
- **Encrypt** Encrypt outgoing packets; decrypt incoming packets.
- **Client Encryption** Accept only if this connection originates from a SecuRemote client.

Track

The Track column defines how information about this session will be recorded. There are several options in the menu when you right-click on this field.

- **Log** Write a log entry regarding this connection.
- **Account** Write an accounting log entry regarding this connection.
- **Alert** Generate a pop-up alert regarding this connection.

- **Mail** Send a mail regarding this connection.
- **SnmpTrap** Generate an SNMP trap based on this connection.
- **User-Defined** Execute the user-defined script as a result of this connection.

Install On

The **Install On** field defines which defined objects will have this policy installed on them. Although the entire policy is installed on each selected object, these objects only enforce the part of the policy that is relevant to them. If no rules are relevant, then no communication will be allowed.

- Enforce on all network objects defined as gateways.
- Enforce on the specified target object(s) only, in the inbound and outbound directions.
- Enforce in the inbound direction on the firewalled network objects defined as Destination in this rule.
- Enforce in the outbound direction on the firewalled network objects defined as Source in this rule.
- Enforce on all OSE devices.
- Enforce on all embedded devices.

Time

In this field, use a time object to restrict the connection to certain specified intervals, or leave the default of **Any.**

Comment

This field is used to describe the rule, its purpose, and its functionality. It is highly recommended that you do not leave this field blank!

Global Properties

While the brunt of your security policy will reside in the rulebase, there are other places you have to pay attention to. In order to fully secure your enterprise, you will need to at least be familiar with the Global Properties, and most likely you will need to alter them. You do this by accessing the Global Properties from the Policy menu. We'll spend the next few sections discussing these properties. Figure 3.32 displays the initial panel of the Global Properties.

Figure 3.32 Global Properties

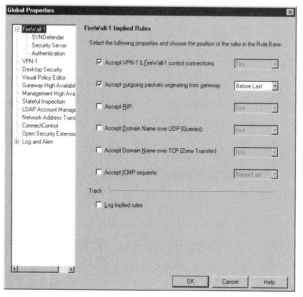

FireWall-1 Implied Rules

FireWall-1 has a feature that many find mysterious at first blush. That feature is the "implied" rule base. This rule base is made up of settings in the Global Properties, as opposed to the one explicitly created by you, the firewall administrator. Once you understand this, the mystery is removed, and you'll see that they are actually pretty simple. They are shown, by the way, in Figure 3.32. What you select is up to your security policy, but I highly recommend that you enable the logging of these rules.

One important thing to understand is the implication of the option values. If you select a rule to be included within the implied rule base, you'll need to decide where to place that rule. You have three choices here.

- First
- Last
- Before Last

You'll need to select the location in the rule base where the selected rule will be placed. This is a critical decision, and you should understand how a packet passes through the rule base in order to assist your decision. Furthermore, not all implied rules are as simple as they may seem. The first implied rule, Accept VPN-1 and FireWall-1 control connections, for example, enables a service group containing 17 services. You probably don't need to worry about this too much, but it is a good thing to be aware of.

Viewing Implied Rules

There are two methods of viewing implied rules. Certainly, you can view them within the Global Properties window, but this is often cumbersome and difficult to do in a cohesive flow. When you want access to these rules while editing the rest of your rule base, the easiest way is to select the **View** menu and then select **Implied Rules**. You'll see something like what is displayed in Figure 3.33. Note that the implied rules are unnumbered and arehighlighted by their different color.

Figure 3.33 Implied Rules

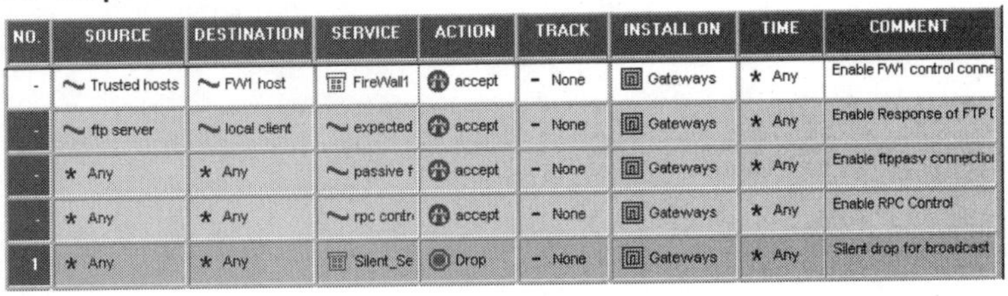

NO.	SOURCE	DESTINATION	SERVICE	ACTION	TRACK	INSTALL ON	TIME	COMMENT
-	~ Trusted hosts	~ FW1 host	FireWall1	accept	- None	Gateways	★ Any	Enable FW1 control conne
	~ ftp server	~ local client	~ expected	accept	- None	Gateways	★ Any	Enable Response of FTP [
	★ Any	★ Any	~ passive f	accept	- None	Gateways	★ Any	Enable ftppasv connectio
	★ Any	★ Any	~ rpc contr	accept	- None	Gateways	★ Any	Enable RPC Control
1	★ Any	★ Any	Silent_Se	Drop	- None	Gateways	★ Any	Silent drop for broadcast

SYNDefender

SYNDefender is a feature used to guard your network from the dreaded SYN flood. Note that this isn't really designed to prevent such an attack against your firewall, but for what it is intended to do it is very handy. It has two modes of operation: SYNGateway and passive SYNGateway. In SYNGateway mode, the firewall actively intercepts SYN packets, completes the three-way handshake, and only then forwards the connection to the true destination. In passive mode, the firewall monitors the connection. If the timeout period is reached, a RST (reset) packet is sent to both the originator and the destination.

Configuring SYNDefender is simple. Simply navigate to the proper submenu and select the method, timeout, and maximum connections.

Designing & Planning…

Defending against the SYN attack

The SYN attack is one of the simplest Denial of Service (DoS) attacks to initiate. Unfortunately, it is also one of the most difficult to defend against. The reasons for these truths are identical. The basic operation of a SYN flood is to send hundreds of thousands of connection requests (SYN, or synchronize, packets) to the target server. The target server will send an acknowledgment of that SYN packet, allocate a bit of memory in a pending connection queue, and then wait, for a predefined timeout period, for the final part of the connection process to complete. Herein lies the rub.

There are two problems here. The first is that the sending of a SYN packet is completely normal. A high-volume server might see thousands of SYN packets in any given time period. The second problem is that the server tends to be too generous in its timeout period, giving the client plenty of time to complete the connection. For example, default config-uration of Microsoft Windows 2000 will wait 189 seconds. That's over three minutes **per connection** of resource consumption. While the memory allocated is small, the cumulative impact can be severe enough to gobble up all the resources on the target server.

While firewall tools like SYNDefender can help you keep the bogus SYN packets from reaching the server, you need (and have available) a better method. Since most SYN attacks use spoofed IP addresses, ingress and egress filtering by large ISPs could go a long way to mitigate the dangers of SYN attacks.

Security Server

The Security Server panel allows the entry of welcome messages for many of the most common Internet services. This is accomplished by pointing to the appro-priate file containing the message. You can also configure the HTTP Next Proxy, although this is better done in the workstation object, assuming a version of FireWall-1 of NG. Earlier versions still require entry in this field.

Authentication

The Authentication panel enables you to specify the tolerance for failed login attempts. There are parameters for rlogin, telnet, client authentication and session authentication. There is also a section for configuring session timeout, wait mode and logging/alerting for backlevel modules.

VPN-1

The VPN panel controls the configuration of items like security association (SA) renegotiation, as well as CRL and SecuRemote grace periods.

Desktop Security

The Desktop Security panel contains a lot of information regarding the behavior of your firewall with regard to SecuRemote client requests. The settings you select here are highly dependant on your own security policy, but again, I strongly recommend that you log violation notifications and **not** respond to unauthenticated topology requests. We'll cover Desktop security in Chapter 11.

Visual Policy Editor

The Visual Policy Editor provides a very slick interface to view your objects and their interrelations, as mentioned in the beginning of this chapter. This panel enables you to display the VPE or conceal it from view. Note that if you disable the VPE, no topology calculations will take place within the firewall inner-workings.

Gateway High Availability

Gateway High Availability is the process in which multiple modules can act as one for the sake of redundancy. This panel lets you enable or disable the feature. I've discussed HA a bit here in this chapter, and it'll be discussed in more depth later on in Chapter 12.

Management High Availability

Management High Availability is similar to that for gateways, except that it allows the management modules to exhibit some redundancy. This panel allows for you to select the synchronization time of the management servers participating in the HA configuration.

Stateful Inspection

Stateful Inspection is the heart of FireWall-1. This panel does not allow you to change that, but instead enables you to specify some timeout settings for the TCP sessions and to configure stateful UDP and ICMP behavior.

LDAP Account Management

The LDAP account management panel allows the enabling of LDAP for account management. Here you can also set some session timeouts and password rules. We'll cover LDAP in depth in chapter 6.

Network Address Translation

The NAT panel configures some general NAT behavior such for the Automatic NAT rules and NAT pools for SecuRemote connections. NAT will be covered in chapters 5 and 12.

ConnectControl

The ConnectControl panel allows the configuration of this very handy feature. On this panel, we can set the interval that VPN-1/FireWall-1 will wait between server checks (commonly known as heartbeat checks) and the number of retries before a server is considered unreachable. We can also set the persistency timeout. This is the time within all connections from the same source ip will be forwarded to the same server. Finally, you configure the listening address of the server agent used to measure server load and the pooling interval for that.

Open Security Extension

The OSE panel allows configuration for "implied rules" that are applied only to OSE compliant routers.

Log and Alert

This panel enables you to configure the responses taken when a packet matches a rule. This topic is covered in depth in Chapter 9.

SecureUpdate

SecureUpdate is a tool for the easy management of both versioning and licensing for both Check Point and OPSEC products. Chapter 8 will cover the version management and upgrade features, but I wanted to touch on the licensing here. This component can be a real lifesaver, as you'll understand if you've ever had to manually upgrade several dozens of licenses.

The GUI interface features two panels, one for Products and one for Licenses. These can be selected by clicking on the appropriate tab within the window. Figure 3.34 illustrates this GUI panel.

Figure 3.34 SecureUpdate GUI

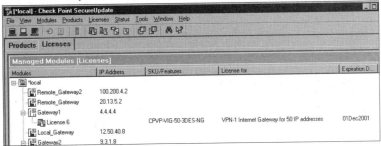

The real blessing of the SecureUpdate tool is that of centralized management and authority. Using this product, you can apply updates to your Check Point modules in a timelier manner, update licenses, and modify the currently licensed machines. Before you begin doing this, however, you should know about a new feature of FireWall-1 NG. This feature is called Central Licensing and uses what is known as a license repository.

In previous versions of FireWall-1, you had only one licensing option, that of a local license. Local licensing mandated that the license be tied to the IP address of the module. This model wasn't very flexible and made upgrades very difficult and migrations nearly impossible. Central licensing binds the license to the address of the management server and allows several benefits.

- When you change the IP address of the firewall module, the license remains useable. This has not always been the case.

- All licenses are bound to only one IP address. This allows great flexibility in your FireWall-1 deployment. Imagine the scenario where your network boundaries are migrated from one provider to another, and with that comes a new network block. Using central licensing makes that address change a piece of cake. Licenses can be taken from one module and given to another and managed from this central location.

Note that while local licenses can still be used with FireWall-1 NG, you won't be able to use them like central licenses. This means that they can't be detached from their module after they have been installed.

Before you can begin using the functionality of SecureUpdate product, some common-sense things have to be in place. Obviously, there needs to be connectivity between the management module and the modules that are being maintained. For your purposes, connectivity implies both IP connectivity and FW-1 connectivity (SIC). Once this is all in place, you are on your way to licensing bliss.

Licenses can be added to the license repository in one of two ways. The first, more tedious method is to copy the license details by hand. This is annoying and can lead to typographical errors, (although support exists to paste the license details from the clipboard, obviating the need to hand-type) so you probably will not want to add licenses in this way. The second method is to import a file created by the Check Point User Center. To begin, select **Licenses | New License** from the SecureUpdate tool bar. This will allow you the choice of adding manually or importing from a file. Figure 3.35 illustrates this menu option.

Figure 3.35 Adding a License

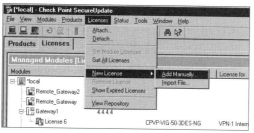

If you opt to add the license manually, you'll see a window with a slew of fields that you'll need to fill out, or as mentioned previously, you can paste the values from the clipboard. If you select **Import File**, you'll see the standard file browse window. Also under this menu option is the ability to view the License Repository. The Repository is a listing of all installed licenses and allows a filtered view. It can show you all licenses, all attached licenses, or all unattached licenses. This is a handy way to get a feel for what spare licenses you have, as well as enableing you to attach and detach central licenses. Remember that the old style licenses can't be detached once they are installed. (SecureUpdate automatically attaches them to the proper module when they are imported.) Figure 3.36 shows us the license repository.

Figure 3.36 License Repository—View All Licenses

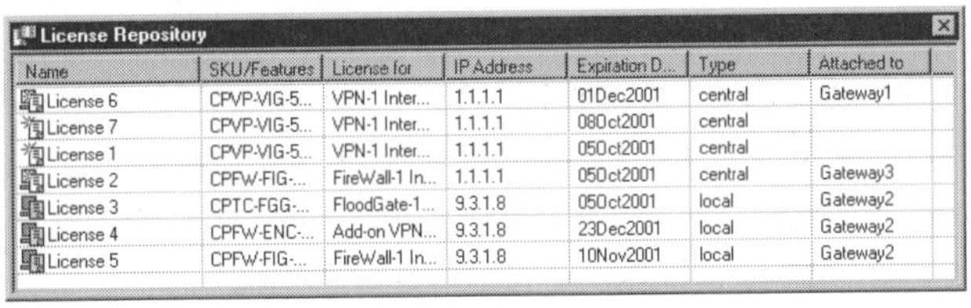

License Repository
Name | SKU/Features | License for | IP Address | Expiration D... | Type | Attached to
License 6 | CPVP-VIG-5... | VPN-1 Inter... | 1.1.1.1 | 01Dec2001 | central | Gateway1
License 7 | CPVP-VIG-5... | VPN-1 Inter... | 1.1.1.1 | 08Oct2001 | central
License 1 | CPVP-VIG-5... | VPN-1 Inter... | 1.1.1.1 | 05Oct2001 | central
License 2 | CPFW-FIG-... | FireWall-1 In... | 1.1.1.1 | 05Oct2001 | central | Gateway3
License 3 | CPTC-FGG-... | FloodGate-1... | 9.3.1.8 | 05Oct2001 | local | Gateway2
License 4 | CPFW-ENC-... | Add-on VPN... | 9.3.1.8 | 23Dec2001 | local | Gateway2
License 5 | CPFW-FIG-... | FireWall-1 In... | 9.3.1.8 | 10Nov2001 | local | Gateway2

Using the Repository, license administration is as easy as right-clicking. In the illustration above, you'll see all licenses. Notice that several of them are not attached to a specific module. To use these licenses, simply right-click on its entry and select **Attach.** At this point, you'll see a listing of the defined workstations with Check Point modules. Select the desired system and select OK. It couldn't be easier.

One other very helpful feature is the ability to view expired licenses. To do this, right-click anywhere within the Repository window and select **Show Expired Licenses**. This presents a window (shown in Figure 3.37) listing the licenses that are no longer valid. Selecting an expired license entry and clicking on **Properties** shows you what module the expired license is attached to. With this tool, you'll never be in the dark about the status of your enterprise.

Figure 3.37 Expired Licenses

Expired Licenses
The following Licenses have expired:
Name | SKU/Features | IP Address | Expiration D...
License 6 | CPVP-VIG-5... | 1.1.1.1
License 7 | CPVP-VIG-5... | 1.1.1.1
License 1 | CPVP-VIG-5... | 1.1.1.1
License 2 | CPFW-FIG-... | 1.1.1.1
License 3 | CPTC-FGG-... | 9.3.1.8
License 4 | CPFW-ENC-... | 9.3.1.8
Delete
Properties
OK
Help

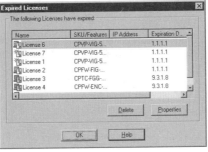

Log Viewer

The Log Viewer is your interface to the log data recorded by VPN-1/FireWall-1. Log data is created by your rule base, by firewall activities, by your own actions (accounting log), and by several other sources. Viewing this data regularly is a key to good security enforcement, and this GUI will make the task of observing the log data much more pleasant.

Upon startup, the Log Viewer begins display of the active security log. You can also use the GUI to view older logs, which may have been rotated out and placed into archive for later review. Note that the name of the log file being viewed is displayed in the upper-left portion of window title bar, as shown in Figure 3.32. This is helpful in the aforementioned case where you are viewing archived data.

The log viewer has three modes of operation, which are accessed by the pull-down menu shown in the figure, or alternatively, via the **Mode** menu option. These modes are **Log**, **Active,** and **Audit**. Active mode displays currently active connections being tracked by the firewall. The active mode is most often used when performing real time-monitoring of traffic, or when you wish to block a connection via SAM. (Block Intruder is a feature we'll discuss in Chapter 9.)

Audit mode is very handy for keeping track of who did what on your firewall. The "who," in this case, is your group of firewall administrators, and the "what" are administrative actions. Examples of these are logging in, creating or deleting objects, and so on. You can also view specific details for any log entry by right-clicking that entry and selecting **Show Details**. Note that the audit data is stored in a separate file, `fw.adtlog` stored in the $FWDIR/log directory of the firewall installation.

Log mode is the most common method of interacting with the log data, and is the most comprehensive way to view the security events. What events you actually see is entirely up to you, as FW-1 allows extensive customization of what is called **Selection Criteria**. This criterion defines what data is extracted from the log data and is displayed to you. You can save your favorite selections and reuse them frequently, or you may opt to use one of the built-in views.

The default views are available via the toolbar or via the **View** menu. These views select some of the more commonly accessed information for display. For example, there is a predefined selection for VPN-1 data, which shows you such entries as Key Ids, encryption method, VPN peer gateway, etc. But the real power of the Log Viewer is in its ability for customization. We see the log viewer GUI in Figure 3.38.

Figure 3.38 Check Point Log Viewer

Column Selections

In order to alter the data displayed, you have to do no more than click **Selection | Customize**. You will be presented with the window shown in Figure 3.39. Using this window enables you to select or deselect any of the available data fields. You can also change the column width using this window. By pressing the **Selection** button, you have access to very granular methods of defining information. I highly recommend that you spend a few minutes looking into this feature on your firewall.

Figure 3.39 Column Options window

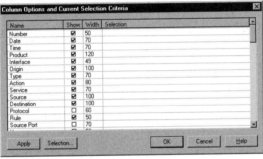

Of course, you probably are looking at the Log Viewer and noticing some familiarity to most common spreadsheet applications. If you feel comfortable with that, then you should feel instantly comfortable interacting with the Log Viewer itself. You can resize columns not only from the options window, but also directly from the viewer main menu.

Right-clicking anywhere within the column you want to modify will bring up a context menu, which enables you to do things like hide that column and resize the width. You can also resize the width by dragging the border of the title header. Once you have tailored the view to your liking, you can begin gathering the information.

The Log Viewer features a very handy search utility, accessed by selecting the **Edit** menu and then **Find**. This enables you to specify the column or columns you want to search through, and the entry of the search criteria. You can also specify a search direction.

System Status

The System Status GUI allows a quick peek at the overall health of your security infrastructure. Real time monitoring, along with status alerting, is featured to assist in the integrity of your enterprise. The System Status viewer is a friendly, lightweight interface. You are presented with a three-pane window, with two of those shown in Figure 3.40.

Figure 3.40 System Status GUI

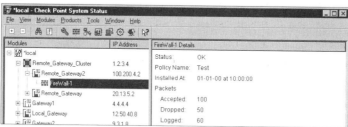

The left-hand pane, known as the **Modules View**, lists the installed and monitored modules. These modules can be either Check Point or third-party OPSEC modules. The right-hand pane, known as the **Details View**, lists the status for the module selected in the **Modules View.** Finally, there is a **Critical Notifications** pane (not shown in the figure) that keeps you updated on any status alerts generated.

The **Modules View** window is further broken down into three columns: Modules, IP Address, and Status. Their meanings are self-explanatory. You can also select specific components to query for status using either the **Products** menu or the button bar across the top of the window. You can query the following components for status (left to right on the button bar).

- SVN Foundation Details
- FireWall-1 Details
- VPN-1 Details
- FloodGate-1 Details
- High Availability Module Details
- OPSEC Application Details
- Management Details

Summary

Are you tired? We've just completed a marathon look at the GUI provided for access to VPN-1/FireWall-1. We looked at the process to create each of the possible object types available for use within your enterprise security policy. This includes network objects, as well as servers and resources. You should now feel comfortable creating objects to support your own implementations.

We also looked at the Policy Editor, and saw how to use these newly created objects to create rules. These rules will be the embodiment of your written security policy, and are the definitions that FireWall-1 enforces. We also saw how FireWall-1 has included something called an "implied rule," how to edit them, and how to view them. Speaking of editing, we covered the various methods of editing our rule base, including adding new rules, deleting existing ones, and rearranging the rule base with cut/paste functions.

We also looked briefly at the Global Properties, and learned a little about how these settings impact the behavior of the firewall. We finished with a peek into some of the additional tools provided with VPN-1/FireWall-1. We saw the Log Viewer and the System Status view, as well as the SecureUpdate tool.

I hope that you feel more at ease with what can often be a daunting and complex task, specifically the representation of your network and the creation of rules to protect it.

Solutions Fast Track

Managing Objects

☑ Don't be stingy: Create as many objects as necessary to support your rule base. You only need to do it once, but you can use them dozens of times.

☑ Save time and complexity by using groups of objects and users.

Adding Rules

☑ Remember that the order in which your rules are displayed is the order they are enforced!

☑ Save time by using cut/paste when creating similar rules. It's easier to edit one field than to create a new rule.

☑ Remember that your security policy is enforced on more than just your firewall modules. Routers and other OPSEC devices may also be impacted.

Global Properties

☑ Be aware of the default settings within the Global Properties and how these may impact the operation of your firewall.

☑ Make sure that you tailor the Implied Rules to suit your site's needs. Don't live with the default entries; they probably won't be just what you need.

Secure Update

☑ Use SecureUpdate to track license and version information enterprise-wide from a single point.

☑ Take advantage of the Check Point VPN-1/FireWall-1 central licenses to ease the crunch of enterprise management.

Log Viewer

☑ Don't live with the default view. Take advantage of the customizations offered to create views that suit your needs.

☑ Remember that the Log Viewer is also home to the Block Connection feature; keep it close at hand.

☑ Don't be afraid to try experiments with new and advanced features!

System Status

☑ Make sure that you do use this tool!

☑ System Status is as important to your enterprise as any other factor. This tool enables you to keep an eye on the health of your infrastructure, which is never a bad thing.

Frequently Asked Questions

The following Frequently Asked Questions, answered by the authors of this book, are designed to both measure your understanding of the concepts presented in this chapter and to assist you with real-life implementation of these concepts. To have your questions about this chapter answered by the author, browse to **www.syngress.com/solutions** and click on the **"Ask the Author"** form.

Q: I see that there is a Read-Only option when I log into the GUI client. Is there a way to force a user to be read only all the time?

A: Yes. Using the `cpconfig` utility, you can add/delete/modify administrators. You can assign Read-Only permissions here. Note that, depending on the installed products, you may see a slightly different configuration panel. This panel also features a custom selection option, which allows different permissions for different Check Point components.

Q: I've installed my FireWall-1 inspection module on a separate machine as my Management module, and I'm having trouble connecting to manage it now.

A: Make sure that you've properly set up the communication infrastructure. To do this, access the General panel of the workstation properties and select the Communication button. Verify that the Trust State is indicated as initialized.

Q: In older versions of FireWall-1, I could manually edit the objects.C file to alter or add objects. Can I still do this on FireWall-1 NG?

A: The easy answer is no. Previously, there were two copies of the objects.C file. One existed with the management module, the other with the firewall module. This is no longer true. In Check Point FireWall-1 NG, the firewall module objects.C is created dynamically based on the objects_5_0.C file found on the management module. The preferred method of editing this file is through the use of the dbedit command. Consult your documentation for the command reference.

## Chapter 4

Creating a Security Policy

Solutions in this chapter:

- Reasons for a Security Policy
- How to Write a Security Policy
- Implementing a Security Policy
- Installing a Security Policy
- Policy Files

☑ Summary

☑ Solutions Fast Track

☑ Frequently Asked Questions

Introduction

This chapter covers an important topic, which is how to define a security policy. This is something you need to do early on so that you can find the right solution for your specific environment. Once you determine how you want to enforce security in your company, then you will know whether you really need to spend the time and effort involved in setting up user authentication, or whether you'd rather use your existing LDAP server, which would save you a lot of trouble. Once you have created a security policy for your company and have planned to introduce security into your network, then choosing your implementation strategy should be fairly straightforward.

We will then discuss how to implement your policy into the FireWall-1 policy editor. Of course, if you are using private IP addresses inside your firewall, then you may need to read the next chapter on Network Address Translation before you can put your firewall in place, but this chapter will get your firewall ready to enforce your policy and start passing packets in your network.

We will walk you through the setup of a Firewall object, and a step-by-step procedure of adding the services outlined in your Information Security Policy into the FireWall-1 Policy Editor interface. Then we'll discuss some additional ways in which to manipulate your rules as well as how to finally install your policy so that it is enforced.

Reasons for a Security Policy

You are probably deploying Check Point NG to protect something. Do you know what you are protecting, what you are protecting it from, and how you are protecting it? Before you can effectively deploy any security control, especially a powerful tool like Check Point NG, you need to have an Information Security Policy. This is not to be confused with the Check Point Security Policy, which, according to Check Point is defined in terms of a Rule Base and [FW-1 NG] Properties. No, we are talking about an enterprise-wide information security policy that includes an Executive Security Policy, accompanied by standards, guidelines, and procedures for implementing and maintaining an information security program.

Many organizations are now seeing the need to have an articulated information security policy. Having such a policy is making organizations more effective in their preventative, detective, and responsive security measures. Moreover, as a result of government regulations, organizations in certain vertical industries are required to have formally documented information security policies.

In addition, an information security policy is also extremely beneficial to the security manager because it provides, at an executive level, a mandated framework for ensuring the confidentiality, integrity, and availability of an organization's information assets. What this means is that the security manager has some weight in his or her corner for budget requests when he or she has an approved information security policy.

Finally, for the security administrator, having a written and approved policy can ensure that you are able to deploy Check Point NG in a way that it minimizes disruption to business. Think of the written policy as a recipe to ensure that you configure everything correctly. Not to mention that a policy is the best way to ensure you will keep your job, should something happen.

How to Write a Security Policy

To completely write an entire Information Security Policy could take months of work with involvement from the legal department, and the various business units. However, in order to implement Check Point NG, you need at a minimum an Executive Security Policy and a Perimeter Network Security Policy. Typically, the Executive Security Policy is a high-level document of about three to five pages that points to relevant standards, procedures, and guidelines. Because the highest levels of management or the board of directors must adopt the Executive Security Policy, it should be written without details about technologies, people, or methods. This will ensure that as technology changes or as people change, the document will not become obsolete. Think of the Executive Policy as a declaration of the importance of security to your organization. However, choose your words carefully because it is a legal document in many respects.

Designing & Planning...

Executive Support

Executive support and approval is critical to the success of your Information Security Policy. When the CEO has to follow the same rules as everyone else, it makes policy enforcement much simpler.

The Executive Security Policy is important because without an executive endorsement of your security policy, enforcement may become difficult. In order to write an effective Executive Security Policy you must identify early on the departments with an interest in maintaining information assets like R&D, Finance, and IT. Approach the managers and request their involvement in drafting an executive-level security document. In addition, you will want to include the legal department and an executive sponsor.

The final document should have language such as: "Because of the nature of our business, customer non-public information is frequently transmitted or stored on our information systems. As a result, we will employ appropriate controls and safeguards including encryption to ensure that non-public information is adequately protected against unauthorized disclosure while in storage or transit." I know at this point that our policy seems rather vague and legal. However, resist the impulse to say, "We must use Triple DES encryption on all private data that is stored or transmitted." This is important because technology changes and this document will eventually be presented to management for approval. Management doesn't want to see you once a month asking for changes to the security policy. As a guiding principle, the Executive Security Policy should address why security is important and delegate the further implementation of appropriate standards, guidelines, and procedures to the appropriate individuals or groups.

Designing & Planning...

Get Trained

Use the security policy to help you do your job better and get the things you need. For example, use the policy to ensure that you get security training. Include a statement in the policy that says, "To ensure that we are adequately controlling and anticipating current and new threats, the security manager and his or her team must attend security training on a semi-annual basis in the form of conferences, seminars, symposiums, and workshops." As you can see, the security policy can be your friend.

Drafting the second part of your overall Information Security Policy, the Perimeter Network Security Policy, is somewhat different. The Perimeter Network Security Policy is a document that includes specific standards, procedures, and guidelines for implementing and maintaining perimeter network security. The first step in drafting a Perimeter Security Policy is to obtain a network map. The network map will help you to better identify resources that need protecting and how to architect your security solution. Depending on the size of your organization, you may elect to do this yourself or to obtain the assistance of individuals with specific knowledge regarding their environment. Although there are a number of software tools to assist you in automatically mapping the network, it will still be necessary to manually validate.

After mapping the network, determine once again the departments or business units with a specific interest in network perimeter security, and assemble the representatives for a meeting. The best approach in this meeting is to identify what is needed and then, by default, disallow everything else. It is at this point that successful security managers recognize the purpose of security to meet business needs. Although it would be great from a security perspective to disconnect the business from the Internet, to stay in business the connection must be maintained. In this meeting you need to specifically ask the representatives if you were to put up a firewall today and block everything, what would need to be changed and configured to allow the business to continue. This step is called defining requirements. For example, some of the requirements that might be voiced include the following:

- We **need** a Web site that has dynamic content

- We **need** to have an e-Commerce storefront

- We **need** to be able to get and send email.

- We **need** to secure all of our internal information from external attacks.

- We **need** to be able to access the Internet securely using HTTP, HTTPS, and FTP from the LAN.

- We **need** to secure our critical information from internal attacks or destruction.

In addition, you will also want to identify any wishes the representatives have. This could be your opportunity to look like a hero when you say, "Yes, we can do that." Examples of wishes are as follows:

- We **would like** to have Instant Messaging

- We **would like** to be able to have Sales reps connect remotely to download order status.

You may find that most needs are simple and can use further refinement. For example, the requirement to send and receive email begs the questions, "From where do you need to send email? Do remote users need to send and receive email? Should there be any additional restrictions on email?" In addition, you should ask questions about what types of communication to log.

Designing & Planning…

Community Involvement

Make sure that everyone who has an interest in the implementation and maintenance of a security policy is involved in its creation. This may involve representatives from HR or even the custodial staff. Involvement from these departments will ease acceptance of the new policy and make the actual implementation much smoother.

The next stage in the drafting of the Perimeter Security Policy is risk assessment. Every requirement and wish has a risk attached to it. As a security professional you must be able to identify those risks and communicate those to the involved parties so they can be weighed against the benefits.

Security Design

After identifying the requirements and risks you are willing to accept, you must design security solutions. Having knowledge of the features and abilities of FireWall-1 NG will help you to determine what you can and can't do. In addition, be aware of the other types of controls that can be used to maintain perimeter network security. There are three main categories of controls: technical controls, physical controls, and administrative controls. Each category of controls has three functions that include preventative, detective, and responsive as shown in Table 4.1. The firewall is primarily a technical control of a preventative and detective nature. That is to say, the firewall prevents unauthorized access and can be used to detect unauthorized access. However, do not dismiss addressing physical and administrative controls in your Perimeter Network Security Policy.

Table 4.1 Categories of Security Controls

	Technical	Physical	Administrative
Preventative	Check Point NG VPN-1	Locked data centers Identification badges	User ID/Password policy Change management
Detective	Check Point NG	CCTV	Log and report review Rule base audits
Responsive	Check Point NG	High availability	Incident response procedures

Other policies that FW-1 NG can help you enforce are the following:

- NAT Security
- QOS Security
- Desktop security
- Monitoring

Firewall Architecture

Before writing the policy, one thing you need to explore is whether you will need to have different policies for different locations or if you will have only one. If you have one security policy, Check Point can enforce the same policy on all firewall modules from a central management station. Otherwise you will have to maintain a different policy for different locations. Although for business reasons this might be necessary, it can add a level of complexity to your environment that could decrease your overall effective security. If it is necessary, then make sure that it is thoroughly documented.

Writing the policy

Now that you know what is necessary, you can write your Perimeter Network Security Policy. As you can see in Figure 4.1, writing a security policy is a logical progression of steps.

Figure 4.1 Steps to Writing a Security Policy

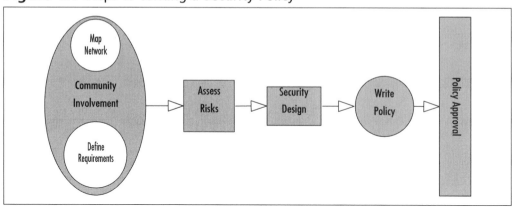

Briefly, the structure of the policy should include the following:

- **Introduction** In this section, you should state the purpose of this policy. What is the objective of the policy? Why it is important to the organization?

- **Guidelines** In this section you should detail guidelines for choosing controls to meet the objectives of the policy. These are the basic requirements. Typically you will see the word "should" in these statements.

- **Standards** In this section you should detail the standards for implementing and deploying the selected controls. For example, this section will state the initial configuration or firewall architecture. This section tends to detail the requirements given in the meeting with the interested departments and business units. This section is written with the words such as, "It is the policy that..."

- **Procedures** In this section you should detail the procedures for maintaining the security solution, such as how often the logs should be reviewed and who is authorized to make changes.

- **Deployment** The purpose of the deployment section is to assign responsibilities and specific steps for the implementation of the policy. Think of it as a mini project plan. In a Perimeter Network Security Policy, this is the section that translates the standards and guidelines into language that the Security Administrator can enforce on the firewall.

- **Enforcement** Many policies lack this component, however, all policies require a method for enforcement. A popular and effective method for enforcement is auditing. In this section you could state that the firewall rulebase would be subject to an external audit yearly. In addition, this section should detail the enforcement and consequences if someone were to circumvent the firewall or its rules.

- **Modification or exceptions** No policy is perfect, and the policy may require modifications or exceptions. In this section you will want to detail the methods for obtaining modifications to the policy or exceptions.

Here is a sample Perimeter Network Security Policy:

Introduction

Due to CompanyX's required connection and access to the public Internet, it is essential that a strong perimeter firewall exist that sufficiently separates the internal private LAN of CompanyX and the public Internet. The firewall should provide preventative and detective technical controls for access between the two networks.

Guidelines

The implementation of any firewall technology should follow these basic rules:

- The firewall should allow for filtering of communication protocols based on complex rule sets.

- The firewall should provide extensive logging of traffic passed and blocked.

- The firewall should be the only entry and exit point to the public Internet from the CompanyX LAN.

- The firewall operating system should be sufficiently hardened to resist attack both internal and external.

- The firewall should fail closed.

- The firewall should not disclose the internal nature, names, or addressing of the CompanyX LAN.

- The firewall should only provide firewall services. No other service or application should be running on the firewall.

Standards

The implementation of any firewall must follow these basic rules:

- It is the policy that only the identified firewall administrator is allowed to make changes to the configuration of the firewall.

- It is the policy that all firewalls must follow the default rule: That which is not expressly permitted is denied.

In addition, the following standards for perimeter networks are as follows:

- The deployment of public services and resources shall be positioned behind the firewall in a protected service net.

- The firewall shall be configured to disallow traffic that originates in the service net to the general LAN.

- Any application or network resource residing outside of the firewall and accessible by unauthorized users requires a banner similar to the following:

> A T T E N T I O N! PLEASE READ CAREFULLY.
>
> This system is the property of CompanyX. It is for authorized use only. Users (authorized or unauthorized) have no explicit or implicit expectation of privacy. Any or all uses of this system and all files on this system will be intercepted, monitored, recorded, copied, audited, inspected, and disclosed to CompanyX management, and law enforcement personnel, as well as authorized officials of other agencies, both domestic and foreign. By using this system, the user consents to such interception, monitoring, recording, copying, auditing, inspection, and disclosure at the discretion of CompanyX. Unauthorized or improper use of this system may result in administrative disciplinary action and civil and criminal penalties. By continuing to use this system, you indicate your awareness of and consent to these terms and conditions of use. LOG OFF IMMEDIATELY if you do not agree to the conditions stated in this warning.

Procedures

Firewall will be configured to allow traffic as defined below.

- TCP/IP suite of protocols allowed through the firewall from the inside LAN to the public Internet is as follows:

- HTTP to anywhere
- HTTPS to anywhere
- TCP/IP suite of protocols allowed through the firewall from the inside LAN to the Service Net is as follows:
  - HTTP to Web Server
  - SMTP to Mail Server
  - POP3 to Mail Server
  - DNS to DNS server
- TCP/IP suite of protocols allowed through the firewall from the Service Net to the public Internet is as follows:
  - DNS from DNS server to anywhere
- TCP/IP suite of protocols allowed through the firewall from the public Internet to the LAN is as follows:
  - None
- TCP/IP suite of protocols allowed through the firewall from the public Internet with specific source, destination, and protocols is as follows:
  - SMTP to Mail Server
  - HTTP to Web Server
  - FTP to Web Server

Deployment

The security administrator will define the rule base and configure the firewall as defined above, in addition to other industry standard properties as appropriate.

Enforcement

Traffic patterns will be enforced by the firewall's technical controls as defined by the firewall administrator. Periodically, an external vulnerability assessment will be performed to assure the proper configuration of the firewall. Additionally, an independent third party will annually audit the configured firewall.

Modifications or Exceptions

Request for modification to the firewall configuration must be submitted via email to the security manager and firewall administrator, accompanied by justification and the duration of the requested change.

Implementing a Security Policy

Now that you have a written Information Security Policy and a Perimeter Security Policy, you can begin configuring and deploying Check Point NG by translating your organization's policies into a policy that can be enforced by Check Point NG.

Default and Initial Policies

Let's start by understanding the default and initial policies in FireWall-1 NG. The default and initial policies taken together comprise boot security for FireWall-1 NG. Unlike previous version of FireWall-1, FireWall-1 NG automatically applies the default policy upon restart. The default policy is intended to protect the firewall and the networks behind it by blocking all traffic while it is loading the firewall services. Additionally, boot security will disable IP forwarding to keep the O/S from routing traffic while the firewall is booting. However, there are some things that the default filter will allow. Specifically, the default filter will allow the following:

- Outgoing communication from the firewall itself
- Incoming communications that are a response to communications initiated by the firewall.
- Broadcasts

Because the firewall is allowing something, the firewall also enforces anti-spoofing measures to ensure that the allowed FireWall-1 NG communications are not spoofed on any of its interfaces.

As FireWall-1 NG boots up and the default filter takes effect, the interfaces are configured and the FireWall-1 services are started. At this point, FireWall-1 applies an initial policy made up of implicit rules. The purpose of the initial policy is to add rules that will allow a GUI to be trusted and connect to the firewall. After the GUI is able to connect to the firewall, a new security policy can be installed. The initial policy is only installed on a module after *cpconfig* is executed and there is no security policy. The initial policy is replaced after a regular policy is written and installed by the administrator to the module. Thereafter, the enterprise security policy will follow the default filter and interface configuration. The enterprise security policy will be composed of the defined rule base and implicit rules. This process is illustrated in Figure 4.2.

Figure 4.2 Boot Security

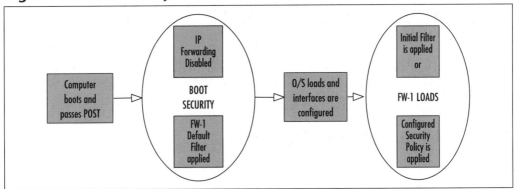

Boot security ensures that at no time is the firewall left unprotected. Ensuring that FireWall-1 starts at boot will allow boot security to be enforced. It is possible to alter boot security and enable IP forwarding and disable the default filter. However, this is not recommended.

Translating Your Policy into Rules

At this point you can take your written policy and your network map and start translating your documented security policy into a policy that Check Point FireWall-1 NG can enforce. Remember that the FireWall-1 NG policy is composed of global properties, which are implicit as shown in Figure 4.3 and an explicit Rule Base. Now let's begin translating and building a security policy.

The first thing you have to do is to create a new policy. To create a new policy, choose from the File menu in Policy Editor and select New.

In the new policy dialog as shown if Figure 4.4, you can see that you have a few options. First type a name for the policy. Now select Security and Address Translation as your Policy Type. This will now enable the Helpers portion of the dialog. In Check Point NG there are three ways to begin defining your new policy: Wizard, Template, and Empty Policy.

Figure 4.3 Global Properties Implied Rules

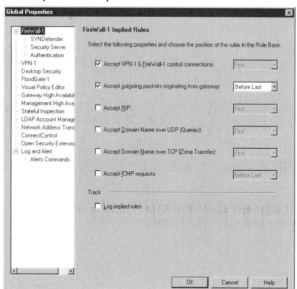

Figure 4.4 New Security Policy Dialog

The wizard method is based on four template networks:

- **Starter network** Dual-homed firewall with one connection to the external network. SMTP mail server is on the internal network. The wizard will walk you through allowing SMTP traffic from the Internet to your mail server.

- **Publisher network** Dual-homed firewall with one connection to the external network. Mail server, FTP, and Web servers are located on the internal network. The wizard will walk you through allowing SMTP traffic in to the mail server, allowing FTP traffic to the FTP server with or without authentication, and allowing HTTP or HTTPS traffic to the Web server with or without authentication.

- **DMZ network** Three-homed firewall with one connection to an external network, one to a service net, and one to an internal network. In this template you can configure permitted services from the internal network to the external network. The wizard will walk you through allowing SMTP traffic in to the mail server, allowing FTP traffic to the FTP server with or without authentication, and allowing HTTP or HTTPS traffic to the Web server with or without authentication.

- **Secure mail network** Three-homed firewall with one connection to an external network, one to a service net, and one to an internal network. In this template you can provide for secure access to the mail server by SecuRemote users.

Using the template method, in contrast to the wizard method, creates an incomplete rule set. Although the Rule Base gets created, the objects remain undefined until you edit each one individually. In fact, all objects will require definition before you can install the policy. The wizard and template are very similar. However, the wizard walks you through the entire setup and makes you define all of the objects up front.

The wizards and templates are an easy way to get things configured to support basic services, or for new administrator with small networks. However, having a security policy that is fine-tuned for your organization is going to require that you do some manual definitions and ordering of objects and rules. So, let's start with an Empty Policy and begin building the policy from scratch.

Defining A Firewall Object

The first step in translating the policy into an enforceable policy is to define the relevant network objects. After creating the network objects, you can create and/or modify the firewall workstation object. Having the networks defined first will enable you to configure anti-spoofing on the firewall object. The firewall object is something you must define before you can install your FireWall-1 Security Policy.

If you have initially installed the FireWall-1 Module, Management Server, and GUI on the same box, then the firewall object will be created and partially configured. If the components are installed in a distributed environment, however, you will have to create the firewall workstation object. You will start by logging into your Management server via the Policy Editor GUI. If you haven't opened the Workstation Properties yet, as shown in Figure 4.5, you may do so by selecting the firewall object from the Objects List at the bottom of the window, right-clicking, and choosing **edit** by double-clicking the firewall object from the Objects List, or by going through the **Manage | Network Objects** menu. You will need to create one firewall object for each firewall module that will be enforcing a security policy and that will be managed by this management server.

If you are creating the firewall object for the first time, then you can right-click on the **Network Objects** in the Objects Tree and choose **Workstation** from the New menu. The first field you will be challenged with is the name of the firewall. This field should be the firewall module's TCP/IP host name. For better performance, it is recommended that DNS is configured to resolve this name to the firewall's external IP address, or at least have it set up in the host's file on the firewall. The next field should contain the external IP address of the firewall. If DNS is configured and you click "**Get address**," DNS will be queried and the address will be filled in for you. Otherwise you can just type in the value. In the next field, the Comment field, be as descriptive as possible. Using comments is a good way to document what you are doing so that others can understand more quickly and easily. The next decision is what color to give the object. This should be based on a scheme that will help you to read the rules and logs more easily.

Figure 4.5 Workstation Properties with Check Point Products Installed

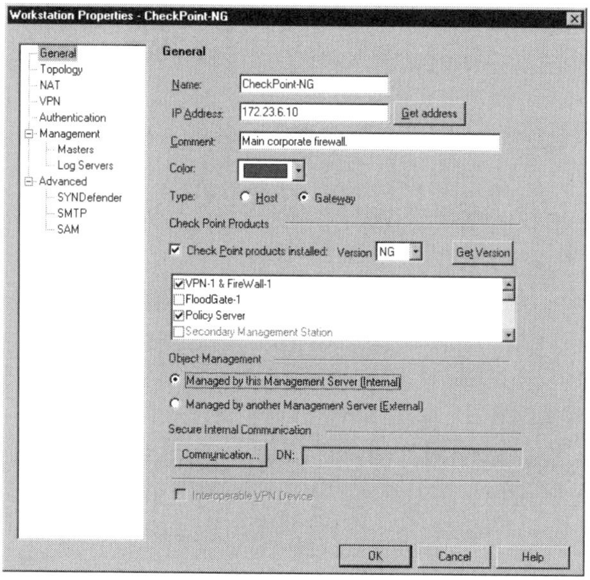

Now let's make this workstation a firewall. If it hasn't been checked already, check the box that reads **Check Point products installed** and select the version "**NG.**" This will enable the next list of product modules. Choose from the list the modules that are installed on this host. Next, in the section Object Management, you must select whether the Management Server for this firewall is Internal or External. Basically, by checking **Internal**, you signify that this Management Server will be able to install policies on this FireWall-1 module, and when you view the System Status GUI, this firewall object will be displayed. If the Management Server and firewall module are on different hosts, then you will need to configure Secure Internal Communication (SIC) to establish communication between these two machines. To do so, click on the **Communication** button and enter a shared password. If this object was created for you, Check Point already knows what products you have installed and has made the selection for you. Please double-check that the selection is correct before you continue. Finally, if an external Management Server manages this firewall module, then you will be able to use this external firewall in the rule base and configure it as a VPN endpoint, but you will not be able to install policies to it (another Management Server will do that), and it will not be displayed in the System Status Viewer. In short, you do not manage external firewall objects from this management server.

The second branch on the Workstation Properties is the **Topology** window. This enables you to define the networks reachable behind the internal and external interfaces that exist on your firewall object. Figure 4.6 illustrates this configuration window.

To define the interface, make sure that you have selected the right one. After selecting an interface to define in Figure 4.6, click on Edit. This will open up the dialog in Figure 4.7.

If you are configuring an interface manually, it is important to use the proper name. For example, the name as displayed by the *ifconfig -a* Unix command. Failure to properly define the interfaces may cause features such as anti-spoofing to not function, and may leave the network open to attack. If you are running SNMP on the object, then you have access to the **Get Interfaces** feature, which will query the system for its interface information and is the recommended method of gathering this information.

Not only will you be able to specify this interface as internal or external, but you can also specify the range of addresses that reside behind the interface for enforcing anti-spoofing and generating NAT rules. This is done while manually adding or editing interface information from the topology tab, as illustrated in Figure 4.7.

Figure 4.6 Topology Window

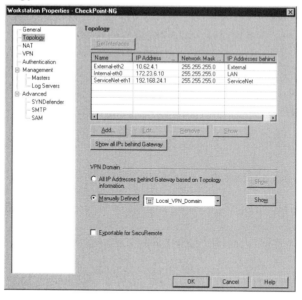

Figure 4.7 Topology Definition

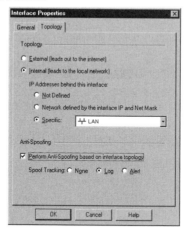

If the interface is internal, then it is very important to define the addresses that reside behind the interface. The first option, **Not Defined**, generally should not be used. If selected, anti-spoofing will be disabled on this interface. Generally speaking, it only makes sense to have anti-spoofing configured either for all or none of the interfaces. If you select the second option, then these addresses will be calculated based on the address and subnet mask for this interface. Lastly, you can specify an explicit range of addresses or groups of networks. Anti-spoof tracking can also be defined on a per-interface basis.

The **Management** branch is quite important for your FireWall-1 configuration. The Management window enables you to specify logging options. These options are broken down into two varieties: Local Logging Options and Advanced Settings. This branch is covered in more detail in Chapter 8.

The **Advanced** window allows the configuration of SNMP settings. If you expand out the **Advanced** branch, you will see three sub-menus. These are as follows:

- SYNDefender
- SMTP
- SAM

The SYNDefender branch is used to configure the firewall options to defend and respond to SYN attacks. Attackers may try to create a Denial of Service (DoS) by initiating a SYN Flood attack. Taking advantage of the connection-oriented nature and initial three-way handshake of TCP/IP, an attacker can keep requesting connections that a server will accept until it is out of resources. FireWall-1's SYNDefender option is disabled by default. To enable it, select SYN relay, SYN gateway, or Passive SYN gateway. These options are displayed in Figure 4.8.

Figure 4.8 SYNDefender Options

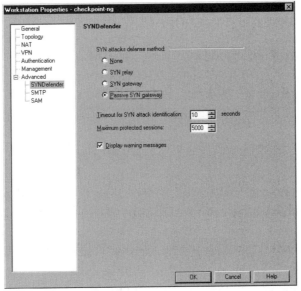

SYN relay monitors all connection attempts, and verifies that the attempt is valid before sending the initial SYN to the server. SYN gateway monitors all connection attempts as well as after the server responds with a SYN-ACK; the firewall also sends an ACK to the server and opens the connection so that the server's backlog queue is available to accept more connection requests. The timeout setting determines how long the firewall will wait before either receiving a response from the client and allowing the connection or closing the connection with the server by sending a RST (reset) packet. Lastly, the Passive SYN gateway monitors all connection attempts like the gateway option, but it does not send an ACK to open the connection to the server. Instead, the passive method waits the allotted timeout period, and if the connection is not valid, it will send a RST to the server. For firewall modules prior to NG, the SYNDefender setting is configured under the Global Properties, FireWall-1 branch. Check Point recommends using the SYN gateway method if you are susceptible to these types of attacks.

SECURITY ALERT

A TCP/IP connection is established when a client requests the connection by sending a SYN packet to the server. Once the server receives the request, it will respond with a SYN-ACK acknowledging the client's SYN packet. Finally, the connection is established when the client sends an ACK back to the server completing the three-way handshake. When a SYN Flood attack is underway, then a malicious client is sending multiple SYN packets to a server with spoofed source IP addresses so that when the server responds with a SYN-ACK, it does not receive a response in return to complete the connection. The server will save these initial sessions in its backlog queue and wait for a response. A SYN Flood attack works by filling up this backlog queue with bogus requests, which causes any valid connection attempts to fail, thereby creating a DoS.

The SMTP page enables you to set local options on how the SMTP security server handles mail. Typically, the defaults on this page are appropriate, although you may have to define the postmaster name. These values are stored in the firewall's $FWDIR/conf/smtp.conf configuration file.

On the final page, you will not need to modify anything unless your SAM server is external to your Management Server. In most cases, you will skip this section. Changing these values will affect the firewall's $FWDIR/conf/fwopsec .conf configuration file.

Define Rule Base

Now let's use our Perimeter Network Security Policy to create a Check Point FireWall-1 NG enforceable policy. The first step is to map things out and identify the objects that will compose the Rule Base. Below is the relevant excerpt from the policy.

- TCP/IP suite of protocols allowed through the firewall from the inside LAN to the public Internet is as follows:
  - HTTP to anywhere
  - HTTPS to anywhere
- TCP/IP suite of protocols allowed through the firewall from the inside LAN to the Service Net is as follows:
  - HTTP to Web Server
  - SMTP to Mail Server
  - POP3 to Mail Server
  - DNS to DNS server
- TCP/IP suite of protocols allowed through the firewall from the Service Net to the public Internet is as follows:
  - DNS from DNS server to anywhere
- TCP/IP suite of protocols allowed through the firewall from the public Internet to the LAN is as follows:
  - None
- TCP/IP suite of protocols allowed through the firewall from the public Internet with specific source, destination, and protocols is as follows:
  - SMTP to Mail Server
  - HTTP to Web Server
  - FTP to Web Server

Reading through your policy, it refers to the LAN, the Internet, and a Service Net. These are all network objects, which will need to be defined before you can continue. Next, traffic is flowing anywhere, to the Web server, mail server, DNS server, and through the firewall. These three servers on the Service Net will be defined as hosts or workstations. Now that you know what objects are needed, you can create them. Based on the work you did in the previous chapter, you should be able to create these on your own.

Now that you have all of the objects defined, it's time to create the rule base. For your first rule, it is best to create the "Clean-up rule." By default, anything that is not explicitly permitted is dropped. However, it would be nice to log those events, and the only way to accomplish that is to define an explicit drop rule in the policy and enable tracking. For your first rule, select **Add rule** from the Rules menu in Policy Editor. This is your first rule, so bottom or top does not matter, although eventually this rule will be the last rule in the policy. From the rule that appears, confirm the following: source **Any**, destination **Any**, service **Any**, action **Drop**, and **Log.** The only thing you will need to change is the track cell from **none** to **Log**, and add a comment in the Comment field of "Clean-Up Rule." At this point, your rule base should consist of one rule and look like the example in Figure 4.9.

Figure 4.9 The "Clean-Up Rule"

9	★ Any	★ Any	★ Any	● Drop	🗏 Log	🗐 Gateways	★ Any	"Clean-up Rule"

Another good rule to have in your rule base is the "Stealth Rule." This rule is defined to protect the firewall and alert you of traffic that is directed to the firewall itself. This time, create the rule from the Rules menu by clicking **Add rule** and choose **Above**. From the newly created rule, change the destination field by right-clicking and selecting **Add** from the context menu. From within the Add dialog, select your firewall object. Next, in the Track field select **Alert**. This rule should read **Any**, **Firewall**, **Any**, **Drop**, **Alert** as illustrated in Figure 4.10. Add the comment "Stealth Rule" in the Comment field.

Figure 4.10 The "Stealth Rule"

NO.	SOURCE	DESTINATION	SERVICE	ACTION	TRACK	INSTALL ON	TIME	COMMENT
1	★ Any	🗐 checkpoint-ng	★ Any	● drop	⏺ Alert	🗐 Gateways	★ Any	"Stealth Rule"

Great! Now you have the beginnings of a good rule base. Let's start adding some rules that are based on your policy.

The first element in the security policy states that you allow HTTP and HTTPS to anywhere. Because your policy doesn't call for any user authentication, you can leave your "Stealth Rule" at the top. Let's place this next rule beneath the "Stealth Rule." Click on the icon in the toolbar that represents **Add**

Rule below Current. Your current rule will always be the rule that is high-lighted in white, instead of being gray like all the other rules. You should see a new rule sandwiched between your two previous rules. There are many ways to create this rule. However, the best way is to select **LAN** as the Source. For the Destination, select the **Service Net**. I'll explain why in a minute. Under the service field, add **HTTP** and then **HTTPS**. Make sure you select **accept** in the Action field. The Track field can be left at **None** for this rule. Now right-click on the **Destination Service Net** and choose **Negate**. A red "X" should now appear on the Service Net object in your Rule Base. What you have done is cre-ated a rule that allows LAN users the use of HTTP and HTTPS to everywhere *but* the Service Net. The reason you had to do this is because the policy doesn't allow HTTPS from the LAN to the Service Net, as you will see in the next couple rules. In the Comment field, write in "Permits LAN access to http and https on the Internet."

Second, you must define what is allowed to the Service Net from the LAN. In these rules, you will allow the LAN access to the mail server for POP-3, and the DNS server for DNS queries. Let's leave SMTP and FTP for later. Start cre-ating the next rule by right-clicking on the number two from the previous rule and choosing "**Add Rule below**." Just like the previous rule, the Source is the **LAN**; however, the Destination is now the **Email_Server**. In the Services field, add **pop-3** and select **accept** in the Action field. As far as the Track field is con-cerned, there are no requirements to log this traffic, and it might make the logs pretty large anyway, so leave Track as **None**. In the Comments field, write in "Permits LAN access to retrieve email via pop-3." Since the next rule will prob-ably generate a lot of traffic (DNS queries), place it just below your stealth rule. So, add a new rule below rule one, and enter **LAN** in the Source field, **DNS_Server** in the Destination, **domain-udp** as the Service, and **accept** in the Action field. Again, let's not log this traffic because domain queries can be quite numerous and we don't need to log it. Enter "Permit LAN access to DNS server for DNS name resolving" in the Comment field.

Next, let's create a rule that allows your DNS server in the Service Net to per-form queries to the Internet for domain name resolution. Add this rule beneath the rule you just finished. Set the rule to read Source-**DNS_Server**, Destination-**LAN** (Negate), Service-**dns**, Action-**accept**, Track-**None**, and Comment, "Permits DNS server access to Internet for domain name resolving."

Now for your final rules, what will you allow in from the Internet? According to the policy you will allow SMTP to the mail server and HTTP and FTP to the Web server. Create a new rule beneath the current rule. This new rule number four should be defined as Source-**Any**, Destination-**Email_Server**, Service-**smtp**, Action-**accept**, Track-**Log**, and Comment, " Permit anyone to send email to the email server via smtp." Notice that this rule also permits your LAN users to connect to the mail server for SMTP. The next rule, Rule number 5 should be defined as Source-**Any**, Destination-**Web_Server**, Service-**http**, Action-**accept**, Track-**Log**, and Comment, "Permit anyone access to web pages via http on the web server." This rule also allows access for your LAN. Add one more rule below 5, and define it as Source-**LAN** (negated), Destination-**Web_Server**, Service-**ftp**, Action-**accept**, Track-**Log**, and Comment, "Permit anyone on the Internet access to ftp on the web server." Since your policy doesn't allow your LAN to connect to the Web server for ftp, you had to negate it in the source.

Now you are pretty much done. Your rule base will have nine rules and should look like the FireWall-1 Rule Base shown in Figure 4.11. You should do a **File | Save** or click on the Floppy Disk Icon to save your finished policy.

Figure 4.11 Rule Base from Security Policy

NO.	SOURCE	DESTINATION	SERVICE	ACTION	TRACK	INSTALL ON	TIME	COMMENT
1	★ Any	FireWall-1_NG	★ Any	Drop	! Alert	Gateways	★ Any	"Stealth Rule"
2	LAN	DNS_Server	UDP domain-udp	accept	— None	Gateways	★ Any	Allow DNS Queries from LAN to DNS Server.
3	DNS_Server	LAN	dns	accept	— None	Gateways	★ Any	Allow DNS server to perform lookups and zone tr
4	★ Any	Email_Server	TCP smtp	accept	Log	Gateways	★ Any	Allow any SMTP to Email Server.
5	★ Any	Web_Server	TCP http	accept	Log	Gateways	★ Any	Allow any HTTP to Web Server.
6	LAN	Web_Server	TCP ftp	accept	Log	Gateways	★ Any	Allow all except the LAN to FTP to Web Server.
7	LAN	DMZ_net	TCP http TCP https	accept	— None	Gateways	★ Any	Allow the LAN HTTP and HTTPS access everywh
8	LAN	Email_Server	TCP pop-3	accept	— None	Gateways	★ Any	Allow the LAN POP-3 access to Email Server
9	★ Any	★ Any	★ Any	Drop	Log	Gateways	★ Any	"Clean-up Rule"

Now, with these rules, the ordering is critical. Keep in mind that the firewall matches packets on the first three columns (Source, Destination, and Service) by using top-down processing. Each packet starts at the top rule and moves down until a rule matches. When a packet is matched, no further processing is performed. This is called top-down processing. If you wrote your rule base directly from a piece of paper, then there may be a few problems to sort out. There will always be more than one way to define your policy; the trick is finding the best method for your organization.

As you fine-tune your policy, you can try to simplify the way you say things. By moving rules, consolidating rules, or just by stating rules differently, you can improve the effectiveness and performance of your rule base. You will also need to install your rule base when you are satisfied that is it set up properly. Any changes that are made through the Policy Editor do not take effect on the firewall module until the Security Policy is installed. The Policy menu will be explained later in this chapter.

Manipulating Rules

FireWall-1 features a very flexible rule base. It provides the ability to alter both content and context very simply. The next few sections focus on manipulating the rule base.

Cut and Paste Rules

Rules can be cut and paste in a way that will be instantly familiar to anyone. You simply select the rule (by clicking on its number), and either copy or right-click and select cut from the menu. The menu is shown in Figure 4.12. Alternatively, you can select from the edit menu. Pasting a rule is just as easy, but there is one additional selection to make. When you select paste from the edit menu, you'll have to also decide on the placement of the rule. Your choices are top, bottom, above, or below, with the choices indicating a relation to the currently selected rule.

Figure 4.12 Context Menu for Manipulating Rules

Disable Rules

Disabled rules are one step from being deleted. They are not part of your security policy and are not installed when you install the policy. They are, however, displayed in the rule base window. Disabling rules is a handy method of troubleshooting, providing an easy way of recovering the rule's functionality. To disable a rule, simply right-click on that rule's number and select **Disable Rule** from the menu. To re-enable the rule, right-click the rule's number and deselect **Disable Rule**.

Notice the big red "X" in Figure 4.13 signifying a Disabled Rule.

Figure 4.13 Disabled Rule

Delete Rules

Deleting a rule eliminates it from both the security policy and your rule base view. To delete a rule, simply select the rule's number and select **Cut** from the edit menu. You can also select **Cut** from the right-click menu. While it is true that you can delete a rule outright, I recommend getting into the habit of cutting rules, since if you mistakenly delete the wrong rule, you can recover it quickly.

Hiding Rules

Sometimes, especially with a large rule base, you don't really need to see every rule all the time. Luckily, FireWall-1 allows you the ability to hide rules. These rules are still part of the security policy and are still installed when that policy is loaded, but they are not shown in the rule base window.

To hide a rule, select the rule by clicking on its number. The easiest way is to right-click and select **Hide** from the menu, or you may select **Hide** from the Rules menu. A hidden rule is replaced with a thick, gray divider line, giving you an easy visual indication that a hidden rule exists.

In Figure 4.14 you can see the thick, gray line between rules 4 and 6. Notice how the rule numbers stay the same. Rule 5 still exists; you just don't see it.

Figure 4.14 Hidden Rules

NO.	SOURCE	DESTINATION	SERVICE	ACTION	TRACK	INSTALL ON	TIME	COMMENT
1	★ Any	FireWall-1_NG	★ Any	Drop	Alert	Gateways	★ Any	"Stealth Rule"
2	LAN	DNS_Server	UDP domain-udp	accept	– None	Gateways	★ Any	Allow DNS Queries from LAN to DNS Server.
3	DNS_Server	LAN	dns	accept	– None	Gateways	★ Any	Allow DNS server to perform lookups and zone tr
4	★ Any	Email_Server	TCP smtp	accept	Log	Gateways	★ Any	Allow any SMTP to Email Server.
5	★ Any	Web_Server	TCP http	accept	Log	Gateways	★ Any	Allow any HTTP to Web Server.
7	LAN	DMZ_net	TCP http TCP https	accept	– None	Gateways	★ Any	Allow the LAN HTTP and HTTPS access everywh
8	LAN	Email_Server	TCP pop-3	accept	– None	Gateways	★ Any	Allow the LAN POP-3 access to Email Server.
9	★ Any	★ Any	★ Any	Drop	Log	Gateways	★ Any	"Clean-up Rule"

You also have the ability to both view and manage hidden rules. To view hidden rules, select **View Hidden** from the Rules menu. Managing hidden rules is even more flexible, as it enables you to create and apply masks to the rule base. These masks can be applied or removed to alter the view of the rule base. For example, suppose you have hidden all of the rules with a specific destination. You can store this view as a mask by selecting **Rules-> Hide->Manage hidden** and then storing this view. Later, if you choose **Unhide All** from the Rules menu, you can easily reapply the filters via the same menu options. The options for working with Hidden Rules are in Figure 4.15.

Figure 4.15 Hidden Rules Options

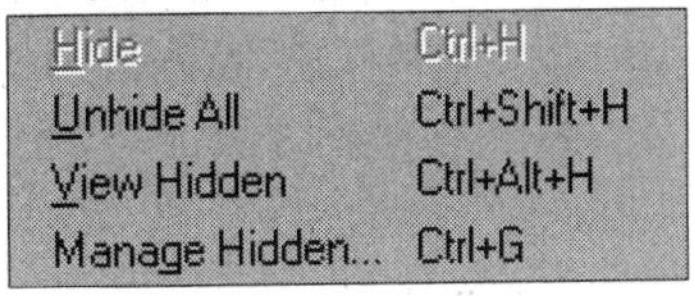

Hide	Ctrl+H
Unhide All	Ctrl+Shift+H
View Hidden	Ctrl+Alt+H
Manage Hidden...	Ctrl+G

Drag and Drop

There are several ways in which you can manipulate the rules by dragging and dropping within the Policy Editor. You can move a rule to a new location in the rule base by simply clicking on its rule number, and dragging it to the new position. You can also drag network objects and services into your rules from the Object List pane and drop them in the appropriate fields. You can even drag an object from one rule into another. This could save you some time when adding new rules or editing your existing rule base. It's worth your time to play around with this feature a little and start to get the hang of it.

Querying the Rule Base

The rule base enables you to view it in many different ways. Sometimes it is beneficial to view it in its entirety, while at other times you may need to see only specific items. This is especially true when dealing with a very large rule base on a very complex network. One way to achieve this narrower view is through the ability to query the rule base.

To query the rule base, select **Query Rules** from the **S**earch menu. A query builder will appear. This window lists defines queries and allows the addition, deletion, or modification of these queries. Select **New** to define a new query. A window will appear that enables you to strictly define the criteria to query against. Enter a name for your query, and then click **New** again to begin entering search clauses. This window, the **Rule Base Queries Clause** window, is similar to that presented when creating a group. Simply select the column you wish to query, add the objects you wish to include in the query to the **In List** box, and you're done. You also have the ability to create a negation, that is, a query that will match only if the specified criteria are not present. The final option is to enforce the query explicitly. What this means is that the match must be exact. For example, if you select **Explicit**, then a query that contained a workstation object would not match a rule that used a group containing that workstation.

Policy Options

Once you have created your security policy, you are ready to put it into action. The next few sections describe the options available for working with the policy you have built. Access to these options is available by selecting **Policy** from the Policy Editor menu.

Verify

Verify is used to test the policy. It compiles the objects and prepares them for installation, but it does not actually perform the install. This is useful when you are in the process of editing and modifying your security policy, and wish to make sure that you aren't doing something wrong; for example, if you have a rule on top that accepts telnet to anywhere, and then below that you create a rule to allow telnet to a specific host. Selecting **Verify** from the Policy menu would tell you that "rule 1 blocks rule 2 for service telnet." This means that rule 2 is redundant, and will never be matched on a packet, and therefore it is misplaced.

Install

This option actually performs the install. You'll be presented with a list of possible firewall objects and can select the proper firewall or firewalls to install on from this list. The policy is then compiled and pushed out to the selected modules. You have a choice as to how these modules are treated.

- **Install on each selected Module independently** This is useful when you are dealing with a large number of gateways. With this option, each module is treated as a single entity, and failure to install policy on one will not impact the others negatively.

- **Install on all selected Modules** This is an all-or-nothing proposition. If you are concerned with configuration integrity, this is the option for you. Failure on any single module will preclude the installation on any module.

- **Install on all the modules of the selected Gateway Cluster** This applies to Gateway Clusters and is identical in behavior to the above Install on all selected Modules.

You will need to install your security policy whenever you make changes through the Policy Editor and wish for those changes to be enforced. Nothing you do in the Policy Editor will take effect until you push the policy to the appropriate firewalls.

Uninstall

This removes the policy from the objects that you select. The object selection method is identical to that when installing policy.

View

The **View** option enables you to view the compiled security policy; that is, it enables you to view the inspect statements, which allows you to view and save the actual inspect scripts. Saved files can be manually altered and loaded with the CLI of FireWall-1.

Access Lists

This is used to incorporate rules into an OSE compliant device, such as a router. When a rule is installed on a router, the firewall actually is generating an ACL for that router and applying it as needed. You can also import the existing ACL entries for the OSE device and verify and edit them. This menu option allows for all three functions. When selected, the **OSE Device Access List Operations** window is displayed. This window enables you to select the OSE device you want to interact with and perform the specified operation. When fetching an ACL, you can further specify the direction you are interested in, and the format you wish the ACLs to be presented in (ASCII or GUI). This requires additional licensing.

Install Users Database

This option, available from both the Policy menu and the User Management function, propagates the user database defined on the management server to the selected modules. Note that the user database is also loaded when a security policy is published (pushed/installed) to the modules, but this manual process allows the updating of user information without interfering with the firewall operations.

Management High Availability

This option of the Policy menu enables you to modify the behavior of your Management High Availability groups. This feature allows multiple Management Modules to synchronize and support each other, just as with HA FireWall-1 Modules. This option loads a maintenance panel, which allows for both manual synchronization and preempting of the primary Management Server.

When performing a manual synchronization, you have two modes of behavior to select from.

- **Synchronize Configuration Files Only** If this is selected, only the database and configuration files will be synchronized between Management Modules.

- **Synchronize Fetch, Install and Configuration files** This mode also synchronizes the Fetch and Install files, allowing the interaction with a standby management server.

You can also change the current state of the Management Module, from Primary to Standby and vice versa.

Installing a Security Policy

After you have defined all objects and composed the rule base, it is time to install the policy on your chosen modules so that it can be enforced. Remember that anytime you modify network objects, rules, or Global properties, you need to install the policy for the changes to take effect. The install policy process does a few things before your rules get enforced.

When you select **Install** from the Policy menu, first Check Point saves your objects and rules. Next, Check Point verifies your rule base to ensure that you don't have any conflicting rules, redundant rules, or rules with objects that require definition. Alternatively, before you install, you can verify the policy by choosing **Policy** and then selecting **Verify**. Check Point NG will then parse your rule set. After the verify process returns the results that "Rules Verified OK!" Check Point NG asks you to select on which network object and module to install the compiled policy.

Select the object that you wish to install this policy on, and an installation window will come up. The progress of the compile and install will be displayed here. When the policy install is completed, you can click on the "**Close**" button at the bottom of the window as shown in Figure 4.16. If you wish to cancel the installation, press the button while it reads, "Abort."

Figure 4.16 Install Policy Progress Window

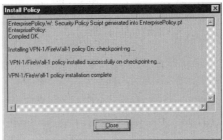

Alternatively, you can install the policy on the firewall modules at the command prompt with the use of *$FWDIR/bin/fw load*. For example, if I want to install the policy named Standard.W on a firewall module defined with an object named Gatekeeper, then I would run the following load command from the Management server's $FWDIR/conf directory:

```
$FWDIR/bin/fw load Standard.W all.all@Gatekeeper
```

To confirm the installation of your policy at the command line, execute $FWDIR\bin\fw stat. This will display the host, policy, and time of install.

Policy Files

In the process of compiling your security policy, Check Point NG takes the contents of the rule base file *.W that you created through the Policy Editor GUI, to create an INSPECT script with the same name adding a .pf extension. The *.pf file is compiled into INSPECT code designated as a file called *.fc (where the * represents the name given to your policy in the initial dialog). The INSPECT code is then applied to the network objects (firewalls) specified in the install. Keep in mind that when you install a policy on a module that has no rules to enforce, the default implicit "deny all" will be in effect for that host and module.

To back up your policy, you should make and keep a separate copy of the files listed below:

- $FWDIR\conf\objects_5_0.C
- $FWDIR\conf*.W

- $FWDIR\conf\rulebases_5_0.fws
- $FWDIR\database\fwauth.NDB★

The objects_5_0.C file stores all the network objects, resources, servers, services, and so on. The ★.W files are each individual policy file that you named via the Policy Editor. The rulebases_5_0.fws file is the master rule base file that holds each of the individual ★.W policies in one place. If you needed to restore your policies, then you would not necessarily need to replace each .W file, but just the rulebases_5_0.fws. When you log in to the Policy Editor, this file will open and create the .W files that were not already in the conf directory. This fws file gets called whenever you do a **File | Open** from the Policy Editor, and you can rename or delete policies from this file via the **Open** window. Deleting a policy from here does not remove it from the hard drive; it just simply removes it from the rulebases_5_0.fws file. The fwauth.NDB★ files contain the user database.

Configuring & Implementing...

Editing Files Manually

The *.W file can be edited with a text editor. Editing this code does not affect the GUI representation of rules. However, it will be used to create the INSPECT script and may introduce inconsistencies between the GUI interface and the installed policy. As an alternative, the *.def file can be edited instead.

Summary

In this chapter we have discussed the importance of a security policy and how to write one for your organization. Remember that the most important aspect of defining a security policy is involvement. Because the default policy of Check Point NG is to deny everything, with community involvement you can better define the requirements, and as a result, only permit communication that is necessary for business activities while denying all other.

As you implement and translate your written policy into something that can be enforced by Check Point NG, you will have to define network objects. Much of this information should have been gathered during the design of your policy and includes items like workstations, gateways, users, and services. Eventually, the rules you write will use these objects to match packets for processing and applying actions.

A firewall object must be defined for each firewall you are installing a policy on. In a simple, standalone installation where the management server and firewall module resides on the same machine, the firewall object is created for you during software installation. You will need to configure the interfaces topology and anti-spoofing and possibly SYNDefender within your firewall object definition.

FireWall-1 provides several tools to manipulate the security policy. You have several different methods of adding a rule to the rule base, disabling rules, cutting and pasting rules, and querying the rule base. Once you have the policy defined and you are ready to start the firewall enforcing the policy, you must install the policy onto the firewall objects that you have previously defined.

The installation of a policy is a process that converts the GUI rule base, which is represented as the *.W file, into an INSPECT script language *.pf file. The *.pf file is then compiled into INSPECT code, and is represented as a *.fc file that can be understood and enforced by the specified Check Point NG modules.

Solutions Fast Track

Reasons for a Security Policy

☑ A written security policy is becoming a requirement for some industries as mandated by government regulation, including financial and healthcare organizations.

☑ Having a written security policy can help the security manager and administrator perform their jobs better and to receive executive-level support for technologies and training.

☑ Developing a security policy before implementing security products will help to ensure that the deployed product meets the requirements of the business and is properly configured.

☑ A written security policy will provide an organization with direction and accountability in the implementation and maintenance of an information security program.

How to Write a Security Policy

☑ One of the most important aspects of writing a security policy is community involvement. Everyone with a stake or interest should be involved in the writing of certain aspects of the security policy.

☑ Writing a security policy should reflect your business needs and how you will manage the risks posed by those needs.

☑ An Executive Information Security Policy should be simple, readable, and accessible to users.

☑ An Information Security Policy is composed of an Executive Security Policy and specific standards, guidelines, and procedures. In addition to the Executive Security Policy, a Perimeter Network Security Policy or a Firewall Security Policy can detail specific standards for implementing a firewall and procedures for maintaining it.

Implementing a Security Policy

☑ The translation of a written policy to a Check Point NG policy is a step-by-step process. First, define your network objects. Then compose rules that enforce your written policy, specifying the actions to be taken when a packet matches the defined criteria.

☑ When creating a Rule Base, the ordering of rules is critical. Because packets are evaluated against the rules in the Rule Base from the top to the bottom, incorrect positioning can have undesirable consequences.

☑ The initial policy of Check Point NG is to deny everything. Use this to your advantage and configure your security policy from the perspective that you will only allow what is needed and everything else will be disallowed. This is much more secure than the approach to allow everything and only disallow that which you know is harmful.

☑ Consider putting the most-often matched rules near the top of the Rule Base to increase performance.

Installing a Security Policy

☑ When you install a policy, it will be verified by Check Point NG and then compiled into INSPECT code.

☑ Firewalls are modules that you install a policy on, but if the policy contains no relevant rules for that firewall or module, then it will enforce the default policy to deny all.

☑ When you choose **install policy** from the GUI, it executes the `fw load` command.

Policy Files

☑ The *.W file is derived from the GUI Rule Base. It can be edited with a text editor.

☑ The *.pf file is INSPECT script created from the *.W file in the install process.

☑ The objects_5_0.C file contains object definitions.

☑ The rulebases_5_0.fws file is an aggregation of all the *.W files.

Frequently Asked Questions

The following Frequently Asked Questions, answered by the authors of this book, are designed to both measure your understanding of the concepts presented in this chapter and to assist you with real-life implementation of these concepts. To have your questions about this chapter answered by the author, browse to **www.syngress.com/solutions** and click on the **"Ask the Author"** form.

Q: Why can't I just write a policy? I know, better than anyone, what our network needs.

A: Community involvement is essential. You can't enforce a policy that is your personal opinion. Besides, do you really want the blame when something goes wrong? In addition, having too strict of a policy could encourage users to back-door the network and bypass the firewall.

Q: We are pretty small and don't have legal counsel on staff. Is legal counsel a necessity in writing the policy?

A: It depends on your potential liability. A security policy can be the standard you are held to in court, so if there is a possibility that may happen, then you should seek legal counsel.

Q: My logs are filling up with a bunch of broadcast stuff. How do I filter it out?

A: You can write a rule that drops or accepts the broadcasts but doesn't log them. The rule will probably state that from any source to destination gateway with protocols netbios, drop. However, make sure the rule appears before the rule that logs them. Netbios is a common protocol to filter out because it is so noisy.

Q: Where do I find all the firewall's configuration files?

A: They are located at *$FWDIR/conf*. (/var/opt/CPfw1-50/conf in Solaris or the default install for Windows is c:\winnt\fw1\5.0\conf)

Q: We are using some protocols that aren't listed in the services menu. They are custom and I don't know anything about them. What can I do?

A: Find out from the vendor the protocol and destination port and source port number. If this doesn't work, then a search on the Internet will yield some results. Or you can just set up a sniffer such as TCP Dump or Ethereal to sniff the traffic. You can then create the new service in the Policy Editor via the Services management window.

Q: How do I know my policy is working?

A: Using vulnerability assessment tools or port scanners, you can check your firewall to ensure it is properly configured. Good tools include nMap, Nessus, or Languard network scanner.

Q: What is the difference between a drop and a reject in the FireWall-1 Rule Base?

A: When the firewall drops a packet, it just discards into the bit bucket and does not respond to it in any way. When the firewall rejects a packet, however, it sends a "Connection Refused" back to the requesting client, thereby ending the connection attempt. If a telnet connection is getting dropped, for example, then the client will wait until the telnet times out. If the telnet connection is getting rejected, however, the client will get a "Connection refused" message right away and will not continue to try the connection. In most cases, it is best to use Drop because it's best that the firewall not respond to port scan requests, as opposed to letting the scanner know that a device is there and refusing the connections.

## Chapter 5

Applying Network Address Translation

Solutions in this chapter:

- **Hiding Network Objects**
- **Configuring Static Address Translation**
- **Automatic NAT Rules**
- **NAT Global Properties**

☑ **Summary**

☑ **Solutions Fast Track**

☑ **Frequently Asked Questions**

Introduction

Another method to secure your internal network or DMZ network behind the firewall is to assign it a network or subnet from one of the reserved IP network numbers for private addressing. These address ranges were set aside by the Internet Assigned Numbers Authority (IANA) to conserve the limited amount of address space available as defined in RFC 1918. These numbers are assigned for reuse by any organization, so long as they are not routed outside of any single, private IP network. This means that they cannot be routed over the Internet, which provides you with a network more easily secured from outside attack.

Even if you are not using one of the IANA-reserved addresses for private networks, you can still utilize Network Address Translation (NAT) to hide your internal network and servers from the Internet. If you are using a private address internally, then you must use some external, Internet-routable network for Internet communications.

We will show you how to set up hiding NAT on your network objects and one-to-one NAT on your workstation objects in this chapter. We will also show you how you can set up some port address translation and other interesting NAT rules by manually adding rules under the Network Address Translation tab in your Policy Editor. If you read the previous chapter on creating your security policy, then once you're done with this chapter, you should have a fully functional Check Point VPN-1/FireWall-1 Next Generation firewall to put on the wire and start passing packets. There are several other important topics in the chapters to come, such as user authentication and managing your policies and logs.

Hiding Network Objects

Because of the incredible and unpredictable speed at which the Internet has expanded, acquiring IP addresses for your organization has become more difficult over time. As a result, it has become increasingly important to use wisely the address space that is available. Using hide-mode NAT is one easy way to conserve address space while not limiting the functionality of your network.

Hide-mode NAT enables you to hide an entire range of reserved address space behind one or more routable IP addresses.

The advantages of hiding network objects extend beyond simply conserving address space: hidden objects are not directly reachable from external hosts, and are therefore far less susceptible to attacks or unauthorized access attempts.

Even though hidden objects benefit from this protection, you may still grant them full access to the Internet. FireWall-1 will translate packets originating from your hidden objects so that once their traffic leaves your firewall, they appear to be originating from a routable address. In turn, when the external host responds, the incoming packets are again translated by the firewall back to the original reserved address, allowing your hidden object to receive the response without knowing any translation took place.

Because Firewall-1 translates source port as well as destination port, it is able to determine what internal host should receive an incoming connection, even if there are multiple connections destined for the firewall's external address. The firewall maintains a translation table, and from the source port in this table, it is able to direct incoming connections appropriately.

The following example will demonstrate how this process works, and how you can configure FireWall-1 to accomplish hide-mode NAT.

One of the most common uses of hide-mode NAT, and where you will want to consider using it, is connecting your office workstations to the Internet. In order to accomplish this, you should assign your office workstations reserved IP addresses; we will use 10.96.1.0/24 for this example. This means that your workstations will use 10.96.1.1 as their default gateway, and you will configure this address on one of your firewall's internal interfaces. Then, each of your workstations will be assigned an address in the range of 10.96.1.2 to 10.96.1.254 (either manually or with a DHCP server).

One important issue to keep in mind is that your firewall must be licensed for sufficient hosts to encompass your DHCP scope, plus any statically assigned addresses. If you end up using more addresses than your Firewall-1 license contains, you will see repeated error messages in the system log on your firewall.

Now your workstations will be able to communicate with the internal interface of the firewall. Be sure to enable IP forwarding on your firewall; otherwise, packets will not be forwarded from one interface to another, and your workstations will not be able to gain connectivity.

The next step is to look at the Address Translation tab in the Check Point Policy Editor, as shown in Figure 5.1.

The rules in this tab can be generated automatically, as we will discuss later in this chapter, or manually. In this case, we are going to add a manual rule to take care of hiding your office network. First, add a new rule by selecting **Rules** and then **Add Rule** and **Bottom** from the menu bar. This will insert a blank rule to the bottom of the current rule base.

Figure 5.1 Address Translation Tab

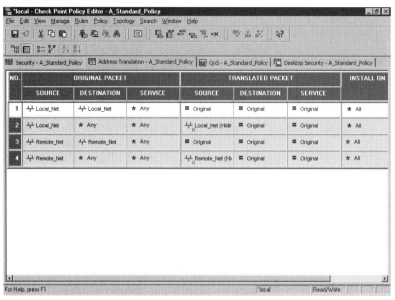

The address translation rule base has two main sections: original packet and translated packet. When a connection comes through the firewall, it compares the packet for a match with the source, destination, and service of the original packet section. If a match is made, the firewall then alters the source, destination, and service as specified in the translated packet section.

Just as in the standard rule base, rules in the translation rule base are processed in the order that they appear. This means that you need to be careful about where you insert new rules. In this example, you are adding a rule to the end of the rule base, but you need to ensure that whatever the location you are inserting a rule, it will not be cancelled out by a previous rule.

Before you can configure this rule, you need to be clear on what network objects are involved. The first object you need is one representing your internal office network (10.96.1.0/24). This will be called "Local_Net." The second object required is one representing the routable IP address that you are going to hide the office network behind. In this case, you are going to hide the internal network behind the external IP address of the firewall, so it is not necessary to create a separate object for this—you will use the existing firewall object called "FireWall_ExtraNet." Note that you can hide a network behind other addresses besides that of the firewall's external interface. To do this, you would simply create another network object representing this address. However, you may have to deal with some routing issues that are discussed below.

Now that we know what objects we are going to use, it is time to create the NAT rule. To do this, start with the **Original Packet** section of the new rule we created. Add **Local_Net** to the Source column, which means this rule will apply to all traffic originating from any of your workstations. Destination should remain as **Any**, since we want to do translation no matter what destination the workstation is trying to reach. Service should also remain as **Any**, since we are not restricting this translation to any particular service type.

In the **Translated Packet** section, set the Source to **FireWall_ExtraNet** by choosing **Add (Hide)** from the pull-down menu. This means that all traffic originating from your workstations will appear to external hosts to be originating from the firewall's routable external address. Again, Destination and Service should remain unchanged, as **Original**, since we are only worried about translating source addresses here, not about destinations or services. Install On should be set to include any firewall we are configuring, and it is always a good idea to add a comment to describe the rule—"Hide rule for Local_Net" is a good description. See Figure 5.2 for the completed rule.

Figure 5.2 Completed NAT rule

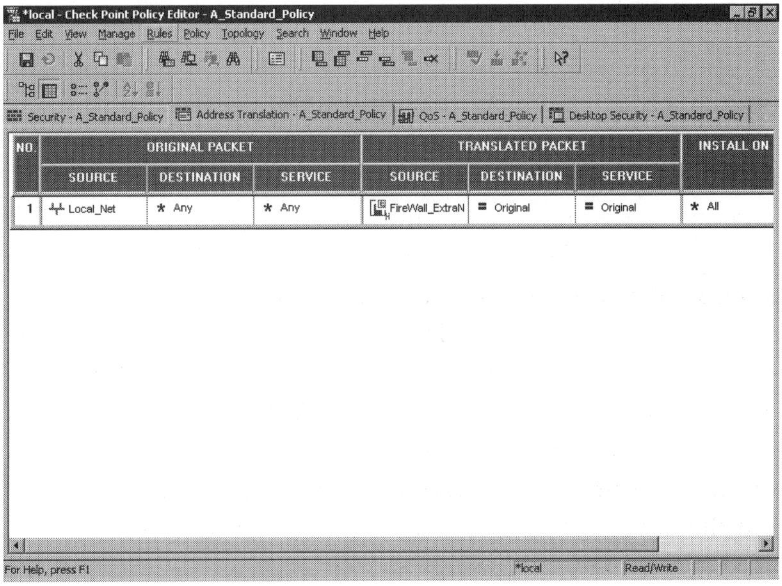

In addition to adding the translation rule, you must also ensure that the security policy will allow your workstations to pass traffic; the translation rule itself does not imply that packets going to and from your network will be allowed. Figure 5.3 displays what this rule should look like.

Figure 5.3 Rule to Allow Outbound Traffic

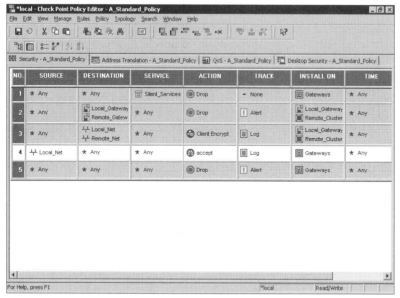

This rule, rule 4 in Figure 5.3, has source **Local_Net**, destination and service **Any,** and action **Accept.** This means that all traffic originating from any of your workstations will be allowed outbound. Of course, because we have already configured the translation rule, once the firewall accepts traffic from any of these objects, it will then go on to translate the packets as specified.

Routing and ARP

Address Resolution Protocol, or ARP, translates IP addresses to hardware MAC addresses, and vice-versa. In the example above, where we used hide-mode NAT to translate packets going to and from your internal network, we used the firewall's external IP address as the translated address. In this case, there are no ARP issues to consider because the firewall will respond to requests directed to its own external address.

However, if we were to use another routable address as the translated address, we would have to ensure that this address is published, so that when external hosts send-traffic to this address, the firewall responds. To do this, you must add a static ARP entry to the host on which the firewall is installed.

On a Solaris system, use the following syntax to add the static ARP entry:

```
arp -s <translated IP> <MAC address> pub
```

The MAC address to use here is the MAC address of the external interface of your firewall. You can determine this address using the *ifconfig -a* command. Note that this ARP entry will only exist until the system is rebooted. To have the ARP entry remain permanently, you will have to added to the appropriate start-up file on your system.

As an example, we will say that the IP address for Firewall_ExtraNet is 198.53.145.5, and that the MAC address on the external interface of the firewall is 00:01:03:CF:50:C9. The ARP command you would use in this case is as follows:

```
arp -s 198.53.145.5 00:01:03:CF:50:C9
```

Similarly, in Windows NT, you would also need to add a static ARP entry. However, NT does not allow this via the *arp* command, and so you must edit the file $FWDIR\conf\local.arp (in earlier versions this file was located in the $FWDIR\state directory). In this file, add a line as follows:

```
<translated IP>      <MAC address>
```

Or, in our example:

```
198.53.145.5         00:01:03:CF:50:C9
```

On both Windows and Solaris, you can display a list of current ARP entries by issuing the command *arp -a*. This will include any manual ARP entries you have created, as well as all other ARP entries the system has learned.

Separate the fields with a space or tab. After editing this file, you will need to stop and start the FireWall-1 service to activate your changes.

If you are using a Nokia, to configure a static ARP entry go to the Voyager GUI, and under **Config** choose **ARP**, and add the entry. You should select type **Proxy Only**. Note that if you are using VRRP, and you use the virtual IP address as the hiding address, there is no need to add a static ARP entry because the firewall already knows that it should respond to this address.

In addition to ARP issues, you need to keep routing issues in mind when configuring any type of NAT. Our example above does not present any obvious routing issues, assuming the workstations are all directly connected to the firewall, and are used as a gateway. However, if there was a router or any other layer-3 device between the workstations and the firewall, you would have to ensure that the router forwarded traffic between the workstations and the firewall properly.

One other routing issue to take into account is that if the IP address you are using as your hiding address is not part of your firewall's external interface, external routers may not know how to reach this address. If traffic does not reach the firewall, then the ARP entry you created for that address will do no good. To ensure that traffic reaches the firewall, you will have to have the router responsible for announcing your networks also publish the network you are using for NAT. This may involve contacting your internet provider if you do not manage your own router.

Configuring Static Address Translation

Static address translation translates an internal IP address to an external IP address on a one-to-one ratio. This is be in contrast to hide-mode translation, which translates many internal IP addresses to one external IP address (many-to-one).

Situations especially suited to static-mode translation include cases where external hosts on the Internet need to initiate connections with hosts on your internal network. Using hide-mode translation would not allow for this—internal hosts are hidden, as the name suggests, and therefore cannot be contacted directly from external sources.

Static address translation is also useful in situations where hide-mode will not work, such as with certain VPN clients or other specialized applications.

Static address translation rules come in two flavors: static source and static destination. Rules are generally generated in pairs—you will want matching source and destination rules for each internal object involved with static translation.

We will now go into detail about the two types of static translation rules, and go through an example of configuring your firewall to make use of these rules. The example here will be of a Web server sitting behind your firewall, called "Web_Server," on an internal IP address, 192.168.24.5. Our objective here is to use static address translation to allow external users to access this web server. To do this, we will first create a static source rule, followed by a static destination rule.

Static Source

The first step in configuring static address translation for your Web server is to ensure that packets originating from the Web server are able to exit your network and reach their destination on the Internet. This is the purpose of static source mode.

Just as in hide-mode address translation, where a reserved IP address is translated into a routable IP address before it leaves the firewall, we must do the same here. The difference is that with static source mode there is a one to one relationship between reserved addresses and routable addresses. That is, each reserved address is translated into a unique routable address.

Static source rules, like hide rules, can be configured either automatically or manually. Here we will focus on manual rule configuration, but see the "Automatic NAT rules" section for information on how to generate these rules automatically.

To configure a static source rule, open the policy editor, and go to the **Address Translation** tab. Select **Rules** and then **Add Rule** and **Top**. Again, depending on what rules are already present, you may need to add the rule elsewhere in the rule base. This will add a new, blank rule to the top of the rule base. We will now configure this rule; see rule 1 in Figure 5.4.

Figure 5.4 Static Source Rule

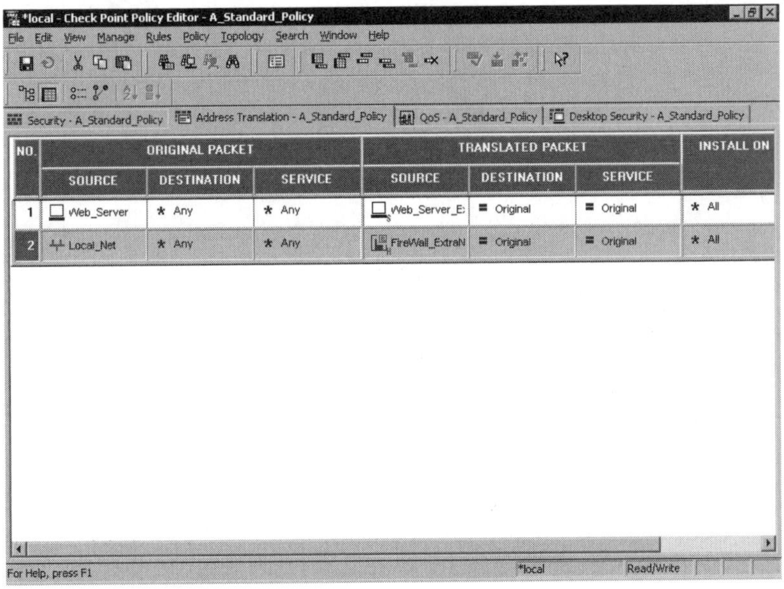

Before you configure this rule, you will need to add an object representing the routable IP address you are going to use to translate the Web server's internal address. Create a standard workstation object with a valid routable IP within your address space, and call it "Web_Server_Ext," as in Figure 5.5.

Figure 5.5 Web Server External Object

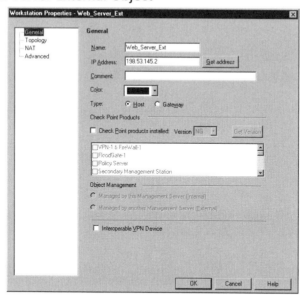

Now, back to the translation rule. In the Original Packet section, under **Source**, add the *Web_Server* object—double-check that this object has an internal address. Leave the Destination set to **Any**, since we want to apply this rule no matter what external host the Web server is attempting to contact. Also leave the Service as **Any**, since we are not going to restrict the destination port for this rule. Note that you could specify "http" or "https" here, depending on your specific application.

In the Translated Packet section, set Source to **Web_Server_Ext**, and double-check that this object is set to the routable address you are using for translation. Again, leave Destination and Service unchanged, as **Original**, since we are only interested in translating the source address, not in the destination or service.

Set Install On to **All,** or if you are only planning to use this rule on a subset of your available firewalls, then set this to match that set. Be sure to add a descriptive comment, such as "Static source for Web_Server," so that you will be able to identify this rule later.

The last step to enable static source translation is to ensure that your standard rule base will allow traffic from the web server outbound. See rule 5 in Figure 5.6.

Set the Source to **Web_Server**, destination to **Any**, and service to **http**. Action will be **Accept**, and track should be **Long**.

Figure 5.6 Outbound Rule for Web Server

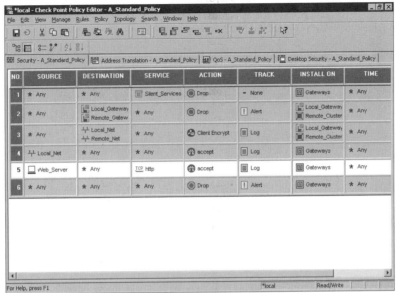

Once you install the policy, you will have a working static source translation rule for this Web server. Remember that this rule only takes care of allowing the Web server to reach external hosts; without any further configuration there is no means by which inbound traffic can reach the server. In general, the functionality of a Web server requires external traffic to reach the server, and so static source rules are usually created in pairs with static destination rules, which are described next.

Static Destination

Creating a static destination rule is very similar to creating a static source rule, except for the order of the objects. See rule 2 in Figure 5.7.

Again, add a rule to the translation rule base by going to **Rules** and then **Add Rule**. Here you should place this rule above or below the static source rule. In this case, in the Original Packet section, set the Destination to **Web_Server_Ext**, and leave Source and Service as **Any**. In the Translated Packet section, set the Destination as **Web_Server**, and again leave the other two columns as **Original**. The reason we are modifying the destination in this case and not the source is that we are worried about incoming traffic, which has the Web server as destination.

Figure 5.7 Static Destination Rule

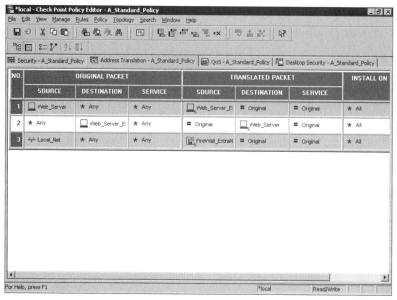

Finally, you must ensure that your standard rule base will allow incoming traffic to hit the routable address. If not, this traffic would be dropped before it even had a chance to go through your translation rule. See rule 6 in Figure 5.8.

Figure 5.8 Rule for Incoming Traffic to Web Server

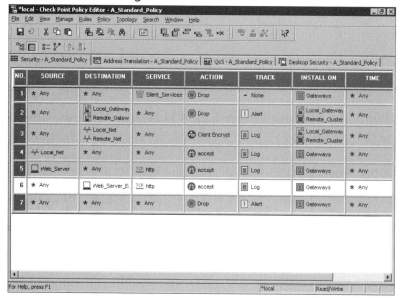

Here, set Source to **Any**, Destination to **Web_Server_Ext**, Service to **Any**, and Action to **Accept**. Note that you could specify specific services, such as http or https, and you could also narrow down the acceptable remote hosts that can access the Web server by adding them to Destination.

After you install the policy, you will have a working static destination setup. What you can do then is configure your DNS so that the name by which you want people to access this Web server, for example www.yourcompany.com, points to the same address as you have assigned to Web_Server_Ext.

When this name is accessed on the Internet, traffic will be directed to your firewall, which will then translate and forward the packets to your Web server's internal address (the same one assigned to the object *Web_Server*). The Web server will recognize these packets as belonging to itself, and will respond to the request. When the response reaches the firewall, the firewall will again translate the packets back to the routable address, and forward them back toward the client. The client will see the response as originating from the same address to which they sent the request, and will not even know translation took place.

Routing and ARP

Just as in hide-mode address translation, there are ARP and routing issues to take into account for static source and static destination modes.

Static source mode requires the same ARP configuration as hide mode; the routable address you are using (in this case the one assigned to Web_Server_Ext) must be configured on the firewall host. This is necessary so that incoming traffic bound for this address is recognized by the firewall as belonging to itself, and processed rather than forwarded elsewhere.

On a Solaris system, use the following syntax to add the static ARP entry:

```
arp -s <translated IP> <MAC address> pub
```

On a Windows NT system, edit the file $FWDIR\conf\local.arp (in earlier versions this file was located in the $FWDIR\state directory). In this file, add a line as follows:

```
<translated IP>      <MAC address>
```

In both cases, use the translated IP assigned to Web_Server_Ext and the MAC address of your local network card. Be sure to start and stop the firewall process after making these changes.

If you are using a Nokia, add an ARP entry in the Voyager GUI under **Configure** and then **ARP**. Here, add a permanent ARP entry with type "Proxy Only."

Static destination mode requires that you take into account routing the packets destined for the Web server. Specifically, the firewall will not know which interface to use to transmit the packets unless told explicitly. This may seem confusing, since you may think the translation rule will take care of routing the packet properly. However, if you upgraded your firewall to NG from a previous version, then translation takes place *after* the packets are routed. I like to think of this as the packet header getting rewritten just as the packet is on its way out of the firewall's interface. So, it must be going out of the correct interface before the address is translated. New installations of NG will translate before the packets are routed. See the section on NAT Global Properties for more info.

To add a static route on a Solaris system, use the following command:

```
route add <routable address> <internal adress>
```

Note that in Solaris, this route, as well as any ARP entries you have added statically, will only remain present until the system is rebooted. You will need to ensure that you add this route to the appropriate startup file prior to the next reboot.

To add a static route on a Windows NT system, use the following command:

```
Route add <routable address> <internal address> -p
```

Here, the route will remain intact following a reboot due to the "-p" option, which stands for persistent. In both cases, the "routable address" is the address assigned to Web_Server_Ext, and the "internal address" is the address assigned to "Web_Server" or the next hop router.

To add a static route on a Nokia, open the Voyager GUI and go to **Configure** and then **Routing Configuration** followed by **Static Routes**. Add the route here, and then apply and save your changes.

Now that you have taken care of all outstanding ARP and routing issues, you can be sure that your static source and static destination translation rules will allow the Web server to function normally, while still being protected by the firewall.

Automatic NAT Rules

In additional to creating translation rules manually, FireWall-1 gives you the ability to generate these rules automatically. Generating automatic translation rules saves you time, and reduces the opportunity for error. You can create both hide-mode and static-mode translation rules automatically.

Automatic Hide

As above, we are going to configure hide-mode translation to hide your office network, 10.96.1.0/24, behind one routable address.

To configure automatic hide-mode translation, open the Policy Editor and choose **Manage** and then **Network Objects**. Edit the properties of Local_Net, and go to the NAT tab, as per Figure 5.9.

Figure 5.9 NAT Tab of Network Object

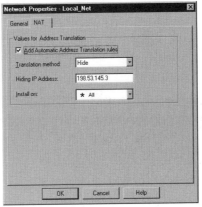

Select **Add Automatic Address Translation Rules**, which will activate the rest of the settings in this window. For Translation Mode, choose **Hide,** and for **Hiding IP Address**, enter the routable IP address you are going to use to hide this network. Note that here you can also specify "0.0.0.0," which will result in the firewall using its external IP address. Install On should include the firewalls that will require this rule, or should be set to **All.**

Once you press **OK**, FireWall-1 will automatically generate the required rules for this hide-mode translation. See Figure 5.10.

Rules 1 and 2 here have been generated by the *Local_Net* object's automatic translation settings. Rule 1 ensures that traffic traveling within Local_Net will not be affected by translation; this traffic does not require translation since it is not leaving your network. Rule 2 resembles the manual translation rule we created earlier. It translates all traffic originating on your network into the routable IP address you specified, and then translates the destination of incoming packets back into their original addresses.

Figure 5.10 NAT Rule Base with Generated Rules

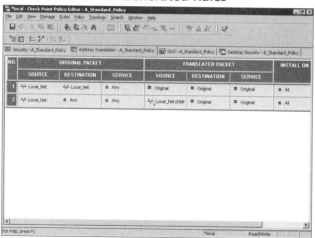

The final step to activating hide-mode translation is to ensure that your general rule base will allow traffic to flow as expected. The rules to create here are the same as when you configured manual hide-mode translation.

Automatic Static

Configuring static rules automatically is similar to creating hide-mode rules automatically. In this example, we will again be configuring translation to allow *Web_Server* to be accessed from the Internet.

To configure automatic static-mode translation, open the Policy Editor and go to the properties of the object you are configuring, in this case *Web_Server*. See Figure 5.11.

Go to the **NAT** tab, and enable **Add Automatic Address Translation rules**. For Translation Method, choose **Static**, and for Valid IP Address, enter the routable IP address you are going to use in this case. Install On should include the firewalls for which this rule is appropriate, or be set to **All.**

Once you press **OK**, FireWall-1 will automatically generate the required rules for this static mode translation. See Figure 5.12.

Here, rules 1 and 2 have been generated by the *Web_Server* automatic translation settings. These rules will resemble the static source and static destination rules we created earlier. Rule 1 translates traffic originating from the Web server to the routable IP address, and rule 2 translates incoming traffic from valid, routable address back to the internal address for incoming traffic.

Figure 5.11 NAT Tab of Web Server

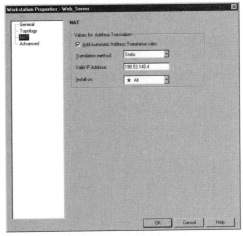

Figure 5.12 Generated Address Translation Rules

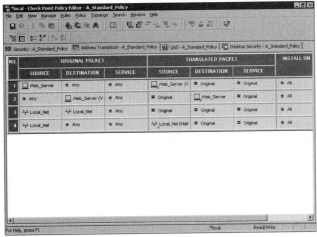

Again, the final step is to ensure that your general rule base will allow traffic to flow to and from the Web server. The rules to create here are the same as when you configured manual static-mode translation.

Static NAT in Win2k

The static NAT feature may not work properly on a Win2k Server. There is a Check Point SecureKnowledge article on the resolution for this problem, which is sk699.

1. Disable RRAS

2. Reboot

3. Edit the following registry entry:

`HKEY_LOCAL_MACHINE\SYSTEM\CurrentControlSet\Services\Tcpip\Parameters`

Change the Dword key from "1" to "IPEnableRouter"

4. Reboot

Automatic ARP will need to be enabled under the **Policy | Global Properties** window.

Routing and ARP

With automatic NAT, you also need to keep routing and ARP issues in mind. The procedures for ensuring packets reach their intended destination are the same as with manual NAT.

Configuring & Implementing...

Automatic ARP

A new feature to FireWall-1 is automatic ARP configuration. This feature eliminates the need for manual ARP entries. When enabled, via the NAT tab in global policy properties, FireWall-1 will automatically create ARP entries for all required addresses. This includes single IP addresses and address ranges, but applies only to automatic NAT.

If there is a router on your internal network, and you are using reserved address space, you need to ensure that static routes (and default routes) exist on the router so that packets will reach the firewall.

For static source and hide-mode NAT, you must ensure that proper ARP entries exist on the firewall for the hiding or static source address. If you have upgraded to NG from a prior version of FireWall-1, then for static destination you need to add a static host route on the firewall to direct the traffic out the proper interface since routing will take place before NAT.

Configuring these ARP and routing tasks should be done just as when you configure NAT manually, or by enabling some of the options available in the NAT Global Properties, which we will talk about next.

NAT Global Properties

FireWall-1 has some global NAT settings that affect the firewall's behavior. To access these settings, open the Policy Editor and go to **Policy** and then **Global Properties**, and choose **Network Address Translation,** as in Figure 5.13.

Figure 5.13 NAT Global Properties

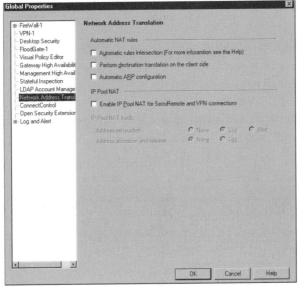

The **Automatic rules intersection** setting, when checked, will apply when there is more than one NAT rule that applies in any given situation. Automatic rules intersection means that in this case the firewall will combine or intersect the rules, thereby applying them both. When this box is not checked, the firewall will only apply the first matching NAT rule, and will ignore any subsequent matching rules.

For example, if a packet matches one translation rule's source and other rule's destination, the firewall would translation both the source and destination.

When **Perform destination translation on the client side** is checked, the firewall will perform static destination mode NAT on the client side of the connection, as opposed to the server side. With this option enabled, the need to add static host routes on the firewall is eliminated since address translation will take place before routing.

Configuring & Implementing...

Destination Translation

Previous versions of FireWall-1 performed destination mode NAT on the server end. This sometimes created routing and anti-spoofing issues. As a result, this version of FireWall-1 defaults to handling destination mode NAT on the client end, unless you are upgrading from a previous version of FireWall-1, in which case it defaults to server side.

Automatic ARP configuration avoids the necessity to configure ARP entries manually on the firewall, as discussed in the routing and ARP sections. This applies only to automatic NAT, not to manual NAT rules. This setting causes the firewall to automatically generate ARP entries for all configured translated IP addresses, enabling the firewall to respond to these addresses. This occurs on the firewall module that is enforcing the translation policy, and you can view the firewall's ARP table with this command:

```
fw ctl arp
```

Summary

Network address translation is an effective way to protect your network, while at the same time conserving valuable IP address space. Hosts that are protected by NAT are far less vulnerable to attack or compromise by external threats, since they are not directly reachable from the Internet.

FireWall-1 provides you with two main methods of doing NAT: hide mode and static mode.

Hide-mode translation is most useful for situations when you need to translate an entire range of private IP space into one routable address. A common example is an office LAN: multiple office workstations, none of which need to be accessible externally, can be hidden with hide-mode NAT.

Static-mode translation, divided into static source and static destination, is suited to cases when the device you are hiding must be accessible from the Internet. In static mode, there is a one-to-one relationship between internal and external addresses.

For both hide- and static-mode translation, FireWall-1 enables you to define NAT rules manually, or to have them generated automatically. The end result is the same—which method you use to define rules is up to you, and will depend on the situation and on how comfortable you are with the NAT rule base.

Now that you understand how to configure network address translation with FireWall-1, you have a powerful tool available that will enable you to create a highly secure, yet functionally uninhibited environment. Using NAT effectively is a key to building an optimal security policy.

Solutions Fast Track

Hiding Network Objects

- ☑ Hide-mode NAT is used to hide an entire range of private addresses behind one routable address.

- ☑ With hide-mode NAT, internal hosts are not accessible from external hosts, but internal hosts can still retain full access outward.

- ☑ When configuring hide-mode NAT, you need to take ARP issues into account, and may have to add manual ARP entries to your firewall.

Configuring Static Address Translation

☑ Static-mode NAT is used when internal hosts need to be accessible from the Internet.

☑ With static-mode NAT, there is a one-to-one ratio between internal and external addresses.

☑ There are ARP and routing issues to take into account when configuring static mode NAT. You may need to add static routes if you have a router between your workstations and firewall, as well as static ARP entries.

Automatic NAT Rules

☑ NAT rules in FireWall-1 can be created manually via the NAT rule base, or automatically via each network object's NAT tab.

☑ Configuring FireWall-1 rules automatically may simplify your configuration tasks, and allow you to more easily visualize your environment. The end result, though, is the same.

☑ Even when configuring NAT automatically, you need to keep the same ARP and routing considerations in mind.

NAT Global Properties

☑ FireWall-1's global NAT properties help you to configure rule intersection behavior, know where to perform destination translation, and help with automatic ARP configuration.

☑ Automatic ARP configuration is an especially useful feature, which eliminates the need for manual ARP entries on the firewall. FireWall-1 will create ARP entries for all required addresses.

Frequently Asked Questions

The following Frequently Asked Questions, answered by the authors of this book, are designed to both measure your understanding of the concepts presented in this chapter and to assist you with real-life implementation of these concepts. To have your questions about this chapter answered by the author, browse to **www.syngress.com/solutions** and click on the **"Ask the Author"** form.

Q: Should I configure NAT rules manually, or use FireWall-1 to generate them automatically?

A: No matter how you configure NAT, the end result should be the same. In fact, if you configure NAT automatically, you should still check the NAT rule base to ensure that the rules ended up as you expected. So, the answer to this question really depends on your familiarity and comfort level with NAT and with FireWall-1 in general.

Q: How do I know when to use hide-mode and when to use static-mode NAT?

A: As a general rule, use static-mode NAT only when the internal device needs to be accessible from the Internet. This includes devices such as Web servers, FTP servers, or any other server you want external users to have access to. Also, some forms of VPN and some other specialized application require static-mode NAT. Hide-mode translation should be used when the internal device needs access outbound, but does not need to be reached externally.

Q: When will the firewall use an ARP entry as opposed to a route?

A: ARP entries are used for devices that are on the same network as the firewall, while routes are used otherwise. For devices on the same network, when the firewall tries to reach an IP address, it first checks to see if it already has an ARP entry for that host. If not, it sends out an ARP broadcast, received by all devices on the same network, requesting the MAC address for the given IP. For devices not on the same network, the firewall simply checks its routing table for a route to that host, and uses the default route if none is found.

Q: I have a lot of NAT rules, and it takes a long time to compile my security policy. What can I do to speed things up?

A: If you have several sequential networks or subnets defined for your hiding NAT networks, then you can combine these into one network object with a subnet that will cover all (or as many as possible) of your networks. For example, if you have 10.1.1.0, 10.1.2.0, 10.1.3.0…10.1.128.0, and you have automatic NAT turned on for each of these networks, that could equal 256 NAT rules. Instead, you can create one object with address 10.1.0.0 and subnet mask 255.255.128.0 and add the automatic NAT to this one object. Then you can remove it from all the others.

Q: My management console is managing several firewalls, and we have an assortment of 10.x.x.x networks on our internal network networks spread out across different locations. How can I keep my NAT rule base simple?

A: Create one network object for 10.0.0.0 with netmask 255.0.0.0, and add hide NAT with a translation address of 0.0.0.0. Using this address will hide the traffic behind the firewall's IP address that the traffic is leaving out of.

Q: I can't access my remote network over our Virtual Private Network because the firewall is hiding our local network. What do I need to do?

A: Sometimes it is necessary to create manual address translation rules that *do not* translate. If you should not be translating your internal network to your remote office, then you could add a rule where the Original Packet fields match these VPN packets, and the Translated Packet section keeps all three columns (Source, Destination, and Service) as **Original.** This would need to be added above any rules in the rule base that translated this source or destination.

Q: How can I troubleshoot my NAT configuration?

A: Perform these steps to verify that you have things configured properly for static address translation. If you cannot determine a problem with ping, check your Log Viewer for dropped or rejected packets.

  1. From the firewall, ping the internal IP address of the host/server. If you cannot, then check the cabling.

  2. From the firewall, ping the routable, external IP address of the host/server. If you cannot, then check the host route on the firewall. If the host route looks right, then check the network object for your workstation; the IP address or Address Translation may be incorrect.

3. From the host, ping the internal IP address of the firewall. If you cannot, then check the cabling.

4. From the host, ping the firewall's external IP address. If you cannot, then check the default route on the host, and the default route of any intervening routers.

5. From the host, ping your Internet router (or the firewall's default gateway). If you cannot, then check the address translation on the workstation's network object in the Policy Editor. If that looks fine, then check the ARP on the firewall (local.arp in NT).

Q: Why can't I get to any servers on my DMZ that are configured with static NAT after rebooting the firewall?

A: If you are on a Windows firewall, then check that the static-host route was added with a −p switch, which stands for persistent or permanent. This makes sure that the routes are added into the registry and restored whenever the system is rebooted. If you are on a Solaris firewall, then make sure that your ARP and route statements are added in a startup file. If you have a Nokia firewall, make sure that you make any route and ARP change through the Voyager GUI, and that you SAVE your changes after you apply them.

## Chapter 6

Authenticating Users

Solutions in this chapter:

- **FireWall-1 Authentication Schemes**
- **Defining Users**
- **User Authentication**
- **Client Authentication**
- **Session Authentication**
- **LDAP Authentication**

☑ **Summary**

☑ **Solutions Fast Track**

☑ **Frequently Asked Questions**

Introduction

There are many reasons that your organization may decide to implement user authentication at your firewall. Perhaps you want to allow different departments access to various resources on your DMZ, or maybe you are using DHCP inside your network, and IP addresses are changing every week when their leases expire. If you want to keep track of who is going to what Internet web sites for whatever reason, then you could authenticate your users at the firewall, so that it can accurately log the user's login identity. Then you don't have to rely on IP addresses to determine who is going where.

VPN-1/FireWall-1 Next Generation provides you with several different authentication schemes and user authentication methods, and you should be able to choose one of them to suit your organization's needs. We will describe the various options you have, and provide some examples of how you might implement them into your current security policy structure.

Some of the options you have to authenticate your users are S/Key, SecurID, RADIUS, AXENT Pathways Defender, TACACS, OS password, and VPN-1/FireWall-1 authentication. You can choose to authenticate your users by one of these methods, and then you can pick from several authentication options in the policy, which we will cover in this chapter.

FireWall-1 Authentication Schemes

Authentication is a cornerstone of any firewall. Without authentication, we would not be able to distinguish authorized users from unauthorized users, and all other security policies would be of no use. FireWall-1 gives you the option of several different authentication schemes. Some of these schemes make use of external products or servers, while others are internal to FireWall-1.

All of these schemes can be used in conjunction with user, session, and client authentication, which will be discussed later in this chapter. Note that to use each of these schemes, you must enable them in your firewall object's "Authentication" tab. See Figure 6.1.

Turning on each of the schemes merely gives you the option of using them for a particular user; it does not force you to use this scheme. You can also use this tab to configure User Authentication session timeout, which is the amount of time that must pass before a user is required to authenticate again. The "enable wait mode for Client Authentication" option will be discussed below, under Client Authentication.

Figure 6.1 Firewall Object Authentication Tab

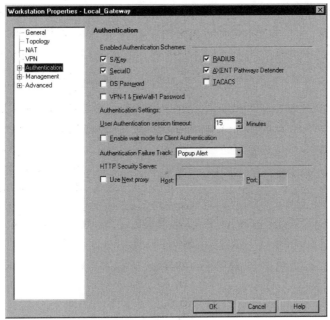

S/Key

S/Key authentication eliminates the possibility of an unauthorized user finding out an authorized user's password. This is possible because S/Key uses a one-time password scheme, whereas the password used for each authentication attempt is used once, and then never again.

On the client side, the user must use an S/Key password-generating application in order to generate his or her one-time passwords. The password is calculated based upon a secret password (this is not a one-time password) and a sequence number, and then passing this through a MD4 or MD5 hash function. The result is a one-time password, in the form of a string that the user will enter to authenticate.

In order to configure your firewall for S/Key authentication, open the Policy Editor and go to **Manage | Users | Authentication**. See Figure 6.2.

On this tab, fill in the following:

- **Seed** A random string

- **Secret Key** The user's chosen password (this is not the one-time password!)

- **Length** The number of one-time passwords that will be generated
- **Installed On** Set this to your firewall object
- **Method** Choose either MD4 or MD5 for the hash method

Figure 6.2 S/Key Configuration Tab

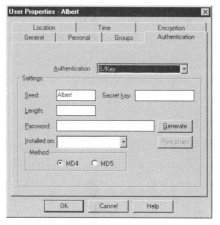

SecurID

SecurID is a two-factor authentication method, meaning two pieces of information are required before access is granted: a password and a token. The token is generally generated by a SecurID token—a small electronic device the user keeps with them that displays a new number every 60 seconds. Combining this number with the user's password allows the SecurID server to determine whether or not the user should be granted access.

In order to configure SecurID, your FireWall-1 server must be configured as an ACE client. Please refer to your ACE server documentation for further information. To enable SecurID authentication in FireWall-1, ensure that it is enabled in the firewall object's Authentication tab. There are no settings for SecurID in the Policy Editor; you simply need to set the authentication scheme for the user you are configuring to "SecurID" in the user's Authentication tab.

OS Password

Authentication via operating system password means that FireWall-1 will refer to the user's account in the operating system for authentication. This may be a convenient method for you if all the users you want to configure for firewall authentication already have accounts on the system.

One example of this is that you may want to authenticate your users with their domain passwords. To do this, your firewall must reside on your NT domain, so that the firewall can access the domain user database. Be aware of the possible security risks of locating your firewall on the NT domain; if security is breached on the domain, it may also be breached on the firewall.

However, OS password authentication may not be appropriate in all situations. For example, if you are running FireWall-1 on a standalone appliance, it is unlikely that users will have local accounts on the appliance.

In order to configure FireWall-1 to use OS password authentication, ensure that it is enabled in the firewall object's Authentication tab, and simply choose it as the authentication scheme for the user you are configuring; there are no other settings for this scheme.

Designing & Planning…

OS Password Authentication

If you are using OS password authentication, be careful about users who have OS accounts but whom you do not want to grant access to through the firewall. If you have defined a default "generic*" user, you may inadvertently grant access to more users than you intended. If this is the case, you can create users with authentication schemes set to "Undefined", which will deny those users access. If a significant amount of your OS users should not have access, consider using a different authentication scheme.

VPN-1 & FireWall-1 Password

If your users do not have accounts on the local FireWall-1 server, but you do not want to use an external authentication scheme such as SecurID or a more complicated scheme such as S/Key, then your best option is FireWall-1 password.

Using a FireWall-1 password simply means that you assign the user a password within FireWall-1, and the user must enter a matching password to authenticate.

To configure VPN-1 and FireWall-1 password authentication, ensure that this option is enabled in the Authentication tab of your firewall object. Then, go to the **Authentication** tab of the user you are configuring, choose **VPN-1 &**

FireWall-1 Password, and enter a password of eight characters or less. FireWall-1 will ask you to confirm the password.

RADIUS

RADIUS, which stands for Remote Authentication Dial-In User Service, is a convenient way of managing usernames and passwords. In order to use this authentication scheme, you must have a functional RADIUS server, which contains a database of all the users you would like to authenticate.

To configure RADIUS authentication in FireWall-1, the first step is to add a workstation object to represent your RADIUS server. To do this from the Policy Editor, go to **Manage | Network Objects | New | Workstation**. Create the object with the IP address of your RADIUS server.

The next step is to add a *RADIUS server* object. To do this, open the Policy Editor, and go to **Manage | Servers**. Select **New** and then **RADIUS**, and refer to Figure 6.3.

Figure 6.3 RADIUS Server Configuration

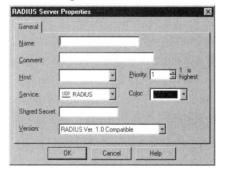

Fill in the following fields:

- **Name** A descriptive name for your RADIUS server.

- **Comment** A descriptive comment about your RADIUS server.

- **Host** The physical server on which your RADIUS server is running. Note that you need to define this host as a network object prior to this configuration.

- **Priority** Specify "1" if you only have one RADIUS server. If you have more than one RADIUS server, then you have the option of ranking them by priority so that certain servers are always contacted first. See below for a discussion about configuring multiple RADIUS servers.

- **Color** Select a color for your RADIUS server icon.

- **Service** Select **RADIUS**.

- **Shared Secret** Enter a secret password. You also need to configure this password on the RADIUS server; see your RADIUS server documentation for details.

- **Version** Select either version 1.0 or 2.0, depending on the version of your RADIUS server.

Now that you have configured your RADIUS server and have told FireWall-1 about it, enabling RADIUS authentication for a user is simple. Ensure that **RADIUS** is selected as an enabled authentication scheme in your firewall object's Authentication tab, and then select **RADIUS** as the authentication scheme in the user's Authentication tab. Then, when prompted for a RADIUS server to use, select the server you configured above.

You also have the option of configuring multiple RADIUS servers. The advantage of this is that if one RADIUS server fails, users will continue to be able to authenticate via the backup servers.

To configure multiple RADIUS servers, add each RADIUS server to FireWall-1 under the **Manage** menu and select **Servers**. Be sure to configure each server with an appropriate priority, depending on the sequence in which you want the servers to be queried; lower numbers indicate higher priorities.

Once you have all your RADIUS servers configured, create a RADIUS Group in your list of Servers, and add each RADIUS server to this group. Then, when configuring each user, select this group in their Authentication tab after choosing RADIUS authentication. You will see that you also have the option of selecting **All,** which means all available RADIUS servers will be queried. This has the same effect as adding all your servers to a RADIUS group and using that group.

AXENT Pathways Defender

Another available external authentication method is to use an AXENT Pathways Defender. Before configuring FireWall-1 for Defender authentication, ensure that your Defender server is set up and configured properly.
The first step to configuring FireWall-1 for Defender authentication is to define a workstation object with the Defender server's IP address. This is done in the Policy Editor, under **Manage Network Objects | Workstations | New**.

Then, to add your Defender server to FireWall-1, open the Policy Editor and go to **Manage | Servers | New | Defender**. Refer to Figure 6.4.

Figure 6.4 Defender Server Configuration

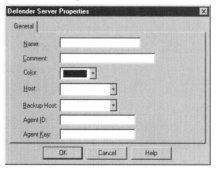

Fill in the following fields:

■ **Name** A descriptive name for your Defender server.

■ **Comment** A descriptive comment for your Defender server.

■ **Color** Select a color for the icon that will represent your Defender server.

■ **Host** The physical server on which your Defender server is running. Note that you need to configure this server as an object prior to this configuration.

■ **Backup Host** If you have a backup Defender server, specify it here. Note that this also needs to be configured as an object prior to this configuration. Also, the Agent ID and key need to be the same on both servers.

■ **Agent ID**: Enter the Agent ID that you configured on your Defender server for FireWall-1.

■ **Agent Key**: Enter the Agent key as specified by the Defender server. This key can be thought of as a hash, used to encrypt traffic between your firewall and your Defender server.

Once your Defender server is defined, to enable AXENT Pathways Defender authentication for a user you should ensure that "AXENT Pathways Defender" is enabled in the Authentication tab of your firewall object, and then choose "AXENT Pathways Defender" in the Authentication tab for the user you are configuring. There are no other options to specify in this tab.

TACACS

TACACS, which stands for Terminal Access Controller Access Control System, is another external authentication scheme you can use to authenticate your users. Configuring TACACS is similar to configuring RADIUS.

First, you need to ensure that your TACACS server is set up and configured correctly. Then, add a workstation object to the firewall with the TACACS server IP address. Next, in FireWall-1's Policy Editor, go to **Manage | Servers**. Choose **New** and **TACACS**, and refer to Figure 6.5.

Figure 6.5 TACACS Server Configuration

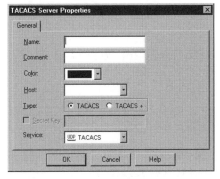

Fill in the following fields:

- **Name** A descriptive name for your TACACS server.

- **Comment** A descriptive comment for your TACACS server.

- **Color** Choose a color for the icon that will represent your TACACS server.

- **Host** Choose the physical server on which your TACACS server is configured. Note that this server should already be configured as a firewall object prior to this configuration.

- **Type** Choose TACACS or TACACS+, depending on the version of your TACACS server.

- **Secret Key** This option is only available for TACACS+ servers. If you have configured a secret key on your TACACS+ server, check this box and enter the same key here.

- **Service** Choose **TACACS**. Note that if you select **TACACS+** for **Type**, this option is not available.

Now that your TACACS server is defined, you need to ensure that TACACS is enabled in the Authentication tab of your firewall object. Then, choose **TACACS** in the Authentication tab of the user you are configuring, and select the TACACS server you defined.

Defining Users

To perform authentication, you will need to define users. Defining users enables you to make use of any of the above authentication schemes, as well as decide upon several other useful properties for each user.

In FireWall-1, users are defined based on templates. Templates enable you to reduce the amount of custom configuration you need to do for every user, by predefining as much of the configuration as possible.

We will now go through the details of how to most effectively manage your user base. All user configuration is done from the Policy Editor, under **Manage** and then **Users...**, or via the Object Tree, by clicking on the **Users** tab.

Creating a Wildcard User

All of FireWall-1's authentication schemes we discussed earlier in this chapter are divided into two categories: internal and external. Internal schemes, including S/Key, FireWall-1 password, and OS Password, have all of their users defined within the FireWall-1 user database. External schemes, including SecurID, RADIUS, AXENT Pathways Defender, and TACACS, inherently have their own user-management systems. It would therefore create an unnecessary amount of overhead if you were required to add all users using external authentication schemes to FireWall-1's user database, too.

To avoid this, FireWall-1 enables you to define a wildcard user that will be used for external authentication schemes. As long as you have a wildcard user defined for a particular external scheme, you do not need to define all users within the FireWall-1 user database.

To create a wildcard user, open the Policy Editor, and go to **Manage | Users | New | User by Template** (see below for more information on templates) and select **Standard User**. In the **General** tab, enter "generic*" as the Login Name. This will enable you to make use of external authentication schemes without duplicating your work in defining users.

If you have a handful of users that you do not want to authenticate, then you can use the generic* user to match the majority of your users and define those users in the FireWall-1 user database that you don't want to authenticate and set their Authentication method to "Undefined". This will essentially disable their account in the firewall.

Users can also be imported and exported to and from your FireWall-1 user database by using the **fw dbimport** and **fw dbexport** commands. If you are importing users into FireWall-1, you must have the users defined in a file in a specific format. The first line of the file must be any subset of the follow set, as long as the "name" attribute is included: {name; groups; destinations; sources; auth_method; fromhour; tohour; expiration_date; color; days; internal_password; SKEY_seed; SKEY_password; SKEY_gateway; template; comments; userc}. Each additional line should contain a value for each user associated with the attribute list you provided on the first line separated by the same delimiter character (; by default).

A value list should be included within curly brackets and separated by commas, such as {MON, TUE, WED, THU, FRI, SAT, SUN}. Acceptable values for auth_method are: Undefined, S/Key, SecurID, Unix Password, VPN-1/ FireWall-1 Password, RADIUS, or Defender. Time format is hh:mm and date format is dd-mmm-yy.

Creating and Using Templates

All users in FireWall-1 are defined via templates. Templates are also a convenient way to eliminate having to define the same user properties repeatedly; you define the user properties once, and create subsequent users with the same settings by simply choosing that template.

It is important to note that templates do not restrict you from changing individual users' settings. Even though you may define two users based on the same template, you are free to change any of the properties of one user without affecting the other user or the template itself.

To create a new template, open the Policy Editor, and go to **Manage | Users | New | Template**. See Figure 6.6.

Although you are prompted for "Login Name" here, what you are actually defining is the template name. Enter a descriptive name for this template, such as "Accounting Department." Next, let's look at the Personal Tab, in Figure 6.7.

Here, you can define an expiration date for users defined with this template. When a user's account expires, FireWall-1 will no longer allow them to authenticate. This is useful in scenarios such as when you know a user will only require access for a limited amount of time, and you don't want to worry about remembering to disable their account. The comment field enables you to enter any additional information regarding this user that might be useful to you, and

"Color" enables you to define a unique color for the icon that will represent this user.

Figure 6.6 User Template

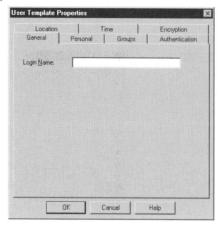

Figure 6.7 User Personal Properties

We will discuss user groups next, so let's move to the Authentication tab. Earlier, we discussed the various authentication schemes, both internal and external, available in FireWall-1. In a template, authentication can also be left undefined, meaning that you will define authentication for each user you create, rather than globally for all users defined via this template.

Next is the Location tab, as in Figure 6.8.

The location tab enables you to restrict both the sources and destinations that are acceptable for this user. Defining a source means that the user will only be permitted to authenticate if their connection originates from the network object(s) you define. Defining a destination means the user will only be permitted to access the object(s) you specify. Note that you can also control the objects a user is permitted to access via the standard rule base.

Figure 6.8 User Location Tab

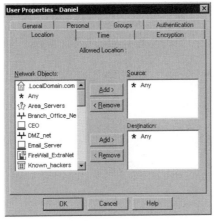

If you would like the user to have access to all objects, be sure to specify **Any** for both source and destination. Otherwise, by default, the user will not have access to anything if these are left blank.

In addition to location-based restrictions, you also have the option of defining time-based restrictions via the Time tab, as in Figure 6.9.

Figure 6.9 User Time Tab

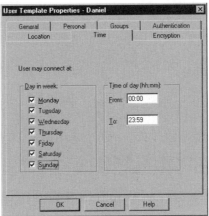

Here, you can define both the days of the week as well as the times of the day that the user is permitted to authenticate. This can be useful to provide increased security, since you can ensure that a user's account is only available when you know they will be attempting to authenticate.

Finally, let's look at the Encryption tab, as in Figure 6.10.

Figure 6.10 User Encryption Tab

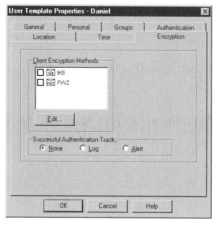

FireWall-1 enables you to choose one of two available client encryption schemes: IKE and FWZ. Note that you can enable both here, in which case the actual encryption scheme used depends on the settings of the user's VPN client. For each encryption scheme, you can define various properties of that scheme by choosing **Edit**. Here you can also choose how FireWall-1 should track successful authentication attempts.

Now that you have defined a template, you can easily create new users. Back on the main Users screen, simply choose **New** and then the name of your template, in this case **Accounting Department**. You will then see a User Properties screen that is identical to what you configured for the template. Feel free to change any settings that are unique to this user, or if this user follows the template exactly, then all you have to do is enter the login name, possibly a password, and you're done.

Creating Groups of Users

Grouping users is an effective way of aligning users into categories for when adding them to rules. Users are not added to rules individually, but as part of a group, which can consist of one or more users.

To create a group of users, open the Policy Editor and go back to **Manage |
Users**. Select **New**, and choose **Group**. See Figure 6.11.

Figure 6.11 Group Properties

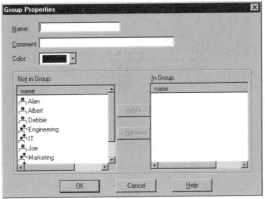

Here, you see a list of all your current users. Select each user that you want to
be a member of the group, and choose **Add**. You will see that user move from
the left side—"Not in Group"—to the right side—"In Group."

In addition to adding users to a group, you can also add other groups to a
group. When you do this, you will be asked by FireWall-1 whether or not you
want to add each member of the group individually, or not. Adding each user
individually means that if you make a change to the group you are adding, that
change will *not* be reflected in the group being added to. If you do not add users
individually, then changes to the group you are adding *will* be reflected in the
group being added to.

User Authentication

User authentication is one of three FireWall-1 authentication types, used to
authenticate users for HTTP, telnet, FTP, and rlogin. This type of authentication
can be used transparently, meaning that the user does not have to invoke a separate connection to the firewall in order to authenticate.

One important aspect of user authentication to note is that there is no facility
to restrict authentication based on source address. This means that if a user's login
credentials are compromised, unauthorized users could use this information to
gain access to your network.

User authentication is available only for HTTP, telnet, FTP, and rlogin
because FireWall-1 proxies all of these connections. This means that you can only

set up user authentication for services for which FireWall-1 has a built-in security server. Also note that since the firewall is acting as a proxy, all traffic will appear to come from your firewall's IP address and any Network Address Translation you configure will not be implemented for these connections.

There are some advantages and disadvantages to using a proxy server. One advantage is that the packet is inspected at the application layer, which means you can open the packet up and view the data. This allows you to utilize third party virus scanners and URL filtering servers (see Chapter 7), which we are not using in your basic user authentication scenario, but you will be able to get more data out of your logs, if you desire to do so. With every User Auth connection, if you specify Long log, the Log Viewer will display their username and the info field will display the exact location of their connection, down to the file they are getting from an FTP connection or the URL they are accessing in their Web browser.

A disadvantage to using a proxy server is that they can easily choke on the data that is presented to them. This is because there are no strict standards in how Web pages are designed, and they are not often checked with any kind of analyzer, which can detect misconfigurations or bad coding. Also, there are different versions of the HTTP protocol (v1.0 or 1.1) and with so many new plug-ins all the time, it's hard to design the perfect proxy server to handle all of these Web sites and varying configurations. A problem arises then, in which a proxy server will not be able to display the content of certain Web sites. This is something that happens to the best of proxy servers, and so far there doesn't seem to be a way to resolve this problem. So, if you are going to implement User Authentication, these are some of the things that you should be aware of before you begin.

To configure user authentication, first define your users in the Policy Editor, under **Manage | Users**, as we discussed above. Your users can be configured with any type of authentication scheme—internal or external—as long as that scheme is enabled in the Authentication tab of your firewall object's properties.

Once your users are defined, and before you can add the users to a rule, you must place them in groups. This is because FireWall-1 does not allow you to add individual users to rules—only groups. If you want to add just one user, simply create a group with only that user as a member. Alternatively, you can use the "All Users" default group, which FireWall-1 has predefined to mean any and all users in the user database. If you use "All Users" in your rule base, then your users do not necessarily need to belong to any groups.

To configure user authentication, create a new rule in your rule base, right-click on the **Source** section, and choose **Add User Access**. See Figure 6.12.

Figure 6.12 User Access

Here, you will see a list of your current user groups. Choose the group you want to add to this rule. You also have the option of setting location restrictions, which will limit the sources from which the user can connect. Figure 6.13 displays the completed rule.

Figure 6.13 User Authentication Rule

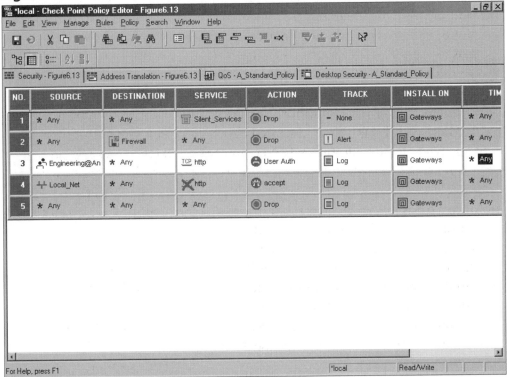

Here, rule number 3 is our user authentication rule. This rule states that all users in the Engineering group, when connecting to any internal host, using service HTTP, must authenticate with user authentication.

One important thing to note is that if there is a less restrictive rule below the user authentication rule in the rule base, the firewall will use the less restrictive rule and will not perform user authentication. For example, if you had an "accept" rule below rule 3 in this example that allowed all traffic from the user's source to any destination, the user would have access without being required to authenticate. This is the only exception that I am aware of where FireWall-1 will not match on a rule in consecutive order as expected.

Next, right-click on **User Auth**, and choose **Edit properties**. See Figure 6.14.

Figure 6.14 User Authentication Action Properties

The purpose of the Source and Destination fields is to resolve any conflicts in configuration between the user database and the rule base. Remember earlier, when we discussed defining users, you had the option of restricting a user's access to certain Source and Destination addresses. You also have the ability to control this aspect of a user's access via the standard rule base. What happens if the two conflict? This setting decides how the firewall should react.

Choosing **Intersect with User Database** means the firewall will match the settings in the user definition and the standard rule base. The connection must match both for the firewall to authorize the connection. Choosing **Ignore User Database** means that the firewall will use the settings defined in the standard rule base alone.

In addition, you have the option here of setting HTTP access to be to "All servers" or "Predefined servers". This setting relates to the settings in the Authentication tab of your firewall object's properties, as in Figure 6.15.

Figure 6.15 Firewall Object Authentication Tab

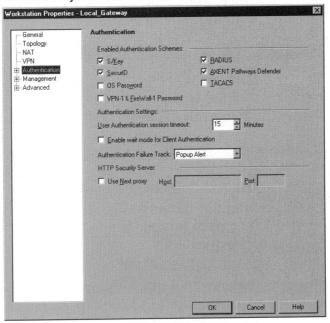

Under Authentication Settings, the value for *User Authentication session timeout* defines how much time may elapse before a user is forced to reenter their login credentials. Back in the User Authentication Action Properties window, setting HTTP access to be to All servers essentially disables the User Authentication session timeout. Setting HTTP access to Predefined servers activates the timeout. Predefined servers would be defined under the **Policy | Global Properties | FireWall-1 | Security Server** window.

Note that these settings apply to both inbound and outbound authentication. If you are going to have users authenticate to external servers on the Internet, which is likely, your only option here is to set the HTTP access in the authentication action properties window to **All servers**, since it is not practical to define each external server users may access. This is a common gotcha when configuring User Auth, since the default setting is Predefined servers.

Once you have configured these settings, you are ready to have your users authenticate with user authentication. Due to the fact that User Auth requires users to authenticate per session, they will need to add the firewall as a proxy server within their web browser's configuration. This will cause their web browser to first hit the firewall, which will challenge the user for their authentication credentials, and if they authenticate successfully, it will then pass the user on to the web server. See Figure 6.16 for the proxy configuration in a Netscape 6.2 browser.

Figure 6.16 Web Browser Proxy Setting

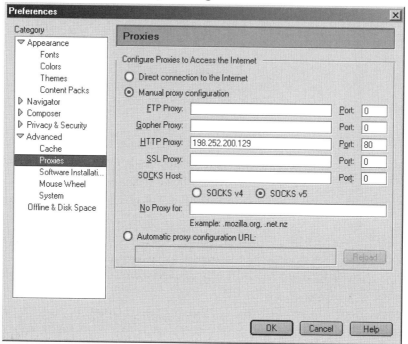

If users do not configure the firewall as a proxy in their web browser's configuration, they can still use user authentication, but they will be asked to authenticate multiple times even when accessing one Web site. This is because, unless the web browser uses the firewall as a proxy, it does not cache the authentication data, and User Auth by nature requires authentication per session. The advantage to this is that if other users gain access to the authorized user's workstation, they will not have unprotected access to the site the original user was accessing. However, the continuous re-authentication may be time consuming and tedious for authorized users. See Figure 6.17 for a preview of User Authentication in action.

Using user authentication for other services, such as FTP or telnet, is done a little differently. In these cases, since the user will not use a web browser to connect, the FTP or telnet client, when transmitting usernames and passwords, will actually get intercepted by the firewall first, allowing it to verify authentication parameters, before passing the connection on to the real destination.

Figure 6.17 User Authentication Prompt

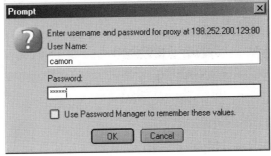

When logging in to an FTP server, users will have to use a special username and password format, so that the firewall understands which username and password is to be used for what purpose. The username is of the format "remote_user@FireWall-1_user@remote_host." For example, to use a remote username of "anonymous," a local username of "Joe," and a remote host of "ftp.checkpoint.com," the user would enter "anonymous@Joe@ftp.checkpoint .com" as their username. When prompted for a password, the password format is remote_password@FireWall-1_password. Check with your FireWall-1 documentation for the syntax for telnet logins.

A practical alternative to using User Authentication and setting the firewall as a proxy in the users' Web browsers is to use Partially Automatic Client Authentication. This will authenticate the user by his or her IP address for a specified period, yet still incorporate the convenience of the User Authentication interface. Another primary advantage that Client Auth has over User Auth is that it does not use the FireWall-1 security servers, therefore, you will not run into any of the problems inherent to running a proxy server, and you can authenticate your users for any service/protocol. Read below for more information on Client Authentication, and how to configure it in your firewall.

Client Authentication

In contrast to user authentication, client authentication is used to grant access based on source address rather than users. Client authentication is also not restricted to any particular service—it can be configured to work with all applications and services.

Client Authentication can be configured to authenticate transparently, like User Authentication does, however, we will first discuss the non-transparent method of using this authentication scheme. In order to authenticate via client authentication using the "manual" method, users must connect to the firewall with either telnet (port 259) or HTTP (port 900). The firewall will challenge the user for username and password and will use the response to determine whether that user is authorized to connect from their source address.

Configuring client authentication is similar to configuring user authentication. Again, the first step is to define your users in the user manager. Then, create a rule in the rule base, as in rule 17 in Figure 6.18.

Figure 6.18 Client Authentication Rule

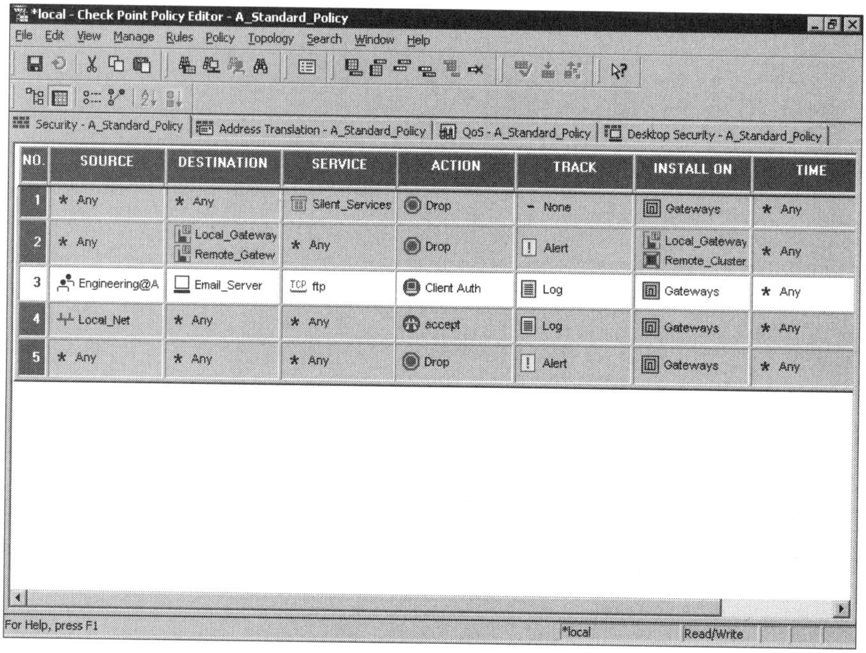

Here, we are allowing all users in the Engineering department, when originating from the "Branch Office Net," to connect via FTP to "Email Server." Just as in user authentication, there are action properties for client authentication, accessed by right-clicking **Client Auth** and choosing **Edit Properties**. See Figure 6.19.

The source and destination options behave the same as they do in user authentication. "Verify secure configuration on Desktop" only applies to users who are using the SecureClient VPN client, which will be covered in chapter 11. This setting ensures that the user's desktop settings are secure as defined by the **Policy | Global Properties | Desktop Security** window.

Figure 6.19 Client Authentication Action Properties

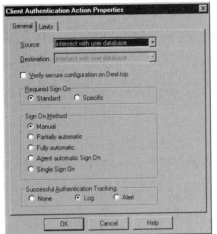

"Required Sign On," when set to "Standard," means that once a user has authenticated one time, they are permitted to access all services, as long as they are allowed to do so according to the rule base. When set to "Specific," users must authenticate again for each new service they attempt to access.

"Sign-On Method" has the following five options:

- **Manual** Users must use either telnet to port 259 on the firewall, or use a Web browser to connect to port 900 on the firewall to authenticate before being granted access.

- **Partially Automatic** If user authentication is configured for the service the user is attempting to access and they pass this authentication, then no further client authentication is required. For example, if HTTP is permitted on a client authentication rule, the user will be able to transparently authenticate since FireWall-1 has a security server for HTTP. Then, if this setting is chosen, users will not have to manually authenticate for this connection. Note that this applies to all services for which FireWall-1 has built-in security servers (HTTP, FTP, telnet, and rlogin).

- **Fully Automatic** If the client has the session authentication agent installed, then no further client authentication is required (see session authentication below). For HTTP, FTP, telnet, or rlogin, the firewall will authenticate via user authentication, and then session authentication will be used to authenticate all other services.

- **Agent Automatic Sign On** Uses session authentication agent to pro-vide transparent authentication (see session authentication below).

- **Single Sign-On System** Used in conjunction with UserAuthority servers to provide enhanced application level security. Discussion of UserAuthority is beyond the scope of this book.

Once you have configured Client Authentication in your Policy Editor, then you are ready to start authenticating your users. As we mentioned before, your users can connect to the firewall to login or logout. Even if you have configured one of the automatic sign on methods, your users can still use one of the manual methods, if they wish. Figures 6.20 and 6.21 illustrate the standard sign-on method using telnet on port 259 to the firewall.

Figure 6.20 telnet to Firewall on Port 259

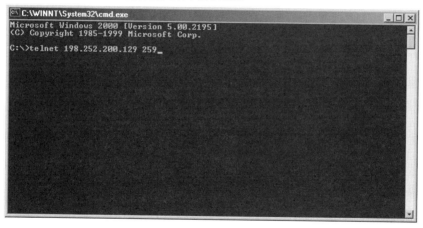

Figure 6.21 Client Auth Standard Sign-On

1. First your users will telnet to the firewall on port 259. For example:

   ```
   telnet 172.16.1.1 259
   ```

2. Next your users will enter their username and password to authenticate to the firewall.

3. Once a user has successfully authenticated, they are presented with three choices to either use the Standard Sign-on method, which allows them to use any rules and any services that were configured in the Policy Editor Rule Base. They could choose to Sign-off, which would de-authorize them and log them out of the firewall. Finally, they could choose the Specific Sign-on method, which allows them to authenticate for specific services to specific hosts. When a user selects option (3) Specific Sign-on, the firewall will prompt them for the service they wish to use i.e. ftp, and then will prompt them for a Host: i.e. ftp.checkpoint .com. Once they are done, they must enter <CTRL-D>, and then they will be authorized for the specific services, which they specified.

The alternative to a telnet session is to have your users use their Web browser to authenticate to the firewall on port 900. See Figures 6.22, 6.23, 6.24 and 6.25 for the screens your users will be presented with if they choose this method instead.

1. First your users will type in the firewall's IP address, then a colon, then 900 for the port they wish to connect on. For example, http://172.16.1.1:900.

2. Next your users will be presented with the first login screen for Client Authentication show in Figure 6.22.

3. After submitting their username, they will be prompted for their password as in Figure 6.23.

4. Once they enter this information, they will be authenticated and presented with their Sign-on options. They may choose Standard Sign-on (default), Sign-off to logout or Specific Sign-on as illustrated in Figure 6.24.

5. Finally, they will see one more screen that verifies the option they selected has been activated as seen in Figure 6.25 for the Standard Sign-on method. Now they may begin using the firewall for the services in which they are authorized to use.

Figure 6.22 Client Auth Port 900 User Prompt

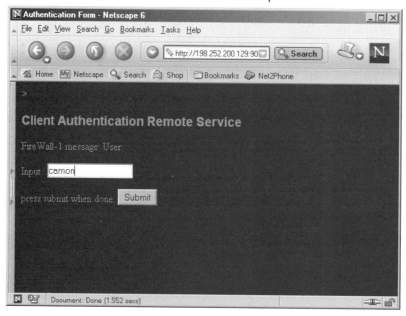

Figure 6.23 Client Auth Port 900 Password Prompt

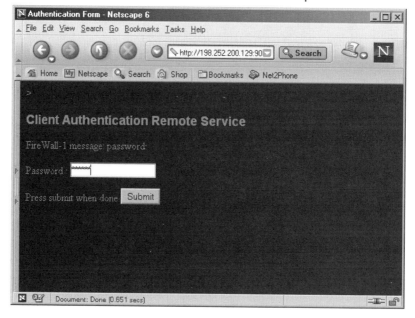

Figure 6.24 Client Auth Port 900 Standard Sign-on

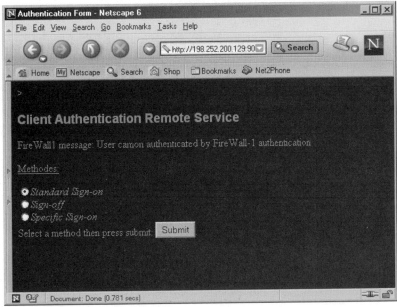

Figure 6.25 Client Auth Port 900 Authorized

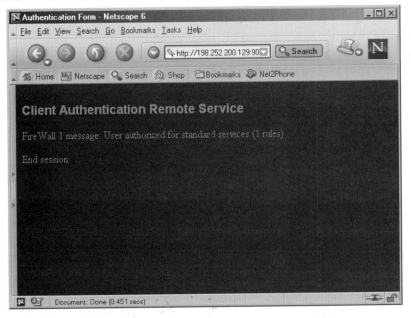

Client Authentication versus User Authentication

Client Authentication gives you many advantages over User Authentication. First of all, you will not be invoking the firewall's built-in security servers; therefore, you will not have any of the problems inherent to using a proxy server for your connections. Also because of the absence of the security servers, you can authenticate any protocol or service with Client Auth, giving you greater flexibility in granting users access. Client Auth also gives you the ability to transparently authenticate users via the User Authentication interface if you configure it for Partially Automatic in the User Auth Action Properties window within the Rule Base. Table 6.1 compares various aspects of user authentication and client authentication.

Table 6.1 Client Authentication versus User Authentication

Authentication Property	User Authentication	Client Authentication
Restrict on source IP	No	Yes
Restrict on Username	Yes	Yes
Transparent	Yes	Optional
Services Available	HTTP, FTP, telnet, rlogin	All

Session Authentication

The third type of authentication available is session authentication. Session authentication enables you to grant users access to any service, without requiring them to originate from the same source IP.

In order to accomplish this type of authentication, the user must run a session authentication agent on a Windows PC. This agent is responsible for receiving the authentication request from the firewall, prompting the user for their login credentials, and transmitting that information back to the firewall. This means that you must install the Session Authentication Agent on each workstation that will need authentication. As you can see in Figure 6.26, the Session Authentication Agent can be installed from the Check Point Next Generation CD under the Mobile/Desktop Components option. This application does not require any special licensing in order to utilize it.

Figure 6.26 Session Authentication Agent Installation from CD

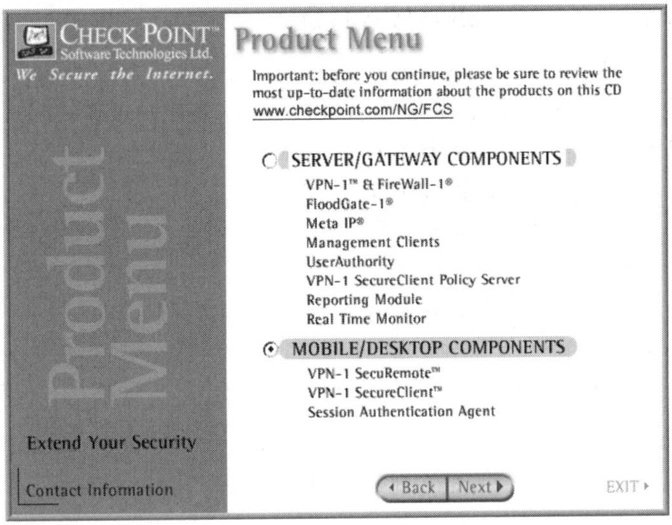

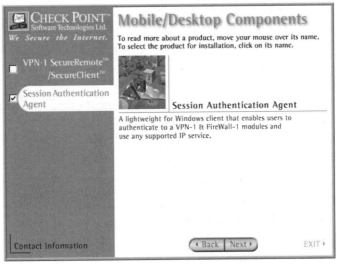

After you select the Mobile/Desktop Components and click **Next**, you will need to choose the Session Authentication Agent software as illustrated in Figure 6.27. After this, the installation will proceed without needing much more input. The only question that you'll need to answer is whether to install to the default destination folder or not.

Figure 6.27 Session Authentication Agent for Windows

Configuring session authentication within the VPN-1/FireWall-1 Policy Editor is similar to configuring client or user authentication. First, ensure that your users are configured in the user manager. Then, add a rule to the standard rule base as in rule 3 in Figure 6.28.

Figure 6.28 Session Authentication Rule

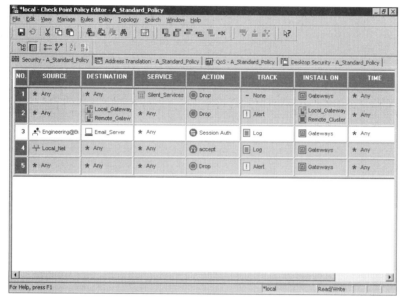

Here, the rule is similar to our previous rule for client authentication. Note that it is not required to restrict session authentication to a service, which is also the case for client authentication. Again, there are action properties available for session authentication, accessible by right-clicking on the **Session Auth** icon and choosing **Edit properties**. See Figure 6.29.

Figure 6.29 Session Authentication Action Properties

Source and destination behave just as they do in client or user authentication. "Contact Agent At" enables you to specify where the authentication agent is running. In general, the agent will be running on the user's workstation, which is located at the source of the connection, so this setting should be left as "Src." In special cases, when the authentication agent is installed elsewhere, you can specify that location via this setting.

"Accept only if connection is encrypted" enables you to reject connections, even if the authentication information is valid, unless the user is connecting over through an encrypted VPN connection.

"Query user identity from UserAuthority" enables you to integrate session authentication with a UserAuthority server.

Once you have configured Session Authentication in your Policy Editor and installed the Session Agent on your users' workstations, then you are ready to start using it. The agent is running if you see the blue icon with the yellow and green arrows pointing right and left respectively in the bottom right hand corner of your Windows Desktop. You can bring up the Session Auth Agent configuration by double clicking on this icon. The default setting on the Passwords tab is illustrated in Figure 6.30. In this window, you can configure the frequency with which a user will be prompted to authenticate.

Figure 6.30 Session Auth Agent Password Configuration

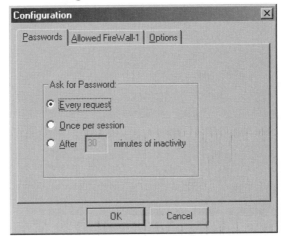

The agent can also be configured to accept authentication requests from only certain FireWall-1 modules. The first time a request comes in from a new firewall, the agent will prompt the user to verify that they are connecting to the correct firewall (Figure 6.33). Once they accept the firewall's IP, then it will be displayed in the Allowed FireWall-1 tab in Figure 6.31.

Figure 6.31 Session Auth Agent Allowed FireWall-1

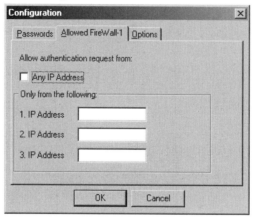

The final configuration tab available for the agent is the Options tab. This tab, shown in Figure 6.32, will determine whether clear passwords will be allowed and whether addresses should be resolved.

Figure 6.32 Session Auth Agent Options

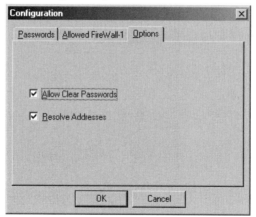

So now your user has the agent installed and configured. Now they try to bring up their Web browser and connect to the Internet. The first thing that will happen is the firewall will query the session authentication agent on the client's PC. The client will receive a pop up window asking them if they want to communicate with your firewall at a given IP as shown in Figure 6.33.

Figure 6.33 Session Auth FireWall-1 IP

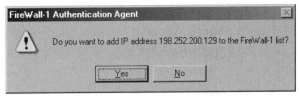

If they accept the firewall's IP address by clicking **Yes** here, then their session auth agent will prompt them for their username and password as seen in Figures 6.34 and 6.35.

Figure 6.34 Session Auth User Login

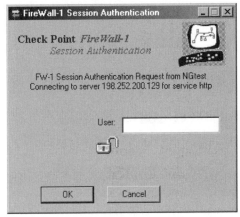

Figure 6.35 Session Auth Password

When they are finished entering their login info, then they click **OK**. The authentication agent will verify with the firewall that the user is authorized to make the connection. If this succeeds, then the user will see a screen like that in Figure 6.36, and then their connection will be allowed through.

Figure 6.36 Session Authentication Successful

Session Authentication versus Client and User Authentication

Like Client Authentication, Session Authentication does not require the use of the FireWall-1 security servers. Therefore, you can configure session authentication to work with any services/protocols. The biggest disadvantage to using Session Auth or the other methods is the fact that you have to install an authentication agent on each and every machine you wish to grant access from, and the agent is only supported on Windows. You can use the Session Agent with Client Auth if you enable Fully Automatic or Agent automatic Sign On in the rule base action properties. Table 6.2 compares various aspects of session, client, and user authentication.

Table 6.2 Session Authentication versus Client and User Authentication

Authentication Property	User Authentication	Client Authentication	Session Authentication
Restrict on source IP	No	Yes	No
Restrict on Username	Yes	Yes	Yes
Transparent	Yes	Optional	Yes

Continued

Table 6.2 Continued

Authentication Property	User Authentication	Client Authentication	Session Authentication
Services Available	HTTP, HTTPS, FTP, telnet, rlogin	All	All
Agent required	No	No	Yes

LDAP Authentication

LDAP, or the Lightweight Directory Access Protocol, is used for a bevy of purposes. With regards to FireWall-1, this server object is used for the purposes of user management. Although setting up an LDAP server is outside the scope of this book, we will guide you in implementing the use of an LDAP server in your FireWall-1 user authentication environment.

To begin configuring LDAP in FireWall-1, open the Policy Editor, go to **Policy | Global Properties | LDAP**, as in Figure 6.37.

Figure 6.37 LDAP Properties

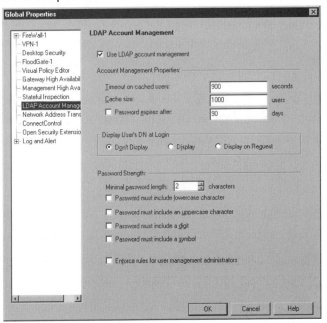

Here, check **Use LDAP Account Management**, which indicates that you plan to use the Account Management functionality in FW-1. You can adjust the timeout if required, and modify the cache size depending on the number of users you plan to have. If you would like to force users to change their passwords periodically, check **Password Expires After**, and specify a number of days.

Only normal passwords will expire. Pre-shared secret passwords, such as those used with the IKE encryption scheme, do not expire, no matter what you choose for this setting.

For **Display User's DN at Login**, choose the following:

- **Don't Display**, if you *do not* want the distinguished name (DN) to be displayed to users after they log in.

- **Display**, if you *do* want the DN to be displayed to users after they log in.

- **Display on Request**, if you only want the DN to be displayed to the user after they log in if they request this information.

Displaying a DN at login is important if you would like your users to verify that the account they are attempting to login to actually belongs to them. There may be some cases where, because of duplicate names, users may be confused unless they are permitted to see the full DN.

The password strength settings enable you to specify how secure your users' passwords must be. It is always a good idea for users to choose hard-to-guess passwords, and these settings allow for them to do so by using uppercase, numeric, and symbolic characters.

Checking the **Enforce rules for user management administrators** means that all the previous settings also apply to administrators, in addition to normal users. This is a good idea; administrators should not be exempt from proper security practices!

Now that you have configured the general LDAP settings, you need to create an LDAP account unit object, as described in the next section. You will then be able to manage external users directly from the Policy Editor. Previous versions of FireWall-1 used a separate Account Management Client (AMC), but in NG this tool has been incorporated into the Policy Editor for even easier Account Management.

LDAP Account Unit

To configure LDAP in FireWall-1, you need to set up an LDAP Account Unit. To do so, open the Policy Editor and go to **Manage | Servers | New | LDAP Account Unit**. Figure 6.38 illustrates the *General* panel for LDAP configuration.

Figure 6.38 LDAP Account Unit Properties

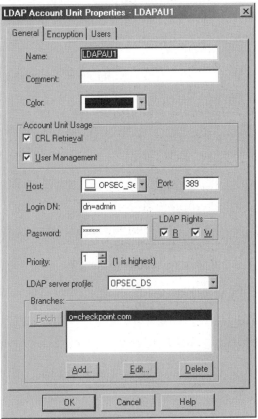

Aside from the four common fields, you have some specific options to select. First, you must specify the Port on which the LDAP server is listening, and the distinguished name (Login DN) that will be used to bind (connect) to the account unit and the password that will be used. Also, in the section labeled *LDAP Rights* you will need to select the rights that this login will attempt to assume (R for read and/or W for write). Note that if **W** is checked, then users will be able to update their VPN-1/FireWall-1 passwords via this account unit.

You'll also need to specify the **LDAP server profile** from the drop-down list to facilitate the proper communication between the firewall and the LDAP server. Check Point's LDAP now supports Microsoft Active Directory, choose Microsoft_AD here if you are configuring the LDAP server to communicate with an Active Directory server. The other options in this window are Netscape Directory Server or OPSEC Directory Server.

The final task on this tab is to select the **Branches** that will be searched within the LDAP server. If you fail to fetch the branches from the server, you may Add them into the Branches: window yourself.

The **Encryption** tab (Figure 6.39) is used when connecting with a server over SSL, and has some specific options available if this need should arise for you.

Figure 6.39 LDAP Account Unit Encryption Tab

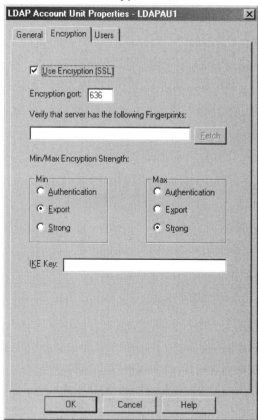

Note that if **CRL Retrieval** is selected within the **Account Unit Usage** section, you'll only have to specify a host, port, and branches for a proper config-uration. If, however, you select **User Management**, then you'll have a third panel to configure. Note that User Management is available only if **Use LDAP Account Management** is checked in the **LDAP** tab of the Global Properties window (shown in Figure 6.37). If selected, you will see a Users tab. This panel, illustrated in Figure 6.40, is used to define basic parameters for user authentication via LDAP.

Figure 6.40 LDAP Account Unit Users Tab

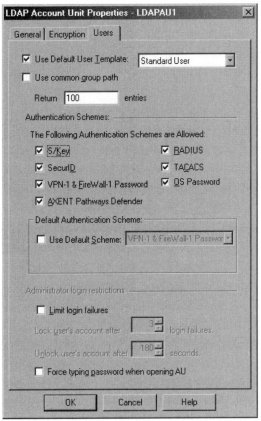

The first section of this panel offers two checkboxes: Use Default User Template and Use Common Group Path. The default user template is used to "fill in the blanks" when using a third-party LDAP server for user management. Since an LDAP server does not offer all of the information needed to describe a user, this feature allows the combination of the VPN-1/FW-1 information with the LDAP information to form a complete user definition. Note that user specific information should not be included in this default template, only generic data.

Next, you must select from among the supported authentication methods. These are the following:

- S/Key one time passwords
- SecurID
- OS Password
- VPN-1/FW-1 Password
- RADIUS
- AXENT Pathways Defender
- TACACS

You also have the option of specifying a default scheme. This default scheme is used when no other authentication scheme is defined for the specific user within the account unit. This option will not be available if you decide to use a default user template, since authentication information will be part of that template.

The next section is Administrator Login Restrictions. This section enables you to enhance the security of your system by supplying some parameters designed to limit the effectiveness of a brute force or other password-cracking attack. These parameters are as follows:

- **Lock user's account after** Specify the number of failed attempts before an account becomes blocked out.
- **Unlock user's account after** Specify the time (in seconds) that the account will remain locked out.

LDAP Administration

There are a few more points that we should touch on in this section before we cut you loose to configure LDAP in your FireWall-1 user authentication environment. First of all, we need to explain about schema integration between Check Point and the LDAP server. Then we will explain how simple it is to manage LDAP users from the Check Point Policy Editor.

Schema Configuration

If you plan to create or manage users on you LDAP server through the Check Point Policy Editor, Check Point has several proprietary attributes for LDAP schema. When you are first configuring your firewall with an LDAP server, you will need to disable schema checking in the directory server so that it won't complain about all the proprietary Check Point attributes, which are not defined in the directory schema. If you have upgraded to NG and you had updated your LDAP server with the Check Point schema before, then you will need to do it again because NG has added a few new attributes such as:

- fw1userPwdPolicy
- fw1badPwdCount
- fw1lastLoginFailure
- memberoftemplate

Some of the object classes were changes as well. You can always enable schema checking later, once you have imported the new attributes and classes into the LDAP server directory.

In order to update the schema for the Netscape Directory Server, you should first take a full backup of the LDAP directory server before you begin. There is a file in the $FWDIR/lib/ldap directory called update_schema.ldif which will add the new attributes, remove the old object classes and insert the new object classes. Use the ldapmodify command to import the new schema.

In order to update the schema for a Microsoft Active Directory server, you should first take a full backup, and then you need to modify a registry entry before you can make any changes to the schema. Choose the HKLM\System\CurrentControlSet\Services\NTDS\Parameters and add a new DWORD key named "Schema Update Allowed" with a value of "1". Next you will need to delegate control of the directory server to a user or administrator, by default administrators do not have the ability to manipulate the directory. Finally, you can add attributes to the Microsoft Directory server after you reboot. You can use the schema_microsoft_ad.ldif file (the file is called update_schema_Microsoft_ad on a Unix firewall) located in $FWDIR\lib\ldap to populate the Microsoft AD server with the Check Point attributes and classes with the ldapmodify command.

For more information on setting up LDAP schema and other LDAP configurations, please read the User Management Guide available on Check Point's Web site at http://www.checkpoint.com/support/downloads/docs/firewall1/ng/UserMgmt.pdf.

Managing LDAP Users

Managing LDAP users is very similar to managing internal VPN-1/FireWall-1 users. You manage users by opening the Policy Editor, and going to the Users tab in the Object Tree window. From here, you will see your LDAP account unit. Begin by double clicking on the name of the account unit, or you can right–click on it and select **Open**.

Now you will see the LDAP branch that you will be managing. Right click on the branch name and select, **Create The Object**. Once you do this, you will now be able to manage users under this branch. Right click on the branch name again and select **New | New User** to create a new LDAP user. See Figure 6.41, the general tab allows you to configure the user's login name.

Figure 6.41 LDAP User Properties

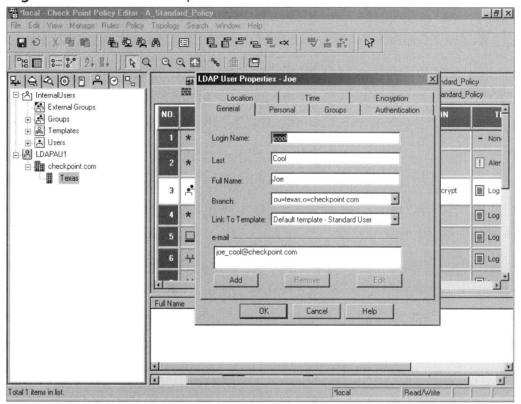

The Personal tab is illustrated in Figure 6.42. Each of these LDAP tabs will allow you to choose to use the information from the template listed on the General tab, or you can specify certain information for each specific user separately here. The default setting is to use the template for all. Figures 6.43, 6.44, 6.45, 6.46 and 6.47 take you through each LDAP user configuration screen. Notice that they are almost exactly the same as a standard Check Point user screens.

Figure 6.42 LDAP User Personal Tab

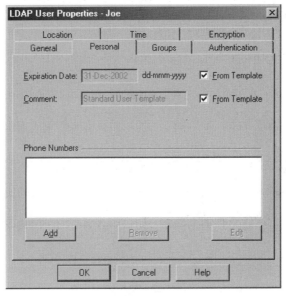

Figure 6.43 LDAP User Groups Tab

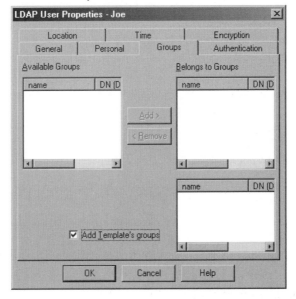

Figure 6.44 LDAP User Authentication Tab

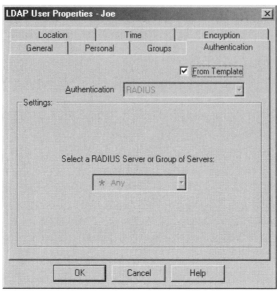

Figure 6.45 LDAP User Location Tab

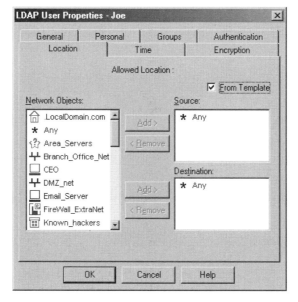

Figure 6.46 LDAP User Time Tab

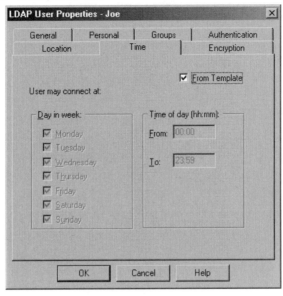

Figure 6.47 LDAP User Encryption Tab

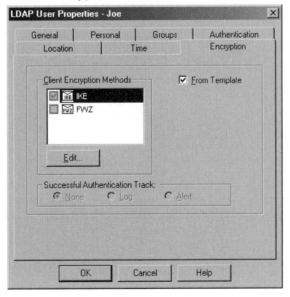

If you need to import users from FireWall-1 to an LDAP server, you may do so by using the **fw dbexport** command utility with the following options:

```
fw dbexport -l [-d delim] [-a {attrib1, attrib2, ...}] -s
subtree [-f file] [-k IKE-shared-secret]
```

This will create an LDIF format file, which you can use to import users into your LDAP server. This is a text file, so you may modify the file before you import it into your LDAP server using the ldapmodify command. For more information on importing and exporting LDAP users, please read the User Database Management section of the NG FP1 Check Point Reference Guide available online here: www.checkpoint.com/support/downloads/docs/firewall1/ng/CPRef.pdf.

Summary

Authenticating users in a reliable, consistent, yet straightforward manner is key to the success of your security policy. No matter how secure the rest of your policy is, you need the ability to authenticate users so that only those who are authorized to access specific resources are given that access.

The various authentication schemes we discussed provide you with different ways of challenging users for their credentials, providing the firewall with a means of determining if they are who they say they are.

Some of the schemes are very simple, such as FireWall-1 password, which simply requires a username and password for successful authentication. Others, such as S/Key or SecurID, present more elaborate challenges to the user before granting access.

Schemes can also be divided into internal and external. Internal authentication schemes, such as FireWall-1 password or S/Key, are based entirely within FireWall-1; they do not interact with any external servers to provide their services. In contrast, external authentication schemes, such as RADIUS or TACACS, query servers outside the firewall to obtain the information they require to authenticate users.

To use these authentication schemes, you must create a database of users. This can be done within FireWall-1, as we discussed when we looked at the FireWall-1 user manager, or you may choose to integrate FireWall-1 with an LDAP server. Using LDAP to integrate an external database of users is especially useful in cases where other components of your network also require access to the user database.

FireWall-1 provides for three types of authentication: user, client, and session. User authentication is used to authenticate users transparently for HTTP, HTTPS, FTP, telnet, and rlogin. Client authentication is more flexible—it works for all services—but is not necessarily transparent. Users must manually authenticate via telnet or HTTP before they are granted access. Session authentication also works for all services, and is transparent, but requires an extra piece of software on the client's end: the session authentication agent.

Another method for managing users is by utilizing an LDAP directory server. Check Point integrates well with Microsoft Active Directory, Netscape Directory Server, and other OPSEC certified directory services. Having a central user database, and the ability to manage those users from within FireWall-1 gives you the flexibility to easily integrate and extend your user authentication to the firewall.

Now that you are familiar with all of FireWall-1's authentication schemes, user-management functions, and authentication types, you will be able to ensure that authorized users have straightforward access to your network, while still protecting your environment from unauthorized users.

Solutions Fast Track

FireWall-1 Authentication Schemes

☑ FireWall-1 authentication schemes include S/Key, FireWall-1 Password, AXENT Pathways Defender, RADIUS, TACACS, and SecurID.

☑ Each user you want to authenticate uses one of these authentication schemes.

☑ Before you can use any scheme, it must be enabled in your firewall object's authentication tab.

Defining Users

☑ Defining users enables you to make use of the authentication schemes mentioned at the beginning of this chapter, as well as decide upon several other useful properties for each user.

☑ All users in FireWall-1 are defined via templates. Templates are also a convenient way to eliminate having to define the same user properties repeatedly; you define the user properties once, and create subsequent users with the same settings by simply choosing that template.

☑ You can use the commands **fw dbimport** and **fw dbexport** to import and export users from the FireWall-1 user database.

User Authentication

☑ User authentication works only for HTTP, HTTPS, FTP, telnet, and rlogin.

☑ It does not require any additional software on the client end.

Client Authentication

☑ Client authentication works for all services, but is not transparent.

☑ Client Auth can be configured with Partially Automatic authentication in order to prompt the user for their login ID and password.

☑ Users must use telnet on port 259 or HTTP on port 900 to authenticate to the firewall prior to being granted access. No additional software is required on the client end.

Session Authentication

☑ Session authentication also works for all services, and is transparent.

☑ The session authentication agent must be running on the client end, which communicates with the firewall and provides authentication credentials.

LDAP Authentication

☑ LDAP can be integrated into FireWall-1 to enable you to have an external user database for authentication.

☑ To configure LDAP, set up your LDAP server, ensure that it is operating properly, and then add an LDAP Account Unit to your list of Servers.

☑ Be sure to disable schema checking when you are first configuring the firewall to communicate with an LDAP server. You can later import the schema with the ldapmodify command and the appropriate LDIF file from $FWDIR/lib/ldap.

Frequently Asked Questions

The following Frequently Asked Questions, answered by the authors of this book, are designed to both measure your understanding of the concepts presented in this chapter and to assist you with real-life implementation of these concepts. To have your questions about this chapter answered by the author, browse to **www.syngress.com/solutions** and click on the **"Ask the Author"** form.

Q: I don't want to use a single-phase authentication scheme, but my users are getting confused with S/Key. What are my options?

A: You may want to consider using SecurID. Outfitting your users with SecurID tags will simplify their authentication process, while still providing a dual-phased authentication approach.

Q: I am using external authentication schemes, and it seems redundant to have to define all my users in FireWall-1. How can I get around this?

A: Create a default user, called "generic*." This avoids the requirement of creating all users locally as well as externally.

Q: I am receiving the following error in my Web browser after configuring User Auth: "Error 407" "FW-1 at <firewall>: Unauthorized to access the document." Then it continues to say:

- Authorization is needed for FW-1

- The authentication required by FW-1 for <username> is: <Password method>

- Reason for failure of last attempt: <Password method> not supported

A: This means that you did not configure your firewall's workstation object with the authentication method defined for this user. You should also have a reject message in your Log Viewer, and the info field will read "reason: <Password method> not supported on gateway". Edit your firewall object, and go to the Authentication configuration window and enable the authentication schemes. After making changes, you must install your security policy.

Q: I'm using User Auth in the rule base, so why do my users keep getting prompted for authentication over and over again in their Web browsers?

A: Configure your users' Web browsers to point to the firewall as a proxy server for HTTP connections. User Auth requires that each session is authenticated, but if you use the proxy setting, the user's Web browser will cache their password until the next time they run the browser. You may want to consider Partially Automatic Client Auth as a feasible alternative.

Q: I just got done configuring my firewall as a proxy server in my Web browser. Why do I receive the following error at every Web site I try to visit, "Error: FW-1 at <firewall>: Unknown WWW Server"?

A: You need to configure DNS on your firewall. When you use the firewall to proxy the connection, the firewall uses DNS to resolve the Web site address. If it cannot resolve DNS, then you will receive this error. On Solaris firewalls, you create an /etc/resolv.conf file and enter "nameserver 10.10.10.1" on each line for each DNS server. Then edit the /etc/nsswitch.conf file and add dns to the end of the line for hosts: so that it reads, "files dns".

Q: I'm using User Auth in my Security Policy, so why can't my users authenticate to a web server on the Internet?

A: This is a known problem with using User Auth for HTTP connections. Partially Automatic Client Auth would be a good alternative as it has many advantages over User Auth.

Chapter 7

Open Security (OPSEC) and Content Filtering

Solutions in this chapter:

- **OPSEC Applications**
- **Content Vectoring Protocol (CVP)**
- **URI Filtering Protocol (UFP)**
- **Application Monitoring (AMON)**
- **Client Side OPSEC Applications**
- **Other Resource Options**

- ☑ **Summary**
- ☑ **Solutions Fast Track**
- ☑ **Frequently Asked Questions**

Introduction

Check Point's Open Platform for Security (OPSEC) model enables you to implement third-party vendor applications into your firewall environment. Based on open protocols, the OPSEC model enables vendors to easily design their applications to conform to this standard, and therefore interoperate with the VPN–1/FireWall-1 product.

You may be asking how this can benefit you, so let us provide some examples. The most notable examples are your content filtering options. You can use other vendors' virus scanners that support the CVP protocol (e.g. Aladdin's eSafe Protect Gateway) to easily implement virus scanning of SMTP mail, HTTP, and/or FTP traffic, just by adding some objects and rules to your Security Policy.

Other content-filtering applications use Web site databases, which are broken into categories, so that you can easily block your users from going to adult entertainment sites or to shopping and chat sites while on the job. Several schools that provide Internet access for their young students utilize this technology to prevent them from accessing certain categories that are considered inappropriate for children.

We will talk about other OPSEC applications, and show you how to configure CVP and UFP applications in this chapter, and also how you can use the resources available in Check Point VPN–1/FireWall-1 to implement limited content filtering without needing a third-party application.

OPSEC Applications

Realizing that no single product or vendor could address network security completely, Check Point designed the OPSEC standard to enable security managers to easily extend the functionality of VPN–1/FireWall-1 with third-party applications designed for specific security requirements. By using a standard set of Application Programming Interfaces (APIs) and open protocols, OPSEC applications are able to easily move data in and out of the VPN–1/FireWall-1 infrastructure.

An OPSEC session is defined as "dialog between two OPSEC entities," and usually is between VPN–1/FireWall-1 and a third-party application that performs a specific task on the data received from the firewall. For a list of available applications, check the OPSEC Alliance Solutions Center at www.checkoint.com/opsec.

The properties of the OPSEC session are defined in the OPSEC Application's object properties in the Security Policy Editor database. As you can see in Figure 7.1, there a three major types of OPSEC servers using the CVP,

UFP, and AMON protocols, as well as six client options using the ELA, LEA, SAM, CPMI, OMI, and UAA APIs.

Figure 7.1 OPSEC Application Properties General Panel

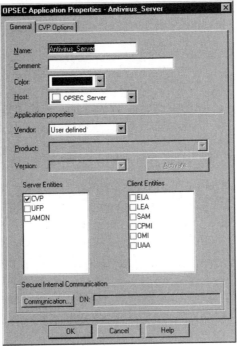

Besides the required naming information, the General panel of the *OPSEC Application* Properties dialog requires you to specify the host that this server is running on. You must create the host object before creating a new *OPSEC Application* object, as you will not be able to create a new workstation object while application properties window is open. You then need to define the application properties, located in the section of that same name. To set the application properties you can select **User defined** from the **Vendor** pull-down menu, and then manually select both the server and client entities, or you can select a specific vendor, product, and version here. Vendors and products available from the Vendor menu include the following: Computer Associates' SafeGate product, Finjan Software's SurfinGate, as well as a variety of solutions from Trend Micro, F-Secure, Aliroo, and Aladdin Knowledge Systems. A complete list of OPSEC certified CVP Vendors/products can be found at www.checkpoint.com/opsec/security.html#Content_Security. After selecting a predefined Vendor from the list, the appropriate Server and Client Entities sections will be filled in automatically.

If you selected **User Defined** from the **Vendor** menu, the next step in defining a new *OPSEC Application* object for use in your Security Policy is to select the **Client** or **Server** entry that matches how the application functions. As shown in Figure 7.1 with **CVP** checked, once you select the appropriate application type, the second tab of the *OPSEC Application* Properties dialog, which contains application-specific communication configuration information, will change to match your selection. Your final step on this panel is to configure SIC, or Secure Internal Communication, by selecting the **Communication** button. Setting up SIC for OPSEC applications is identical to setting up SIC for firewall modules.

Over the next few pages, we'll look at each of these communication methods in detail and hopefully give you a sense for the flexibility and ease of integration that the OPSEC standard offers.

Content Vectoring Protocol (CVP)

Content Vectoring Protocol (CVP) is normally used to move data, such as Web pages or e-mail messages, from VPN-1/FireWall-1 to another server for validation. For example, CVP could be used to move all inbound Simple Mail Transfer Protocol (SMTP) e-mail messages to a content-scanning server that will check for malicious Active-X code. Most commonly, CVP is used to virus-scan file data from e-mail messages or files downloaded from the Internet as they pass through the firewall.

Defining Objects

There are three steps involved in creating a new CVP object to use in your Security Policy.

1. Create a standard *Workstation* object for the server. The *Workstation* object enables you to assign an IP address and name to the server that hosts the application you will be sending data to.

2. Create a new *OPSEC Application* object to define the properties of the service you're enabling. This can be done by selecting **OPSEC Applications** from the **Manage** menu, and then clicking **New,** or by right-clicking in the **OPSEC Applications** tab of the **Object Tree** and selecting **New**, and then **OPSEC Application**. When you complete the General tab of the *OPSEC Application* Properties dialog, you will be using the *Workstation* object you created for the resources' Host. Figure 7.1 above shows the completed General tab.

3. Configure the *CVP* properties, this is done on the CVP panel that appeared when you checked the **CVP** option under the **Server Entities**. The CVP panel is used to define how this application communicates with the firewall. As shown in Figure 7.2, CVP applications only require a few options be set, consisting only of a Service dropdown and an optional directive to utilize backwards compatibility.

Figure 7.2 CVP Panel Options

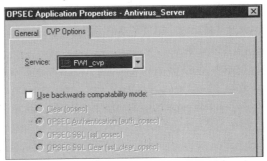

The **Service** selected on the CVP Options tab defines the port on which this application will be listening for connections from the firewall, and is almost always set to FW1_cvp (TCP port 18181). The "Use backwards compatibility mode" section replaces the function of the fwopsec.conf file that was used in the version 4.x of FireWall-1. If your OPSEC vendor has supplied instructions relating to that file, then this is the area you need to implement them. Generally, applications based on the OPSEC Software Development Kit (SDK) version 4.1 or lower will require that you use backwards compatibility.

Creating a CVP Resource

Now that you've defined your OPSEC Application server, you'll want to start sending it data from your Security Policy through a Resource definition. There are four Resource types that can be used in your Security Policy to send data to a CVP Server:

- **URI** Universal Resource Identifier Resources are mostly used to manipulate HTTP requests.

- **SMTP** Simple Mail Transport Protocol Resources enable you to filter and modify e-mail message data as it passes through your firewall.

- **FTP** File Transfer Protocol Resources provide the tools needed to control you users' FTP sessions.

- **TCP** The TCP Resource enables you to work with other Transmission Control Protocol services that are not covered by the other resources.

The Resources listed above are implemented by the VPN-1/FireWall-1 Security Servers. Each Security Server is a specialized module that provides detailed control for specific services. Located just above the Inspection Module in the firewall daemon, the Security Servers have the ability to monitor and manipulate SMTP, Telnet, FTP, and HTTP traffic, providing highly tunable access control and filtering capabilities.

Since each Security Server has full application awareness of the protocols it supports, it is capable of making control decisions based on the data and state of the session similar to how proxy firewalls work. In addition to doing specific content filtering, the Security Servers provide a conduit to send and retrieve data to and from third-party severs, allowing VPN-1/FireWall-1 to use other security applications in the traffic control process.

When invoked by a Resource, the Security Servers will proxy the affected connections. Aside from the possibility of adding latency to the session (normally only measurable on very busy firewalls) and additional load to the firewall, Network Address Translation cannot be used with data allowed (or dropped) using Resources. Since the firewall must proxy the connection, all data will appear from the address of the firewall that is closest to the server

To help understand how CVP servers can be used as part of the Security Policy, let's look at how to integrate virus scanning into the Security Policy. Later on, we'll examine in detail how FTP and other resources match data streams that we can send to our CVP server, but for now let's just look at how to set up a simple FTP resource that enables users to retrieve files from the Internet and scans those files for viruses before sending them to the user. There are three steps involved in setting up this simple Resource:

1. Create the Resource object by selecting **Resources** from the **Manage** menu, clicking **New**, and then **FTP**. Set up the object name, comment, and color on the resulting FTP Resource Properties dialog. The other two tabs of this dialog will enable you to specify the details for the resource's filter and allow you to send data to the CVP server.

2. Set **Method** to **GET** on the **Match** tab. This instructs the VPN-1/ FireWall-1 FTP Security Server to only allow users to download files via FTP, since uploading would require the use of the PUT command.

3. The CVP tab, shown in Figure 7.3, is the most interesting aspect at this point since it enables you to select the antivirus server object and define how it will function for this resource.

Figure 7.3 FTP Resource CVP Tab

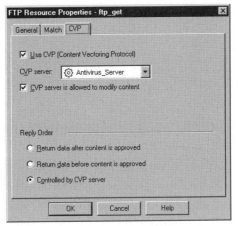

Aside from the **Use CVP** checkbox, which enables the **CVP Server** pull-down menu where you select the server to use, the CVP tab has two other important options that control how the CVP server functions in your resource. The **CVP server is allowed to modify content** check box controls whether or not VPN-1/FireWall-1 will pass on data that has not come back from the CVP server in its original form. This option is particularly useful for virus scanning where an infected file may be sent to the antivirus server and cleaned before being returned. This option would allow the VPN-1/FireWall-1 Security Server (which enforces the FTP Resource definition) to accept the cleaned file. If the **CVP server is allowed to modify content** option was not checked, the antivirus software would only be allowed to report that the file was infected, causing the Security Server to discard the file completely.

The Reply Order option controls when and how the CVP server will scan data being passed to the user. The three options for controlling how data is scanned are listed below.

- **Return data after content is approved**. This option sends the entire file or data stream to the CVP server to be checked after the Security Server has validated the content. In our example, the 'GET' request would be validated before the file was checked for viruses.

- **Return data before content is approved**. Some packets are returned to the Security Server before the CVP server has approved them. This option is especially useful for resources that may deal with large files. Trickling some of the data stream before it has been approved may help stop problems with FTP or HTTP sessions timing out while the CVP server downloads and then checks the requested file.

- **Controlled by CVP server**. The CVP server makes the decision on whether to wait and collect all pieces of a file or data stream before scanning and returning the data to the Security Server or to scan each piece and return the data stream as it's received.

The method used will depend greatly on what function your CVP server performs on the data, and on how the application is designed. In the antivirus server example, the CVP server controls the reply order. This allows the antivirus software maximum flexibility for scanning files and raw data differently if desired, since the application could decide to assemble a complete binary file before scanning, but scan HTML packets individually. Note that your CVP application must support this option, so check the documentation that came with your application before creating the resource to ensure compatibility.

Using the Resource in a Rule

The final step in using a CVP server, after creating the *OPSEC Application* object and using it in a Resource definition, is to build it into a rule in your Security Policy. Creating a Security Policy rule to use a resource is almost identical to creating a normal rule. The only exception is in the service column where, instead of selecting **Add** after right-clicking, you will select **Add With Resource**. Figure 7.4 shows the "add Service with Resource" dialog that enables you to configure the resource to be used in the Security Policy.

The Service with Resource panel enables you to select from the supported Services and define which resource to use with that service. In the case of our virus-scanning example, we'll be using the FTP service with the ftp_get resource. Figure 7.5 shows the completed rule that allows local network traffic to FTP data from the Internet using the resource that limits access to FTP GETs only, and will use the CVP server we defined to virus scan all files before passing them to the user. You'll notice that in the destination field I have used both my local and remote network objects (representing all the trusted networks in my policy), and then I've negated that field. This enables me to control access to known networks separate from access to the Internet as well as to strictly adhere to the security principle of least access. If I had left the destination field set to **Any,** I would have inadvertently opened FTP access to the network represented by the *Remote_Net* object even though my intention was just to allow FTP GETs from the Internet. You will also notice that the icon used in the Service column indicates that we're allowing the FTP service with the ftp_get resource.

Figure 7.4 Service with Resource Dialog

Figure 7.5 Security Policy Rule Using Resource

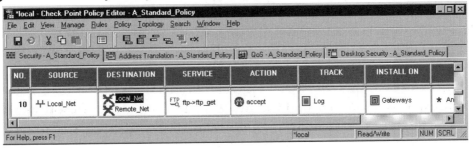

The important thing to remember when using resources is that data is matched or denied on a per-packet basis. You could, for example, select to scan only files of type "*.exe" downloaded via HTTP, with an "accept" rule that uses a CVP resource. However, this will only accept the files downloaded, not the pages you must browse to find the file you want. To make this work, you must specify a rule to match all other HTTP traffic, otherwise the HTTP-browsing traffic will fall through to the Cleanup rule and be discarded.

CVP Group

As with most other objects in the Security Policy, *CVP* objects can be grouped. When you combine two or more OPSEC applications into a group, additional options for load balancing and chaining become available. Figure 7.6 shows a CVP group configuration panel being used to enable load balancing across two antivirus servers.

Figure 7.6 CVP Group Properties

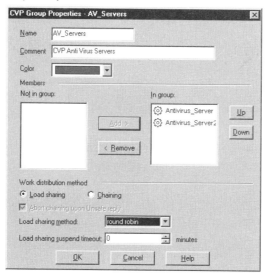

Creating a new CVP group can be done easily by right-clicking in the **OPSEC Applications** tab of the object list selecting **New**, and then **CVP Group**. After defining the group's name, adding a descriptive comment, and assigning the color you want for this object, you'll need to select the servers that will be members of this group. Note that groups don't have to be of identical object types. You can have a group consisting of a UFP server (which we'll look at next) and a CVP server to enable application chaining.

Once the components of the group have been defined, you'll have to select the function of this group by making the appropriate selection in the **Work distribution method** section. You have two choices:

- **Load sharing** When selected, the workload is distributed among the servers in the group. There are two distribution methods allowed: round robin or random.

- **Chaining** Chaining allows a data stream to be inspected by several servers that perform different functions. For example, a chaining group consisting of an antivirus scanner and a Web content scanner could be employed to check your incoming e-mail traffic for viruses and appropriate language. If you select chaining, you'll have an option to abort the chain when any individual server detects a violation, or to allow all the servers to inspect the data before making a control decision.

Once you have the CVP group created, it can be used in the Security Policy to create a Resource rule, just like any other group object would be used to create a standard rule.

Configuring & Implementing…

Load Balancing Chained Servers

CVP Chaining enables you to tie servers with different functions together to apply multiple levels of control to a single data stream. For example, you may chain an antivirus and content filtering server together to inspect and clean files downloaded by your users. Load sharing enables you to spread the work to be done across multiple servers for efficiency and redundancy, but what happens if you want to do both?

You cannot load balance chained servers since load balancing must be done between two or more servers with similar functions, and a chain contains multiple servers all doing different functions. You can, however, chain load balanced servers, enabling you to achieve a similar effect.

Consider that you have two antivirus servers and two content-filtering servers that you want to load balance and chain. To create this, you first must create two URI groups that use load sharing, one for the antivirus servers, and one for the content filters. Then all you need to do is create a third URI group that chains the first two groups together. This provides load sharing between similar servers and enables you to chain the servers together.

URI Filtering Protocol (UFP)

A Uniform Resource Identifier (URI) most commonly defines how to access resources on the Internet. URI Filtering Protocol (UFP) is used to enable passing data between VPN-1/FireWall-1 and a third-party server for URI classification.

The most common example of UFP is to pass HTTP Uniform Resource Locators (URLs) to a server running Websense or a similar product, to check that the requested URL is allowed by your corporate acceptable Internet usage policy. Since the term URI (described in RFC 1630) and URL (RFC 1738) essentially deal with the same thing (especially when discussing HTTP), it is common to see the terms interchanged. Which term you use (URL or URI) is more a matter of preference than being technically correct, as there seems to even be disagreement between the industry standards organizations as to which is correct when.

Defining Objects

Creating an UFP server object is almost identical to creating a CVP object. Both objects require that you define a workstation object with at least a name and IP address for the server and that you use that workstation in the *OPSEC Application* object. Figure 7.7 shows the General tab of the *UFP server* object that enables you to define the application you are using. You can choose from the predefined list that includes vendors such as WebSense, Symantec, SurfControl, Secure Computing, and 8e6_Technologies, or you can use the User Defined option to customize your *UFP server* object. A complete list of UFP applications from OPSEC certified vendors is available at www.checkpoint.com/opsec/security.html#URL_Resource_Management.

The difference in setting up a CVP server compared to a UFP server starts when you select **UFP** (as seen in Figure 7.7) in the **Server Entities** section of the *OPSEC Application* Properties window, which makes the UFP Options panel seen in Figure 7.8 available.

The Service pull-down menu defines which port the UFP service will be listening on; for most UFP applications, this is set to FW1_ufp (TCP port 18182). The Backwards Compatibility options for UFP servers are the same as for the CVP server you looked at earlier, enabling you to configure options that, in previous versions of VPN-1/FireWall-1, were set in the now nonexistent fwopsec.conf file.

Figure 7.7 UFP Server Object General Panel

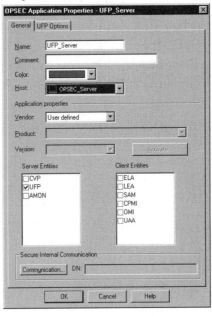

Figure 7.8 UFP Panel Options

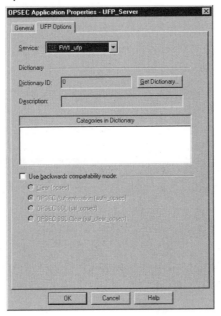

The Dictionary section of the UFP panel will show the category list from the UFP server. In order for the UFP server to function with VPN-1/FireWall-1, the servers' Dictionary ID and category list is required. Once you've set up the server object on the General panel and set the Service to match your UFP Server, you can click the **Get Dictionary** button to retrieve category list and ID number from the UFP server. The category list is displayed here to help you verify that the connection to the UFP server is established and to show you which categories are available on that server, but the categories in this window cannot be manipulated here. To select which categories you would like to filter incoming URLs against, you must create a URI Resource that uses UFP.

Creating a URI Resource to Use UFP

Unlike a CVP Server that can be used with SMTP, TCP, FTP, and URI, a UFP Server can only be used with URI Resources. A URI is made up of two basic parts: a scheme or protocol, and a path. The scheme is the first portion of the URI, located to the left of the colon. Common schemes are HTTP, FTP, TFTP, LDAP, and so on, and can be thought of as a protocol identifier. The remainder of the URI specifies the path to the resource, and often has scheme-dependant syntax. Part of the path may contain a method, such as GET, POST, or PUT, which the UFP server may use to make filtering decisions.

Although the UFP Server actually scans the URL and makes a control decision, it's the URI Resource that tells VPN-1/FireWall-1 where and how to send the URI to be scanned. Figure 7.9 shows the *URI Resource* Properties window that is used to create the resource that will enable you to validate URLs through the UFP Server created above.

Figure 7.9 URI Resource – General Panel

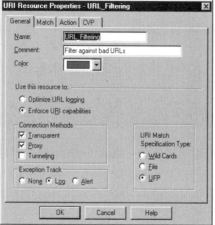

Aside from the generic object identifiers, you have some interesting options for URI Resources to select from. The first is the **Use this resource to:** radio button set, which affects how the URI Resource functions. If you select the first option, all of the remaining options will gray out, and the object will only be used to log HTTP URLs into the VPN-1/FireWall-1 log. In order to use this resource as a conduit to an UFP server, you must select the **Enforce URI capabilities** option, which enables all the remaining configuration choices.

The **Connection Methods** option defines what modes FW-1 will use to examine traffic. If **Tunneling** mode is selected, you will not have access to the CVP tab and will not be able to use any URI filtering or UFP servers, since tunneling only allows the Security Server to inspect the port and IP address information, not the URI that you're interested in. **Transparent** mode is used when the users' browser configuration does not contain proxy server information. In this configuration, the firewall must be your network gateway that handles Internet traffic. As your users request resources from the Internet, the firewall will send the URIs to the UFP server to be checked as part of the Security Policy. In **Proxy** mode, the firewall must be specified in the user's browser as a proxy server. This configuration is very useful if you want to direct Internet service requests (such as FTP and HTTP) to a firewall that is not the default gateway for your network, as the Security Server will provide proxy services to Internet requests. Using the proxy option also enables you to manually load balance your Internet traffic by directing users' traffic to different firewalls, or to separate traffic based on type (for example FTP to one firewall, HTTP to another) if required.

The *URI Match Specification Type* radio group tells VPN-1/FireWall-1 how you want to inspect the URIs matched by this object. We'll be examining the File and Wild Cards options later in the chapter, but for now we're only interested in the UFP option. Once you select the **UFP** option, then the **Match** tab, as seen in Figure 7.10, will provide you with additional UFP options needed to enable the UFP server.

The **Match** tab enables you to select the **UFP Server** to use, as well as set operating parameters to control the interaction between the firewall Security Server and the filtering application. The **UFP caching control** enables you to increase the performance of the URI Resource by reducing the number of URLs sent to the UFP server. There are four caching options.

- **No Caching** With caching disabled, the UFP server is used to check each URI. Although turning off the cache has a negative impact on performance, as every request must be checked by the UFP Server, this option is useful if your UFP server configuration changes frequently and if you want to ensure that each request is filtered using the newest options.

- **UFP Server** This option allows the UFP server to control the caching. The UFP server may choose to check each URL or it may maintain its own cache to speed up the checks.

- **VPN-1 & FireWall-1 (one request)** The VPN-1/FireWall-1 Security Server controls UFP caching. Unique URIs will be sent to the UFP server only once before being added to the cache. This option provides the greatest performance by significantly reducing the number of URIs sent to the UFP server.

- **VPN-1 & FireWall-1 (two requests)** URIs previously checked by the UFP server will be sent a second time before being added to the cache. Reduced performance is traded for the added security of checking each URL twice.

Figure 7.10 UFP Options for URI Resources

The **Ignore UFP server after connection failure** option controls how the Security Server will react if the UFP server is not available to service requests. Leaving this option unchecked can have a severe impact on performance if your UFP server fails, since the Security Server will attempt to send each URI to the failed server, and will not allow traffic to pass until the server responds with an accept message. If this option is unchecked and your UFP server fails, then you most likely will experience a Denial of Service condition, as even acceptable sites cannot be checked. The telltale sign of this condition will be messages in your logs that read, "Unknown error while trying to connect to UFP," and users calling your help desk complaining of a lack of access. Enabling the "Ignore UFP server after connection failure" option enables you to specify the "Number of failures before ignoring the UFP server" option that controls how many attempts are made before considering a UFP server offline. The "Timeout before reconnect to UFP server" value instructs VPN-1/FireWall-1 on how long to wait before considering the connection to the UFP server lost.

The final tab, shown unless **Tunneling** is selected on the General tab, is CVP. As we examined earlier, CVP enables you to hand data off to a third-party server for validation. In addition to the antivirus example we looked at before, CVP servers like Symantec's Igear Web content scanner can provide you with fine-tuned content control for Web applications.

Using the Resource in a Rule

Using a UFP server to validate URIs as part of your security policy is similar to using a CVP server in a resource rule. Using the example from above, scanning URL requests to Internet sites, the final step is to add the URI Resource we've created, which uses the *UFP Server* object, as the resource in a new (or existing) rule. As with the CVP rule we created earlier, the only difference between a rule that uses a resource and a normal Security Policy rule is what is defined in the service column. Instead of selecting the **Add** option for the service, use the **Add with Resource** dialog to enable you to select the URI Resource that contains the UFP Server configuration you need. Figure 7.11 shows the final rule in the Security Policy being used to drop unacceptable data requests. Notice that the Service column shows both the scheme being used (HTTP) and the name of the URI Resource (URL_Filtering).

Figure 7.11 Security Policy Rule Using UFP Server in URI Resource

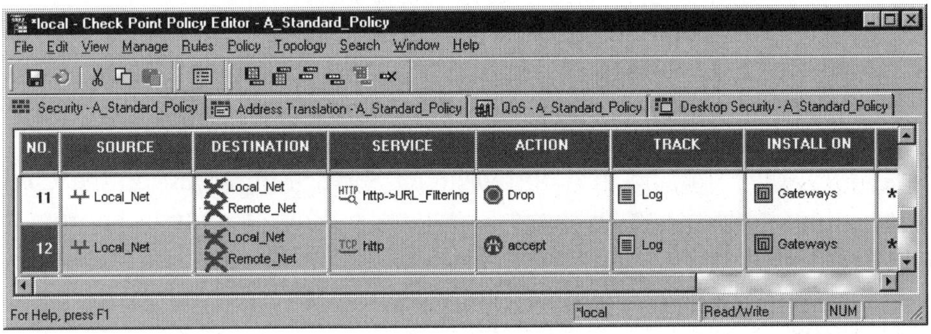

As with CVP Resources, it is necessary to remember that "match" is made on the packet, not the session. For example, with UFP, you will typically create a drop or reject rule to match on the categories you want to disallow. As you can see in Figure 7.11, you must have another rule with which to accept the traffic that you want to allow, or else it will be dropped on the Cleanup or "Drop All" rule. This second rule is necessary because the resource rule only deals with dropping traffic, not with allowing it. You could, of course, use a UFP resource in the rule base to allow based on category rather than drop it, to get around this second rule requirement. The only problem with this approach is that the allowed list is often longer that the drop list, and is therefore is harder to maintain.

UFP Group

A UFP group is similar to a CVP group except that it does not support chaining. The configuration of a UFP group is common with the other generic group configuration screens, in that you enter a name, comment, and select the appropriate color and then simply move UFP servers from the "Not in group" window to the "In group" window.

Your choices for load balancing between servers in a UFP group are either **Random** or **Round Robin**. Using **Up** and **Down** buttons will enable you to change the order in which servers are used in the Round Robin configuration, but since the server being used will change with each incoming session, changing the order will only slightly affect how the object performs. The final option, **Load sharing suspend timeout**, enables you to configure the time to ignore a failed server before attempting to reestablish communication with it. You can set this time anywhere from 0 (ignore the failure, attempt to use server normally) to 10,000 minutes.

Application Monitoring (AMON)

Using OPSEC Applications as CVP and UFP resources in your Security Policy makes those servers an integrated part of your security environment. To allow for easy monitoring of OPSEC products that function alongside of VPN-1/FireWall-1, Check Point developed the Application Monitoring (AMON) API.

AMON is the third and final option under Server Entities list on the *OPSEC Application* Properties dialog (as shown in Figure 7.12), and allows supported applications to report status information to VPN-1/FireWall-1. This status information is then available in the Check Point System Status Viewer alongside the real-time status of your Check Point applications.

Figure 7.12 AMON Application General Tab

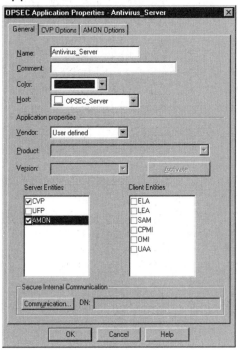

Enabling AMON is as simple as checking the **AMON** option under **Server Entities**, and then setting the **Service** and **AMON Identifier** information on the AMON tab. As seen in Figure 7.13, the **Service** option is usually set to FW1_amon (TCP port 18193), but you should check the documentation that came with your application to ensure that this is the port the application is listening on. The **AMON Identifier** field contains the Management Information Base (MIB) identifier, which also must be provided by your applications' vendor.

Figure 7.13 OPSEC Application AMON Configuration

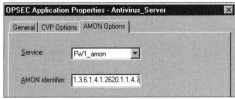

Client Side OPSEC Applications

In addition to the UFP and CVP application servers and the AMON monitoring service, there are six client application APIs that extend the functionality and management of VPN-1/FireWall-1 to third-party applications. Although complete configuration and implementation details for each of the six APIs will be dependant on which third-party application you're using, we'll have a quick look at each to discuss the capabilities of the API and to show the integration options possible for OPSEC certified products.

Event Logging API

The Event Logging API (ELA) allows third-party applications to send log data to the VPN-1/FireWall-1 log database. Sending log data to the central log has two main advantages: log consolidation and alert triggering.

In many networks, the firewall gateways are the security focal point, making the VPN-1/FireWall-1 logs the primary data source for security auditing. By extending the log to third-party products with the ELA, Check Point has enabled you to collect your security logs into a single location, making it easier to analyze and trend your security infrastructure's performance. An added benefit of consolidating logs from other products into the central log is that products using ELA will be able to trigger the VPN-1/FireWall-1 alert mechanism. This allows products like Stonesofts' StoneBeat high-availability solution to send logs and alerts to the Check Point Management Console when a FireWall-1 product has failed over to a standby machine.

Log Export API

To securely and efficiently access the Check Point log database, third-party products can use the Log Export API (LEA). The LEA allows access to the log in a real-time or in a historical access mode. In order to use LEA, the product vendor must write a LEA Client that will access data from the Management Console that is running the LEA Server. Using the LEA Client/Server model, OPSEC Applications reduce the need to try and access the locked, proprietary formatted logs directly or having to export the Check Point logs out to plain text before being able to work with the log data.

For example, products like the WebTrends Firewall Suite can set up a secure connection to the VPN-1/FireWall-1 log database to pull in historical information for report generation. Since LEA supports encryption, you can be assured that the information used to generate the reports was not copied or corrupted during the transfer from one application to another.

Real-time data retrieval using LEA is most useful for generating alerts, based on firewall events, with a non–Check Point application. For example, LEA could be used to funnel firewall events into an Enterprise Security Manager (ESM) product that could correlate data with other security products, to generate trends and alerts based on a bigger view of the security infrastructure.

Suspicious Activities Monitoring

The SAM, or Suspicious Activities Monitor, was designed to provide a method for Intrusion Detection System (IDS) software to communicate with VPN-1/FireWall-1. This provides a method for an IDS application to create dynamic firewall rules to block traffic that the application believes is malicious.

Using a SAM-enabled application allows you to add some level of reflexive access to block previously allowed traffic. The key to realize here is that the access can only be granted with the static Security Policy rules, not the SAM application's dynamic rules. For example, if an IDS system detected something suspicious like a connection attempt to a closed port, it would be able to close all access to all resources from the IP address in question for a configurable period of time. This would block traffic, such as browsing your Internet Web site, that may be explicitly allowed in your Security Policy. The action taken by the firewall is configurable and can include anything from making an entry in the logs, disconnecting a session in progress, or blocking all further access from the offending host. You need to be especially careful when allowing SAM applications to create firewall rules. If not configured properly, you can inadvertently create a Denial of Service (DOS) situation on your own servers. For example, if you block all data from any host that has tried to connect to a closed port for one hour, an attacker may send connection requests to your servers with spoofed IP addresses, to cause your own firewall to block traffic from your customers.

Object Management Interface

The Object Management Interface (OMI) allows OPSEC applications to interact with the Management Server. The OMI has been replaced by the Check Point Management Interface, and has only been kept in NG for backwards compatibility. New applications being developed with the NG OPSEC Software Development Kit (SDK) will use CPMI.

Check Point Management Interface

Replacing OMI in the NG OPSEC SDK, the Check Point Management Interface (CPMI) allows OPSEC applications access to the Management Servers' Security Policy and objects database. This can enable you to use objects already defined with the Policy Editor in other applications. Additionally, this secure interface can provide other applications access to create objects in the VPN-1/FireWall-1 database. The CPMI has three main benefits that OPSEC applications can take advantage of.

- CPMI can allow access to authentication information, enabling vendors to design single sign-on security solutions that take advantage of the authentication information already known to the firewall.

- Access to the Check Point object database can allow for report generation and alerting based on changes to monitored objects.

- Some management tasks can be automated, allowing software products to modify VPN-1/FireWall-1 in response to a security event.

UserAuthority API

The UserAuthority API (UAA) is designed to extend the firewall's knowledge of users' VPN and LAN authentication to other applications. In addition to providing the information that applications need in order to enable a single sign-on model, the UAA can also be used to provide information needed to develop billing and auditing applications that track individual users, instead of just sessions.

The UAA also allows third-party applications to take advantage of the Secure Virtual Network's (SVN) openPKI infrastructure for authentication. This reduces the vendor's need to develop their own authentication methods, which not only speeds development time for new applications, but also ensures compatibility with and leverages the investment in your existing infrastructure.

Other Resource Options

When we examined CVP and UFP resources, we touched on the basics of URI and FTP Resources to show how to use the third-party servers in the Security Policy. URI Resources can be used to filter based on wild-card matches and can be configured using specially formatted files, which you could create or purchase. After covering the remaining URI filtering methods and functions, we'll have a closer look at the FTP Resource that we used in the virus-scanning example earlier, as well as examine Simple Mail Transport Protocol (SMTP) and Transmission Control Protocol (TCP) resources.

The URI, SMTP, FTP, and TCP Resources can be used in the rule base in the same fashion as a normal service (such as HTTPs). The difference is in how the firewall handles the resource. When a packet matches a rule that uses a resource, the connection is handed off to the appropriate Security Server to make a control decision after inspecting the connection's content. This means that the packet must be approved by the Resource before the rule's action will take effect. This is important to keep in mind when creating your rules, as you don't want to waste time virus-scanning files with a Resource that will be dropped by the rule that caused the scan to be performed.

URI Resources

In addition to the Resource we examined earlier (Figure 7.9) to use a UFP server in the Security Policy, there are two other types of URI Resources. URI File Resources enable you to use a specially formatted file to load in complete URL strings, while Wild-Card Resources enable you to create completely custom-match strings that may be as simple as looking for all executable files.

When you select the type of URI Resource you are creating on the General tab, the Match tab will change to offer specific options for that type of object (Wild Card, File, or UFP). We've already looked at the UFP match tab (Figure 7.10), and will examine the File and Wild Card options next, but it's worth noting that regardless of which **URI Match Specification Type** you choose, the Action and CVP tabs remain unchanged.

As we saw when we looked at CVP Servers, the CVP tab (Figure 7.3) enables you to configure the Resources' interaction with the CVP server. The Action tab, shown below in Figure 7.14, enables you to specify some interesting things to further control and filter URI requests. Here you can enter a **Replacement URI**, which redirects the user's session to a site of your choice, if the rule that matches this object sets the action to drop or reject. Many companies use this option to redirect users to the corporate acceptable Internet-use policy when certain blocked URLs are requested.

Limited content filtering is available through the use of **HTML Weeding** on the **Action** tab. You have five options for removing Active X, JAVA, and JAVA Script code from the HTML data.

- **Strip Script Tags** Remove JavaScript information from the selected Web page.

- **Strip Applet Tags**   Remove Java Applet information from the selected Web page.

- **Strip ActiveX Tags**   Remove ActiveX information from the selected Web page.

- **Strip FTP Links**   Remove links destined for an FTP site from the selected Web page.

- **Strip Port Strings**   Remove port strings from the selected page.

Figure 7.14 URI Resource Action Tab

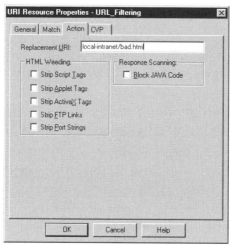

Although removing the above data from the HTML code before the user sees it does reduce the risk of malicious code being sent to your users, the data stripping is non-selective, so all tags are removed. In addition, you have the option, under the **Response Scanning**, to block all Java execution. You need to consider how these settings may reduce the functionality of some pages that could have a negative impact on your users before enabling this type of filtering. To achieve more granular control over these data types, you need to look into the services provided by a good CVP or UFP application.

URI file

After selecting **File** from the **URI Resource Properties** General tab (Figure 7.15), the Match tab will display the import and export options, as seen in Figure 7.16, that enable you to load the match string definitions from disk rather than having to create complicated match strings manually.

Figure 7.15 URI File General Tab

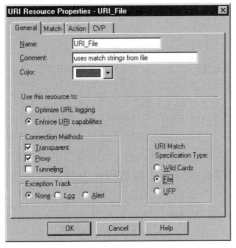

Figure 7.16 URI File Configuration

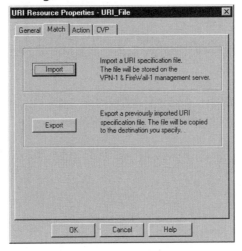

Clicking **Import** will enable you to specify the directory and filename of the file that contains the URIs you want to filter on. The **Export** option will create a file containing the currently filtered URIs.

A URI specification file can be bought from companies that specialize in URL classification, or you can create your own. When creating a URI specification file, be sure to use an ASCII editor that uses a \n as the new line character, as this is the character the Security Server expects at the end of each line. There are three parts to each line in the URI Specification:

- The IP Address of the blocked server.

- An optional path to filter.

- A category number. Although this is not used at this time, it is a required field. Normally, I just set each line to 0 (zero), but you can pick any number you like. Be careful when applying service or feature packs to your firewall, as it is possible that Check Point may start using this field in the future, so you may need to adjust it to an acceptable value.

The completed line will look similar to this: 192.168.0.1 /home 0, which will deny any data request for information under the /home directory on the 192.168.0.1 server. Your firewall will require access to a Domain Name Service (DNS) server if you use the name of the blocked resource rather than the IP Address. Also, note that you could be generating a considerable amount of DNS traffic if you have a busy firewall and are using names rather than IP addresses, since each URI must be resolved before being checked.

URI Wild Cards

When you select the **Wild Cards** option from the **General** tab of the **URI Resource Properties** dialog (Figure 7.17), you are offered several options on the Match tab that will help you build a customized string to search for.

Figure 7.17 URI Wild Card Resource General Tab

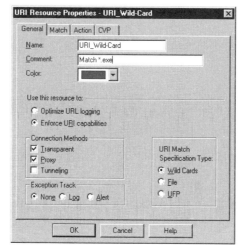

Figure 7.18 shows the predefined check box options available on the Match tab. As well as the commonly used schemes and methods provided, the **Other** option can be used to provide even greater flexibility.

Figure 7.18 URI Wild Cards Match Specification

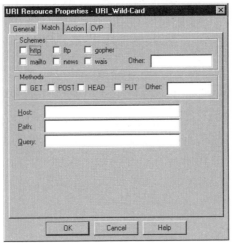

Under the **Schemes** section, you can select from the predefined common schemes of HTTP, FTP, Gopher, mailto, NEWS, and WAIS. If what you're looking for isn't among the six schemes provided, you can specify exactly what you need in the Other field. Most commonly, you'll be entering complete schemes to catch such as HTTPs, but this field also supports wild cards, so you can, if needed, specify something similar to *tp in the Other field. This would enable you to catch any scheme that ended in the string 'tp' such as FTP, NNTP, SMTP, and HTTP, among others. You need to choose your wild cards carefully to ensure that you're not blocking or allowing something that you hadn't intended with a poorly written search string.

Similar to the Schemes area, the Methods section provides the most common HTTP methods in a predefined set of options:

- The GET method is used to retrieve all the information specified by a URI. It is commonly used to download a complete HTML file as part of a Web browser session.

- POST is used to ask the server to accept a block of data, and is usually found in forms to send input from the user back to the server for processing.

- The HEAD method functions almost exactly like GET, except that the entire requested resource is not returned. HEAD is commonly used to validate URL links and to check time and date stamps for modification (normally to see if a cached copy is still current).

- PUT is used to place data (normally files) into the location specified by the URI, and is unlike the POST method, which sends data to an application as input.

The Other field, under Methods, supports the following less-common methods as well as wild cards that can be used to specify a custom pattern to match.

- **OPTIONS** This method can be used to determine the parameters available and supported at a specified URL. The OPTIONS method is commonly used to retrieve information about the server or specific resources without using a method like GET or HEAD that would attempt to retrieve the actual object.

- **PATCH** Functions like PUT except that only a list of changes or differences between the file specified in the URL and the clients' copy is sent. This method is most likely to be found when dealing with large files that only receive small updates, so sending only the changes is more efficient than sending the entire file again.

- **COPY** The COPY method specifies a second URL in the request headers and instructs the server place a copy of the specified resource at the location defined in the headers. This would enable the user to copy data from one server to another without having to download a copy of the data first, and is commonly used if the network between the servers is faster than between the client and the servers.

- **DELETE** Instructs the server to delete the resource (normally a file) specified in the URL.

- **MOVE** The MOVE method will first copy the data to another specified URL then delete the original.

- **LINK** Enables you to create relationships between resources and is similar to the *ln* command on Unix systems.

- **UNLINK** Deletes the relationships created by LINK.

- **TRACE** The TRACE method is normally used for testing and will cause the server to echo back the information it receives from the client.

This enables the client to analyze the information that was received by the server and compare that to what was sent.

The final section of the Match panel enables you to specify the Host, Path, and Query options to match. The host option can be specified by name (such as www.syngress.com) or by IP address. If you specify the host by name, you will need to ensure that the firewall has access to a DNS server to resolve the name to an IP address. You can use wild cards to help build the pattern to match if needed.

The path option must include the directory separation character (normally /) in order for a match to be made. When you define the path to match, you must specify the complete path, down to the individual file, or use wild cards to match all files or directories. Table 7.1 shows common strings used in the path field and how they will match to incoming data.

Table 7.1 Path Field Search Examples

String	Results
/home	Will match a file called home in any directory. For example: /home and /mysite/mydir/home would both be matched. In either case, if home was a directory, no match would be found.
/home/*	This pattern will match all files and directories under the home directory. For example, /home/index.htm and /home/files/index.htm would be matched.
/home/	This will match any URI that contains the directory home, so files in /home would be matched as well as files in /mydir/home/mysite.
*/index.htm	This will match the file index.htm in any directory.
/.mp+	This pattern will match three character file extensions that start with "mp," such as mp3 and mpg.
/.{exe,zip,gz}	Will match all files that end in .exe, .zip, and .gz in any directory.

The Query field can be used to match on any string of characters found after a question mark (?) in a URL. Since wild cards are supported here as well, it is not necessary to know the exact placement of the key words you are looking for in the query. For example, this will enable you to block or redirect searches for keywords that are in violation of your Internet acceptable-use policy.

When working with URI Resources, it is common to use a single asterisk in the three match fields (Host, Path, and Query) so that all possible requests can be matched. However, when using CVP servers, it is often useful to do specific file matching with wild cards in the patch field to ensure that only supported data types are sent to the server to be scanned.

SMTP Resources

The SMTP resource defines the methods used by FW-1 to control and manipulate incoming and outgoing e-mail. There are many options, including the ability to remove active scripting components, rewriting fields in the envelope (such as to: or from:), or filtering based on content. The configuration of a SMTP Resource is similar to that of URI Resources, including the ability to use a CVP server to provide third-party content filtering. Figure 7.19 shows the General panel of the *SMTP Resource* Properties window that is used to set basic operational parameters for the resource.

Figure 7.19 SMTP Resource General Panel

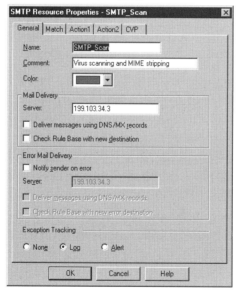

This panel includes the standard initial object setup of name, comment, and color. You also should specify the name or IP address of a server for mail delivery, if you want to simply forward all messages to another server or enable the "Deliver messages using DNS/MX records" to allow the security server to deliver the message directly. The **Check Rule Base with new destination** option can be used to instruct the Security Server to recheck the SMTP message's destination server against the Security Policy after being modified by the

SMTP Resource. Identical settings are available for the handling of error mail messages if the option to **Notify sender on error** is selected.

The Match tab, shown in Figure 7.20, has only two option fields that control how to match messages being examined by the Security Server. The Sender and Recipient option fields are used to define the addresses you want to work with. Wild cards are supported in these fields to provide the ability to specify all addresses (using ★) or all users in a specific domain (with ★@domain.com) if needed.

Figure 7.20 SMTP Resource Match Tab

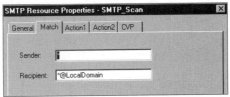

When you create a new SMTP Resource, the Sender and Recipient fields are blank, and must be filled in before the Resource will function. You need to be careful with these options, though; it's common to just set the Recipient field to an asterisk to save time. You need to keep in mind that the Resource defines how the Security Server will function, and by placing an asterisk in both the sender and recipient fields, you could be allowing external hosts to bounce mail off your firewall. This makes your firewall into a "open relay" for SMTP traffic, and aside from the possibility of your server being used to send unsolicited bulk e-mail (spam), many domains and even some ISPs may refuse to accept SMTP traffic from your domain if it's known that you have an open relay. For information on blocking open relays from your domain, or checking to see if you've become blacklisted, check an open relay database site such as www.ordb.org.

The Action1 tab has only a few simple options that enable you to re-address messages and change limited content. The Sender and Recipient address rewriting fields enable you to re-address messages on a single-user basis, or, by using wild cards, translate addresses for an entire domain. The Field option enables you to modify data in any of the other standard SMTP fields such as the carbon copy (cc), blind carbon copy (bcc), or subject. Once you've specified the field to change, you need only specify the string to look for, and what to replace it with. Shown in Figure 7.21, this tab is very useful if you have recently changed your SMTP domain name but still have a few messages coming to the old domain. Using the simple rewrite options shown, you could easily translate an address joe@olddomain to joe@newdomain.com.

Figure 7.21 SMTP Resource Action Tab Showing Address Rewrite

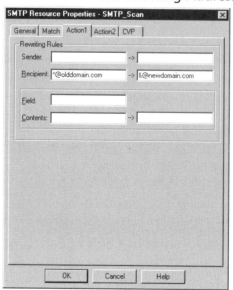

The Action2 tab allows the removal of information found within the body of the message. The "Attachment handling" section of this panel provides two simple methods of discarding attachments from messages. There are seven supported options, as defined in RFC 2046, for removing specific file types for messages with the Strip MIME of type.

- Text
- Multipart
- Image
- Message
- Audio
- Video
- Application

You can use the "Strip file by name" field to remove files based on a pattern, using wild cards if needed, rather than by Multipurpose Internet Mail Extension (MIME) type. I find that this field is often used to stop "zero day" or new viruses and worms that spread via e-mail. It's often faster to start the firewall filtering the attachment name (once known) of a new virus, than updating the virus signatures throughout your entire enterprise. If nothing else, this function will buy you enough time to update your signatures properly while you block new infections from entering (or leaving) your network. The next section of the Action2 panel, seen in Figure 7.22 for reference, enables you to control the maximum message size and the allowable characters in messages (either 7- or 8-bit ASCII). The Weeding section enables you to remove JAVA, JAVA Script, Active X, FTP URI links, and Port strings from the message's headers and body.

Figure 7.22 SMTP Resource—Action2 Panel

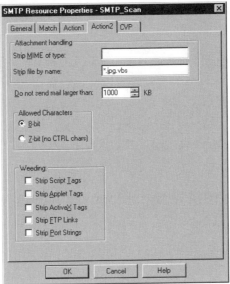

One common mistake made when creating SMTP Resources is not checking the **Do not send mail larger than** field. By default, the messages larger than 1000 KB will be dropped. Many attachments will be larger than this limit of just under one megabyte. Aside from irritating users, failing to check this option often results in e-mail administrators spending hours troubleshooting lost SMTP messages, since the Security Server will discard the entire message.

The CVP panel of the SMTP Resource Properties window provides the standard options we discussed when examining CVP Servers. The only exception, as noted in Figure 7.23, is the addition of a single SMPT-only option to **Send SMTP headers to CVP server**. This option enables you to have the CVP server scan the messages full headers in addition to the message body.

Figure 7.23 SMTP Resource CVP Tab

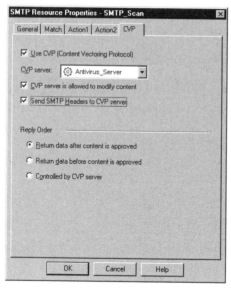

FTP Resources

We looked at FTP resources briefly when we first examined CVP servers. In addition to enabling you to send FTP data streams to another server for content filtering, FTP Resources can be used without a CVP server to just control FTP sessions.

The *FTP Resource* Properties, General tab (Figure 7.24,) enables you to specify the normal *VPN-1/FireWall-1* object information, but the interesting options (aside the CVP tab) are on the Match tab.

Figure 7.24 FTP Resource General Tab

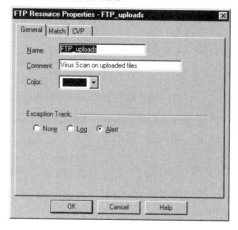

The Match tab, shown in Figure 7.25, contains three options that enable you to control the actual FTP session. The Path field enables you to specify specific file paths, using wild cards if desired, to perform actions on. The most interesting, and useful, part of the FTP Resource is the next two options: GET and PUT, since they enable you to control FTP functions. Using these options will enable you to control the commands that your users can issue to remote servers. Allowing your users to GET but not PUT will prohibit them from pushing data out of your network, while still allowing them to download files as needed. Allowing PUT but not GET would be a good solution for a publicly accessible FTP server used to receive files from your business partners, since they could upload files to you, but could not download anything.

Figure 7.25 FTP Resource Match Tab

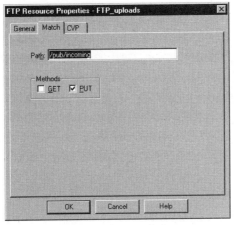

The FTP Resource CVP tab enables you to specify a CVP server to send matched data to, and defines the interaction between the FTP Security Server and the CVP Server. Similar to the example you looked at when examining CVP server objects, Figure 7.26 shows how to virus-scan incoming files. By enabling the **CVP Server is allowed to modify content** option, you have allowed infected files to be cleaned. If this option were unchecked, any infected file would be discarded.

TCP

The TCP Resource enables you to work with services not handled by built-in Security Servers, and has only two methods of operation. You can use the TCP Resource as a generic daemon, providing an alternative to the HTTP Security Server, for interaction with a CVP server.

Figure 7.26 FTP Resource CVP Tab

Additionally, you can use the TCP Resource to screen URLs via a UFP server without the intervention of the Security Server. Note that the UFP server must support this sort of interaction, as the format of its incoming data stream will not be in full URI format, as only the IP-based URL is available without the Security Server. The TCP resource has three possible panels, with only two being displayed. The **Type** option on the **General** tab (Figure 7.27) enables you to select either **UFP** or **CVP**, and controls which second panel is offered for configuration.

Figure 7.27 TCP Resource General Tab

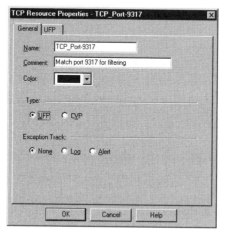

After checking **UFP** on the **General** tab, you can then select the **UFP** tab (shown in Figure 7.28) and configure the associated panel. The UFP configuration on this panel is similar to other resources that use UFP Servers. You need only to select the UFP server that this resource will be using, configure the caching method, and select the categories against which this data stream will be checked from the supplied list.

Figure 7.28 TCP Resource UFP Tab

If you select **CVP** on the **General** tab, you will be presented with the CVP tab (Figure 7.29) that will enable you to configure the resources' interaction with the CVP server. You will need to specify which CVP server to use from the drop-down list on the CVP panel. The other options on this panel are identical to the CVP objects you've looked at before, and will enable you to configure options, such as whether the CVP server is allowed to modify the content passed to it, and to specify the method in which data is returned to the Security Server.

Figure 7.29 TCP Resource CVP Tab

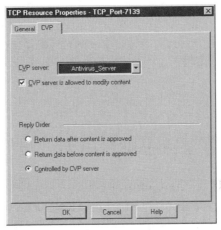

Summary

Check Point's OPSEC standards program certifies that third-party applications meet minimum integration and compatibility requirements with the VPN-1/FireWall-1 products. This, in essence, extends the reach of your VPN-1/FireWall-1 security infrastructure to encompass areas where highly specialized or customized solutions are required to meet the needs of your network.

Through the use of CVP and UFP application servers, you are able to extend the information used by VPN-1/FireWall-1 to make data-control decisions to include input from third-party solutions. In addition to providing you with greater flexibility, this enables you to build best of breed solutions into your firewall from vendors that specialize in the task you need to perform.

Content Vectoring Protocol is used to send an entire data stream, such as a downloaded file, to another server to be validated either as a whole or in parts. This validation can be as simple as checking the file for viruses or using image recognition software to discard images that may not be acceptable in your environment. In many cases, such as a virus scanner, the CVP server may modify the data before returning it to the Security Server to be passed along to its final destination. CVP objects can be grouped together to share load among servers performing a similar function, or servers can be chained together to perform multiple actions and validation checks on the data before returning it to the firewall.

URI Filtering Protocol is used to check the scheme and path of data resource requests. UFP is most commonly used for HTTP traffic to control access to sites that may not be appropriate in a corporate setting, but can also be used with other protocols. UFP servers enable you to choose from predefined categories to specify which sites are to be filtered or denied from the data requests passing through the firewall. UFP applications often come with a subscription service that will provide updates to the database of sites and categories known to the product, as well as enabling you to specify your own so that your protection is kept up-to-date. As with CVP Resources, you can group UFP servers together to provide high availability and load sharing among servers providing the same service. You cannot, however, chain UFP servers together.

The Application Monitoring (AMON) API is new for the NG version of VPN-1/FireWall-1, and provides a method for third-party servers to report status information to the firewall products. This enables you to monitor the status of other security devices using the Check Point, or other vendor tools that you're already using to keep an eye on your firewalls.

OPSEC Applications can also access VPN-1/FireWall-1 information and resources by using one of the six client APIs provided.

- Log Export API (LEA)

- Event Logging API (ELA)

- Suspicious Activities Monitor (SAM)

- Object Management Interface (OMI)

- Check Point Management Interface (CPMI)

- UserAuthority API (UAA)

These client applications are not normally used in the data control process as OPSEC Servers are, but often make use of the status, log, and object databases to report on and manipulate VPN-1/FireWall-1 devices and applications.

There are four major types of resources in VPN-1/FireWall-1: URI, SMTP, FTP, and TCP. URI is the most common and offers the greatest flexibility, since URI resources can be created using wild cards or from specially formatted files that define the pattern to match on. Most commonly, URI Resources are used with CVP or UFP servers as a method to move data between the Security Policy and third-party servers.

SMTP Resources enable you to manipulate e-mail messages and provide a method to replace or substitute information in certain fields as messages pass through the firewall. FTP resources enable you to control FTP sessions down to the level of being able to specify whether users can issue GET or PUT commands, as well as the ability to stop users from accessing specific paths on the server. Both SMTP and FTP Resources support using CVP servers to validate data coming into or leaving your protected networks. The TCP resource enables you to use either a UFP or a CVP server with TCP data that is not handled by one of the built-in Security Servers.

Solutions Fast Track

OPSEC Applications

☑ Using third-party OPSEC Certified applications enables you to build onto your existing Check Point security infrastructure to address specific security needs, while ensuring compatibility and interoperability.

☑ There are three types of OPSEC Server applications: CVP, UFP, and AMON. UFP and CVP servers interoperate with VPN-1/FireWall-1 by passing data back and forth and participating in the control process, whereas AMON is used by other applications to report status information back to the firewall management server.

☑ OPSEC Client applications, as a general rule, either send data to or pull data from VPN-1/FireWall-1, and generally do not affect the control process directly as servers do. There are six methods for OPSEC Clients to send or receive data from VPN-1/FireWall-1: LEA, ELA, SAM, OMI, CPMI, and UAA.

☑ ELA allows third-party applications to send log data to the VPN-1/FireWall-1 log database for consolidation and alerting functions.

☑ LEA provides a method for applications to extract, historically or in real time, log data from the central log database.

☑ SAM provides a conduit for IDS devices to signal and make changes to the current Security Policy, such as blocking traffic from a specific host.

☑ The OMI provides support for legacy applications that need to access the VPN-1/FireWall-1 object database.

☑ CMPI replaces OMI in the NG version of VPN-1/FireWall-1. CPMI allows applications to access the object database as well as authentication information known to the firewall. CPMI also provides the needed APIs to allow third-party applications to make limited changes to the Security Policy.

☑ The UAA can be used to access VPN and LAN authentication information from VPN-1/FireWall-1. This allows applications to be designed to use existing logon information to provide single sign-on capabilities.

Content Vectoring Protocol (CVP)

☑ CVP is normally used for sending data, such as binary files or e-mail messages from VPN-1/FireWall-1, to a third-party server to be scanned. The results of the scan have a direct impact on the control decision for that data, which can include blocking the data entirely or just modifying it to an acceptable format (in the case of removing a virus).

☑ CVP Resources are created using an *OPSEC Application* object as the server to send data to, and contain configuration settings for what actions the CVP server is to perform on the data.

☑ CVP Groups enable you to load share between servers or chain multiple CVP servers together to perform different tasks one after another.

☑ Load sharing splits the incoming work to be done evenly among the defined servers, using the method that you specify.

URI Filtering Protocol (UFP)

☑ A Uniform Resource Identifier (URI) describes how to access a resource and is made up of two parts. The scheme defines which protocol (such as HTTP) to use and is separated by a colon from the path to the desired resource.

☑ UFP can be implemented through the use of URI Resources in the Security Policy, and enables you to examine and filter URIs passed from the VPN-1/FireWall-1 Security Servers as part of the control decision.

☑ UFP is commonly used to verify that requested or returned URLs conform to an acceptable standard, by classifying URLs into categories and enabling you to choose which categories are permissible in your environment.

☑ UFP Groups enable you to share load between multiple UFP servers to increase efficiency and provide availability, if a UFP server should fail.

Application Monitoring (AMON)

☑ AMON allows supported applications to report status information to VPN-1/FireWall-1. This status information is then available in the Check Point System Status Viewer alongside the real-time status of your Check Point applications.

☑ Enabling AMON is as simple as checking the **AMON** option under **Server Entities**, and then setting the **Service** and **AMON Identifier** information on the AMON tab.

Client Side OPSEC Applications

☑ In addition to the UFP and CVP application servers and the AMON monitoring service, there are six client application APIs that extend the functionality and management of VPN-1/FireWall-1 to third-party applications. These include:

- Event Logging API

- Log Export API

- Suspicious Activities Monitoring

- Object Management Interface

- Check Point Management Interface

- UserAuthority API

☑ Complete configuration and implementation details for each of the six APIs will be dependant on which third-party application you're using.

Other Resource Options

☑ URI File Resources allow you to use a specially formatted file to define the URIs that you want to filter on. This option is commonly used when you have many URIs to filter but do not want to use a UFP server.

☑ URI Wild Cards enable you to build a completely customized URI string to match to incoming data. The flexibility of wild cards enables you filter on a specific file extension or even specify entire IP address blocks.

☑ SMTP Resources enable you to inspect and modify e-mail traffic passing through your firewall. You can, for example, modify sender or recipient information in addition to the data within the body of the message. It is also possible to perform limited screening for potentially malicious content by removing Active X and/or JAVA code from the messages. For more granular screening capabilities, the SMTP Resource enables you to send e-mail messages, with complete headers, to a CVP server to be analyzed.

☑ FTP Resources enable you to control FTP data streams. In addition to looking for certain paths or file names being requested, you can control when and where your users can use the FTP GET and PUT commands to control data moving into or out of your network.

☑ The TCP Resource enables you to send data from TCP protocols not covered by the normal Security Servers to a CVP or UFP server for inspection.

Frequently Asked Questions

The following Frequently Asked Questions, answered by the authors of this book, are designed to both measure your understanding of the concepts presented in this chapter and to assist you with real-life implementation of these concepts. To have your questions about this chapter answered by the author, browse to **www.syngress.com/solutions** and click on the **"Ask the Author"** form.

Q: My URI Specification file looks okay, but it doesn't work properly. What should I look for?

A: There are three major parts to each line in the URI Specification file. After you've entered the IP address, path, and category, you must end each line with a new line character (\n). If you use a Windows-based computer to build your file, ensure that you use an editor that uses only \n when you end a line. The WordPad application or Edit (run from a cmd.exe window) will create the file properly, whereas the Notepad application may not.

Q: What are the valid wild-card characters?

A: There are only four characters that can be used as wild cards in resource definitions, such as a URI Wild Card object:

- The asterisk (*) can be used to match any number of characters.
- The plus sign (+) can be used to match a single character only. For example, '+tp' will match 'ftp' but not 'http.'
- The ampersand (&) can only be used with SMTP addresses and enables you to manipulate information on either side of the @ symbol for address replacement objects. For example, changing from "jim@yoursite.com" in an object to "&@yournewsite.com" results in "jim@yournewsite.com."
- A list of strings may be separated with commas (,) to match any one of the specified strings. The case of "hr,sales," "@yoursite.com" will match "hr@yoursite.com" and "sales@yoursite.com."

Q: What OPSEC applications are available?

A: The list of OPSEC certified applications grows everyday. At the time of this writing, there are over 300 certified OPSEC vendors, each with one or more certified applications. This means that when you're looking for a third-party product to fill a specific security need in your organization, odds are that there is an OPSEC-certified one available. The current list of OPSEC certified products and vendors can be found at www.checkpoint.com/opsec.

Q: How do I block the latest virus that is spreading today?

A: If the virus is spread through http/ftp downloads and/or through e-mail attachments, then you can use FireWall-1 resources to block these connections. Using the Nimda virus as an example, you could use the SMTP file and/or MIME stripping to match MIME attachments of type "audio/x-wav" and the filename of "readme.exe." Then use a URI wild-card resource to match HTTP, GETs to any host and any query match. Fill in the Path field with the following string: {*cmd.exe,*root.exe,*admin.dll,*readme.exe, *readme.eml,default.ida}. Then just use these resources in rules that drop or reject the connections. For more information on blocking Nimda, see Check Point's public knowledge base (support.checkpoint.com/public) article sk7473.

Q: Why do my users receive the error, "FW-1 Unknown WWW Server," intermittently?

A: If your firewall cannot resolve the Web site name to an IP (DNS), then it will present this error when a Web browser has the firewall defined as a proxy. Sometimes other problems with the HTTP security server may result in this error as well. You may want to try some of the objects_5_0.C changes below or contact support for assistance.

Q: My users are complaining that they cannot connect to certain sites and they are receiving the following message: "Web site found. Waiting for reply..." All of these sites seem to include a double slash in them. Is there a problem with the firewall?

A: If the site your users are trying to access contains a double slash within in the URL GET command, then the GET command does not conform to RFC 2616 standards (according to Check Point), and the security server will not allow a connection. Your only option (if you must pass the site) is to bypass the security server by creating a HTTP-accept rule specifically for this destination above any HTTP resource rules defined in your FW-1 Security Policy. See Check Point's public knowledge base article skI3834 for more information.

Q: In FireWall-1 4.1, there were several objects.C file modifications for the HTTP security server that resolved several problems. Are the same changes available in NG?

A: Yes, most of the changes that you implemented in 4.1 can be used in NG as well. To edit the objects_5_0.C file, you need to use the dbedit utility in NG. Some changes are as follows.

```
:http_disable_content_type (false)

:http_disable_content_enc (true)

:http_enable_uri_queries (false)

:http_max_header_length (8192)

:http_max_url_length (8192)

:http_avoid_keep_alive (true)
```

These are the default settings that are in the objects.C file in NG HF1:

```
:http_allow_content_disposition (false)

:http_allow_double_slash (false)

:http_allow_ranges (false)

:http_avoid_keep_alive (false)

:http_block_java_allow_chunked (false)

:http_buffers_size (4096)

:http_check_request_validity (true)

:http_check_response_validity (true)

:http_cvp_allow_chunked (false)

:http_disable_ahttpdhtml (false)

:http_disable_automatic_client_auth_redirect (false)

:http_disable_cab_check (false)

:http_disable_content_enc (false)

:http_disable_content_type (false)

:http_dont_dns_when_star_port (false)

:http_dont_handle_next_proxy_pw (false)

:http_failed_resolve_timeout (900)

:http_force_down_to_10 (0)

:http_handle_proxy_pw (true)

:http_log_every_connection (false)
```

```
:http_max_auth_password_num (1000)
:http_max_auth_redirect_num (1000)
:http_max_connection_num (4000)
:http_max_header_length (1000)
:http_max_header_num (500)
:http_max_held_session_num (1000)
:http_max_realm_num (1000)
:http_max_server_num (10000)
:http_max_session_num (0)
:http_max_url_length (2048)
:http_next_proxy_host ()
:http_next_proxy_port ()
:http_no_content_length (false)
:http_old_auth_timeout (0)
:http_process_timeout (43200)
:http_proxied_connections_allowed (true)
:http_query_server_for_authorization (false)
:http_redirect_timeout (300)
:http_servers (
        :ers ()
        :Uid ("{6CAC812A-202F-11D6-AB57-C0A800056370}")
)
:http_session_timeout (300)
:http_skip_redirect_free (true)
:http_use_cache_hdr (true)
:http_use_cvp_reply_safe (false)
:http_use_default_schemes (false)
:http_use_host_h_as_dst (false)
:http_use_proxy_auth_for_other (true)
:http_weeding_allow_chunked (false)
```

Chapter 8

Managing Policies and Logs

Introduction

In this chapter we will strive to give you some basic firewall administrator knowledge and show you how to administer this enterprise security software package, VPN-1/FireWall-1 Next Generation, so that it doesn't get too big for you to handle. It's very easy for several administrators to be involved in policy development and manipulation, but if you have too many people involved in a security system such as a firewall, then you need to keep strict vigilance and record who is making changes when and why. Otherwise, you could end up with a misconfigured firewall, which could compromise the security it is meant to provide.

Besides monitoring administrator activities, you should also keep software up-to-date. You should frequently check Check Point's Web site for the latest security patches and software updates. Sometimes these updates require you to modify configuration files or to stop and start your firewall services, and we will discuss how to go about doing that in this chapter.

We will cover performance related to your security policy and logs, and discuss what to do when you have multiple firewalls in various locations. Then we'll tell you about your firewall's log files, and give you some ways to administer your logs so that you don't run into disk space issues. We'll equip you with several command line options that you can use when performing maintenance or troubleshooting on your firewall.

As a Check Point NG administrator, you have three main goals with respect to administration. They are as follows:

- **Performance** Because the Check Point NG firewall is the point that all traffic flows through when going to or from the unprotected to protected network, performance is critical. A poorly performing firewall will get quick complaints from users and eventually from your boss.

- **Effectiveness** The effectiveness of the firewall is a vital concern. If the firewall isn't doing its job at controlling and monitoring access, it isn't any good. In fact, an ineffective firewall could open your organization up to multiple vulnerabilities.

- **Recovery capability** Because the Check Point NG firewall is such a crucial piece in your network architecture, forget about rebuilding a firewall from scratch to its pre-crash state, duplicating the many rules and properties from memory. You need to be able to recover your configuration and security policy quickly and effectively should a disaster strike.

Administering Check Point VPN-1/ FireWall-1 NG for Performance

With FireWall-1 NG, Check Point has made a number of improvements over previous versions. One major improvement is with INSPECT XL, which is responsible for evaluating packets based on rules. The new version of INSPECT XL is supposed to be optimized and much more efficient because it uses only one state table, as opposed to earlier implementations that used multiple state tables. Despite these improvements, ensuring that your firewall is performing up to your expectations as well as everyone else's is important. There are a number of "best practices" that you should keep in mind when configuring and administrating your firewall to ensure that Check Point NG performance is at its optimum.

Configuring NG for Performance

There are a number of things that you can do when initially configuring FireWall-1 NG so that it provides optimum performance for your environment.

- Use hosts files on management servers and remote enforcement modules.
- Disable decryption on accept.
- Modify logging Global Properties.

The recommendation, to use hosts files, should be part of every installation. To clarify, every time you install a policy, the management station must resolve its name to an IP address and each of the enforcement modules it is installing policy onto. By using hosts files, the host will parse the hosts file first for IP address mappings and not make a network query. This will speed up the install of security policy. On Unix systems, the hosts file is located at /etc/hosts. On Windows NT/2000 the hosts file is located at %SystemRoot%\System32\drivers\etc. For example, if the name of your FireWall-1 object in the Rule Base GUI is FW_TAMPA, then you must be sure that the name FW_TAMPA is mapped to an IP address in the hosts file. Additionally, let's say that part of your policy installs policy on to a remote firewall name FW_DALLAS. The mapping of FW_DALLAS must also be defined in the hosts file. Here is a sample hosts file:

```
127.0.0.1 localhost
192.168.3.30 FW_TAMPA
192.168.3.20 FW_DALLAS
```

Configuring & Implementing…

NT Name Resolution

Windows NT 4 uses Netbios name resolution to find services on the network. WINS is a dynamic name registration service that a workstation can use to resolve Netbios names to IP addresses. Additionally, the LMHOSTS file located at %SystemRoot%\System32\drivers\etc can be used to statically map Netbios names to IP Addresses. The Netbios name and TCP/IP host name can be two different names on an NT 4 workstation, although this is not recommended. Despite Microsoft's dependence on Netbios names, your FireWall-1 NG relies on TCP/IP host names.

Windows 2000 uses host name resolution to find services on the network. DNS is the network service that a Windows 2000 workstation can use to resolve name to IP addresses. However, the hosts file will always be parsed first; if there is no mapping the host will attempt DNS resolution.

Another setting you can change right off the bat is **decryption on accept**. If you are not using encryption, then you should uncheck **Enable decryption on accept**. This option can be found in Global Properties under the VPN-1 tab, as shown in Figure 8.1. This prevents FireWall-1 NG from attempting decryption of packets even when the rule doesn't require it. Doing so will allow FireWall-1 NG to free up some resources to other tasks.

Other Global Properties that you should consider changing are related to Logs and Alerts as shown in Figure 8.2. Although the default settings are generally effective, depending on your environment you may need to make changes. For example, you can limit the amount of activity that gets logged to the log file by decreasing the Excessive log grace period. This is the period in seconds that FireWall-1 NG will not log the same activity multiple times. Decreasing this number will probably reduce the number of resources that the Log Unification Engine uses to consolidate activity into the log view.

There are also a couple of performance tweaks that will not affect firewall throughput but that have an effect on overall performance. One such setting is the Log Viewer resolver timeout. Decreasing this value will decrease the amount of time in seconds that FireWall-1 NG spends resolving IP addresses to names for log entries. If names are not critical to your understanding of the logs and DNS queries frequently timeout, then this would be good to decrease. This increases the Log viewer, but not the firewall throughput.

Figure 8.1 Global Properties

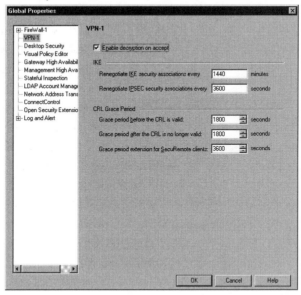

Figure 8.2 Log and Alert Global Properties

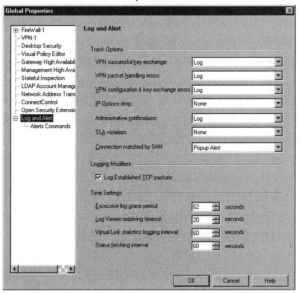

And finally, you can decrease the Status fetching interval to decrease the frequency in seconds that the management server queries the modules that it manages for status. If your environment is pretty static, this could be reduced. Again, this will not affect firewall throughput and will not even be an issue if the System Status window is not open and querying modules.

Administering NG for Performance

In addition to the initial configuration of FireWall-1 NG, there are a number of administration "best practices" that you should keep in mind to ensure that the firewall is performing up to expectations and its capabilities.

- Keep the rule base simple.
- Put the most frequently applied rules near the top of the Rule Base.
- Keep accounting to a minimum.
- Use the active log mode sparingly.
- Use logging wisely.
- Consider limiting the use of security servers.
- Implement NAT wisely.
- Avoid the use of domain objects.

The first recommendation, to keep the Rule Base simple, will probably have the greatest impact on overall performance. Unfortunately, it is the most difficult to define and control. The reason this is so important is because every packet that isn't a part of an existing connection must be evaluated against the Rule Base sequentially, from the top to the bottom, until a match is arrived at. A long, complex policy will introduce latency into the processing of packets, not to mention that a long, complex policy is hard to administer. When making modifications to the Rule Base, you should consider the best way to write the rule and where to place it. For example, instead of writing an extra rule to give FTP to the internal network, if you already have a rule for HTTP, then just add FTP to the HTTP rule. Just remember that there is almost always a simpler way to write rules. Keep the number of rules as low as possible.

Designing & Planning…

Top Performers

On the top end, Check Point has posted a number of top performance numbers for throughput, concurrent firewall connections, and other data. According to Check Point, it is possible to have in between 315 and 765 Mbps in a software installation. A firewall appliance optimized installation can see throughput around 3 Gbps.

FireWall-1 Throughput

Platform	Mbps
Windows NT Xeon 1.7 GHz	457
Solaris Dual UltraSPARCIII 750 MHz	315
Linux Dual Xeon 1.7 GHz	765
Linux Celeron 400 MHz	200
Nortel Alteon Switch Firewall System	3,200

Putting this in perspective, keep in mind that the average Internet connection is around T1 speeds of 1.54 Mbps. Unless your firewall is protecting enclave networks internally running at Gigabit speeds or an OC12 connection to the Internet, the firewall will not be a performance bottleneck.

Another statistic, concurrent connections, is the number of connections maintained between hosts on either side of the firewall. The number of connections is highly memory dependent. On an installation with 512 mb of memory, Check Point NG can support 1,000,000 concurrent connections. That same installation with 512 mb of memory can support 20,000 VPN tunnels. You will probably run out of bandwidth before you exceed one of these limiting factors. I hope we have proven that FireWall-1 architecture can meet the most demanding environments. In fact, performance issues are typically a result of administration or configuration issues. If you would like more performance information you can visit www.checkpoint.com/products/security/vpn-1_firewall-1_performance.html.

Also interesting, Check Point recently announced that a $400 open PC/server equipped with an Intel Celeron processor and Red Hat Linux operating system, version 2.2 running Check Point NG, achieved

Continued

> throughput of 200 megabits per second. According to Check Point, the system was tested running 100,000 concurrent connections and is capable of 3,000 new connections per second.

Remember in Chapter 4 in which we had a security policy that allowed our internal users the use of HTTP to anywhere and the use of HTTPS everywhere but the local service net? We chose to write the rule as Source-**LAN**, Destination-**Service Net**, Service-**HTTP/ HTTPS**, Action-**Accept**, and Track-**None** with the Destination-**Service Net Negated**. And because another element of our policy allowed everyone HTTP access to the Web server in the service net, we wrote a second rule as Source-**Any**, Destination-**Web Server**, Service-**HTTP**, Action-**Accept**, and Track-**Log**. This rule could have been much more complicated. For example, we could have written our Rule Base to look like Figure 8.3.

Figure 8.3 A Bad Example

NO.	SOURCE	DESTINATION	SERVICE	ACTION	TRACK	INSTALL ON	TIME	COMMENT
1	✱ Any	CheckPoint-NG	✱ Any	Drop	! Alert	Gateways	✱ Any	Stealth Rule
2	LAN	Web_Server	TCP https	Reject	– None	Gateways	✱ Any	Reject LAN access to
3	LAN	✱ Any	TCP http TCP https	accept	– None	Gateways	✱ Any	Allow LAN access to l
4	✱ Any	Web_Server	TCP http	accept	Log	Gateways	✱ Any	Allow unrestricted acc
5	✱ Any	✱ Any	✱ Any	Reject	Log	Gateways	✱ Any	Clean-up Rule

Translating our policy this way, we used three rules instead of two. If we repeated this process over and over while writing the Rule Base, then we would have 1/3 more rules!

In addition to keeping it simple, put the most frequently applied rules near the top. This will get packets through inspection more quickly and routed by the O/S. Remember that a packet is processed from top to bottom until a match is made on the Rule Base; so, when optimizing, be aware the effect of reordering rules. As a help to optimization, monitoring your logs using the FireWall-1 predefined selection criteria can help you determine the most frequently applied rules. Take a look at Figure 8.4. Here you will see the most activity on Rule number 10, which allows SMTP traffic outbound. Although this isn't enough information for you to decide that Rule 10 should be moved up, this is the kind of monitoring you should undertake. Keep in mind that you need to log all rules to see what is going on, and that some rule order can't be changed, or else it weakens the security policy.

Figure 8.4 Logs and Optimum Rule Placement

No.	Date	Time	Product	Inter.	Origin	Type	Action	Service	Source	Destination	Proto.	Rule	S_Port
0	16Ma...	18:35:09	VPN-1 & FireWall-1	dae...	10.27.10.2	control	ctl						
1	16Ma...	18:35:10	VPN-1 & FireWall-1	El9...	10.27.10.2	control	ctl						
2	16Ma...	18:35:11	VPN-1 & FireWall-1	dae...	10.27.10.2	log	accept	smtp	pc1.mycompany...	10.27.11.5	tcp	2	2693
3	16Ma...	18:35:12	VPN-1 & FireWall-1	dae...	10.27.10.2	log	key install						
4	16Ma...	18:35:13	VPN-1 & FireWall-1	El9...	10.27.10.2	log	drop	bootp		255.255.255.255	udp	0	bootpc
5	16Ma...	18:35:14	VPN-1 & FireWall-1	El9...	10.27.10.2	log	accept	http	10.27.10.11	www.company.c...	tcp	12	1208
6	16Ma...	18:35:10	Multi-product	El9...	10.27.10.2	log	drop		10.27.10.14	10.27.11.32	icmp	1	
7	16Ma...	18:35:16	VPN-1 & FireWall-1	El9...	10.27.10.2	log	accept	http	10.27.10.112	www.other.com	tcp	12	1213
8	16Ma...	18:35:17	VPN-1 & FireWall-1	El9...	10.27.10.2	log	accept	netbios-ssn	10.27.10.55	10.27.11.33	tcp	5	1729
9	16Ma...	18:35:18	VPN-1 & FireWall-1	dae...	10.27.10.2	alert	reject	telnet	10.27.10.76	10.27.11.111	tcp	4	1737
10	16Ma...	18:35:19	VPN-1 & FireWall-1	dae...	10.27.10.2	log	reject	telnet	10.27.10.30	10.27.11.227	tcp	4	1737
11	16Ma...	18:35:20	VPN-1 & FireWall-1	dae...	10.27.10.2	log	encrypt	netbios-ssn	10.27.10.44	10.27.11.100	tcp	7	2411
12	16Ma...	18:35:21	VPN-1 & FireWall-1	dae...	10.27.10.2	log	decrypt	netbios-ssn	10.27.10.44	10.27.11.100	tcp	8	2411
13	16Ma...	18:35:22	VPN-1 & FireWall-1	dae...	10.27.10.2	log	accept	smtp	10.27.10.221	10.27.11.3	tcp	10	1791
14	16Ma...	18:35:23	VPN-1 & FireWall-1	El9...	10.27.10.2	log	accept	smtp	10.27.10.10	smtp.military.mil	tcp	10	1792
10	16Ma...	18:35:25	VPN-1 & FireWall-1	El9...	10.27.10.2	log	accept	smtp	10.27.10.22	smtp.company.com	tcp	10	1794
16	16Ma...	18:35:26	VPN-1 & FireWall-1	El9...	10.27.10.2	log	accept	smtp	10.27.10.89	mail.organization...	tcp	10	1795
17	16Ma...	18:35:27	VPN-1 & FireWall-1	dae...	10.27.10.2	log	accept	telnet	10.27.10.110	10.27.11.82	tcp	3	1734
18	16Ma...	18:35:28	VPN-1 & FireWall-1	El9...	10.27.10.2	control	ctl						

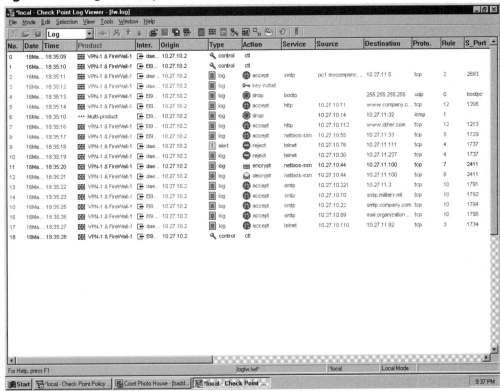

An improved feature in FireWall-1 NG is accounting. In previous versions, accounting decreased performance by 10 to 15 percent. However, because of NG's consolidation of connection tables, accounting information need only be pulled from one table and written to one log. Although this makes accounting in NG much more efficient, the accounting data is still pulled from the logaccount.fwl file and consolidated into the fw.log by the Log Unification Engine. Obviously, this extra work requires resources. Unfortunately still, rules that use *Account* as the *Action*, such as Figure 8.5, have a price and should be implemented only as required by policy and when it is worth the performance hit.

Figure 8.5 Rules That Perform Accounting

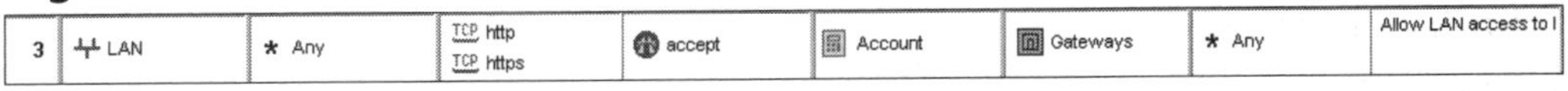

3	LAN	* Any	TCP http TCP https	accept	Account	Gateways	* Any	Allow LAN access to I

Designing & Planning...

Extreme Performance

If you need even greater performance or need to maintain a high number of concurrent VPN tunnels, then you should consider Check Point's SecureXL API technology and hardware acceleration. First, the SecureXL API is an open interface that vendors can use to offload security operations such as state table lookups, encryption, and network address translation. One currently available solution that utilizes the SecureXL API is the Nortel Alteon Switched Firewall and Check Point's own Firewall-1/VPN-1. Secondly, by using optimized hardware cards that offload encryption from the CPU, you can speed up encryption and decryption operations.

Just like accounting, using the active mode log requires that resources be used to consolidate log data. As a result, use the active mode logs only when actively blocking connections. The section on active mode logging will discuss in further detail how to do this.

Although one of the primary functions of the firewall is to monitor and log connections, carefully consider what is being logged. Over-logging not only decreases performance but also may make it hard to review the logs. One hint is to create a special rule that drops and doesn't log noisy services like Netbios or DHCP.

If you decide to use Security servers for HTTP, FTP, SMTP, Rlogin, or Telnet, realize that the kernel will divert all packets that meet the Rule Base demand for content checking or authentication to the Security Servers for processing. The Security Servers then perform any authentication or content checking as required and then, if allowed, establish a second connection to the destination host on behalf of the originating source host. Both the connection from the source to the Security Server and the Security Server to the destination are maintained in the connections table. You can open the fwauthd.conf file in a text editor to view which Security Servers are running. Security Servers are turned on automatically when a rule requires content checking or authentication.

In addition, if you are using the HTTP Security Server you can improve the performance for your users by increasing the number of concurrent processes. Setting this number too high can degrade overall performance, so a good number is usually 4. Keep in mind, however that, Check Point recommends that you have multiple processors if you intend on modifying this value. To make the change for additional HTTP processes, in the fwauthd.conf, modify the corresponding line for HTTP to say the following:

```
80      in.ahttpd    wait   -4
```

Another recommendation is to consider limiting the number of NAT rules in your Address Translation Rule Base. Although this is probably going to be something you will just have to live with, however, realize that NAT requires considerable resources. Fortunately, NAT performance is one of the things that Check Point claims to be improved in NG also, due to the single connection table. Moreover, you can further optimize your usage of NAT by limiting rules and combining objects intended for NAT. For example, if you or the network engineers have efficiently laid out the IP addressing scheme, you can use a subnet mask to combine multiple networks. Here's what I mean: If you have several internal networks that are sequential, like 172.16.1.0, 172.16.2.0, 172.16.3.0, … , 172.16.128.0 all with 255.255.255.0 subnet masks, then you can create these objects separately for use in the security policy rule base if you need to have specific access restrictions for each network. However, if you don't need separate restrictions for each network, then you can "supernet" them by creating one object with the subnet mask of 255.255.128.0 subnet mask. This will cover all the networks 172.16.1.0 through 172.16.128.0 as mentioned above.

And finally, try to avoid the use of domain objects. Domain objects are network objects based on the TCP/IP domain name. This is unwise because every time a packet is matched up with a rule that has a domain object, FireWall-1 NG must do a domain name look-up. This will slow the overall processing of packets. If you must use them, then place them as far down in the policy as possible.

Monitoring NG for Performance

Memory is probably the most important commodity to Check Point FireWall-1 NG, or any other firewall for that matter. According to Check Point, the formula for determining your required amount of memory is as follows:

```
MemoryUsage =

((ConcurrentConnections)/(AverageLifetime))*(AverageLifetime +

   50 seconds)*120
```

Concurrent connection is the number of connections for hosts at one moment in time. Remember that the use of Security Servers will make what seems to be one connection really two. Another definition, average lifetime of a connection, is defined as the number of seconds a session will typically last from handshake to termination. You can use your accounting log to determine this.

No matter what the platform, there are tools specific to FireWall-1 that you can use to monitor your firewall for performance. The easiest tool available is to take a quick look at the System Status Viewer. The System Status Viewer is an application that will show you the license status, alerts, and details from the different modules deployed in your enterprise.

By selecting the SVN foundation object, you can see some performance-related details in the right windowpane as shown in Figure 8.6. From SVN Foundation details you can view CPU usage, memory usage, and disk space. Obviously, high CPU usage that is consistently above 60 percent should be a concern as well as a low amount of free real memory or free disk space.

Figure 8.6 SVN Foundation Details

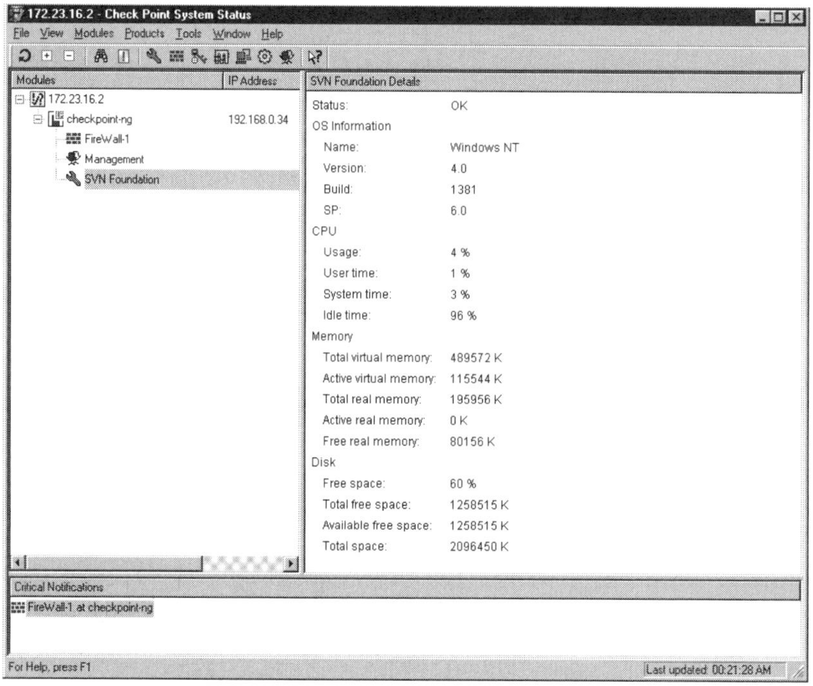

A final method for checking the amount of memory available to the kernel is by executing at a command line:

```
FW ctl pstat
```

Executing this command will show you internal statistics of Firewall-1.

You can modify the amount of memory available to the kernel by following the OS specific instructions for modifying kernel memory.

As indicated by Check Point Technical Support, in Unix, stop FireWall-1 by executing fwstop at the command line and perform the following commands, based on your platform:

- **Solaris** Add to /etc/system "set fw:fwhmem = 0x500000" and reboot

- **SunOS** echo "fwhmem ?W500000" | adb -w $FWDIR/modules/fwmod.32.5.x.o

- **HPUX 9.x** echo "fwhmem ?W500000" | adb -w /hp-ux and reboot

- **HP-UX 10.x** echo "fwhmem ?W500000" | adb -w /stand/vmunix and reboot

- **HP-UX 11.x** echo "fwhmem ?W500000" | adb -w /stand/vmunix and reboot

- **AIX** echo "fw_heap_size?W 800000" | adb -w $FWDIR/modules/fwmod.32.5.x.o echo "fwhmem?W 500000" | adb -w $FWDIR/modules/fwmod.32.5.x.o

Restart the firewall by executing fwstart.

Again, as indicated by Check Point Support in Windows NT, to modify the amount of memory available to the kernel, do the following:

1. Run regedt32 (the registry editor)

2. Go to HKEY_LOCAL_MACHINE\SYSTEM\CurrentControlSet\Services\FW1\Parameters

3. Select from the main menu **Edit -> Add Value**

4. The value's name is Memory, and the data type is REG_DWORD

5. Enter the new amount of kernel memory (in bytes). (NOTE: The value should be in Hex. For example, 600000 equals 6 MB_.)

6. Reboot

There are also command utilities that help you understand how well internally the firewall is performing. An example is fw tab. Issuing the command *fw tab −t connections −s* will show you the connections table as specified by the −t, and in short format, as specified by the −s. This command will tell you how many connections are in the state table. Because the state table has a limit of 25,000 items, if the results are near 25,000 or if you know that you have 10,000 concurrent connections, then you should increase the size of your state table. Changing the size of your state table in Check Point NG is different than in previous versions of FireWall-1. In Check Point NG, the size of the state table is defined in objects_5_0.C, not $FWDIR/lib/table.def. Remember that new to Check Point NG is the use of dbedit to modify objects_5_0.C and other system files. To alter the size of the table follow these easy steps:

1. Close all GUI clients that are connected to the management server.

2. Execute DBEDIT.

3. You will be prompted for the server. (Enter for the localhost.)

4. Next, enter your Check Point NG administrator user ID, followed by the password.

5. At the Enter the Command prompt, type: "modify properties firewall_properties connections_limit [Value]."

6. After pressing **Enter**, on the next line, type: "update properties firewall_properties."

7. After entering the preceding line, you can now end your DBEDIT session by typing "Quit."

8. Next you must reboot the machine. Any time you modify a table with the *Keep* attribute you will have to reboot the machine. You can tell if a table has the *Keep* attribute by typing fw tab -t 'table name' as shown in Figure 8.7.

9. Finally, you must install the policy for changes to take effect.

Figure 8.7 Viewing the 'Keep' Attribute for Tables

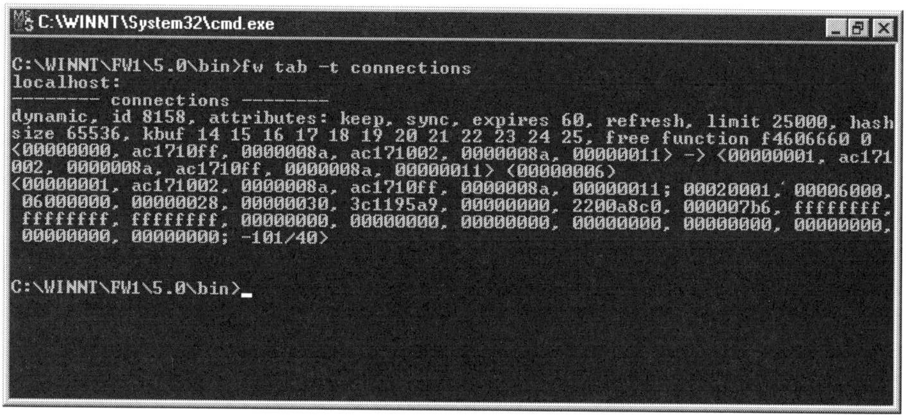

As you are modifying the connections table, you will probably need to modify the hash size as well. The hash size value should be a power of 2 that is as close as possible to the limit on the connections table. As you can see in Table 8.1, if you have modified the connection limit to be 50,000, then you should set your hash size to 65536.

Table 8.1 Relevant Powers of 2

	Hash Size	Connection Limit
2^{14}	16384	4097-24576
2^{15}	32768	24577-49152
2^{16}	65536	49153-98304
2^{17}	131072	98305-196608

NOTE

Check Point does sell a product that integrates nicely into the Check Point framework, called Real Time Monitor. Real Time Monitor is included with FloodGate-1 or can be licensed as a separate product. It enables you to monitor bandwidth, bandwidth loss, and round-trip time in end-to-end VPNs.

Platform Specific Tools

In addition to the Check Point NG tools provided for measuring performance on Windows NT, there are a number of FireWall-1 specific counters that get installed to the NT performance monitor. The counters provided include the following:

- Number of packets accepted
- Number of packets dropped
- Number of current connections
- Number of packets decrypted
- Number of packets encrypted

- Number of packets that fail encrypt/decrypt
- Amount of hash memory currently in use
- Amount of system kernel memory currently in use
- Number of packets logged
- Number of packets rejected
- Number of total packets processed
- Number of packets undergoing address translation

These counters can be invaluable in further tuning your firewall.

Performance Conclusion

And finally, if none of these suggestions improve the performance of your FireWall-1 NG, then consider upgrading your hardware based on the following Table 8.2 and on your own observations of CPU, memory, and I/O usage:

Table 8.2 Quick Recommendations

If you require a large amount of...	Then you need...
Encryption/decryption	CPU
Network Address Translation	Memory
Logging	Memory and I/O
Sessions	Memory
Security Servers	CPU and I/O

Administering Check Point VPN-1/ FireWall-1 NG for Effectiveness

Although performance is important, if a firewall doesn't do what it's supposed to do, then it is no good. In fact, it is easy to trade increased performance for decreased effectiveness or security. In this section we will talk about how to make sure your FireWall-NG is doing its job and securing your network.

Quality Control

One of the best ways to test the effectiveness of the firewall is to assume the role of attacker. Although it is possible to hire a third party to do penetration testing, the initial testing is your responsibility. The simplest way to test the firewall is by using a simple port scanner. Some popular and free port scanners you may want to try include the following:

- **Nmap** A favorite of security professionals and hackers alike. Nmap allows different types of scans, spoofing, decoys, and timing changes. It can be found at www.insecure.org.

- **Languard Network Scanner** A very noisy but full-featured scanner. This tool will pull SNMP information as well as attempt to connect to open services and gather banners. It can be found at www.gfisoftware.com/languard/lanscan.htm.

- **Hping2** An advanced tool that runs on *nix that allows the crafting of custom TCP/IP packets. Hping2 can be used to test firewall rules and even transfer files. Hping2 can be downloaded at www.hping.org.

If you would like to assess your configuration further, you can use a full-featured vulnerability assessment tool. Most even have modules that enable you to test known FireWall-1 vulnerabilities. For recommendations and more descriptions, you can visit www.insecure.org/tools.html.

This sort of quality control has multiple benefits. It helps you to see what ports are open or not filtered from the outside. Also, it may help you to see what patches you might be missing or vulnerabilities you are exposed to. Next, it enables you to test your logging and monitoring. And finally, it enables you to see what an attack might look like and help you detect one from your monitoring.

Designing & Planning...

War Games

Don't underestimate the value of auditing your firewall configuration. Assign someone to periodically audit the configuration with scans from the outside or even simulated attacks. This will enable you to test your monitoring and incident response procedures. It will be much easier to hone your incident response skills under simulation than to respond ineffectively to a real attack, or worse yet, to not detect a real attack underway at all.

Patches and Updates

As a security professional, make sure you sign up to a security mailing list to stay abreast of new developments in security, especially the Check Points newsletter, which will notify you of support issues and relevant patches when available. You can sign up for Check Point's email newsletter at www.checkpoint.com/ newsletter.html.

To obtain updates to your FireWall-1 NG installation, you can use SecureUpdate as shown in Figure 8.8. From the **Help** menu, select **Check Point download center**. This will open your browser to the Check Point site. Here you will be prompted to accept a software license agreement after which you will be required to enter a user name and password.

Figure 8.8 SecureUpdate Utility

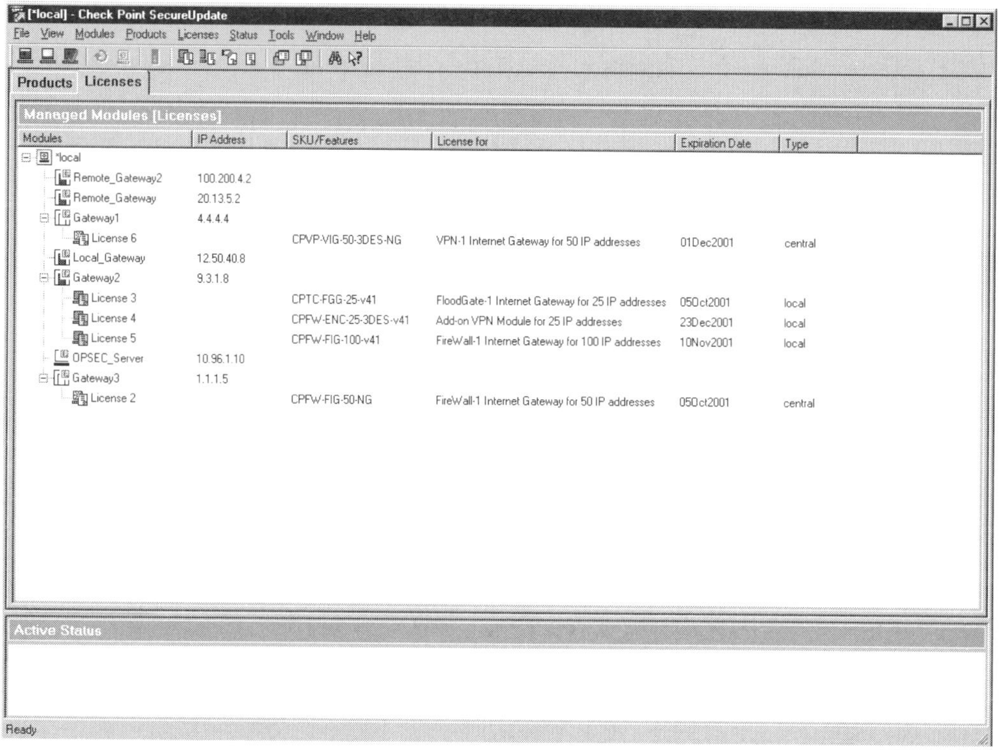

In order to use SecureUpdate to do remote installations and updates centrally, you must be licensed. Beyond that, SecureUpdate tries to make it easy. The first step is to obtain a SecureUpdate package. This can be obtained from the Internet or CD. The Product Repository is managed by using *cppkg* commands. The command to add a new package is the following:

```
cppkg add <package-full-path | CD directory>
```

Next, you must put the package into the Product Repository. After the package is in the Product Repository, you can literally drag and drop packages onto modules from the SecureUpdate GUI interface.

As an alternative, if you are not licensed to use SecureUpdate, you can download updates from http://www.checkpoint.com/techsupport/downloads_ng.html. You will want to pay particular attention to the hot fixes. Download the appropriate Hot Fix just like you would any other file. After extracting it to a directory, you can install the Hot Fix. Make sure that the SVNFoundation (*cpshared_hf*.tgz*) Hot Fix is installed first, and then you can follow with the particular Hot Fix for the products you are running.

Policy Administration

The core of an effective firewall is policy. To help you manage and administrate, there are a number of best practices you will want to implement. One of the most important administrative tasks you will perform is modifying security policy. Additionally, this may be a task you spend a lot of time doing. To assist you here are a number of tips to keep in mind:

- Clean up old policies.
- Use groups.
- Save copy of policy before making changes.
- Use comments.

Whenever you create a new policy and save it, it gets written to a *.W file and to the rulebases_5_0.fws file. The asterisk in the *.W file represents the name of the policy. The rulebases_5_0.fws file is a collection of all *.W files. If you have a lot of policies, the rulebases_5_0.fws can get quite large. Don't be afraid to clean up some of the old policies if you do not need them anymore. The best way to do this is through the Policy Editor interface. Choose **File** from the menu and select **Delete**. This will open a dialog that will enable you to choose the policies you would like to delete. By deleting policies this way, the actual *.W file is deleted as well as the reference within the rulebases_5_0.fws file.

Second, try to arrange network objects into groups. This will help in administration and make the rule base easier to read. As you add new objects to groups, they are automatically included in any relevant rules.

Next, if you are making modifications to a production policy, then before you begin, save the policy under a different name as a backup. If something goes wrong or gets misconfigured, you can then roll back to the saved policy. Also, you may find it beneficial to save the new policy with a meaningful naming convention. One suggestion is to name the policy according to the date of creation and the responsible administrator's initials. For example, a policy created and saved by an administrator named Joe Admin on December 28, 2001, would be 20011228JA. Using a naming convention such as this one would then make it easy to delete the oldest policy whenever a new one is created. By doing this, you can leave a smaller number of policies at a given time in the **File | Open** window, which means a smaller rulebases_5_0.C file.

And finally, it cannot be emphasized enough: Use comments. Using comments in your FireWall-1 Rule Base will help you to understand what certain rules are doing, whom they are for, and when they should expire. This will help you to keep the rule base fit and trim. There is nothing worse than making a modification on the fly and forgetting about it. Making appropriate comments will help you in auditing your Rule Base and network objects from time to time.

Managing Multiple Policies

Although it may be confusing at times, it may be necessary to have multiple policies for multiple firewalls. If this is the case for you, then here are a couple of pointers to help you effectively administrate.

- Use meaningful policy names.
- Delete old policies.
- Properly configure the Install On Field.

When naming policies, use a name that is indicative of its function and enforcement location. This is helpful so that you don't accidentally overwrite the wrong policy.

Deleting old policies will also improve performance because the GUI downloads all policies from the Management Server. This could slow the response of the GUI. Deleting old policies will decrease the amount of data that must be sent to the GUI. As recommended before, delete policies by selecting **Delete** from the **File** menu within the Policy Editor.

Finally, when working with multiple policies, be sure that the Install On field is properly configured. By installing policy on FireWall-1 modules that will not enforce any of the policy, you do two things: Number one, you will slow down the install of the policy because of the process a policy goes through when it is installed. And number two, FireWall-1 modules that have policy installed to them, but that enforce no rules in that policy, will enforce the default rule and reject all communications.

Editing Files

One of the most powerful features of FireWall-1 is the ability to customize or change virtually everything about the way FireWall-1 operates. However, to do so requires that you manually edit certain files. Before we discuss how to go about that, we will identify some of those files and their purposes.

After you create a Rule Base in a new policy, it is written to a *.W file upon saving or installation of the policy. This file can be edited with a text editor as it contains the information displayed graphically in the GUI regarding the Rule Base.

The objects_5_0.C file was formerly called objects.C in earlier versions of FireWall-1. Although, objects.C still exists. The purpose of the objects_5_0.C file is to contain network objects, properties, and configuration information for the management server. It is a master file. The objects.C is pushed to the modules and is created from the master objects_5_0.C when a policy is installed. It is possible to edit the objects_5_0.C with the new DBEDIT utility, which is illustrated as Figure 8.9. The advantage of this utility is that it enables an administrator to search the file based on type and attribute. Moreover, the tool will keep an audit trail of modifications. This is the recommended way to edit the objects_5_0.C. Remember to close all GUI clients and back up your objects_5_0.C before you use debedit to make modifications.

Figure 8.9 Introduction to DBEDIT

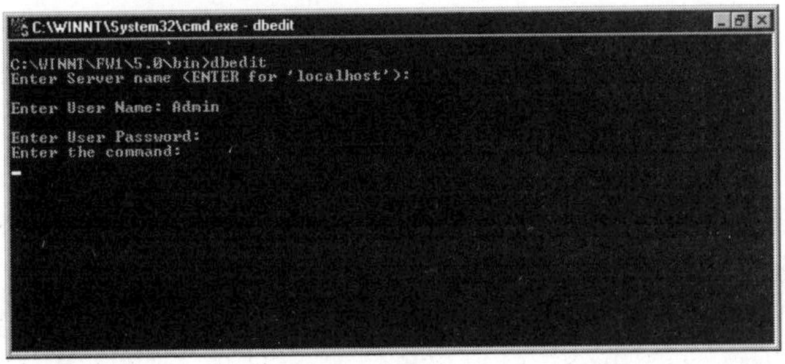

Another file you should become familiar with is the $\star$.pf. The $\star$.pf is the packet filter or Inspection script that results from the $\star$.W file and the objects_5_0.C file when performing a policy install. It is not recommended that you attempt editing this file. You can view the Inspection script for a policy by selecting **View** from the Policy menu in the Policy editor.

During a policy install, the $\star$.pf file is compiled into a $\star$.fc file. The $\star$.fc file is the Inspection code that is installed onto enforcement modules. It is not recommended that you edit this file either. The process of compiling the $\star$.W file into the $\star$.pf and subsequest $\star$.fc is begun by the command `fw load`. This command compiles and installs a policy to the firewall. The whole process of installing a policy is illustrated in Figure 8.10.

Figure 8.10 The Policy Installation Process

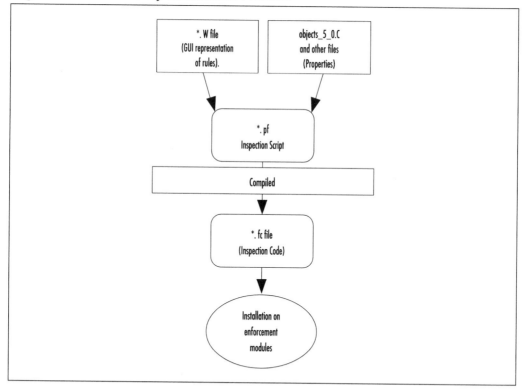

One $\star$.pf files that is of particularly importance is the defaultfilter.pf. This file is responsible for implementing security during the boot process. In FireWall-1, NG IP forwarding is always disabled until a policy is loaded. This is the function of the default filter (default.pf). This policy protects the firewall until the initial policy can be loaded.

The boot process can be summarized as follows:

1. Machine boots up.

2. Default Filter loads and IP Forwarding is disabled.

3. Interfaces are configured.

4. FireWall–1 services start.

5. Initial policy is Fetched from the Local Module if this is the first boot and there is no policy; otherwise the configured policy is installed.

Managing Firewall Logs

Monitoring your logs is an important job for administrators. Logs not only help you to ensure that the firewall is effective, but they can help you to detect an attack. You should probably review your logs on a daily basis at a minimum. Understanding the different types of logs available to you and their purpose will help you review them.

There are basically three log modes in FireWall–1 NG. The three modes are these:

- Log mode
- Active mode
- Audit mode

Log mode is the basic log file that contains all logging information. It is the default log mode. To assist you in reading the log there are seven predefined log views. They are as follows:

- General (loggeneral.fwl)
- FireWall–1 (logfw.fwl)
- Account (logaccount.fwl)
- FloodGate–1 (logfg.fwl)
- VPN–1 (logvpn.fwl)
- Virtual Link Monitoring (loge2e.fwl)
- Secure Client (logsc.fwl)

Obviously each predefined view contains information specific to the view title.

The new Log Unification Engine in FireWall-1 NG is responsible for bringing information from all of these modules into one log (fw.log). The other two logging modes are audit and active.

- Audit mode files are named ⋆.fwo. The audit mode provides an audit trail of administrator actions. This can be helpful for seeing what administrative actions have been performed on a FireWall-1.

- Active mode files are named ⋆.fwa. This mode is used primarily for monitoring current connections and blocking connections. When blocking connections, it doesn't modify the Rule Base and remains in effect until manually removed or until the enforcement module is unloaded. Your choices in blocking as illustrated in Figure 8.11 include the following:

  - Block only this connection.

  - Block access from this source.

  - Block access to this destination.

You can also specify how long the block should last and if the blocking should be enforced by the FireWall-1 that is currently processing the connection or on any other FireWall-1.

Figure 8.11 Block Intruder Dialog

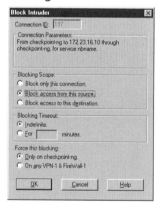

Log Rotations

Rotating your logs will prevent them from getting too big and eating up all of your hard drive space or just too cumbersome to understand. You have two options in performing log rotations from within the Log Viewer application, and those are Log Switch or Purge. If you select **Log Switch** from the File menu, you will save a copy of the log and start a fresh one. If you select **Purge**, then the current log files are deleted, and a new log is started. New to NG is the ability to schedule log rotation. Under your firewall object's workstation properties displayed in Figure 8.12, you can create a logging policy and specify to perform a log switch when the log reaches a certain size or at a certain time. (The default time is midnight.) These options are explained in detail in Table 8.3.

Figure 8.12 Setting Firewall Logging Policy

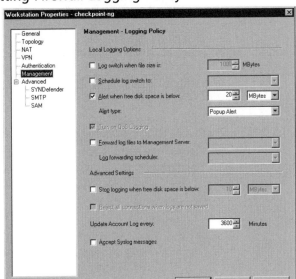

Table 8.3 Logging Options

Local Logging Options	Explanation
Log switch when file size is	Specifies a size, in megabytes, that the log file shall not exceed. When this size is met, the current log file will be closed and a new one created.
Schedule log switch to	Schedules a time (as defined by a predefined time object) when the current log will be closed and a new one created.
Alert when free disk space is below	Send an alert when free disk space falls below this threshold. This also enables you to specify the alert type.

Continued

Table 8.3 Continued

Local Logging Options	Explanation
Turn on QoS logging	Enables logging of Quality of Service related events. This option requires Floodgate-1.
Forward logfiles to management server	Specifies a server to forward locally recorded logs to. Logs are recorded locally when the defined log servers are unavailable. Logs will be forwarded according to the log forward schedule.

Advanced Settings	Explanation
Stop logging when free disk space is below	Specifies a threshold that, when reached, will cause log recording to cease.
Reject all connections when logs are not saved	If selected, all connections that are attempted to a firewall that has ceased logging will be rejected. While this seems foolish, many organizations require verbose logging for purposes of auditing or accountability, and rejecting connections is preferable to unaccounted acceptances.
Update account log every	Specifies the time interval for accounting messages to be logged. Accounting messages contain the information about a connection, such as packets sent. When the accounting message is sent, those counters are reset. Each subsequent message is therefore a recording of the change since the last message.
Accept Syslog messages	If selected, syslog messages will be accepted. This is often necessary when the source of the log data is not an OPSEC compliant device. Note that the firewall must be configured to accept syslog data on UDP port 514 in order for this to function. Also, the CPSyslogD daemon must have been started prior to the start of FW-1.

In previous versions of FireWall-1, the automation of log rotation required some configuration outside of FireWall-1. As an alternative, a security administrator can still schedule a 'cron' or 'at' job depending on the operating system, to execute the *fw logswitch* command. Additionally, you could also perform an export on the log files, such as copy or move the log files to another partition or disk drive or even to another machine.

An example of logswitch script for Solaris is below:

```
#!/bin/sh
#
# Set variables
#
FW_BIN_PATH=/etc/fw/bin
BIN_PATH=/usr/bin
LOG_PATH=/etc/fw/log
TODAY=`$BIN_PATH/date +%d%b%y`
#
# Switch the log files
#
$FW_BIN_PATH/fw logswitch $TODAY
#
# Export the logs
#
$FW_BIN_PATH/fw logexport -d ";" -i $LOG_PATH/$TODAY.alog -o
    $LOG_PATH/$TODAY.alog.txt -r 1000
$FW_BIN_PATH/fw logexport -d ";" -i $LOG_PATH/$TODAY.log -o
    $LOG_PATH/$TODAY.log.txt -r 1000
#
# Compress log files to conserve disk space, and delete pointer files.
#
$BIN_PATH/rm $LOG_PATH/$TODAY.*ptr
compress $LOG_PATH/$TODAY.*log
# EOF
```

This script could be placed in the crontab file and run at midnight every day or as often as required.

An example batch file for NT is as follows:

```
c:\bin\fdate /Ff /o"ddmn3yy" /P"@SET TODAY=" > c:\temp\_tmpfile.bat
call c:\temp\_tmpfile
del  c:\temp\_tmpfile.bat
```

```
cd c:\winnt\fw1\5.0\log
c:\winnt\fw1\5.0\bin\fw logswitch %TODAY%
c:\winnt\fw1\5.0\bin\fw logexport -r 1000 -d ; -i %TODAY%.alog -o
     %TODAY%.alog.txt
c:\winnt\fw1\5.0\bin\fw logexport -r 1000 -d ; -i %TODAY%.log -o
     %TODAY%.log.txt
:end
```

In this batch file, we are using a script called fdate to set the date for TODAY on the system. If you do not specify the format of the date for the *logswitch* command, then the log files will be saved based on the date and time that the switch occurred. This can be tricky if you want to call the log file for an export, but if you are just performing a *logswitch* and are not manipulating the log files after the switch, then the default format is sufficient. To use this script in NT 4, the scheduler would have to be enabled and an 'at' job created to run the file every night at midnight or as often as necessary. To use this script in Windows 2000, the administrator would only have to create a task within the Task Scheduler application.

Log Maintenance

It is possible to see log corruption. If this happens, the log can easily be rebuilt from the fragments of logs used to build fw.log. Executing the command *fw repairlog [-u] <logfile name>* will unify the log, replacing the corruption.

Administering Check Point VPN-1/ FireWall-1 NG for Recoverability

Recoverability is an important issue for most organizations. In some organizations, a down firewall can have a serious impact on business. Being able to recover quickly is essential.

Making Backups

Making backups of your FireWall-1 configuration is relatively easy. In fact, we have already identified most of the critical files you should backup:

- objects_5_0.c
- rulebases_5_0.fws
- fwauth.NDB*

- All *.W files (Not required)

- All *.pf files (Not required)

- fwmusers and gui-clients (Not required)

You should back up these files to a secure and safe location after any modifications made, as well as after any files that have been manually modified such as the base.def or table.def. To restore a firewall, it is as easy as ensuring copying these files over. The *.W and *.pf files are not required because FireWall-1 will recreate them.

In addition to having your configuration backed up, you should consider how to recover if the hardware failed completely. Make sure that if you have a four-hour service response contract, that you can live without a firewall for four hours. If this isn't the case, then you should purchase a hot-swap server or invest in a high-availability solution.

If your firewall does go down and you need to move the installation, follow these easy steps.

1. If your IP address is changing or if your license is based on host ID, then request a license change from Check Point's Licensing User Center. If you need additional licensing features, then contact your Check Point VAR.

2. Install the operating system on the new hardware and patch it, implementing any O/S-recommended hardening measures.

3. Install the FireWall-1 software from a downloaded file or via CD, and install your license.

4. Patch the FireWall-1 software to the same build level as the machine you are copying files over from.

5. Copy the files objects_5_0.c, rulebases_5_0.fws, and fwauth.NDB* into the $FWDIR/conf directory.

6. If you do not want to add your administrators and GUI clients again by hand, then you can also copy over the files fwmusers and gui-clients in $FWDIR/conf as well.

7. You will need to redo any SIC configuration.

8. Install the policy and test connectivity.

9. Last, upgrade the firewall and add any new patches beyond the build you were duplicating.

Performing Advanced Administration Tasks

In this section we will talk about performing some of the more advanced administration tasks that are possible with Firewall-1 NG. These are some of the "tricks of the trade" that can make life easier for you.

Firewall controls

Sometimes the best way or only way to do something is at the command line. Fortunately, many of the things that you can do with the GUI you can also do at the command line. In fact, in case you haven't noticed, many GUI actions invoke command-line functions. In the next section, we will discuss some of the most common command-line options and their purpose.

fwstop

At times you may need to stop and restart the firewall for maintenance or just to bounce it. The easiest way to do this is with the *fwstop* command. Executing fwstop will kill the following:

- The FireWall-1 daemon (fwd)
- The Management Server (fwm)
- The SNMP daemon (snmpd)
- The Authentication daemon (authd)

It is possible to unload FireWall-1 processes but to maintain security by loading the default filter. This enables the FireWall-1 administrator to take down the FireWall-1 processes for maintenance without exposing the firewall machine to attacks while unprotected. The commands to stop FireWall-1 NG and load the default filter are these:

```
fwstop -default
fwstop -proc
```

fwstart

fwstart will load FireWall-1 and start the processes killed by *fwstop*:

- The FireWall-1 daemon (fwd)

- The Management Server (*fwm*)
- The SNMP daemon (*snmpd*)
- The Authentication daemon (*authd*)

No options are needed with *fwstart*.

cpstop

Not to be confused with *fwstop*. In fact, *cpstop* is inclusive of the *fwstop* function. Executing *cpstop* will stop all Check Point applications running. One exception is the *cprid,* which is a Check Point process that is invoked at boot time and runs independently of other Check Point applications.

cpstart

Executing *cpstart* will start all Check Point applications. Similar to *cpstop*, executing *cpstart* implies that *fwstart* perform its function.

cpconfig

The command *cpconfig* is used to configure FireWall-1/VPN-1. In Windows NT, executing this command opens the Check Point Configuration Tool GUI. In *nix environments, the command displays a configuration screen with options that depend on what is installed. In both environments, executing *cpconfig* enables you to Install and update licenses, create administrators, view the management server fingerprint, specify remote clients that can log into the management server, configure SNMP, and register PKCS#11 cryptographic tokens.

cpstat

Executing this command will provide you with status of the target hosts. In NG, *cpstat* is intended to replace *fw stat*.

fw

There are a number of *fw* commands that are helpful for controlling the FireWall-1 daemon. *fw* commands follow this basic syntax:

```
fw [action] [target (default localhost)].
```

fw load

This command will convert the *.W file from the GUI to a *.pf file and compile into Inspection code, installing a Security Policy on an enforcement module. A sample *fw load* command would be as follows:

```
fw load Standard.W all.all@localgateway
```

This will load the Standard.W policy onto the firewall object named *local-gateway*.

fw unload

This command will uninstall Security Policy from the specified target(s). An example of usage is as follows:

```
fw unload localhost
```

This command will uninstall the policy from this firewall.

fw fetch

fw fetch is used to fetch Inspection code from a specified host and install it to the kernel of the current host. An example of usage is as follows:

```
fw fetch 192.168.1.1
```

This will fetch the security policy from the management station located at 192.168.1.1.

fw putkey

This command is helpful if you are integrating an NG Management Server with 4.X enforcement modules. Executing *fw putkey* will install an authenticating password. The password is used to authenticate SIC between the Management Server and the module, the first time the two communicate. For an example of a remote firewall module, type the following:

```
fw putkey –n 192.168.1.2 192.168.1.1
```

The –n option specifies the dotted IP address that will be used to identify this host to other hosts. The second part of the syntax that specifies 192.168.1.1 is the closest interface on the target to which the password will be installed. Additionally, by not specifying the password to be used, you will be prompted for it.

fw ctl

fw ctl is a utility for controlling the FireWall-1 kernel. In addition, *fw ctl pstat* will provide you with internal FireWall-1 statistics. It can also be used for obtaining interface information.

fw tab

Fw tab is used for displaying the contents of FireWall-1's various tables INSPECT tables. As an example, to display the connections table, you would type the following:

```
fw tab -t connections
```

fw logswitch

This command will save the current log and start a new one. This is particularly helpful in rotating logs on remote machines from the Management Server.

```
fw logswitch -h localgateway +old_log
```

This command will rotate the logs on the remote firewall named local-gateway and copy the log to the management server with the name of local-gateway.old_log.

fw logexport

This command dumps the log to an ASCII file. Log files in this format can be processed by third-party tools or imported into databases for further analysis. For example, to export your logs with a semicolon that delimits the output fields and to give the file the name 4analysis, you would type the following:

```
fw logexport -d -o 4analysis.txt
```

fw ver

This command returns the version of FireWall-1 currently running. By adding the *-k* option you can learn the kernel build as well.

```
fw ver -k
```

Firewall Processes

There are a number of operating specific commands you can use to list the processes running on your bastion host.

*NIX

In *nix, executing *ps −ef* will display all currently running processes and full information, including their process ID.

Nokia

For Nokias, using the command *ps −aux* will display running processes.

Windows

In Windows NT, you may view the running processes and their allocated memory by executing the Task Manager. Be aware that all Firewall-1 processes will appear as fw.exe. It is not uncommon to have five or more fw.exe processes running.

$FWDIR\tmp

FireWall-1 writes the process IDs of FireWall-1 processes as they are started, and writes them to *.pid files that correlate with the process started, as you can see in Figure 8.13. For example, opening the file fwd.pid in a text editor would display the process ID assigned to the fw.exe process. This is extremely helpful in Windows when each process is named fw.exe. This process-to-process ID mapping will help you to figure out which fw.exe goes with what firewall process.

Figure 8.13 Process ID Mapping in NT

fwd

The *fwd* process is the FireWall-1 daemon.

fwm

The *fwm* process is the Management Server.

in.ahttpd

in.ahttpd is the name of the process assigned to the HTTP Security Server.

in.asmtp.d

in.asmtpd is the name of the process assigned to the SMTP Security Server.

in.atelnetd

in.atelnetd is the name of the process assigned to the Telnet Security Server.

in.arlogind

in.arlogind is the name of the process assigned to the Rlogin Security Server.

in.aftpd

in.aftpd is the name of the process assigned to the FTP Security Server.

in.aclientd

in.aclientd is the process responsible for client authentication on port 259.

in.ahclientd

in.ahclientd is the process responsible for client authentication on port 900 through a Web browser.

fw kill

The *fw kill* command can be used to terminate any running Firewall-1 process. The syntax is *fw kill [process name]*. For example you can terminate the HTTP security server and restart it to resolve problems with the HTTP proxy by executing the following: `fw kill in.ahttpd`

Summary

We've covered a lot of ground to help you administer Check Point FireWall-1 NG. We've talked about ways you can tune and monitor the performance of FireWall-1 NG. Additionally, we have discussed how to maintain the effectiveness of the firewall by performing audits, using best practices for administration, applying patches, and monitoring the logs. And finally, we gave you details about how to back up and recover from a failed FireWall-1 NG. In summary, as an administrator, your primary job is to make the firewall perform well, effectively, and without fail. Sometimes that may seem like a lot to ask. In fact, at times performance may be at odds with effectiveness or vice versa. However, the primary goal of an administrator is to make the firewall work the way it was designed in the Security Policy. Moreover, the best way to ensure the effectiveness of your firewall is daily administration through log review and performance monitoring.

Solutions Fast Track

Administering Check Point VPN-1/ FireWall-1 NG for Performance

☑ Keep the Rule Base Simple. Enough said.

☑ Keep the most frequently matched rules near the top. Because FireWall-1 uses top-down processing of all packets against the Rule Base, packets that are matched early on are kicked out to the O/S for routing sooner.

☑ Monitor performance periodically using FireWall-1 built in tools. There are also a number of platform specific utilities, such as the NT performance monitor, to gauge the firewall's level of performance.

Administering Check Point VPN-1/ FireWall-1 NG for Effectiveness

☑ Audit your firewall using assessment tools. This will not only test your configuration but also show you in the log how it looks when attackers reconnaissance your firewall.

☑ Subscribe to Check Point's mailing list to be alerted to new patches. Additionally, monitor general security lists for pertinent vulnerabilities.

☑ Monitor your logs on a daily basis and develop a plan for log rotation.

Administering Check Point VPN-1/ FireWall-1 NG for Recoverability

☑ Save a back-up copy of your policy before you modify it. This will enable you to fall back should something go wrong or not work the way planned.

☑ Backup FireWall-1's configuration files after modifications are made. The files you should back up include objects_5_0.c, rulebases_5_0.fws, all ★.W files, all ★.pf files, and fwauth.NDB★.

☑ Evaluate your hardware support contract to see if the time period would be acceptable if the firewall hardware were to fail.

Performing Advanced Administration Tasks

☑ The commands fwstop and fwstart can be used to stop and start FireWall-1 respectively.

☑ The ★.pid files in $FWDIR\tmp can be used to determine the process ID assigned to FireWall-1 processes.

☑ The Security Server binaries are named in the format in.a[application]d. For example, HTTP is called in.ahttpd and FTP is in.aftpd.

☑ When the security servers are running in Windows, they show up as fw.exe processes.

Frequently Asked Questions

The following Frequently Asked Questions, answered by the authors of this book, are designed to both measure your understanding of the concepts presented in this chapter and to assist you with real-life implementation of these concepts. To have your questions about this chapter answered by the author, browse to **www.syngress.com/solutions** and click on the **"Ask the Author"** form.

Q: Users are complaining that the firewall is slow. How do I know if I need a bigger, better, faster box?

A: After making sure that the firewall is appropriately tuned and has a good Rule Base, the best way to determine your need for new hardware is to monitor the CPU, memory, and I/O of the firewall.

Q: If I block a connection, how long will it last?

A: Blocked connections will persist based on what was specified when the blocking action was performed.

Q: How is NG different than previous versions with respect to performance?

A: Performance is one of the big improvements in NG. One of the new performance enhancements is the consolidation of state tables into one. This speeds up the processing of packets.

Q: Why don't I see any Security Server processes running?

A: This is because they haven't been invoked in the fwauthd.conf manually or by a rule that requires authentication or content checking.

Q: How do I know when my Rule Base is too complex?

A: That is a difficult question. What is complex in one environment may be very appropriate in another. It appears that a medium-sized organization should have around 20 rules. However, always the fewer the better, but get the job done first.

Q: How do I get these command-line options to run?

A: You must run them from the $FWDIR\bin. Alternatively, you can add $FWDIR\bin to your path statement. To add the $FWDIR/bin to your path statement perform the following:

In Unix:

1. You must edit the path statements in your `.cshrc` or `.profile` files. (Remember that these are hidden files.) Which file you edit will depend on which shell you use when you log on.

2. If you are editing your .cshrc, add the following line:

```
set path=(. /usr/bin $path etc/fw/bin /usr/etc /etc /local/etc)
```

3. To activate your change, type the following:

```
source .cshrc
```

4. Now type "echo $PATH" to confirm your change. You should see etc/fw/bin in your path statement.

In Windows NT and Windows 2000:

1. Select **Start | Settings | Control Panel.**

2. Double-click the System applet and select the **Environment** tab.

3. Select the **Path** variable from the **System Variables** window.

4. Verify that the Variable field at the bottom of the Environment tab shows "Path," as follows:
Variable: Path
Value: %SystemRoot%\system32;%SystemRoot%

5. Add the FireWall-1 \bin directory path to the current Path variable value, in the following manner. For FireWall-1 5.0:
%SystemRoot%\system32;%SystemRoot%;C:\winnt\fw1\5.0\bin

6. Once the FireWall-1 \bin directory has been added to the Path variable, the value of the Path variable can be checked by running the following command in the command prompt:
set

7. The value of the Path variable will be displayed in the following manner:
Path=C:\WINNT\system32;C:\WINNT;C:\WINNT\fw1\5.0\bin

## Chapter 9

Tracking and Alerts

Solutions in this chapter:

- **Alerts Commands**
- **User-Defined Tracking**
- **Suspicious Activities Monitoring (SAM)**
- **Check Point Malicious Activity Detection (CPMAD)**

☑ **Summary**

☑ **Solutions Fast Track**

☑ **Frequently Asked Questions**

Introduction

One important part of firewall security is being aware of what traffic is going through your firewall. For instance, if you are under an attack, you will be able to react appropriately. Check Point VPN-1/FireWall-1 provides you with the ability to set up alerts based on certain criteria, and you can add some of these alerts directly into your rule base under the Track column in your Security Policy Editor. You can even decide what action to take if a certain alert is raised.

For example, you could put an alert command in the Track column of your Drop All rule, and configure it to page you if it matches 20 drops every five minutes. You would have to be careful about filtering out noisy services like Netbios (nbname, nbsession, and nbdatagram); otherwise you may get paged once every five minutes. Setting up an alarm like this, however, could help you detect port scans on your network.

VPN-1/FireWall-1 NG comes with a Check Point Malicious Activity Detection system, CPMAD for short. This system is enabled when you install the software, and has a basic set of configuration options. We will discuss the configuration files and show you how to modify alert commands in this chapter.

Alerts Commands

Your main day-to-day interaction with the firewall will be the handling of alerts that it generates. These alerts are generated by the rules you have configured, and are also customizable. Using the Policy Editor GUI, you can customize the various alert types. Select **Policy | Global Properties** and then select the **Log and Alert** branch from the left. You'll see a screen like that in Figure 9.1.

Figure 9.1 Log and Alert Main Menu

This panel contains a lot of information, but it is all pretty straightforward. The default settings are shown in the illustration, but may be altered to be any of the valid responses (log, pop-up alert, mail alert, and so on). Let's begin at the beginning.

Using Track Options

The Track Options are very handy for seeing information about administrative happenings, such as VPN information, as well as for a couple of security related issues, such as connections matched by SAM. How is this useful to you? Say, for example, that your organization has placed the burden of configuring a Virtual Private Network on your lap, and now you must troubleshoot while you attempt to establish this VPN with your parent organization. These options could be useful to you while you are in the first stages, by logging or alerting based on the criteria you select here.

- **VPN successful key exchange** This event is triggered by the successful exchange of VPN keys.

- **VPN packet handling errors** This denotes an error in a VPN connection, such as a method mismatch.

- **VPN configuration and key exchange errors** This field defines the behavior that FireWall-1 will exhibit when a VPN configuration or key exchange event fails.

- **IP Options drop** This is triggered by an IP packet with options set. Since options are rarely (if ever) useful in a valid connection, FireWall-1 will always drop these packets. You may, however, do something when you see such a packet. Often, such packets are used to probe a network, so it might be wise to at least log them.

- **Administrative notifications** This action is triggered by a FireWall-1 administrative notification.

- **SLA violation** Used in concert with the Traffic Monitor, this event will alert you when a Service Level Agreement (SLA) has been breached.

- **Connection matched by SAM** This defines action taken when a packet belonging to a SAM inhibited connection is matched. SAM is discussed later in this chapter.

Logging Modifiers

The Logging Modifiers section features only one option. This option instructs FireWall-1 to log information pertaining to packets in an established TCP flow, or packets in a connection that might have been timed out. This selection is enabled by default.

- Log Established TCP packets

Time Settings

The time settings can help decrease the amount of data that you see in your Log Viewer. You can accomplish this by setting thresholds on the packet flows, and recording only the data that is unique within that threshold.

- **Excessive log grace period**   This defines the time in which packets belonging to an established TCP flow are considered uninteresting to FireWall-1 for logging purposes. Increasing this value has a proportionate decreasing impact on your log volume. Packets are considered part of the same flow if they have an identical packet header, meaning that they contain the same source address, source port, destination address, and destination port (e.g. telnet), and that they use the same protocol (e.g. TCP=protocol 6). You can find a list of commonly used protocol numbers on most UNIX systems in the /etc/protocols file. Note that packets will still be inspected and acted on, but the logging of the packet will be suppressed.

- **Log Viewer resolving timeout**   This indicates the amount of time that FireWall-1 will try to resolve IP addresses into hostnames before quitting. If this time is reached, the IP address will be displayed in the Log Viewer instead. If the FireWall-1 Log Viewer GUI is slow at displaying, you could adjust this setting to increase the Viewer's performance.

- **Virtual Link statistics logging interval**   Specifies the amount of time between VL informative packets. This is meaningful if you are using CP Traffic Monitor and if you have properly defined virtual links.

There is also a sub-panel, which is shown in Figure 9.2. This panel enables you to configure your response programs. Generally, most of the information on this panel won't require altering, with the exception of the pointers for user-defined scripts.

With that said, let's look at the default entries on the **Alerts Commands** sub-menu.

Figure 9.2 Alerts Commands Sub-Menu

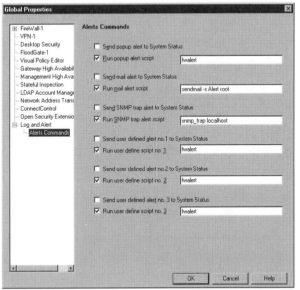

Alerts Commands

The default alert, fwalert, is indicated for both the normal alert handling as well as the three optional user-defined alerts (a nice increase from the single user-defined alert offered by VPN-1/FireWall-1 CP2000). Each field also enables you to interact with the System Status component. Keep in mind that the event is acted on by the machine that records the logs. While, in the majority of cases, this is the Management machine, it does not necessarily have to be. Also note that the actual executables and scripts reside in the $FWDIR/bin directory on the *Management* module. This is also where you would need to save your user-defined alert programs.

- **Pop-up alert script** This is the script that will be executed when you select a pop-up alert as the action for a matched rule. Generally, this should not be altered. One item of special note here is the actual function of a pop-up alert. When you are running the System Status GUI, and a rule is matched whose action is alert, and **Send pop-up alert to System Status** is selected, you will be notified with a window containing details of the alert. These details include the packet information as well as things like the component generating the alert. This window enables you to delete single events or all selected events.

- **Mail alert script**   This specifies the command that will be run to send an email alert regarding the matched event, assuming that this action is the specified one. You may need to change this and the command will be specific to your system.

- **SNMP trap alert script**   Defines the action when a rule with the SNMP trap action is matched. You may decide to alter this to send your traps to alternate locations, such as to a Network Management station.

- **User defined script (No. 1, 2, and 3)**   These allow for you to write your own programs to handle a matched rule, and are very handy. User-defined alerts are covered later in this chapter.

Once you have properly configured the commands to be run, you are ready to begin using them as an action. Your most frequent interaction with them will be in the rules you create on your firewall. When you create a new rule, or wish to modify an existing rule, simply right-click on the **Action** column, and you'll see a Context menu as shown in Figure 9.3.

Figure 9.3 Alert Context Menu

You also may interact with the alerting function within various network objects. For example, Figure 9.4 shows us the User Properties window with the Encryption panel active. Note the field labeled *Successful Authentication Track*. In this field, (which is common to several network objects), you'll be able to configure alerting for this event.

Figure 9.4 Alerting in Use

User-Defined Tracking

FireWall-1 features very robust event handling, but it isn't always able to do exactly what you want. In some cases you need to send multiple alert types, or need to send them to many different people. Check Point foresaw this need and has included the user-defined alert type. With this alert type, VPN-1 /FIRE-WALL-1 provides you the ability to "roll your own" event-handling scripts. You also don't have to learn a new programming language to do so. If you are proficient in C, C++, Perl, WSH, the various Unix shell-scripting languages, or even writing .bat files, then you are well on the way to creating a user-defined response. You also might be able to find an existing script via the Internet that would suite your needs.

The process to write your own script is pretty simple. There are a couple of ways to go about it. Initially, you may be more inclined to use user-defined alerts to generate multiple alert types. Suppose, for example, that you want to send an SNMP trap to a network management console, to a security console, and also mail an alert to yourself. Writing a simple Windows batch or Unix shell script will get this done for you with minimal effort, as shown in Figure 9.5.

Figure 9.5 Simple "Batch" Script

```
snmp_trap 192.168.1.23
snmp_trap 192.168.10.12
mailx -s Warning admin@security
```

alertf

Another option for user-defined tracking is the VPN-1/FW-1 command "alertf." alertf is a program that acts as a wrapper for user-defined scripts. It simplifies the process of launching your user-defined event by allowing some specific criteria. It does this by enabling you to specify a threshold that must be met in order for your user-defined script to be executed. The syntax for alertf is as follows:

```
alertf num_seconds num_alerts program_name arg1 arg2 ...
```

As an example, we would like to see a minimum of 5 events over 2 minutes in order for your user-defined script to be launched. This is a bit tricky to do within the script itself, and may lead to some strange hacks. Using alertf, however, gives you a simple, one-line solution. To accomplish this, you would use the following syntax:

```
alertf 120 5 $FWDIR/bin/program
```

It doesn't get much easier than that! Keep in mind, as usual, that alertf resides on the system running the management module, which is also where your user-defined script must reside.

Advanced User-Defined Alerts

If you want to move into more advanced realms, the first step is to understand what VPN-1/FIREWALL-1 will be sending as input to your script. The format for this input is as seen in this example:

```
10Nov2001 15:00:12 drop    firewall_sparc   >le1 proto tcp
     src 192.168.10.3 dst 192.168.10.4 service 1234 s_port 2345
     len 40 rule 4
```

The various fields are described in Table 9.1.

Table 9.1 Basic User-Defined Alert Input

Field	Example
Date	10Nov2001
Time	15:00:12
Action	Drop
Originating firewall	Firewall_sparc
Traffic Direction and Interface	>le1

Continued

Table 9.1 Continued

Field	Example
Protocol in use	proto tcp
Source Address	src 192.168.10.3
Destination Address	dst 192.168.10.4
Service in use	service 1234
Source Port	s_port 2345
Length of data captured	len 40
Rule matched	rule 4

Note that these are the basic log input values. The values will change depending on your use of NAT, VPN encryption, or the alerting on ICMP packets. For example, an ICMP packet will include field information for the icmp-type and icmp-code. These additional fields are detailed in Table 9.2.

Table 9.2 ICMP and NAT User-Defined Input

Field	Explanation
icmp-type	ICMP type
icmp-code	ICMP code
Xlatesrc	When using NAT, this indicates the source IP that was translated.
Xlatedst	When using NAT, this indicates the destination IP that was translated.
Xlatesport	When using NAT, this indicates the source port that was translated.
Xlatedport	When using NAT, this indicates the destination port that was translated.

Once you understand what VPN-1/FIREWALL-1 will be sending your program, you can then make logical decisions as to what to do with this. User-defined alerting can be very useful as a method to inform various people based on what the rule detects. For example, the script could parse out the destination IP address or system name, compare that information to a database and then, from the database, locate the proper contact information for the responsible individual. Once this person is located, he or she can be notified via any of several means, allowing the person a more rapid response to the attack. Some other common examples use the global WHOIS database to attempt to locate the administrator of the source of the event, and attempt to notify that person as well. Figure 9.6 includes a partial script as an example of how to get started. It's written in Perl, but, as mentioned earlier, the choice is yours.

Figure 9.6 Beginnings of a User-Defined Alert

```
#!/usr/bin/perl -w
#
# Here we'll request strict pragma checking and import a module to
# assist in sending a mail message.
use strict;
use Net::SMTP;

# Good programming practice mandates security!
$ENV{'PATH'} = '/bin:/usr/bin:/sbin:/usr/sbin:/usr/local/bin';
umask (0177);

# Get the log entry and break it up into smaller, useable bits.
my $log = <STDIN>;
my @elements = split (/[ ]+/, $log);

# Identify the most commonly used elements and assign them for frequent
# use.
my $date       = $elements[0];
my $time       = $elements[1];
my $source     = $elements[9];
my $destination = $elements[11];

# The array element to use can vary depending on the use of NAT, among
other factors. Be sure to test.
my $service    = $elements[13];
(...)
```

You can see that it is actually very simple to get the log data. Any program that can gather one line of input and parse it up will do the trick. The only remaining tasks are to install your program in $FWDIR/bin on the machine running the firewall Management Module, and point to it within the firewall configuration. The fact that the alert script runs on the Management Module makes deploying this user-defined script much easier, especially in a large network. And, since it runs in one central location with access to all the firewall logs, you can do some simple event correlation.

Designing & Planning…

Intrusion Detection?

While this book is about VPN-1/FireWall-1, you probably also have Intrusion Detection on your mind as well. Intrusion Detection greatly adds to the overall effectiveness of a firewall, when deployed properly. But what if you can't deploy an IDS suite because of something such as budget limitations?

The usual solution is to cross one's fingers and hope for fair weather, but with VPN-1/FireWall-1, you have better solutions. As we'll detail later in this chapter, you can use the Check Point Malicious Activity Detection to alert you to the presence of some simple probes and attacks, but this feature isn't all that extendable. Another solution is to use user-defined alerts.

Lance Spitzner maintains a guide on how to use user-defined alerts to create a lightweight IDS based on the data collected by VPN-1/FireWall-1 alerts, and even has a script that will do the trick for you. You can visit this guide and download the script (it's distributed under terms of the GPL license, free of charge) by pointing your Web browser to http://secinf.net/info/unix/lance/intrusion.html.

Suspicious Activities Monitoring (SAM)

Check Point, along with their OPSEC alliance partners, has introduced a very powerful feature into VPN-1/FireWall-1. This feature, known as Suspicions Activity Monitoring, or SAM, enables the firewall to interact and be configured by other network devices. Most notable among these OPSEC partners is ISS, with their RealSecure product. Using SAMP (Suspicious Activity Monitoring Protocol) a RealSecure sensor can dynamically update VPN-1/FireWall-1 rules. These changes can be either permanent or time based.

For you, as a firewall administrator, the most interesting element of SAM is not the ability of other devices to restrict connections, but your own ability to block, or "inhibit," a connection. This can be a very powerful reactive measure, and, if properly employed, can greatly enhance your site security. Imagine the ability to block a connection for five or 10 minutes while you do some quick research on the nature of the suspicious connection. Teamed with a user-defined alert script, this can even be done in an automated way.

Connection inhibiting is enabled using the *fw sam* command. This command has some very useful options, most of which are detailed in Table 9.3.

Table 9.3 "fw sam" Command Options

Option	Explanation
-v	Enable verbose mode. In this mode of operation, SAM writes a message to STDERR on each firewall module that is enforcing the action. The message indicates the success or failure.
-s server	The address or registered name of the VPN-1/FireWall-1 system that will enforce the action.
-t timeout	The time period, during which the action will be blocked, specified in seconds. If no value is specified, the action will be in effect indefinitely, or until canceled by you.
-C	Cancel the blocking of the connection specified by the parameters.
-D	Cancel all inhibit and notify directives.
-n	Notify (by recording a log entry) and alert (but do not block) based on the specified criteria.
-i	Inhibit the connection meeting the specified criteria. Connections will be rejected.
-I	Inhibit the connection meeting the specified criteria. Also close all existing connections that match the criteria. Connections will be rejected.
-j	Inhibit the connection meeting the specified criteria. Connections will be dropped.
-J	Inhibit the connection meeting the specified criteria. Also close all existing connections that match the criteria. Connections will be dropped.
-l	Specifies the log format to use when recording an event. Options are nolog, long_noalert and long_alert, with the latter being the default.

This command is very useful if you are writing user-defined scripts, and you should really become comfortable with that process. Another way to interface with SAM is via the Log Viewer GUI. From the Log Viewer, select **Active Mode** from the Mode menu. You will then see entries representing the active connections for the firewall. Each connection will be assigned a Connection ID, as indicated in Figure 9.7.

Figure 9.7 Active Connections—Connection ID

Once you have noted the connection that you wish to do away with, you will select **Tools | Block Intruder** from the menu. You will then see a screen as illustrated in figure 9.8.

Figure 9.8 Specify the Connection ID

Finally, you'll see the actual panel used to block the connection. You have a couple of options to select from on this screen, which is shown in Figure 9.9.

- **Blocking Scope**   Enables you to block this specific connection, all connections from the source noted in the log, or all connections to the destination noted in the log.

- **Blocking Timeout**   Enables you to specify either indefinite blocking or a time period for this block.

- **Force this blocking**   Enables you to enforce blocking this connection on all firewalls or just the firewall that has recorded the event.

You see that the command-line arguments, while a bit more complicated, do allow some greater flexibility. The ease of use of the GUI makes up for this, as scripted execution can be used when you want to be very specific. You'd hate to "fat finger" a command-line version and block your boss' connection.

So, what do you do when you've blocked a connection that shouldn't be blocked, or wish to unblock an existing block? Here's where it gets odd. The

GUI only enables you to unblock *en masse*. It's an all-or-nothing proposition. From the menu bar, select **Tools | Clear Blocking**. This will present you a pop-up message, like the one in Figure 9.10, warning you that ALL inhibited connections will now be cleared. If you've made a mistake and blocked the wrong connection (assuming you have other, valid blocks in place) your only real recourse is to use the command-line syntax to clear a specific block.

Figure 9.9 SAM Block Intruder Screen

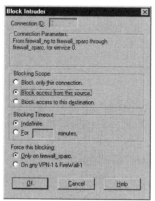

Figure 9.10 Clear Blocking Confirmation

Check Point Malicious Activity Detection (CPMAD)

FireWall-1 features a handy log analyzer known as Check Point Malicious Activity Detection, or CPMAD for short. This feature aids in the detection of unusual, potentially dangerous activities across a range of firewall modules. To accomplish this, the software analyzes the log data from either single or multiple firewall modules and compares the log information to rules that have been con-figured for alerting. Consequently, CPMAD only runs on the management server, and not within the firewall module itself. Following your VPN-1/FireWall-1 installation, CPMAD is disabled and must manually be enabled.

CPMAD also has some limitations. Primarily, CPMAD only runs on the Windows, Solaris, Red Hat Linux, and Nokia platforms. Also, it has severe limitations in the attacks that it can detect, as these are preconfigured within the VPN-1/FIREWALL-1 application. Table 9.4 lists these attacks.

Table 9.4 MAD Attack Types and Descriptions

Event Name (default state)	Description
syn_attack (on)	Excessive number of TCP synchronization (SYN) requests.
anti_spoofing (off)	Packets with a spoofed source IP address have been detected.
successive_alerts (on)	VPN-1/FireWall-1 has generated an amount of alerts that exceed the threshold.
port_scanning (off)	Port scanning behavior has been detected. Note that this event records the connection attempt as an attack regardless of the success of the connection attempt.
Blocked_connection_port_scanning (on)	Port scanning behavior has been detected. Note that this event only records attacks that attempt to connect to multiple blocked ports. This setting is less memory intensive than the port_scanning event, but also may miss attacks. Port_scanning and blocked_connection_port_scanning are not meant to be used together. Select one or the other.
login_failure (on)	A single source IP address has registered an amount of login failures that exceeds the threshold.
successive_multiple_connections (off)	A single source IP address has initiated a number of connections to the same destination IP address/port number which exceeds the threshold.
land_attack (on)	A "land attack" has been detected.

Another limitation is that MAD only analyzes the existing log data. In short, this means that if you don't log an event, MAD will have no idea that it happened. For example, the *port_scanning* behavior cannot be detected unless you have a rule that will generate a log entry for connection attempts.

Several of the listed attacks have prerequisite settings within the FW module itself. These settings enable the generation of the log entry that CPMAD alerts are based upon. These prerequisite settings are as follows:

- **Syn_attack** The FW module must be set as either a SYN Gateway or a Passive SYN Gateway.

- **Anti_spoofing** The interface properties must be set to alert (Interface Properties | Security Tab)

- **Login_failure** "Authentication Failure Track" must be set to alert (Properties Setup | Authentication Failure Tab)

CPMAD Configuration

CPMAD, as mentioned earlier, must be enabled on the management server before any events will be alerted on. CPMAD uses three configuration files, two of which are of interest to you here.

cpmad_config.conf

The main configuration file for CPMAD events is cpmad_config.conf. This file can be found in $FWDIR/conf directory. Its format is pretty standard: stanzas of configuration information with the # symbol indicating a comment line. Let's take a moment to examine the contents of this file. Note that a comment line indicating the purpose of the information begins each stanza, and I'll describe the information contained within the stanza immediately following that stanza.

```
# MAD mode
```

```
MAD_system_mode = off
```

This enables or disables CPMAD.

```
# MAD global parameters
```

```
MAD_memory = 75000
MAD_clean_interval = 60
MAD_number_of_connection_attempts = 10
MAD_interval_between_connection_attempts = 60
```

This defines the CPMAD global configuration paramaters. MAD_memory is the amount of memory, in bytes, allotted to the MAD process. Note that if insufficient memory is allocated, MAD will silently exit, giving no indication of the failure. `MAD_clean_interval` defines, in seconds, the amount of time that old attacks will be stored within the MAD memory tables. Increases in this value will result in a proportionate increase in memory requirements, but a lowering of the CPU overhead. `MAD_number_of_connection_attempts` defines the number of times the MAD process will attempt to reconnect to either the ELA or LEA server, should that connection fail. `MAD_interval_between_connection_attempts` defines the wait-period between those reconnection attempts.

The remaining stanzas define attack-specific parameters. All stanzas contain the same settings, in the following generic format.

```
# MAD attacks



# <attack name>

MAD_<attack name>_mode = [on|off]

MAD_<attack name>_resolution = [integer value]

MAD_<attack name>_time_interval = [integer value]

MAD_<attack name>_repetitions = [integer value]

MAD_<attack name>_action = [action]
```

As an example, let's examine the stanza for the `syn_attack` attack. Table 9.5 describes the meaning of the entry line by line.

Table 9.5 CPMAD Configuration Details

Stanza Entry	Description
MAD_syn_attack_mode = on	Enables or disables the processing of this alert.
MAD_syn_attack_resolution = 10	Sets the "resolution" for this attack. Conceptually, a timer is started when the first matching event is recorded. All subsequent matching events within *resolution* seconds will be counted as part of the first event and will not count towards *repetitions* for logging purposes only. Increasing this value lowers memory usage.

Continued

Table 9.5 Continued

Stanza Entry	Description
MAD_syn_attack_time_interval = 60	The amount of time, in seconds, that attack information is stored within the internal MAD memory tables. Similar to the global MAD_clean_interval in purpose, this parameter must be larger than the value set for MAD_<attack name>_resolution in order to be meaningful. Check Point recommends that the ratio between *resolution* and *interval* not exceed 1:5, with 1:10 being recommended.
MAD_syn_attack_repetitions = 100	The number of unique events that must be recorded within *interval* seconds in order for the action specified to be taken.
MAD_syn_attack_action = alert	The action to be taken when the event threshold is exceeded. This corresponds to the alert commands in the Log and Alert field under *Policy*	*Global Properties*. Action choices are alert, mail .snmptrap, and useralert.

CPMAD Problems

It is important to remember that CPMAD, in common with every other piece of software written by us mere mortals, has some problems. Hopefully you can be forewarned here of some of the most bothersome, so that you won't have to discover them on your own. You've already heard mentioned what may be the most glaring problem, that being the tendency for MAD to silently exit if insufficient memory resources are available. Related to this is the fact that little guidance is given as to how much memory is enough. Also, memory isn't the only thing that may cause the MAD process to exit without writing an error. Some other annoyances include the following:

- The ELA proxy being disabled

- The FWDIR environment variable being incorrectly set or not set at all

- Improper settings in the fwopsec.conf file

- Failure of the firewall daemon, fwd

Another thing to keep in mind is that MAD is, in effect, an LEA client. For those who aren't as familiar with OPSEC jargon, this means that MAD uses the OPSEC Log Export API (LEA) to gather information from the management module. It also uses the Event Logging API (ELA) to create log entries in the VPN-1/FIREWALL-1 log file. This means that it requires that the ELA proxy be running on the management module, which is generally the case. It is not a requirement, however; you can disable the ELA proxy on the management module without any negative impact.

Another important thing to keep in mind is that if VPN-1/FIREWALL-1 is stopped and restarted while the ELA proxy is attempting a connection, MAD events are logged to a temp file. When the ELA proxy completes its connection, a log entry is generated, indicating the location of this temporary log as well as the number of entries it contains, but MAD **will not** generate alerts based on the contents of that file.

Designing & Planning…

Where are all the experts?

Here's a place we've all been before: using a new product, perhaps even new to firewalls altogether, and wondering how to get help. Check Point, while putting out what is arguably the best firewall software on the market, does seem to lack a little when it comes to support, and their documentation is, well, sparse. With this in mind, you might be wondering how one does go about truly mastering this software.

One of the best resources is the Internet. VPN-1/FIREWALL-1 has developed quite a following, and with this comes a bevy of online resources developed by third parties, with one of my favorites being the VPN-1/FIREWALL-1 FAQs, located at www.phoneboy.com. Folks from all over contribute these FAQs on almost every topic you can imagine, concerning VPN-1/FIREWALL-1. There is also a very busy mailing list hosted at this site. Point your browser at www.phoneboy.com/wizards/index .html in order to subscribe. Two other very popular mailing lists are also most valuable in the aid they can provide. These lists are the VPN-1/FIRE-WALL-1 mailing list and the Firewall-wizards mailing list. You can get information about each at the following URLs:

- www.checkpoint.com/services/mailing.html
- http://list.nfr.com/mailman/listinfo/firewall-wizards

Summary

In this chapter, we have looked at some of the options you have when dealing with an event recorded by VPN-1/FireWall-1. We examined, in some depth, the ability for you to exercise some strong control over these settings and how their judicious use can greatly enhance the security of your network.

We examined the alerts commands configuration panels and learned about the default settings and how to alter them to better suit your security policy. You saw that you can modify not only the data that is logged, and when it is recorded, but also what action to take based on event criteria.

We went on to learn about the process of defining your own programs to handle an event, and saw some of the increased flexibility this allows you when designing your security policy. We even saw how user-defined alerts can be a sort of "lightweight" IDS system, and learned how to use the command-line interface to Check Point's Suspicious Activity Monitoring to allow your user-defined alerts to have some "teeth."

We also saw the GUI interface to SAM, and how to interface with the Log Viewer GUI to block connections, and how to use the command-line interface to SAM. Finally, we delved into Check Point's Malicious Activity Detection program, CPMAD. We witnessed how this program can warn you of some of the most common attacks your network might face, and how to configure MAD to alert or ignore attacks. All in all, the additional features and function added by the ability to define your own alerts, SAM and MAD make Check Point FireWall-1 a real standout in the firewall market, and I hope that after reading this chapter you'll be more able to take advantage of these features to secure your enterprise.

Solutions Fast Track

Alerts Commands

- ☑ Do not change the default program for a pop-up alert
- ☑ Be very cautious when changing the time parameters, specifically Excessive Log Grace Period. Your company may have log retention policy that mandates verbose logging.
- ☑ Remember that you're if using multiple log hosts, you'll run the possibility of getting multiple alerts.

User-Defined Tracking

- ☑ Make every attempt to put the power of user-defined alerts to work for you.

- ☑ Be sure that you test any user-defined script against all the rules in the Rule Base set to run it as an action. NAT, ICMP (and NAT'ed ICMP), and VPN traffic will have different formats sent as input to the script.

- ☑ Use alertf to extend your script by enforcing limit criteria and cutting down on false positives.

Suspicious Activities Monitoring

- ☑ Use SAM to enhance the power of your user-defined alert scripts.

- ☑ Be sure that you double-check the connection information before performing a block, and consider using the time restrictions.

- ☑ Remember that the GUI method to unblock a connection cannot specify which connection to unblock; it's all or nothing!

Check Point Malicious Activity Detection (CPMAD)

- ☑ Use CPMAD when you need to be aware of events such as a SYN flood or basic port scans.

- ☑ Be sure to modify $FWDIR/conf/cpmad_config.conf to suite your site's needs.

- ☑ Make sure that sufficient resources are available to CPMAD, and (as always) test the system before relying on it to protect you.

Frequently Asked Questions

The following Frequently Asked Questions, answered by the authors of this book, are designed to both measure your understanding of the concepts presented in this chapter and to assist you with real-life implementation of these concepts. To have your questions about this chapter answered by the author, browse to **www.syngress.com/solutions** and click on the **"Ask the Author"** form.

Q: I installed my user-defined script on my firewall, but it isn't doing anything when the rule is matched.

A: Remember that the alertd process is running on the machine acting as the management server. Place the script in the $FWDIR/bin directory of that system and begin testing from there.

Q: I'm trying to block a connection with SAM, but I don't see a Connection ID field in my log viewer, and when I click on **Tools**, the **Block Intruder** option is grayed out.

A: Remember that to use the SAM feature, your Log Viewer must be in **Active Mode**.

Q: Is there a way to see what IP addresses are currently blocked on my firewall?

A: Yes and no. The blocked IP addresses are maintained in a FW-1 table, sam_blocked_ips. The firewall command *fw tab —t sam_blocked_ips* will show you the contents of that table, but it isn't the easiest thing on earth to read.

Q: I'm no programmer, but I'm really excited by the user-defined alert idea. Does Check Point supply any preconfigured user-defined alerts?

A: Not that I have ever seen, but fear not. The Internet is full of helpful people, and a quick search might reveal what you need.

Chapter 10

Configuring Virtual Private Networks

Solutions in this chapter:

- **Encryption Schemes**

- **Configuring an FWZ VPN**

- **Configuring an IKE VPN**

- **Configuring a SecuRemote VPN**

- **Installing SecuRemote Client Software**

- **Using SecuRemote Client Software**

☑ Summary

☑ Solutions Fast Track

☑ Frequently Asked Questions

Introduction

Many organizations are using Virtual Private Networks (VPNs) over the Internet in order to have a secure channel for remote offices, business partners, and mobile users to access their internal networks. For many, the VPN is replacing dedicated frame relay circuits or dial-in VPN services for their organizational needs.

For example, your office headquarters may be in Hartford, Connecticut, but you have a small, remote office located in Tampa, Florida. You could set up a gateway-to-gateway VPN between these two offices so that they can share each other's resources on the network through an encrypted channel over the Internet. The communication between these two branches is secured by the endpoints of the connection, which are the firewalls at each location.

In this chapter, we will discuss the different types of encryption available to you in VPN-1/FireWall-1 Next Generation, and we'll explain this technology to you so that you'll understand how it is working. Check Point makes it easy to set up a VPN using their Policy Editor, and we will show you how to configure VPNs between gateways and to mobile clients. Then we will demonstrate how to install the SecuRemote client software. If you are interested in desktop security for the client, we will be covering that in the next chapter.

A bit of theory is necessary before beginning the process of describing how to set up VPNs with Check Point NG. You need to first understand the basics of encryption algorithms, key exchange, hash functions, digital signatures, and certificates before you can feel comfortable troubleshooting and deploying VPNs.

Encryption Schemes

Encryption is the process of transforming regular, readable data, or plaintext, into "scrambled" or unreadable form, called ciphertext. Decryption is the reverse process, the transforming of ciphertext into plaintext. The process of encryption can be used in various ways to ensure privacy, authenticity, and data integrity:

- **Privacy** No one should be able to view the plaintext message except the original sender and intended recipient.

- **Authenticity** The recipient of an encrypted message should be able to verify with certainty who the sender of the message is.

- **Data Integrity** The recipient of the message should be able to verify that it has not been tampered with or altered in any way while in transit.

Encryption is accomplished using an encryption algorithm, typically a pair of closely related mathematical functions that perform the actual encryption and decryption on the data provided to them. Modern encryption algorithms, including the ones used in Check Point NG, utilize what is called a *key* (or keys) to aid in the encryption or decryption process. There are two types of encryption algorithms: symmetric and asymmetric.

Encryption Algorithms; Symmetric vs. Asymmetric Cryptography

In what is called *Symmetric Encryption*, the encryption algorithm itself is public, while the key is a secret. Anyone discovering the key, with knowledge of the algorithm, can decrypt any messages encrypted with that key. Since both the sender and recipient need to know the secret key before they can communicate, you must have a secure method of exchanging the key. Sometimes you will hear the term "Sneaker Net" used to describe this key exchange process, meaning that the exchange takes place via phone, fax, or in person, since an online exchange cannot be encrypted prior to the sharing of the key. Sometimes you will hear this key referred to as a "shared secret." Symmetric encryption is typically very fast, but has some disadvantages:

- As stated above, anyone discovering the secret key can decrypt the messages.

- Since each sender-recipient pair (we will call them "users") needs a separate secret key, the number of separate keys that need to be managed increases rapidly as the number of users increases. Mathematically, we need $n(n-1)/2$ keys for a network of n users. Using this formula, a network of 500 users requires 124,750 unique keys.

Asymmetric encryption was developed to solve the problem of secure key exchange and to improve key management. It is called asymmetric because the encryption and decryption keys are different. In one form of asymmetric encryption, called "public key" encryption, both the sender and recipient each have two keys, one of which is public and can be openly shared, and another of which is private and is kept secret and never shared. If Alice wishes to send an encrypted message to Bob, she and Bob only need to exchange public keys. The method used for the exchange need not be private in this case. Alice encrypts the plaintext message to Bob using Bob's public key. When Bob receives the message, he decrypts it using his private key. This method of public key encryption was invented in 1976 by Whitfield Diffie and Martin Hellman, and is sometimes called the "Diffie-Hellman" algorithm.

Another form of asymmetric encryption, called RSA encryption, is used by Check Point NG for generating digital signatures.

As we can see, asymmetric encryption solves the problem of key exchanges needing to be done in private. Users need only share their public keys to encrypt messages to one another. Asymmetric encryption does suffer one serious drawback, however: It is much, much slower than symmetric encryption (on the order of 1000 times slower). For this reason, real-life encryption schemes tend to use a "hybrid" form of public key exchange and private (symmetric) key encryption. Check Point NG is no different in this regard. A Diffie-Hellman key pair is used to generate and exchange a shared secret key, which is used for all encryption and decryption after the initial public key exchange. The shared secret key in this case is sometimes called a "session key." The shared key can be regenerated at periodic intervals to lessen the chance of its compromise.

An encryption algorithm's security is completely dependent on its keys and how they are managed. Strong encryption that has a flawed key management algorithm is really weak encryption. You will often hear of an encryption algorithm described as using a "128-bit" key, for example. What this means is that, if implemented properly, someone who tried to enumerate every possible key in order to break your encryption (called a "brute force" attack) would have to try 2^{128} different key combinations to be guaranteed success. This is not computationally feasible for the foreseeable future. In practice, cryptanalysts will typically attack an algorithm's key generation or key management scheme instead, attempting to find a flaw such as a predictable sequence of keys to exploit. The moral of all this is to pay attention to an algorithm's implementation, rather than to its key size exclusively. The latter will not guarantee your security. Note that asymmetric encryption schemes typically have key sizes that are much larger than symmetric ones (1024 bits, for example). The strength of these keys cannot be equated to the strength of symmetric keys, as they use different mathematical principles. The original Diffie-Hellman public key scheme, for example, was based on the difficulty of factoring very large prime numbers.

Check Point makes available several encryption algorithms. They are enumerated below in Table 10.1, along with their shared key sizes and whether or not they are based on a public standard or are proprietary.

Table 10.1 Check Point Encryption Algorithms

Algorithm	Key-Length in Bits	Standard
FWZ-1	40-bits	Check Point proprietary
CAST	40-bits	Public
DES	56-bits	Public
3DES	168-bits	Public
AES	256-bits	Public

Key Exchange Methods: Tunneling vs. In-Place Encryption

The above encryption algorithms can be used in one of two key exchange schemes in FireWall-1: IKE (ISAKMP) or FWZ.

The Internet Security Association and Key Management Protocol (ISAKMP), or Internet Key Exchange (IKE), is an Internet encryption, authentication, and key exchange standard put forth by the IETF. It is widely used in today's Internet when implementing VPNs. Because it is a standard, a Check Point firewall utilizing it will be able to interoperate with other third-party VPN products. I have tested or seen in production use Check Point firewalls that interoperated with Linux gateways (Free/SWAN), OpenBSD, SonicWall, and Watchguard firewall products, as examples. The ISAKMP key exchange process is divided into two phases, and utilizes what are called "Security Associations" (SAs) to facilitate encryption and key generation. Keys and SAs are regenerated on a periodic basis.

IKE uses what is called "tunneling-mode encryption." This means that each packet that is to be sent over a VPN is first encrypted (both header and data payload are encrypted), and then encapsulated with a new header. The new header will differ based on whether the packet is just being encrypted, just being authenticated, or both. This tunneling mode slightly degrades network performance, but is more secure.

FWZ is a Check Point proprietary key exchange scheme that utilizes another proprietary protocol, RDP (reliable datagram protocol, not the same as the one described in RFC 1151) to negotiate encryption and authentication methods between gateways.

FWZ uses what is called "In-place encryption," in which packet bodies are encrypted, leaving the original TCP/IP headers in place. This method of encryption is faster than tunneling mode, but at the expense of security, since original header information is left in a readable state, including IP addresses, which are internal to an organization. Note that because FWZ does not encapsulate packets before sending them through a VPN, FWZ cannot be used in situations where any networks participating in the VPN domain have non-routable addresses.

Hash Functions and Digital Signatures

A hash function, also known as a "one-way function," is a mathematical function that takes a variable-length input and generates a fixed-length output, which is typically much smaller than the input. If we pass a plaintext message through a hash function, we produce what is called a "message digest." A good hash function is one that, if we are given the message digest, it is impossible to "reverse" the function and deduce the original message. It is also one in which for any two different function inputs (two different messages in this context), the output should be unique to the input. To put it another way, the message digests for two different messages should also be different. As we will see below, this principle can be used to ensure the integrity of a message. If a hash function generates the same message digest for two different inputs, we call this a "collision." A good hash function will minimize collisions. When we talk about hash functions, we usually specify the length of the message digest in bits. This roughly corresponds (strength-wise) to the length of a symmetric encryption key. For example, a commonly used hash function, "MD5," produces a 128-bit message digest for any size input it is given.

The output to a hash function is usually much smaller than the original message as well. MD4 and MD5 are good examples of hash functions. You may have heard of an MD5 checksum before. This checksum would be the result of sending a file through the MD5 hash algorithm.

Another important note about hash functions is that the output is unique to the message. If the original message was tampered with in any way, then a different message digest would result. Since you cannot "decrypt" a message digest, you run the algorithm against the message and compare the two digests to verify that the message is intact. This is how data integrity is achieved.

A *digital signature* is an attachment to a message that utilizes a hash function and enables the receiver to authenticate the sender and verify data integrity. Digital signatures can be attached to encrypted messages. Check Point NG generates digital signatures using an RSA private key and a hash function, as follows (assume that Alice wants to send a digitally signed message to Bob):

1. Alice sends the (unencrypted) message through a hash function, producing a fixed-length message digest.

2. Alice encrypts the message digest with her private RSA key, and sends it on its way, along with the encrypted message. The encrypted message is now "signed" by Alice.

3. Bob decrypts the message as usual, and passes it through the same hash function Alice used when it was sent. Bob compares this message digest he just generated with the decrypted message digest sent to him, making sure they match. Alice's public key is used to decrypt the message digest in this case.

A match in this case means that Bob can be sure that Alice sent the message, and that no one tampered with it in transit. We are assuming here that Bob trusts that he is using Alice's public key; this trust is usually provided by a certificate authority who will certify public keys.

The two hash functions offered by Check Point are *MD5* and *SHA-1*. MD5 is a 128-bit hash function, while SHA-1 is considered more secure with a 160-bit message digest length.

Certificates and Certificate Authorities

A certificate authority (CA) is a trusted third party that we can obtain a public key from reliably. A certificate is issued by a CA, and contains reliable information about the entity wishing to be "certified" authentic. This could be a person's or firewall's public key, or a secure Web-server host name and domain.

In the case of Check Point NG VPNs, certificates can be used by encrypting gateways to exchange public keys and to authenticate one another. Typically, the gateways themselves or (in the case of FWZ) the management consoles act as certificate authorities in this regard.

Types of VPNs

There are logically two types of VPNs: *site-to-site* and *client-to-site*. Site-to-site VPNs are what we normally think of when we think "VPN"—two gateways separating an insecure network (usually the Internet), with encrypted traffic passing between them.

Client-to-site VPNs, on the other hand, have a fixed gateway at one end and a mobile client on the other, perhaps with a dynamic IP address. This type of VPN is implemented by Check Point's SecuRemote or Secure Client products.

VPN domains

We can define a *VPN domain* as a group of hosts and/or networks behind a firewalled gateway that participate in a VPN. In a site-to-site VPN, each gateway has its own VPN domain defined, and is also aware of the other gateway's VPN domain. Any traffic coming from one VPN domain and going to the other (behind the opposing gateway) will be encrypted outbound, and then decrypted inbound at the other end.

VPN domains are defined on each gateway's firewall object, and must be set up with certain rules in mind. We will talk about this in more detail when we discuss VPN implementation.

Configuring an FWZ VPN

This section describes how to implement a site-to-site FWZ VPN. We will discuss configuration of local and remote gateways first, and then we will add encryption rules to our rule base. We will show configuration in the common situation of two gateway modules, with the local module acting as a management station for both modules. Since the management station manages both firewall modules, it will be a Certificate Authority for both gateways. We must also decide which networks will participate in our VPN domain. For this example, we will use *Local_Net* and *Remote_Net*. Make sure these network objects are created prior to starting implementation of your VPN. It is worth noting that in order to install a policy with encryption rules, you will need to purchase an encryption license from Check Point. This can be added to an existing license, or included with an original software purchase.

Designing & Planning…

VPN domains

It is important not to include either peer's gateway object in their respective VPN domains, or else traffic to or from each gateway will be encrypted, which is not what we want, nor can it work, as key exchange has not yet taken place. Contrast this with SEP (Single Entry Point) configurations, in which gateways must be a member of each VPN domain. Also, for non-routable VPN domains, make sure opposing subnets are

Continued

not identical. In large deployments, where you may have more than one gateway, each with a unique VPN tunnel, make sure the VPN domains don't "overlap" or include the same hosts/networks in both domains. Both gateways will want to encrypt traffic in cases where traffic passes through more than one gateway on the way to its destination. Better to use a SEP configuration for this, with some dynamic routing protocol inside you local network.

Defining Objects

For any site-to-site VPN, you will need to create and properly configure certain network objects, including both gateways and the networks or group objects representing your VPN domains.

Local Gateway

The first step in implementing your FWZ VPN is to configure your local gateway's encryption parameters. Under the VPN tab of your gateway's Workstation Properties window, select the FWZ encryption scheme and click **Edit**. The FWZ Properties dialog comes up (see Figure 10.1). Choose the management station (itself in this case) from the drop-down box labeled "Key manager management server," and generate a DH key if one is not present.

Next, open the Topology tab of the Workstation Properties window (see Figure 10.2). This is where you will define your VPN domain for the local gateway. Under **VPN Domain**, select **Manually Defined**, and then choose your local network from the drop-down list.

Remote Gateway

The remote gateway is set up exactly as the local gateway, with the distinction that your remote gateway's VPN domain is defined as *Remote_Net*, and your *Key manager management server* is still the local gateway object, since that is acting as the management station for both of your encrypting gateways.

Figure 10.1 Local Gateway's FWZ Properties Dialog

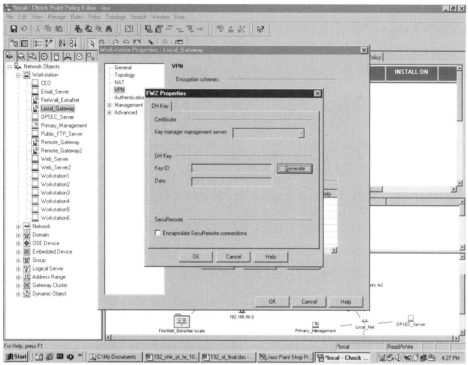

Figure 10.2 Topology Tab of the Workstation Properties Window

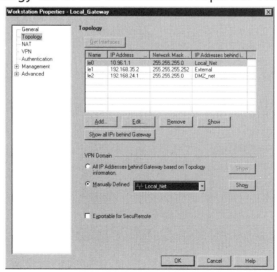

Adding VPN Rules

You want to modify your rule base so that traffic between *Local_Net* and *Remote_Net* is encrypted. This is done rather simply with the addition of two rules to your rule base (see Figure 10.3).

Figure 10.3 Rulebase Encryption Rules

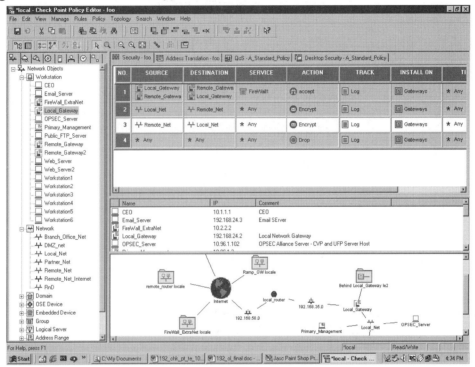

One rule specifies the following:

- **Source** Local_Net
- **Destination** Remote_Net
- **Service** Any
- **Action** Encrypt
- **Track** Log

While the other specifies the following:

- **Source** Remote_Net
- **Destination** Local_Net

- **Service** Any

- **Action** Encrypt

- **Track** Log

If you double-click on the **Encrypt** action in either encrypt rule, you will open the **Encryption Properties** dialog, from which you select **FWZ** and click **Edit** (see Figure 10.4). In the FWZ Properties dialog you can choose your encryption method, allowed peer gateway (e.g. which gateway or gateways you are allowed to establish a VPN with), and a data integrity method. You are limited to MD5 data integrity with FWZ encryption.

Figure 10.4 FWZ Properties Window

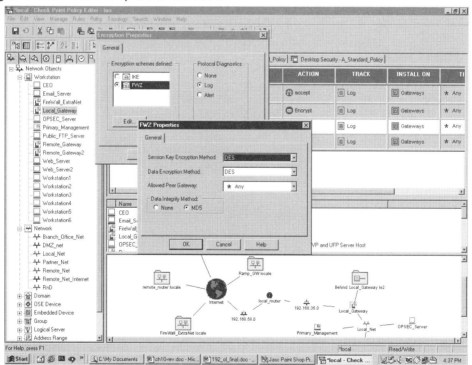

Note that in your encryption rule base, you have Rule 1 defined to allow the "FireWall1" group of services between both gateway endpoints. This rule is not always necessary, but must be added when you have "Accept VPN-1 & FireWall-1 control connections" unchecked in your security policy's Global Properties window (see Figure 10.5). This is checked by default after installation, so, in most cases you won't need a rule 1 as shown above, but it is good to keep in mind, as this allows the key exchange between gateways.

Figure 10.5 FireWall-1 Implied Rules

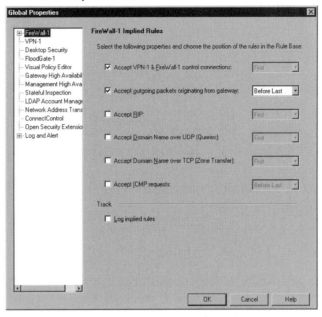

Once the gateway objects are properly configured and the VPN rules are added to the rulebase, the security policy must be installed for the changes to take effect. Once the policy has been installed on both gateways, you can open your log viewer and begin testing your VPN.

FWZ Limitations

Because FWZ is a non-encapsulating protocol, you cannot use it in situations where the networks participating in your VPN domains have non-routable addresses, or where both the source and destination IP addresses are being translated. FWZ will also not interoperate with other third-party VPN products, as it is a Check Point proprietary scheme. If you are in any of these situations, use IKE instead.

Configuring an IKE VPN

We will use the same assumptions as above, that we have two gateways, both managed by the same management station. As before, be sure to define network objects for the networks that will be participating in your VPN domain. We will use Local_Net and Remote_Net again for these networks.

Defining Objects

For any site-to-site VPN, you will need to create and properly configure certain network objects, including both gateways and the networks or group objects representing your VPN domains.

Local Gateway

Under the **VPN** tab of your gateway's Workstation Properties window, select the **IKE encryption scheme** and click **Edit**. The IKE Properties dialog comes up (see Figure 10.6). Notice that you have more encryption and data integrity choices with IKE than with FWZ. Select any and all of the encryption and data integrity methods you want your gateway to support, and check **Pre-Shared Secret** under **Support authentication methods** (you would check **Public Key Signatures** if you were using certificates). You will not be able to edit this secret until you define your remote gateway's encryption properties.

Figure 10.6 IKE Properties Dialog

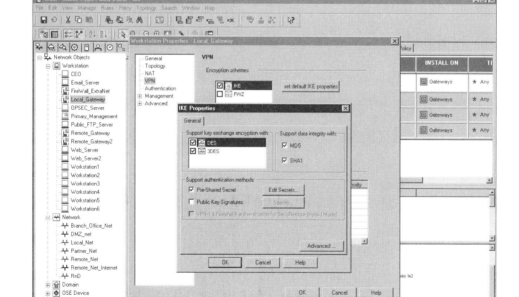

Next, open the **Topology** tab of the **Workstation Properties** window (see Figure 10.2). This is where you will define the VPN domain for your local gateway. Under **VPN Domain**, select **Manually Defined**, and choose your local network from the drop-down list.

Remote Gateway

Configuration of the remote gateway is nearly identical—you just need to make sure that you support the same methods of encryption and data integrity as you did on the local gateway. When you check **Pre-Shared Secret** this time, you can click on **Edit Secrets**, where you should see your peer, the local gateway, in the Shared Secrets List window (see Figure 10.7). You can edit the shared secret by highlighting the peer gateway in the list and clicking **Edit**. Enter the agreed-upon shared secret in the **Enter secret** text field, and click **Set** to define it. Don't forget to define your VPN domain under the Topology tab, by opening the **Topology** tab of the **Workstation Properties** window (see Figure 10.2). Under **VPN Domain**, select **Manually Defined**, and choose your remote network from the drop-down list.

Figure 10.7 Shared Secret Configuration

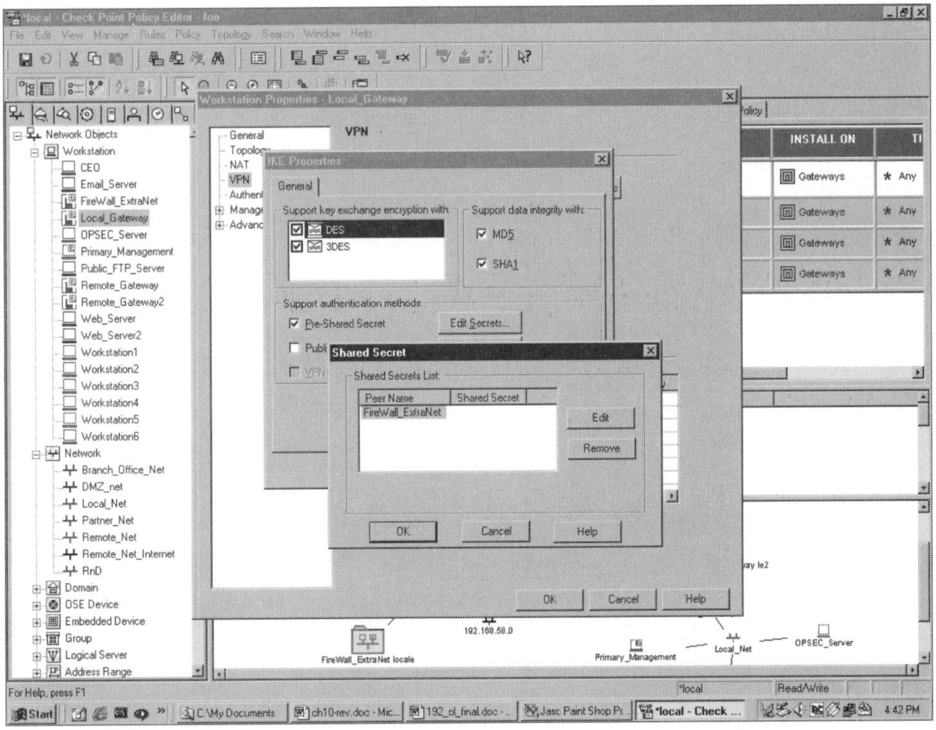

Adding VPN Rules

You will want to modify your rule base so that traffic between *Local_Net* and *Remote_Net* is encrypted. As above in the section on FWZ encryption, this is done with the addition of two rules to your rule base (see Figure 10.8).

Figure 10.8 IKE Encryption Rules

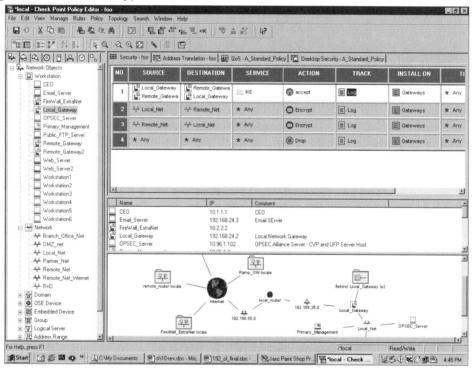

One rule specifies the following:

- **Source** Local_Net
- **Destination** Remote_Net
- **Service** Any
- **Action** Encrypt
- **Track** Log

While the other specifies the following:

- **Source** Remote_Net
- **Destination** Local_Net

- **Service** Any

- **Action** Encrypt

- **Track** Log

Rule 1 allows key exchange to occur between the two gateways by allowing the pre-defined service "IKE" to be accepted bi-directionally. This rule is only necessary if you have "Accept VPN-1 & FireWall-1 control connections" unchecked in your security policy's Global Properties window (see Figure 10.5). This is checked by default, so in most cases you won't need a rule 1 as shown above. Note that the "IKE" service is included in the "FireWall1" service group, so you can use the same rules here that you used above, under FWZ encryption. Specifying only the IKE service here gives you more control over exactly what traffic you wish to allow between gateways, and is especially important when your peer gateway is not managed by you. See the next section for more considerations of this sort.

If you double-click on the **Encrypt** action in either encrypt rule, you will open the **Encryption Properties** dialog, from which you select **IKE** and click **Edit**. (See Figure 10.9).

Figure 10.9 IKE Properties Dialog

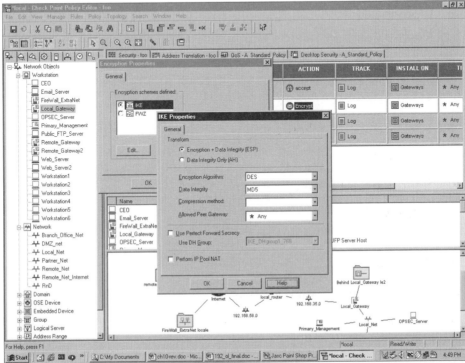

You have more choices here than you did when you used FWZ encryption. Go through the options given here one at a time:

- **Transform** Determines how each packet is encapsulated prior to being transmitted to the peer gateway. "Encryption + Data Integrity (ESP)" is the default, and is probably what you want in most cases. The other option, "Data Integrity Only (AH)," does not provide encryption, only authentication.

- **Encryption Algorithm** Choose an encryption algorithm from the list. Strong encryption is available with IKE (e.g. Triple-DES or AES).

- **Data Integrity** Choose the hash method used to provide authentication. SHA1 is available here, in addition to MD5.

- **Compression Method** Normally, only "Deflate" is available here. This specifies the method used to compress IP datagrams. Select **None** if you do not want the added CPU overhead.

- **Allowed Peer Gateway** Specifies exactly which gateways this one is prepared to establish a VPN with. Defaults to "Any," meaning that you will allow VPN traffic from or to any gateway if the packets source or destination IP address is in the other gateway's VPN domain.

- **Use Perfect Forward Secrecy (PFS)** PFS adds an added measure of security to key exchanges, with some additional overhead.

- **Use DH Group** This enables you to select which Diffie-Hellman group you would like to use for encryption. Selecting a "longer" group means better key security.

- **Use IP Pooling** Allows the use of a pre-defined "Pool" of IP addresses that are assigned to incoming VPN connections. This is typically used to prevent or fix asymmetric routing conditions where inbound and outbound VPN traffic follow different routes.

Testing the VPN

Once the configuration is complete, install the security policy on both gateways. Try to establish a connection from a host in your local VPN domain to a host in the remote gateway's VPN domain. You should see packets with a local source address and a remote destination address being encrypted on the way out the local gateway, and corresponding packet decryptions on the remote gateway (see

Figure 10.10). If this is not immediately apparent, or if you see errors in the log, then see below for some troubleshooting tips.

Figure 10.10 Log Viewer Showing Encrypts, Decrypts, and Key Exchanges

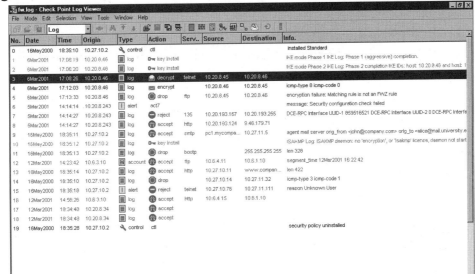

Debugging VPNs

Troubleshooting VPNs has traditionally been rather difficult. There are certain steps you can take to make troubleshooting and testing of VPN deployments easier:

1. Enable implied rule logging in the security policy Global Properties window.

2. Under the security policy "Log and Alert" tab in the Global Properties window, enable all the three encryption-specific log events: VPN successful key exchange, VPN packet handling errors, and VPN configuration and key exchange errors.

3. Disable NAT (Network Address Translation) by adding one or more manual rules to the NAT rule base that force traffic between opposing VPN domains to be "Original", or un-NATed. NAT can be used with VPNs; however, disabling it allows for cleaner testing (see Figure 10.11).

Figure 10.11 Address Translation Disabled Between VPN Domains with Manual Rules

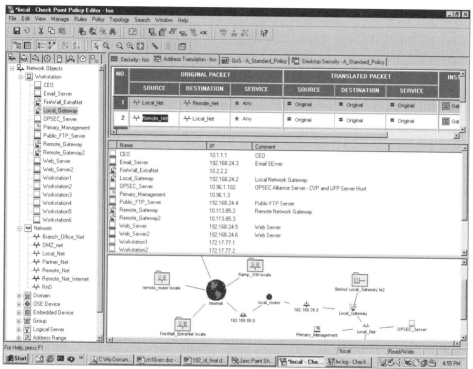

4. Be aware that the gateways participating in the VPN and perhaps the management stations need to communicate prior to the VPN tunnel being established (key exchange, protocol negotiation, etc.). You may need a rule in your rule base explicitly allowing this communication (see FWZ and IKE encryption rule base examples, above). Be aware of where in your rule base your stealth rule is, and how this might impact such communication. Implied rule and VPN logging, above, will show you such communication in a default installation.

5. Remember to test traffic from VPN domain to VPN domain, not from gateway to gateway. Normally, gateways are *not* included in VPN domains, and so they cannot provide a platform for reliable tests.

6. Be aware that using just ICMP (Ping) tests may not tell whether or not a VPN is working correctly. This especially applies if you don't have control over the other VPN endpoint. Administrators are often leery of allowing ICMP through their firewall and/or border routers, and may be

dropping it with implicit or explicit rules before any encryption can take place. A better test, and one which works on any platform with a "telnet" binary, is to telnet to a port other than the traditional port 23, using one that you know is open. So, for example, if your VPN peer has a DNS server in her VPN domain, "telnet <IP of DNS server> 53" would show you that you could establish a TCP connection through your VPN tunnel.

7. Your gateway may attempt to encrypt packets even if key exchange is not complete, causing you to wonder why a VPN is failing to work if encryption is taking place. If you filter your Log Viewer for "Key Install" under the "Action" column, you will see key exchange as it occurs. The "Info" field of each log entry in this case may contain useful error messages relevant to key exchange errors.

8. For every "encrypt" action on your gateway, your partner's firewall should show a corresponding "decrypt" action. You may or may not have access to those logs, so the above tips can help you test in that case.

Considerations for External Networks

It is important that all encryption rules have the same exact parameters defined under their respective encryption properties dialog. Your VPN will fail if they do not. This is easy to check when you manage both the local and remote gateways, but can be harder to verify when the remote gateway is managed by another management station, or even another company. Typically this coordination is done via telephone, agreed upon ahead of time as in "We will use IKE with 3DES encryption, SHA-1 data integrity, key exchange for subnets, and no perfect forward secrecy." Most VPN failures are a result of someone changing his or her respective VPN parameters, causing key exchange, encryption, or decryption to fail.

Configuring a SecuRemote VPN

In this section you will see how to configure your gateway for client encryption with SecuRemote, Check Point's client-to-site VPN tool. First, you will configure your gateway to act as a SecuRemote "Server," and then define the SecuRemote users, including their authentication methods. Finally, you will add the appropriate rules to your rule base to allow the encrypted communication.

Local Gateway Object

SecuRemote clients support both FWZ and IKE encryption schemes. From the Workstation Properties window on your local gateway (the gateway through which SecuRemote connections will pass), you need to make sure that the encryption scheme you are using is supported by checking it off in the VPN tab. When using FWZ with SecuRemote, you have the option of encapsulating the packets prior to transmission—this option is available in the FWZ properties dialog, which you took a look at earlier in the chapter (see Figure 10.1). This will enable SecuRemote clients to access non-routable networks behind the SecuRemote server (gateway) once they are authenticated and a VPN tunnel is established.

Next, you must define your VPN domain, which in this case defines which networks your SecuRemote clients will have access to once they have been authenticated. Set this as usual in the Topology tab of the Workstation Properties window on your local gateway. For SecuRemote, you need to check **Exportable for SecuRemote** on the same tab (see Figure 10.2). This enables clients to download the networks that they will have access to after being authenticated.

Finally, you must choose which authentication methods your gateway will support; for these exercises, you will choose **VPN-1 & FireWall-1 Password** on the **Authentication** tab of the **Workstation Properties** window on your local gateway. If you neglect to check off the appropriate authentication scheme here, your users will all get "Authentication not supported" errors when they attempt to log in.

Note that if you are using FWZ encryption, you must check off **Respond to Unauthenticated Topology Requests** in the **Desktop Security** page of the **Global Properties** window (see Figure 10.12).

User Encryption Properties

Assume for this section that you have a preexisting set of users that you want to configure for client encryption.

Start by opening the Users window by choosing **Users** from the **Manage** menu in the Policy Editor. Select an existing user and click on **Edit**. The "User properties" window appears. Here, you have two choices. If you are using IKE, the user's authentication parameters are defined in the "Encryption" tab. If you are using FWZ, the user's authentication properties are defined on the "Authentication" tab.

Figure 10.12 Desktop Security Window from Policy | Global Properties

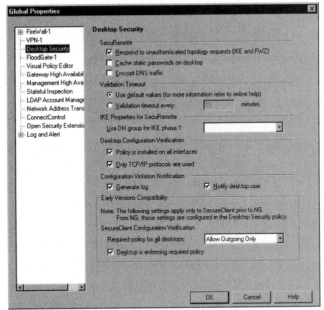

FWZ

For FWZ, once you click on the Authentication tab, you can choose an authentication method from the drop-down list. Choosing **VPN-1 & FireWall-1 Password** will enable you to enter a password in the text box. On the user's encryption tab, select **FWZ** and click **edit.** This will present you with a dialog box, from which you can select encryption and data integrity methods (see Figure 10.13).

IKE

With IKE, you do all of your setup from the Encryption tab of the User Properties window. Choosing **IKE** and clicking on **Edit** here brings up the IKE Properties window. On the **Authentication** tab, select **Password**, and enter the user's password. On the Encryption tab, select the encryption and data integrity methods you will use for the client VPN (see Figure 10.14).

Figure 10.13 FWZ Properties

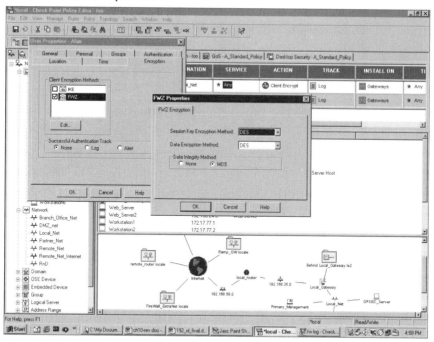

Figure 10.14 IKE Properties

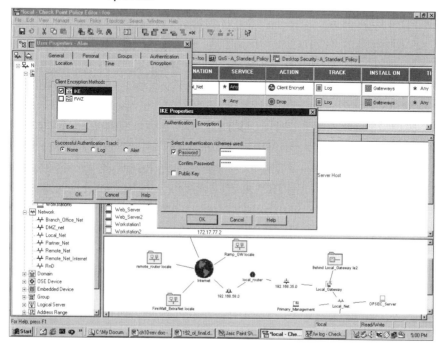

Client Encryption Rules

Your client encryption rule will look as follows (see Figure 10.15):

- **Source** AllUsers@Any
- **Destination** Local_Net
- **Service** Any
- **Action** Client Encrypt
- **Track** Log

Figure 10.15 SecuRemote Client Encrypt Rule

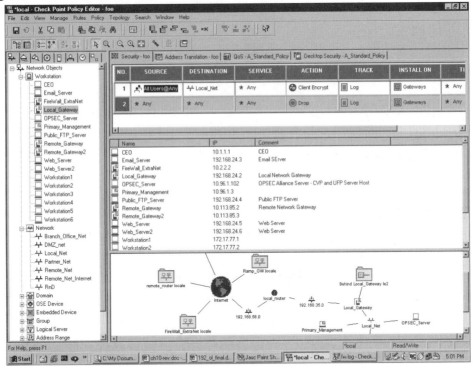

In this case, the Source column must specify a group of users and a location; the location can be "Any," or be a specific allowable source network. Destination must be the VPN domain defined for those users on the local gateway object.

Once the rule is in place, you can edit the Client Encrypt properties by double-clicking on the **Client Encrypt** icon (see Figure 10.16). If the source column of your rule base conflicts with allowed sources in the user properties setup, the client encrypt properties will specify how to resolve the conflict. You can specify that the intersection of the allowed user sources and the rule base determine when to allow access, or to ignore the user database altogether.

Figure 10.16 Client Encrypt Properties

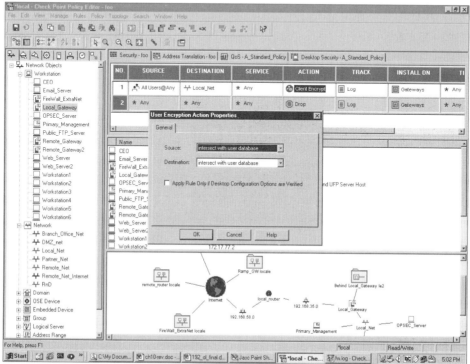

Installing SecuRemote Client Software

The SecuRemote client software must be installed on all the users workstations or laptops whom you as an administrator would like to give mobile access to your VPN domain. SecuRemote presently supports Windows 2000, NT, 98, and ME, and typically requires 32 to 64MB of RAM and about 6MB of disk space to install. It cannot be installed alongside Firewall-1. (As of this writing, SecuRemote version 4.1 SP5 for Windows 2000 can be installed on Windows XP. SecuRemote NG FP1 has a native Windows XP version.) There is also a Macintosh version that supports OS 8 and OS 9.

The client software works by inserting a driver between the client's physical network interface and the TCP/IP stack, in the operating system kernel. This kernel module monitors outbound TCP/IP traffic, and intercepts any packet destined for a VPN domain (from topology downloaded during site creation or update). The packet is then handed off to a user-space daemon, which handles user authentication and key exchange with the SecuRemote server, as well as encryption, should authentication succeed.

Installation is handled by a fairly straightforward graphical setup program; however, there are some points worth noting:

- You only need to install "Desktop Security Support" if you are using Secure Client (see Figure 10.17 and Chapter 11, "Securing Remote Clients").

Figure 10.17 SecuRemote Desktop Security Prompt During Installation

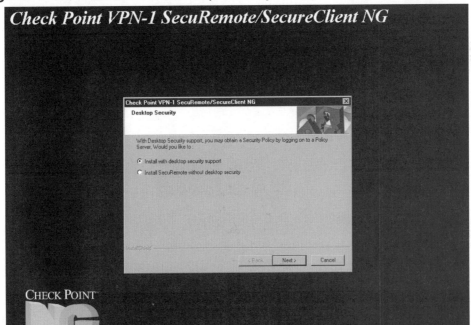

- If you do not install Desktop Security, you will be asked on which adapters to bind the SecuRemote kernel module (see Figure 10.18). You can choose from "Install on all network adapters," (which would include Ethernet *and* dial-up adapters) or "Install on dialup adapters only." The latter would be appropriate for remote users with a dial-up ISP who would never use their Ethernet interface to access the VPN domain from the outside. Mobile sales people often fall into this category; they use dial-up access when on the road, and Ethernet to plug into the LAN when they are in the office.

Figure 10.18 SecuRemote Adapter Configuration Screen During Installation

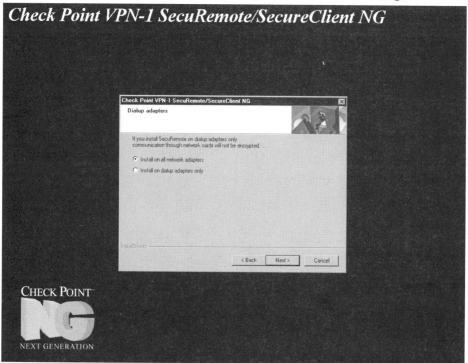

- You can install over an older version of SecuRemote. You will be asked if you wish to update the previous version, (which saves site and password information), or if you would like to overwrite the existing version.

- Although the client software is available for free download, a license is still required to use SecuRemote with CheckPoint NG.

Using SecuRemote Client Software

Once the client software is installed, you can start the SecuRemote GUI by double-clicking in the envelope icon in your taskbar. Before you can use SecuRemote, you must create a new site by choosing **Create New Site** from the **Sites** menu (see Figure 10.19). Enter the IP address or hostname of your SecuRemote server, (which is the gateway through which you will be connecting, or, in a distributed installation, that gateway's management console), and click **OK**. The site key information and topology will be downloaded automatically, and will be stored in a file called "userc.C" on the client, in the SecuRemote installation directory.

Figure 10.19 Creating a New Site

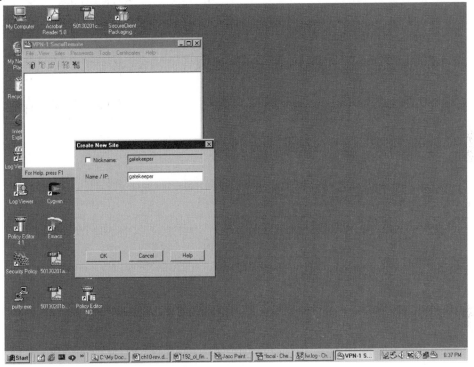

Once a site has been successfully created, you can attempt a connection to something in your VPN domain. You should see an authentication dialog box pop up (see Figure 10.20); here you would enter one of the previously defined user-names and passwords, after which you will be allowed access. Note that IKE encryption is the default, so if you are using FWZ, the client software needs to be reconfigured. Do this by choosing **Encryption Scheme** from the **Tools** menu, and then selecting **FWZ** instead of IKE.

After a topology change, you will need to update the SecuRemote clients so that their topology is in sync with the SecuRemote server. Updating the site can be done manually by right-clicking on the site icon and choosing **Update Site**. This works for a small number of clients, but if you have a large number of remote users, you can enable automatic update (in SecuRemote version 4.1 or NG) in one of three ways:

Figure 10.20 SecureRemote Authentication Window

- Prompt the client to update its topology whenever SecuRemote is started by adding ":desktop_update_at_start (true)" to the :props section of the objects_5_0.C file on the management station. This can be refused by the client.

- Prompt for update of *all* defined site topologies whenever SecuRemote is started by adding ":update_topo_at_start (true)" to the :props section of the objects_5_0.C file on the management station. This can also be refused by the client.

- Force updating of the site topology every *n* seconds by adding ":desktop_update_frequency (*n*)" to the :props section of the objects_5_0.C file on the management station.

Configuring & Implementing…

Making Changes to Objects_5_0.C Stick

Editing the objects_5_0.C file can be tricky—if not done in the right way, your changes will be lost. You should follow these recommendations when making changes to the objects_5_0.C file on your management server. Note that this file is called "objects.C" on the firewall module, as it was in past versions of CheckPoint Firewall-1. Editing this file on the firewall module will have no effect, as it gets overwritten by the objects_5_0.C from the management station during policy installs. Also,

Continued

see Chapter 8, "Managing Policies and Logs," for a discussion of the "dbedit" tool, which can be used to make changes to objects defined in objects_5_0.C.

1. Close all GUI clients.

2. Perform *fwstop* on the management console.

3. Delete or rename the files "objects_5_0.C.sav" and "objects_5_0.C.bak."

4. Back up the original objects_5_0.C.

5. Make the necessary changes to the objects_5_0.C file and save them.

6. Perform *fwstart* on the management console.

7. Install the security policy to all modules.

Secure Domain Login (SDL)

Secure Domain Login (SDL) enables users to encrypt traffic to a windows NT domain controller behind a FireWall-1 firewall. Normally, SecuRemote is activated *after* domain login, meaning that domain login is not encrypted. To enable SDL after installation, choose **Enable SDL** from the **passwords** menu. This will take effect only after a reboot. Note that SDL over a dial-up connection is only supported when using the Windows 2000 or NT clients—the 98 or ME clients only support SDL over an Ethernet adapter.

In order to successfully log in to an NT domain, you need to make sure you have the following client settings:

- Your "Client for Microsoft Networks" has "Log on to Windows NT Domain" checked.

- Your dial-up profile is configured with your internal WINS server address OR.

- You need an LMHOSTS entry that points to your primary or back-up domain controllers.

Designing & Planning...

VPN Management

Easy VPN management is directly related to network topology choices. In general, one VPN endpoint with multiple small VPN domains behind it will be easier to manage than multiple distinct gateways, each with one VPN domain. The need for back-end security can be best solved by using gateways as needed, behind the sole VPN endpoint. Each smaller gateway must then be configured to pass encrypted traffic and key exchange traffic through untouched. You can use Table 10.2 to assist in this:

Table 10.2 Encryption Protocols

Encryption Scheme	Ports/Protocols Used
FWZ	RDP (UDP port 259) HTTP, FTP, IMAP, etc OR FW1_Encapsulation (IP protocol 94)*
IKE	IKE (UDP port 500) ESP (IP protocol 50) AH (IP protocol 51) IKE over TCP (TCP port 500) * UDP encapsulation (UDP port 2476)*
FWZ and IKE	FW1_topo (TCP port 264) FW1_pslogon_NG (TCP port 18231) FW1_sds_logon (TCP port 18232) FW1_scv_keep_alive (UDP port 18233)

* not always necessary

Summary

Virtual Private Networks (VPNs) can be used to provide authenticity, privacy, and data integrity. There are two types of VPNs: site-to-site and client-to-site; both provide two methods of key exchange (IKE and FWZ) and several encryption algorithms. Establishing a site-to-site VPN can be broken down into three steps: configuring the firewall and/or management stations, configuring the VPN domain, and adding encryption rules to the security policy rule base. Establishing a client-to-site VPN is similar, except that users are configured with the proper authentication method, and then the rule base is updated with a Client Encrypt rule. Remote users must install the SecuRemote software and download SecuRemote server topology before they can make use of a client-to-site VPN. Several methods exist for automatically updating site topology.

Solutions Fast Track

Encryption Schemes

- ☑ VPNs can provide Privacy, authenticity, data integrity.
- ☑ Key exchange is public (asymmetric); encryption is symmetric for performance.
- ☑ Beware of the security of proprietary encryption schemes.

Configuring an FWZ VPN

- ☑ Double-check encryption rule properties to make sure they are identical.
- ☑ Make sure key exchange rules (if any) are above your stealth rule.
- ☑ Make sure to encapsulate FWZ for SecuRemote connections.

Configuring an IKE VPN

- ☑ Double-check encryption rule properties to make sure they are identical.
- ☑ Make sure key exchange rules (if any) are above your stealth rule.

☑ It is a good idea to disable NAT for any encrypted traffic between VPN domains.

Configuring a SecuRemote VPN

☑ SecuRemote can be used with dial-up or Ethernet adapters.

☑ Secure Domain Login is possible with SecuRemote.

☑ Several methods exist for automatically updating site topology.

Installing SecuRemote Client Software

☑ Your main choices when installing the SecuRemote client are whether or not to bind SecuRemote to all adapters, or just your dial-up adapter, and whether or not to enable desktop security (see Chapter 11, "Securing Remote Clients").

Using SecuRemote Client Software

☑ The IP address or hostname used when creating your "site" is the IP address or hostname of the firewall gateway through which you will be connecting, or, in the case of a distributed installation, the IP address or hostname of that gateway's management console.

☑ Topology downloads are saved on the client locally in the file "userc.C," in the SecuRemote installation directory.

Frequently Asked Questions

The following Frequently Asked Questions, answered by the authors of this book, are designed to both measure your understanding of the concepts presented in this chapter and to assist you with real-life implementation of these concepts. To have your questions about this chapter answered by the author, browse to **www.syngress.com/solutions** and click on the **"Ask the Author"** form.

Q: Why can't I ping such-and-such host in my peer's VPN domain?

A: This may not be allowed by policy. Check your policy's Global Properties, and make sure that ICMP is not being accepted first, before any encryption rules. Try a different protocol if you have no control over the peer policy (e.g. telnet to port 25 on a mail server in peer's VPN domain).

Q: What does "No response from peer: Scheme IKE" mean when seen in logs during VPN testing?

A: Confirm that fwd and isakmpd are running on your peer gateway. Isakmpd listens on UDP port 500; you can use the "netstat" command to double-check this (on Unix platforms and Windows platforms).

Q: What does the error "No proposal chosen" mean?

A: The two-encryption rule properties differ in some way, or one gateway supports an encryption method that another doesn't.

Q: I want my salespeople to be able to log on and browse my NT/Domain from the field. How can I do this?

A: See the section on "Secure Domain Logon," above.

Q: I have a really large network, with a lot of VPN traffic to and from multiple VPN domains, and notice frequent connection interruptions. Why is this?

A: Check to make sure that "key exchange for subnets" is enabled. Check the size of the connection table. Check gateway memory usage and processor load ('fw tab –t connections –s' and 'fw ctl pstat').

Q: What does "gateway connected to both endpoints" mean?

A: This is usually due to broadcast traffic that is generated on your internal net-work. If your encryption rule has your local network in both the source and destination, and the local network object has "Broadcast address included" checked in the network properties General tab, then you may receive these messages. They are harmless, and are just stating that the source and destina-tion of this traffic match the encryption rule, but both endpoints are con-nected locally, therefore no encryption will take place.

## Chapter 11

Securing Remote Clients

Introduction

If your organization is interested in using a VPN client, but you are concerned about allowing clients' personal computers into your network when you have no control over what they are running on their PCs, then Check Point solves this problem by giving you control of your remote users' desktop security. You can configure specific properties for your mobile users' desktops, which could include prohibiting connections to their PC when they have the remote software running. That way, if they are running a Web server on their PC, you do not have to worry about their server being compromised while they have a connection into your private network.

SecureClient software operates exactly like the SecuRemote software package that we discussed in the previous chapter. The only difference is that you choose to install it with desktop security. This feature provides a personal firewall on your mobile users' PCs, which you control via the FireWall-1 Policy Editor. Within the Policy Editor, you can define detailed policies that the SecureClient downloads when they log in to your firewall's Policy Server.

We will show you how to install and configure a Policy Server in this chapter, and how to configure different desktop policies for your users. A policy server can reside on one of your firewall modules, or it can be set up as a separate server to strictly enforce clients' security policies.

After describing the Policy Server to you in full detail, we will then show you how to install the SecureClient software, and how to use the SecureClient Packaging Tool on the Next Generation CD. The client receives information on its Policy Server when it downloads the topology from the management console. We'll describe how to log in to the Policy Server, and how to use the SecureClient application.

Installing and Configuring a Policy Server

The first step toward ensuring that your remote users' desktops adhere to the security policies you dictate is to install and configure a Policy Server. Once the Policy Server is installed and configured, it will be able to transmit the appropriate security settings to the SecureClients running on the remote desktops.

Install from CD

The Policy Server can be found on your Check Point NG CD-ROM. To install the Policy Server, insert the CD-ROM, and from the **Product Menu,** choose **Server/Gateway Components**. Then, deselect all components except "Policy Server," as in Figure 11.1.

Figure 11.1 Check Point Policy Server Installation

This will load the Check Point installation wizard, which will first check that the VPN-1/FireWall-1 module is installed. If not, you will be required to install the VPN-1/FireWall-1 module prior to continuing with the Policy Server installation.

The Policy Server installation will proceed, and will not require any further input from you. Once it is complete, you need to ensure that you have the appropriate user-group license installed on your firewall. The license must contain sufficient users for the number of actual users connecting to your environment.

Now that the Policy Server component of Check Point NG is installed, you can configure your security policy for its use.

NOTE

New in FP1 is a Software Distribution Server (SDS) that is installed on the Policy Server. NG FP1 SecureClients include a Software Distribution Agent, which will check the SDS for updated software revisions using TCP port 18332.

Configuring a Policy Server

The first step of configuring the Policy Server is to open your Policy Editor and go to **Manage**, and then edit your firewall object. In the example here, the firewall object is called *Local_Gateway*. From the **General tab**, under the **Check Point Products** section, check off **Policy Server** as in Figure 11.2.

Figure 11.2 General Firewall Properties

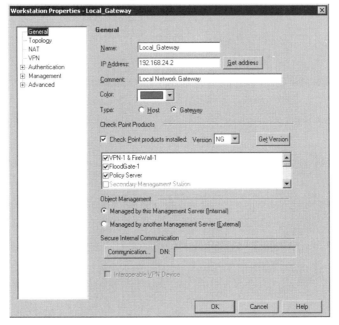

By selecting this option, you are telling the firewall that the Policy Server is installed, and you will then be able to continue configuring its remaining options.

Next, go to the Authentication tab of your firewall object. Here, you will see a new option that only appeared since you installed the Policy Server. Now you can define a group of Users, as in Figure 11.3.

Here, you need to select the user group that the Policy Server is going to manage. This user group must also be licensed by your Check Point group license. Later, you will add all applicable users to this group. Once you install the policy, the Policy Server will start running.

Figure 11.3 Authentication Firewall Properties

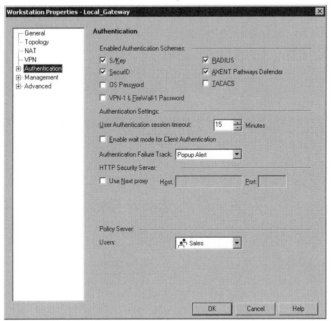

Desktop Security Options

There are two main areas of the Policy Editor important to desktop security: the Desktop Security Policy, and the Desktop Security global properties. Both of these enable you to control various aspects of what will be transmitted to the SecureClient users by the Policy Server.

Desktop Security Policy

Located on the main screen of the Policy Editor, the Desktop Security tab enables you to specify what access your users have. The Desktop Security Rule Base is similar to the standard Security Policy Rule Base, with some important distinctions.

You install the Desktop Policy as you would a standard Security Policy. When you select **Install** from the Policy Menu, you have the option of installing either a Security Policy or a Desktop Security Policy. Both are selected by default, and once you download the desktop policy to the Policy Servers, then they get distributed to the SecureClients as they log in. Only the rules that apply to the user who belongs to the SecureClient desktop will be applied. See Figure 11.4 for an example of a Desktop Security Rule Base.

Figure 11.4 Desktop Security Rule Base

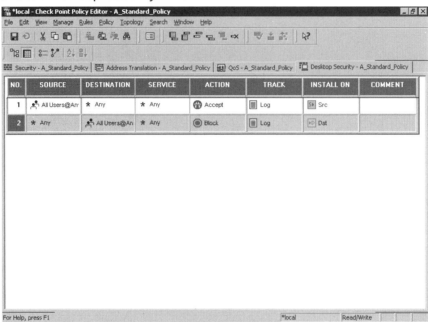

Here, rule 1 allows traffic from all remote users' workstations outbound, to any remote host, via any service. This rule would enable your users to surf the Internet, for example. Rule 2 blocks all traffic from all remote hosts to all users' workstations, which will protect them from external attacks.

Notice that under "Install on" field, FireWall-1 places an indicator as to whether this rule will control source or destination traffic, from the SecureClient desktop's perspective. This is a good reminder to you that these rules are always from the perspective of the SecureClient desktop, and not from the firewall.

Under **Action**, besides the expected **Accept** or **Block**, you also have the option of setting this to **Encrypt.** This causes the firewall to check whether the matched packet is encrypted, and it will drop the packet if not. See Figure 11.5 for an example.

Figure 11.5 Desktop Security Policy with Encrypt

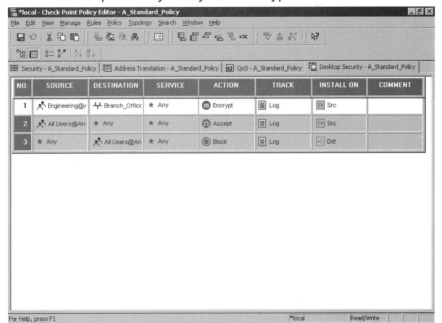

Rule 1 here will ensure that all traffic between the "Engineering" group and "Branch_Office_Net" is encrypted. This is a good mechanism to use to ensure that users are not using clear connections when you believe encrypted connections are required.

The Desktop Security rule base adds an implicit rule to the bottom of the rule base that denies all communication. This means that anything not explicitly allowed in the Desktop Security rule base is blocked. Note that packets that are dropped due to the implicit drop rule are not logged; if you want to log-drop packets, you can add your own explicit drop rule at the bottom of this rule base.

Desktop Security Global Properties

The Desktop Security global properties screen enables you to configure various additional aspects of the SecureClient desktop environment. Keep in mind that SecureClient uses the same Client Encryption software as SecuRemote, and therefore some of the settings shown in Figure 11.6 apply to both sets of users.

Figure 11.6 Desktop Security Global Properties

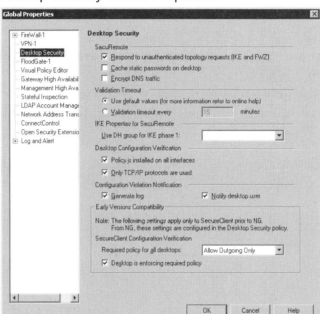

The first section here is for SecuRemote. The options are as follows:

- **Respond to unauthenticated topology requests (IKE and FWZ):** This settings instructs the firewall to respond to topology requests from remote workstations running SecuRemote, even if the request does not come over an encrypted connection. Note that only previous versions of the SecuRemote client require this option; if all your users have up-to-date clients, this can be disabled for added security.

- **Cache static passwords on desktop:** This setting applies to users who have their authentication method set to OS or VPN-1/FireWall-1. When checked, users with these authentication methods will only have to enter their password once per session, and the password will then be cached by their local workstation. If this option is not selected, these users will be required to reauthenticate.

- Encrypt DNS traffic: As expected, this option will force DNS traffic to be encrypted.

Next is the validation timeout setting. You may choose Use default values, which results in different behavior depending on what authentication method your users utilize:

- If you select **Cache static passwords on desktop** above, users with authentication methods of OS or VPN-1/FireWall-1 password using FWZ or IKE will only have to authenticate when SecureClient starts up.

- If you do not select **Cache static passwords on desktop** above, users with authentication methods of OS or VPN-1/FireWall-1 password will have to reauthenticate with each VPN gateway they try to access. They will also have to reauthenticate every hour on each gateway.

- Users authenticating via a certificate will only have to authenticate when SecureClient starts up.

- Users authenticating with one-time passwords (S/Key, for example) must reauthenticate on each VPN gateway they try to access, as well as every hour.

Alternatively, if you choose **Validation timeout every ___ minutes**, then you can configure exactly how much time can elapse before users are required to reauthenticate.

The "IKE properties for SecuRemote" option enables you to select the DH group you want FireWall-1 to use during phase-1 negotiation.

Desktop Configuration Verification

Desktop configuration verification enables you to control two important aspects of the SecureClient desktop:

- Policy is installed on all interfaces: When selected, this option ensures that the Desktop Policy you specify is installed on every physical interface of the SecureClient desktop including LAN cards as well as dial-up adapters. This is important because if the policy is not installed on an interface, there is an increased chance that security of the desktop could be compromised via that interface, and subsequently your own firewall is at risk. However, some users may wish to leave an interface unsecured, so that they have access to other resources while connected to your firewall via VPN.

■ Only TCP/IP Protocols are used: When selected, this option ensures that only TCP/IP protocols are installed on the SecureClient desktop. This option is important because SecureClient is unable to protect the desktop from non-TCP/IP protocols, and so using these protocols could introduce an unwanted security risk.

FireWall-1 also enables you to specify what it should do if desktops are found to be in violation of these policies. If you select **Generate Log**, you will see via the Log Viewer an entry with the offending user's name, IP address, and the violation reason. If you select **Notify Desktop User**, SecureClient will notify the user of the desktop that a violation has been detected.

Early Versions Compatibility

This section of the Desktop Security tab in the Global Properties window in Figure 11.6 enables you to configure policies for versions of SecureClient prior to NG. There are four policy options in the "Required Policy for all desktops" pull-down window, which are the following:

■ No Policy

■ Allow Outgoing & Encrypted

■ Allow Outgoing Only

■ Allow Encrypted Only

You can see from this list how much more granular the new Desktop Security Rule Base is over the "old" way. You can only select one of these policies for all pre-NG SecureClient users, and they will work in conjunction with the other Desktop Configuration Verification options set on this page.

If you select **No Policy**, then there will be no policy loaded on the SecureClient when they log in to their Policy Server. If you select **Allow Outgoing Only**, then only non-encrypted traffic originating from the SecureClient PC will be allowed, and all inbound connection attempts to the SecureClient will be dropped. If you select **Allow Encrypted Only**, then only connections to and from your VPN Domain will be permitted. For example, with the encrypted policy, your mobile users could not browse Internet sites, but they could download their email from the office while the SecureClient software is running. Finally, if you select **Allow Outgoing & Encrypted**, then your users can initiate any connections to either the Internet or to your VPN Domain, and only encrypted traffic will be allowed inbound to the SecureClient.

Client Encrypt Rules

The final step to allowing remote users to use SecureClient securely to VPN is to set up a client encrypt rule in the standard Security Rule Base. This is where the firewall administrator defines the policies that will be installed on the firewall module that will be enforcing the policy and allowing SecuRemote and/or SecureClient users into the VPN domain. To do this, open the Policy Editor and add a new rule to the rule base. See Figure 11.7.

Figure 11.7 Client Encrypt Rule

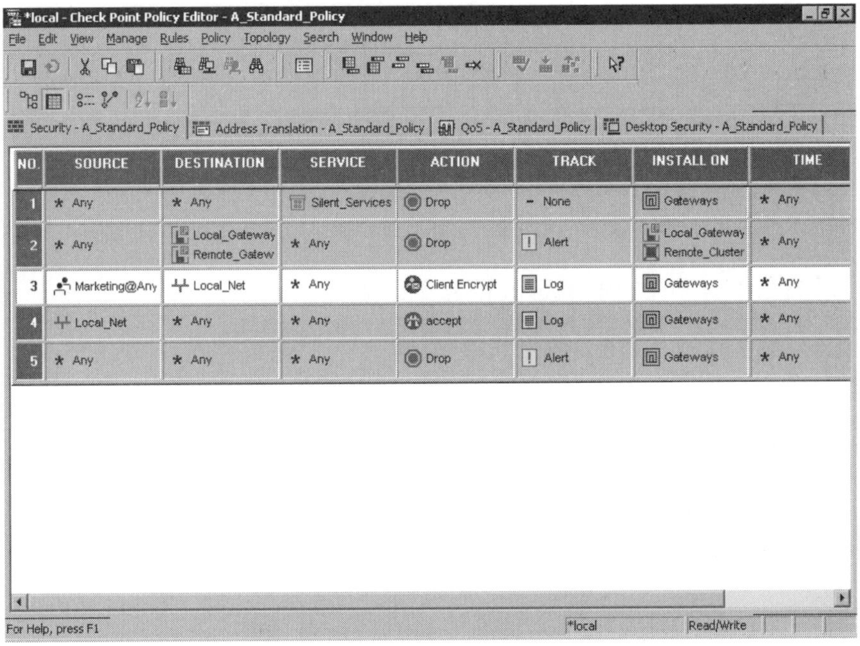

Here, rule 3 is our client encrypt rule. To add the source, right-click on the **Source** field and choose **Add Users Access**. You then have the option of choosing a user group, and optionally restricting this group to connecting from a specified location, as in Figure 11.8.

For this example, choose **Accounting**, and set **Location** to **No restriction**. The Destination field specifies what objects these users will have access to via the encrypted connection, and **Service** enables you to further restrict the connection to particular services. Set **Action** to **Client Encrypt**, **Track** to **Log**, and ensure that Install On includes the appropriate firewalls. You have the option of setting a time restriction to this rule, and adding a descriptive comment.

Figure 11.8 User Access

Now that the rule is configured, there are some additional action properties to consider. To access them, right-click on **Client Encrypt**, and choose **Edit properties**. See Figure 11.9.

Figure 11.9 User Encrypt Action Properties

These options show how to resolve conflicts between location restrictions specified in the user database, and location properties set here in the rule base. If you select **intersect with user database**, the firewall will combine the access location rules in both areas. If you select **ignore user database**, then only the rule base's location restrictions will apply. These options can be specified for both source and destination.

You can also select the option **Apply Rule only if desktop configuration options are verified**, which relates to the desktop configuration verification options you configured earlier. If any of the desktop verifications fail for a particular user, then the firewall will not allow the encrypted connection via this rule. This is an effective way to ensure that only properly secured SecureClient desktop users are authenticating and connecting to your network. If a user does not have the appropriate desktop policy loaded on their client, then they will not have access.

Client Authentication now supports SecureClient connections as well. To enable this, select **Client Auth** in the action field on a rule, and then edit the **Client Auth Action Properties** and select **Verify secure configuration on Desktop**. This would generally be used for clear text (not encrypted) communication from an internal SecureClient PC.

Installing SecureClient Software

Each remote user that will be connecting to your firewall via VPN will need to install the SecureClient software. This software is available on your Check Point NG CD-ROM, and the latest version is also downloadable from the Check Point Web site at http://www.checkpoint.com/techsupport/downloads_sr.html. I highly recommend that you read the release notes prior to installing or upgrading the SecuRemote/SecureClient software.

You may notice that the software package is called SecuRemote/SecureClient. These are both VPN clients, with the important distinction being that SecuRemote does not contain the desktop security components that SecureClient does. This means that with SecuRemote, the user's desktop will not be protected from external attacks, nor will they receive policy updates from your Policy Server. To install the SecureClient software, follow these steps:

1. Run the SecuRemote/SecureClient installation program. If you have a previous version of SecuRemote or SecureClient on your workstation, you will be asked if you would like to upgrade or overwrite the old version, as per Figure 11.10. Upgrading your previous version of SecuRemote/SecureClient preserves your configuration data, so you would be wise to take this option. Overwriting may be necessary if there is something wrong with the previous version, and you want to start with a clean installation. Also, if you want to switch from SecuRemote to SecureClient, or vice-versa, choose overwrite, since upgrading will only upgrade the type of client you already have installed. Whichever option you choose, click **Next** to continue.

2. Next, you will be asked if you want to install SecureClient or SecuRemote, as in Figure 11.11. Unless you have a particular reason not to provide personal firewall functionality for this client, it would be

best to take advantage of these additional security features by installing SecureClient. Fill in the checkbox for "Install VPN-1 SecureClient" and click **Next**.

Figure 11.10 Previous Version Screen

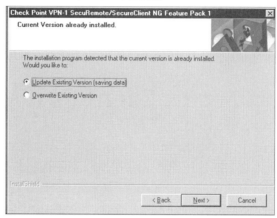

Figure 11.11 SecureClient

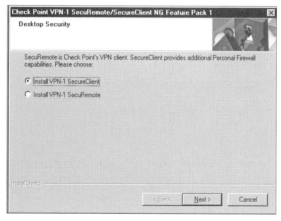

3. Next, you will be asked what network adapters you would like to bind SecuRemote/SecureClient to, as in Figure 11.12. The most secure method of running SecuRemote/SecureClient is to bind it to all adapters. Binding to all adapters means that traffic passing through any physical interface on the desktop will be secured and encrypted. Otherwise, it is increasingly possible for unauthorized access attempts via one of the desktop's other network interfaces. This option also relates to your "Desktop Configuration Verification," where you specified whether

or not the policy must be installed on all interfaces. If you selected this option, and you do not choose to install on all adapters here, this client will be denied access. Fill in the checkbox for "Install on all network adapters" and click **Next**.

Figure 11.12 Network Adapters

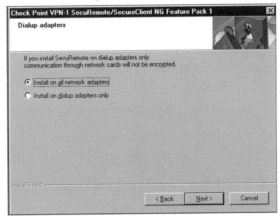

4. Next, the installation wizard will install the SecuRemote/SecureClient kernel into the operating system. This is a fairly intensive process that may take several minutes. By placing itself at the operating system level, SecuRemote/SecureClient can ensure the highest level of security, since it will inspect packets prior to their interaction with applications. Note that during this phase, all of your current network connections will be briefly interrupted.

5. You will then be prompted to restart your system, which is required prior to using SecuRemote/SecureClient.

SecureClient Packaging Tool

In order to reduce the amount of configuration and customization each remote user must perform to his or her VPN client, Check Point provides the SecureClient Packaging Tool. This tool enables you to create a customized SecureClient package that you can distribute to your remote users. The end result is an easy-to-install, self-extracting SecureClient executable file that is designed to your specifications. The SecureClient Packaging Tool is installed from your Check Point NG CD-ROM.

1. Once installed, the SC Packaging Tool is run from the Windows Start menu, in the "Check Point Management Clients" section. Upon loading the tool, you will see the login screen as per Figure 11.13. You will log in to the SC Packaging Tool with the same credentials as you use to log in to the Policy Editor. Note that you also have the option of using a certificate file, which must be located on your system, instead of a login name. This screen also gives you the option of changing the password for your certificate, and enables you to specify whether or not you want to connect to the management server over a compressed connection. Press **OK** to log in.

Figure 11.13 Packaging Tool Login

2. The first time you log in, you will see a blank window. Figure 11.14 shows this window with a list of profiles. You will want to create a new profile. To do this, go to the **Profile menu**, and choose **New**. Click **Next** on the welcome screen.

Figure 11.14 List of Profiles

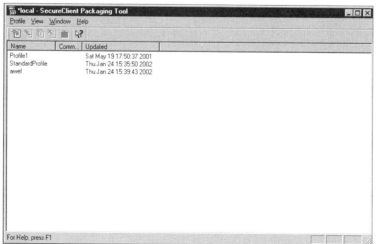

3. You will now see the General configuration screen, as in Figure 11.15. For "Profile Name," enter a descriptive name for this profile. Note that this name can only contain up to 256 alphanumeric characters, and cannot contain any spaces. In this case, you will use "StandardProfile." "Comment" can include a more detailed comment about this profile. Once you have entered these click **Next**.

Figure 11.15 General Properties

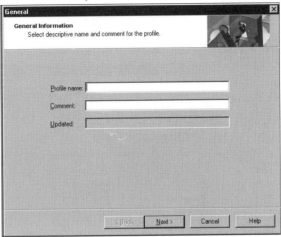

4. You will see the SecureClient configuration window, as per Figure 11.16. Your options on this screen are listed below.

■ **Allow clear connections for Encrypt action when inside the encryption domain** This option, when selected, allows unencrypted connections whenever both the source and destination of the connection are within the VPN domain. When this is the case, clear connections are allowed even if "Encrypt" is specified in the Desktop Security rule base.

■ **Enable DHCP connections if explicitly allowed by the SecureClient Rule Base** By default, SecureClient will accept DHCP connections regardless of whether or not they are defined in the Desktop Security rule base. If you select this option, these DHCP connections will *only* be allowed if they are defined explicitly in the rule base.

■ **Restrict SecureClient user intervention** As described in the window, selecting this object will hide the "Disable Policy" item from the SecureClient menus. This removes the remote user's ability to disable the policy their SecureClient receives from the Policy Server.

■ **Policy Server** The "Prompt the user to choose a Policy Server" option, when selected, will result in the remote user being prompted to choose a Policy Server to log on to. If instead you choose "Choose default Policy Server," the user will not be prompted, and the Policy Server you specify will be used instead.

Click **Next** when you have configured this screen.

Figure 11.16 SecureClient Configuration

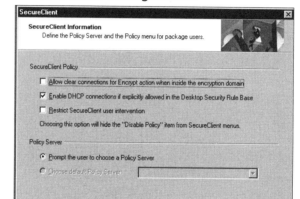

5. You will now see the "Additional Information" options, as in Figure 11.17. Here, you can select the encryption scheme, FWZ or IKE, whichever one you want SecureClient to use to authenticate. If IKE is selected, you also have the option of hiding the FWZ option. "Force UDP encapsulation for IPSec Connections" is useful in cases when the SecureClient is connected behind a NAT gateway; as some NAT gateways are unable to route ESP/AH packets properly for an IPSec VPN. The usual problem is that some NAT devices do not allow you to set up NAT for these protocols. Basically, it can only handle TCP, UDP, and ICMP. ESP and AH use protocols 50 and 51, and these are needed along with the IKE service on UDP 500 for IPSec communication. Table 11.1 shows you which TCP, UDP, and IP protocols each encryption scheme uses. If you have a Policy Server behind a firewall, then these are the ports that you will need to open.

Figure 11.17 Additional Information

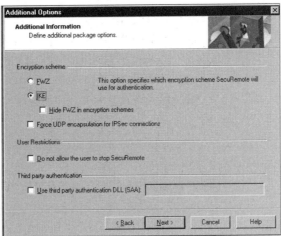

Table 11.1 Encryption Protocols

Encryption Scheme	Ports/Protocols Used
FWZ	RDP (UDP port 259) HTTP, FTP, IMAP, etc OR FW1_Encapsulation (IP protocol 94)*
IKE	IKE (UDP port 500) ESP (IP protocol 50) AH (IP protocol 51) IKE over TCP (TCP port 500) * UDP encapsulation (UDP port 2476)*
FWZ and IKE	FW1_topo (TCP port 264) FW1_pslogon_NG (TCP port 18231) FW1_sds_logon (TCP port 18232) FW1_scv_keep_alive (UDP port 18233)

not always necessary

If using FWZ without encapsulation, then you must allow any specific services through a firewall, such as HTTP, FTP, or IMAP, since this packet data will not be altered, but if you are using FWZ encapsulation, then you only need to allow IP protocol 94 (FW1_Encapsulation) instead.

The option "Do not allow the user to stop SecuRemote" means that the user will not be able to exit SecureClient. This is done by removing the "Stop" option from all menus. You may find this useful if you want to ensure that your users are always using their VPN to connect to the site, and are worried that they may inadvertently exit the client.

Finally, "Use third party authentication DLL (SAA)" enables you to integrate SecureClient's authentication methods with an external vendor's product. When you are done, click **Next**.

6. You will now be brought to the Topology Information screen, as shown in Figure 11.18. The options in the Topology Information screen include the following:

■ Change default topology port to this: Topology information is transmitted by default on port 264. For port conflicts or security reasons, you can change this to an alternative port.

■ Obscure Topology on disk: The topology information, which FireWall-1 stores in the "userc.C" file, can be stored in an obscured format. If so, you must specify this option.

■ Accept unsigned topology: If selected, the firewall will accept topology requests even if there is no security signing in place. This is not recommended, since it introduces a possible security hole.

■ Perform automatic topology update only in "Silent" mode: If enabled, this option causes SecureClient to obtain an updated topology after every key exchange.

Click **Next** when you have made your selections.

Figure 11.18 Topology Information

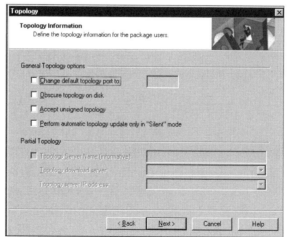

7. This will bring up the Certificates Information configuration screen, as in Figure 11.19. Here, you can select a **Certificate Authority IP Address** and **Port**, which are used to specify the location and port of your Entrust certificate authority server. You can also specify your **LDAP server IP address** and **Port**, which you should use if you are using an LDAP server as part of your configuration. **Use Entrust Entelligence** specifies whether SecureClient should use this proprietary feature of Entrust. When you have made your selections, click **Next**.

Figure 11.19 Certificate Information

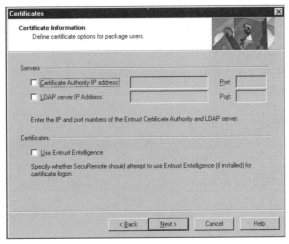

8. Now you will see the Silent Installation configuration screen, as shown in Figure 11.20. The options here specify how many, if any, prompts the user will see when installing the SecureClient package. The **Don't prompt user during installation** option means that the user will see no prompts at all, which is what Check Point calls a silent installation. Alternatively, you can select **Choose prompts that will be shown to users**, and turn on or off the various prompts as per your requirements. Make your choices and click **Next**.

9. You will now see the Installation Options Information screen, as shown in Figure 11.21. Here, you can specify the destination installation folder to use, what adapters you want SecureClient to bind to (see above for details), and whether you want the package to install SecureClient by default, as opposed to SecuRemote. You can also choose whether you want the user's system to be restarted by default after installation. Make your selections and click **Next**.

Figure 11.20 Silent Installation

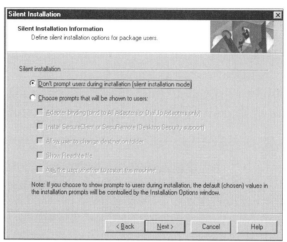

Figure 11.21 Installation Options

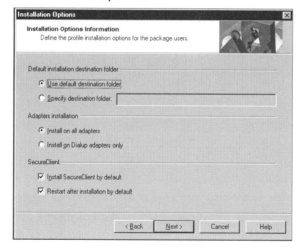

10. Next, you will see the Operating System Logon Information screen, as shown in Figure 11.22. Here, you can choose **Enable Secure Domain Logon (SDL)**, and specify a timeout for SDL. This means that remote users will be able to log on to a Windows NT domain controller. "Enable Roaming user profiles" means users can use the Windows NT roaming profiles feature over their SecureClient connection. Finally, "Enable third party GINA DLL" enables you to use an external vendor's authentication DLL. Make your selections and click **Next**.

Figure 11.22 Operating System Logon

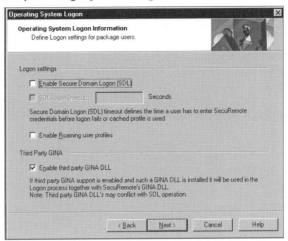

11. You will now be brought to the Finish screen, as in Figure 11.23. Here, you can choose **NO, Create profile only** to have the packaging tool simply create a profile based on the parameters you have specified. Or, if you choose **YES, Create profile and generate package**, the Packaging Tool will generate a complete SecureClient package that you can then distribute to your remote clients. If you choose to generate the package, you will see the SecureClient Packaging Tool wizard, which will prompt you for a "Package Source Folder," which is the location of the SecureClient package on your system. You can either use the package directory on the NG CD or you can place it (unzipped) in a directory on your PC. You will also be prompted for a destination folder, which is where the final package executable file will be placed. Click **Finish** once you have made your selection.

Logging into the Policy Server

Once you create and distribute a SecureClient package to your remote users, they are on their way to securely connecting to your network. After installing the SecureClient package, the Policy Server needs to communicate with the remote client. This occurs when the user logs in to the Policy Server, either explicitly or automatically.

Figure 11.23 Finish

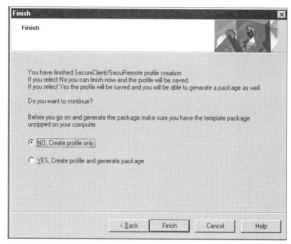

When the remote user first loads SecureClient, it automatically tries to log in to the Policy Server, provided that one is installed on the firewall. The user will be prompted for their login credentials, and then logged on.

> **NOTE**
>
> If a remote user has IP forwarding enabled on his or her desktop, SecureClient will detect this, will display a warning to the user, and may disable some functionality as per your security policy. This is an important feature because having IP forwarding can result in packets entering one insecure interface being transmitted out another interface, which is a security risk.

After successfully logging on, SecureClient will periodically re-log on to the Policy Server in order to transmit any logs, and ensure that it receives any updates to the security policy.

In addition to these automated Policy Server logins, the remote user may also decide to explicitly log on to the Policy Server. This is useful in cases where the user knows the policy has been updated, such as when they are in contact with the firewall administrator and they want to update their desktop's policy immediately.

To explicitly log on to the Policy Server, the remote user should go to the **Policy menu,** and then choose **Log on to Policy Server**. They will see a list of available Policy Servers, and they should choose the appropriate server.

Summary

Any security policy is only as strong as its weakest link. A common mistake by firewall administrators is not considering remote users as a possible source of security breaches. Once a remote user is connected to your network, any compromise of that user's workstation could easily result in a compromise of your network.

Check Point's SecureClient and Policy Server enable you to reduce the risk of a remote user's desktop being susceptible to a security compromise. Because remote users are not necessarily knowledgeable about what their local security policy should be, or how to implement it, the combination of Policy Server and SecureClient enables you, as the firewall administrator, to set the security policy appropriate for remote users, and then push that policy out in a way that is simple and unobtrusive to the user.

The Check Point SecureClient Packaging tool is an additional component, which enables you to distribute preconfigured versions of SecureClient to your users. This eliminates the need for remote users to correctly set up and configure SecureClient, thereby further simplifying the process for remote users to securely connect to the network.

Solutions Fast Track

Installing and Configuring a Policy Server

- ☑ Install the Policy Server from the Check Point NG CD-ROM.
- ☑ Enable the Policy Server as an installed product in your firewall object.
- ☑ Set the user group to use with the Policy Server in the Authentication tab of your firewall object.

Desktop Security Options

- ☑ Set up your desktop security rule base, and configure the global policy properties for desktop security.
- ☑ If desired, configure desktop configuration verification to specify what should happen if the security policy is broken.
- ☑ Add a client encrypt rule to the standard rule base and edit the client encryption action properties.

Installing SecureClient Software

☑ Remote users can install SecuRemote/SecureClient directly from their Check Point NG CD-ROM.

☑ The latest version of SecuRemote/SecureClient software can be obtained from Check Point at http://www.checkpoint.com/ techsupport/downloads_sr.html.

☑ You can use the SecureClient packaging tool to preconfigure SecureClient, and bundle it into a package that remote users can easily install.

Logging into the Policy Server

☑ When a remote user loads SecureClient, it automatically logs into the Policy Server and receives the most recent security policy.

☑ SecureClient periodically logs into the Policy Server (about every 30 minutes) to check for any security policy updates, and send logs back to the Policy Server.

☑ Users can also explicitly log in to the Policy Server through SecureClient.

Frequently Asked Questions

The following Frequently Asked Questions, answered by the authors of this book, are designed to both measure your understanding of the concepts presented in this chapter and to assist you with real-life implementation of these concepts. To have your questions about this chapter answered by the author, browse to **www.syngress.com/solutions** and click on the **"Ask the Author"** form.

Q: Can I install the Policy Server on two firewalls for redundancy?

A: You can configure the Policy Server for high availability, but it is more complicated than simply installing the Policy Server on two separate firewalls. Consult the Check Point NG documentation for details.

Q: What licensing issues should I take into account when installing a Policy Server?

A: In addition to your existing FireWall-1 licenses, the Policy Server requires a separate license on each Firewall module on which it is installed. You also need to ensure that you have sufficient user licenses for the number of remote users that will be connecting. The user licenses are installed on the Management Module.

Q: I want my salespeople to be able to log on and browse my NT/Domain from the field.

A: See the section on Secure Domain Logon in Chapter 10.

Q: I have a really large network, with a lot of VPN traffic to and from multiple VPN domains, and notice frequent connection interruptions.

A: Check to make sure that "key exchange for subnets" is enabled under the firewall workstation object under the Advanced IKE Properties tab. Check the size of the connection table. Check gateway memory usage and processor load ('fw tab –t connections –s' and 'fw ctl pstat').

Q: I have installed SecureClient NG (build 51057) on several WinXP Professional laptops, and I've run into a seemingly random problem that is occurring on some systems but not others. I am able to download the topology and update the site; however, when I attempt to access the VPN domain, I am not getting prompted for authentication. It doesn't matter if I try to use FWZ or IKE. No error messages are received at all…it just does nothing. Do you know how to resolve this problem?

A: Yes, there is a workaround to this problem. Check Point is working on a permanent solution. Here is what you can do:

1. Remove/Uninstall SecuRemote or Secure Client.

2. Reboot.

3. Right-click on **My Network Places** or **Network Properties** in the **Control Panel**, and go to the adapter you are using. Depending on the type of adapter, you should see either "configure" or "properties." This will bring you to the TCP/IP properties for this adapter. In this list, you will see QOS. Highlight it, and then hit the **Uninstall** button. (Note: Just unchecking QOS may render the system unusable, so make sure you uninstall it.)

4. Reboot.

5. Reinstall SecuRemote/SecureClient and test the connection.

The problem is that the QOS (Quality of Service) is changing the registry entries in:

```
HKLM\System\CurrentControlSet\Control\Class\{4D36E972...}\00xx
    \Linkage\Upper Bind from FW1 to PSched.
```

## Chapter 12

Advanced Configurations

Solutions in this chapter:

- **Check Point High Availability (CPHA)**

- **Single Entry Point VPN Configurations (SEP)**

- **Multiple Entry Point VPN Configurations (MEP)**

- **Other High Availability Methods**

- ☑ **Summary**

- ☑ **Solutions Fast Track**

- ☑ **Frequently Asked Questions**

Introduction

The Internet and Internet services have become increasingly important to businesses over time, and several organizations are choosing to implement measures to keep these services highly available to their staff or to their customers. The first task is identifying which services are business critical, and then determining the best solution to keep that service available 99.9 percent of the time. The reason that keeping a service available is an issue at all is because the Internet and networking technology is not fail-proof. Your ISP connection could be down or slow, your internal router could lose its routing table and stop passing packets, or you could have a hardware failure or power failure at any point in the network infrastructure, which could cause any number of service interruptions.

So, what can you do to prevent these outages from happening? Well, you probably can't control them 100 percent of the time, regardless of how much time, money, and effort you put into the project, but you can make a considerable dent in downtime by setting up some redundant systems and configuring them to fail over in the event of a failure.

For example, your company prints a well-known newspaper on the East Coast, and having the Internet available to your reporters is business critical, since they use this source of information for many of their articles. Therefore, it's your job to have a redundant Internet connection with fail-over abilities. You could contract two ISPs, have two routers set up at each end of each ISP connection, have two or four firewalls set up to fail over, and have two routers inside each firewall, all plugged into various UPS. This is a complicated configuration, but it can be an operational means to have a high availability connection to the Internet.

In this chapter, we will discuss the Check Point High Availability module, and discuss a few network configuration models in which Check Point will allow VPNs to fail over. And we'll discuss some of the other options you can utilize with VPN-1/FireWall-1 in order to have a high availability system.

Check Point High Availability (CPHA)

High Availability can be your best friend, both from a network performance and from a security perspective. Many enterprises are concerned about the firewall being their single point of failure, and I've seen more than one contingency plan allowing for the redirection of traffic around a firewall, should it fail. With a highly available solution, this won't be needed.

One of the first questions I am often asked when dealing with high availability is concerning the definition of available. What makes a system available? Is it that the operating system is…for lack of a better term…operating? Is it defined by a daemon on the system, or, like a server group discussed earlier in the book, does it require some sort of agent installed to monitor "upness"? To answer these questions, we'll delve into the mechanics of Check Point High Availability.

Enabling High Availability

Before you can begin using High Availability, or define and join clusters and all of the other neat things, you have to do some preparatory work. Primarily, you need to make sure that you have the proper licensing in place in order to run the High Availability module, and that High Availability is enabled. Then you must begin by defining the configuration and the IP addresses on the future cluster members. The cluster members must have three interfaces, with four interfaces being preferred if you opt to use synchronization. All of the internally facing IP addresses must be the same, as must all of the externally facing addresses. The Check Point High Availability module will make sure that the MAC addresses are identical, so there's no need to play around with ARP entries. Figure 12.1 illustrates what a sample network layout for High Availability might look like. Note that all of the external facing IP addresses are the same in the diagram (noted as .101 to indicate the final octet) as are the Internal IP addresses. The interfaces on the management segment must each use a unique IP address. Also, if state synchronization is opted for, you'll probably want to connect the firewall machines on another interface, one used exclusively for synchronization. We'll discuss synchronization shortly.

The next step toward gaining the benefits of Check Point High Availability is to enable it on the enforcement module. This is a really easy step, and only involves running the cpconfig command. I've run the cpconfig command on my Solaris machine that is running the enforcement module, and have included a sample of the output below. On Windows it's even easier, since the Windows version of cpconfig is GUI based. Access the High Availability tab by selecting **Start | Programs | Check Point Management Clients | Check Point Configuration NG | High Availability tab**. From here, all you need to do on Windows is to place a checkmark in the checkbox, indicating that you are enabling High Availability. Figure 12.2 shows you the output of the cpconfig command on Solaris.

Figure 12.1 Highly Available Cluster

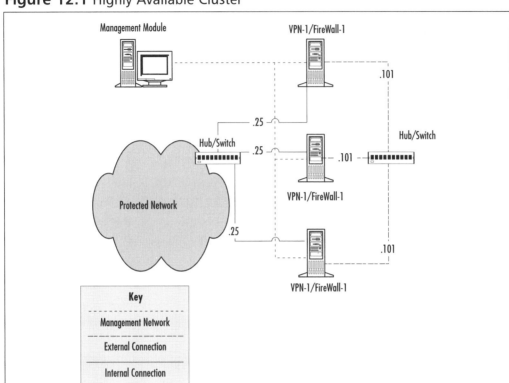

Figure 12.2 Enabling High Availability

```
# cpconfig

This program will let you re-configure

your VPN-1 & FireWall-1 configuration.



Configuration Options:

----------------------

(1)   Licenses

(2)   SNMP Extension

(3)   PKCS#11 Token

(4)   Random Pool

(5)   Secure Internal Communication
```

Continued

Figure 12.2 Continued

```
(6)   Enable Check Point High Availability/State
 Synchronization
(7)   Automatic start of Check Point modules

(8) Exit

Enter your choice (1-8) :6
Configuring Enable Check Point High Availability/State
Synchronization...
============================================================
High Availability module is currently disabled.


Would you like to enable the High Availability module (y/n) [y] ? y
------------------------------------------------------------


You have changed the High Availability configuration.
Would you like to restart High Availability Module now
so that your changes will take effect? (y/n) [y] ? y



************************************************************
The High Availability module is now enabled.
cpconfig will now end. To continue, please run cpconfig again.
```

There are some restrictions when implementing a High Availability solution. The gateways must be running the same version of VPN-1/FireWall-1, and they must be on the same platform (e.g., you cannot synchronize a Solaris firewall with a Windows NT firewall). Also, you must have a separate management server; the management module cannot reside on a cluster member.

Another wise bit of advice is to configure each cluster member offline, that is, off of the network. While it is good security practice to build machines disconnected from the network anyway, there is a different reason here. Since each machine will be sharing IP addresses, it's nice to avoid address conflicts that might be present if the machines were active on the network segment. Finally, if you are configuring an SEP VPN High Availability solution, the VPN domain for the cluster should be a group object containing the cluster member gateways and their respective VPN domains. We'll discuss SEP later in this chapter.

Configuring & Implementing…

How does the HA module select the MAC address?

There are two distinct types of bootups for a HA member. Initially, at the first boot, there are no real elements of the cluster associated with that machine. The policy has not yet been installed, no priority is associated with the machine, and no gateway priority has been defined. In this case, the gateway begins to look for information by listening on UDP port 8116, from an already configured cluster member. If it can't determine information from a configured cluster member, then it looks for information from other machines with its shared IP address. Once it sees that traffic, it will select the MAC address from the machine with the lowest Random ID and use it for its own.

After that initial boot, and after the remaining cluster information has been assigned, the CPHA module looks for packets coming from the Primary cluster machine, compares that machine's MAC to its own, and changes its own, if necessary.

Failing Over

Now that we've seen how to enable Check Point's High Availability, your next question most likely harkens back to our earlier wonderings about what classifies a system as "up." When dealing with Check Point FireWall-1, the answer to this question is up to you.

When using the Check Point High Availability module, you gain access to the functionality of the `cphaprob` command. This command enables you to define services that are considered critical to the operation of the VPN-1/FireWall-1 system. There are also some default conditions that must be met for the system to be considered available. These are as follows:

- The fwd process must be running, and must not report any problems. (For example, the un-installation of the security policy is considered a problem.)

- The network connection must be active.

- The machine must be running.

These are, of course, the most basic of conditions. As you've come to expect (and, I hope, appreciate) Check Point enables you to enhance the granularity of the checking. This is using the aforementioned cphaprob command. This command is used to register additional devices within the firewall machine as critical, so that their failure will cause the preemption of cluster control. The options to this command are displayed in Table 12.1.

Table 12.1 cphaprob Command Options

Command Option	Command Explanation
-d <device name>	Specify a device to be monitored.
-s <status>	The state of the device. Status can be either "ok," "init," or "problem." If the value is anything besides OK, the device is not considered active.
-t <timeout>	Define a timeout value. If the device doesn't report its status before the timeout expires, the device is considered as failed.
-f <filename> register	Allow the specification of a file containing multiple device definitions.
[-l[a]][-e] list	Display the current state of CPHA devices.
Register	Register the device as a critical process.
Unregister	Remove the registration of this device as a critical process.
Report	Display the status of the HA modules.
If	Display the status of interfaces.
Init	Instruct the firewall to reacquire the shared MAC address.

You can also use the cphaprob command with the state argument to see the status of the HA cluster. Example output for a two-member cluster might resemble this:

```
$ cphaprob state
```

```
Number       Unique Address   State


1 (local)   192.168.10.1      active
2            192.168.10.2      standby
```

You can also check your log files for information about both synchronization and failover.

Firewall Synchronization

State Synchronization allows the firewall or VPN module to be really highly available, in the truest sense. Without synchronization, when a failover occurs, the connections that are currently active will be dropped. This may not be that important when dealing with a firewall, for example, when the majority of the traffic through your firewall is destined for the Web, but can be disastrous in a VPN context. You probably never want to be without synchronization when dealing with a VPN.

What synchronization does is maintain an identical state table on all of the machines involved in the gateway cluster. This, obviously, uses resources. The synchronization process consumes memory, CPU, and network resources, and depending on the size of the state table, this could be significant.

How does it work? The first thing to grasp is that the entire state table is not copied from machine to machine all the time. Obviously, the first synchronization involves the entire state table, but subsequent updates only involve the changes since the last update. The updates occur by default every 100 milliseconds, and while this can be changed, the process isn't easy and you'll probably never want to try. Another thing to consider is that processing the updates takes a minimum of 55 milliseconds. If you are maintaining a particularly busy site, one with a lot of HTTP traffic, for example, your state table may have a larger number of changes, and processing may require more time than the minimum. When I say that synchronization consumes resources, I mean it.

Also, synchronization is not available when using a Multiple Entry Point (MEP) VPN solution. This is because, as we will discuss later in this chapter, MEP is designed for use with a disperse VPN solution. Synchronization is most often used with a Single Entry Point (SEP) VPN solution, and you can see a screen shot of the Synchronization panel in the section on SEP. In a truly user-friendly manner, enabling synchronization is as easy as placing a checkmark in the box labeled **Use State Synchronization** on the **Synchronization** tab of the cluster object. Next, you'll need to define the synchronization network by clicking on **Add** on the **Synchronization** panel. Clicking **Add** will show you a panel such as shown in Figure 12.3.

Figure 12.3 Add Synchronization Network

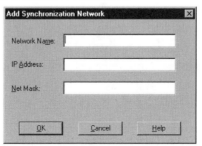

There's a caveat here: Make sure that the synchronization network is trusted. The way I do this is to segment the synchronization traffic from any general-use traffic. I like to use a crossover cable when dealing with a two-member cluster, for example. Next, you need to make sure that FireWall-1 control connections are allowed to pass between the cluster members. Simply make a rule that allows the FW1 service from member to member.

After you have activated synchronization, you'll want to test it to make sure that it is working. There are a couple of different techniques. The quickest way is to check the size of the state tables on each machine. The command to do this is as follows:

```
fw tab -t connections -s
```

While this is quick, it is the least accurate. Remember, the state table is updated frequently, so there is a chance that the table on one machine could change before you can type the command.

The most accurate method (although I've seen it return false information) is the use of the *fw ctl* command. Using the `pstat` option will give you the info on the synchronization process (and other processes as well). A sample bit of the output is shown below.

```
sync new ver working
sync out: on  sync in: on
sync packets sent:
total: 2145 retransmitted: 0 retrans reqs:0 acks: 0
```

```
sync packets received:

total 2473 of which 1 queued and 31 dropped by net

also received 0 retrans reqs and 2 acks to 0 cb requests
```

Another way to check is to see that two or more firewalls are connected to one another via the netstat –an command. I usually run netstat –an | grep 256. On Windows machines you can substitute the "findstr" command for "grep."

The second line is the key to determining the operation of state synchronization. If synchronization is on, then both of these should be on.

What if you are working on a particularly busy boundary firewall cluster, where the vast majority of traffic consists of HTTP and SMTP connections? Each of these connections is relatively short lived, and might not be the best candidates for synchronization. HTTP, for example, is totally stateless by design, so a failover probably wouldn't be noticed. Does the burden of synchronization outweigh the benefits? If so, you are in luck. You don't have to synchronize every protocol. You can selectively weed out those protocols that are hogging too many resources when compared to the necessity of their HA condition. This is done by editing the $FWIDR/lib/user.def file and inserting a line like this:

```
//Don't sync the web!
 non_sync_ports {<80, 6>};
```

The first line is a comment, which is always a wise thing to add. The second line supplies port numbers as arguments a port number (80) and a protocol number (6). After applying that change to all cluster members and restarting the firewall service, you'll no longer be syncing HTTP, and perhaps will be saving a lot of CPU cycles.

Single Entry Point VPN Configurations (SEP)

Single Entry Point VPNs enable your enterprise to deploy a solution that protects what many consider an increasingly critical element of the network. VPNs enable you to extend your enterprise to the remote user, and as more companies look toward telecommuting, remote sales forces, and partner networks, their availability becomes increasingly important. Gone are the days when a VPN was a novelty or a convenience; today it's a necessity. Also, synchronized connections are a must. You wouldn't want users to notice that their VPN connection was just transferred to another gateway.

Another nice feature is the support for SEP (and MEP) VPNs when dealing with both remote clients and with gateway-to-gateway VPNs.

Gateway Configuration

Before you go about configuring a Single Entry Point VPN solution, you need to make sure that Gateway Clusters are enabled on the management server. This is simply done from within the Global Properties in the Policy Editor. Figure 12.4 shows you the means of enabling HA on the Management server.

Figure 12.4 Enabling Gateway Clusters

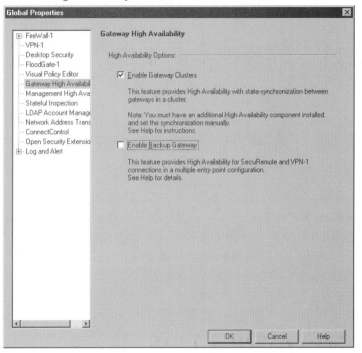

In Chapter 3, you began looking at the means of configuring a High Availability solution. In this section, you'll look at this topic in greater depth. Figure 12.5 is presented here as a memory refresher. It shows you the General panel used for cluster configuration. As covered in Chapter 3, this panel is used to initially identify the information about the cluster, such as the cluster name and IP address and also to specify the Check Point applications installed. Note that the IP address configured here is the cluster IP address. This will be the common IP of the cluster, and should be defined in the interface configuration of each cluster member.

Figure 12.5 Gateway Cluster: General Panel

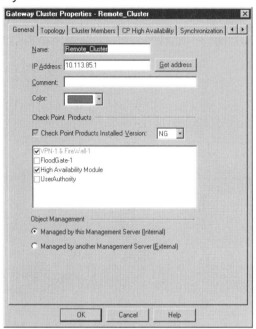

You also can specify, on the topology panel (Figure 12.7), which addresses reside behind this cluster. This is similar to the features on a workstation object's interface properties topology panel. One of the most common uses of a manually defined VPN domain is to define an overlapping encryption domain for the gateway cluster. Figure 12.6 shows you a gateway cluster with an overlapping VPN domain. Note that the VPN domain contains the protected network and all of the cluster members.

You'll first need to define a network object symbolizing the protected network. Then you'll want to define a group object containing each gateway cluster member, as well as the newly created network object. In Figure 12.7, this group is called Remote_VPN_Domain. Specifying this object on the Topology panel as shown is all you need to do to institute a full VPN domain overlap.

The next panel enables you to specify cluster members. This is your next task. Cluster members are the workstations previously defined for inclusion within the cluster. This configuration panel is illustrated in Figure 12.8. Here it is important to note that order is important, as the order that the gateways are listed defines their priority. The order can be shuffled without much effort by the use of the familiar Up and Down sort buttons. Also, new gateways can be added and old ones simply removed, as well. In this case, the Edit button will take you to the

properties panels for the selected gateway, allowing very handy alteration of its
settings information.

Figure 12.6 Overlapping VPN Domain in an SEP Configuration

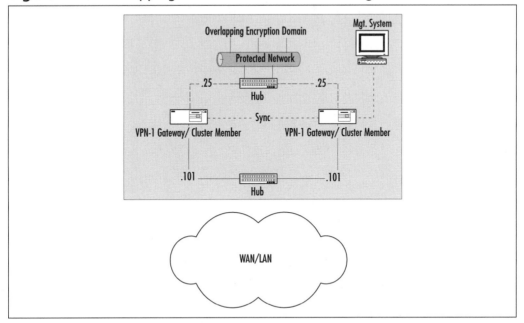

Figure 12.7 Gateway Cluster: Topology Panel

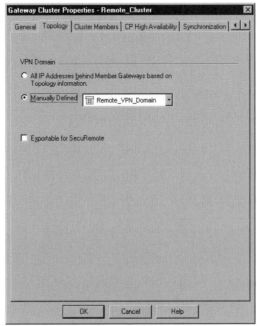

Figure 12.8 Gateway Cluster: Cluster Members

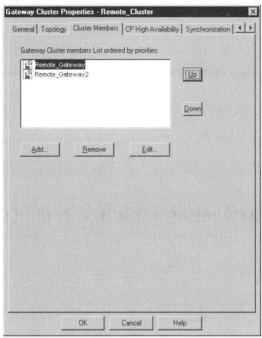

Figure 12.9 shows you how the High Availability settings are defined. The first option, High Availability Mode, tells the HA process how to react when a failed cluster member returns to service. There are two options, which are explained below.

- **Active Gateway Up** In this mode, when a primary gateway has failed and subsequently returned to service, it will not regain control of the cluster. Instead, it will assume the role of secondary. This is useful when you opt not to use state synchronization, as it causes the least interference in these cases.

- **Higher Priority Gateway Up** When the primary gateway in the cluster fails and subsequently returns to service, it will retake control of the cluster, assuming that it has been assigned a higher priority (as sorted in the cluster members panel).

Figure 12.9 CP Gateway Cluster: High Availability Panel

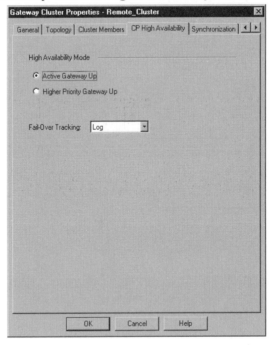

Also defined on this panel is the action to take when a primary gateway fails. The options are these:

- None
- Log
- Alert
- Mail

Figure 12.10 shows you the Synchronization panel. Synchronization is not required for a HA cluster to function, and is, in some cases, better excluded. Synchronization assures that no connections are lost when a primary cluster firewall fails. It does this by maintaining the state table across all cluster members. This table maintenance has an associated resource cost, which, depending on the size of the state table, can be large. The decision to use this feature is up to you. If you opt for its benefits, you'll need to define what Check Point calls a "synchronization ring," or, in common terms, a group of networks. Note that the network listed in this ring will be treated as trusted. The HA module will trust all messages coming from this network, and, as such, it should be segmented from

normal user traffic. If you opt not to use synchronization, simply uncheck the
Use State Synchronization field.

Figure 12.10 Gateway Cluster: Synchronization

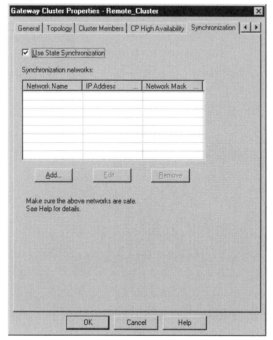

Recall from our earlier discussion of State Synchronization what the purpose
of this mechanism is. Imagine if a user behind your firewall is getting a very large
file via FTP, downloading the newest service pack from Microsoft, for example. If
the primary firewall failed and synchronization was enabled, the secondary firewall would take over the connections and the user wouldn't notice the slightest
difference. Without synchronization, the transfer would need to be restarted, perhaps with the loss of the already downloaded data.

The remaining tabs of the Gateway Cluster are identical to their cousins in
the workstation properties. Hidden in the screenshots are VPN, Authentication,
Masters, and Log Servers tabs (refer back to Chapter 3 for a refresher on the
Workstation object). These allow the setting of the same information as for the
individual member workstations, except that here the information is defined per
cluster. This also means that the information will no longer be configurable on
the individual cluster members.

Policy Configuration

When you have finished configuring the cluster and assigning all the proper members, you still need to allow the FW1 service to pass between the cluster members. As mentioned earlier in the High Availability section, it's best to make sure that the synchronization network is trusted completely. This is easily accomplished by simply not connecting that network to any other machines. You certainly wouldn't want others synching up with your firewalls—that could lead to very bad things. There's only one problem with making this rule. You can't use the cluster object as either a source or destination in the Rule Base. To work around this, you'll need to create a *Workstation* object with the IP address of the interface on the synchronization network, and use that in the rule.

Multiple Entry Point VPN Configurations (MEP)

Multiple Entry Point VPN deployments make use of the VPN-1/FireWall-1 Backup Gateway feature. You should remember that MEP is used primarily to support providing automatic backup gateways to SecuRemote clients. With this sort of implementation, gateways for logically separated networks can be used to connect to the same destination network, assuming that a link exists between those networks. A diagram of a MEP configuration is shown in Figure 12.11.

Figure 12.11 Simple MEP Illustration

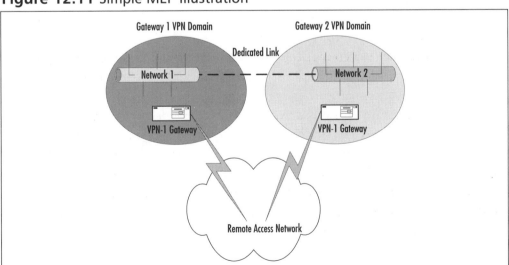

I consider MEP configurations to be more of a redundancy solution than a true High Availability solution. Since the networks are logically (and often geographically) separated, firewall synchronization is not possible. With this being the case, connections cannot be maintained as they can be with a SEP configuration. Instead, when the SecuRemote client's gateway fails, there is a brief pause before the backup gateway is connected to. This will cause an interruption in the connection from a user's perspective. Usually this isn't a big deal. A user browsing the Web, for example, will simply hit the refresh button to continue as normal. Something like an SSL-secured Web page, however, would be more of a bother.

The first step toward setting up a MEP solution is to enable backup gateways on the Management server. This is done by altering the **Global Properties | Gateway High Availability** by placing a checkmark in the box labeled **Enable Backup Gateway**, as shown in Figure 12.12.

Figure 12.12 Enabling MEP

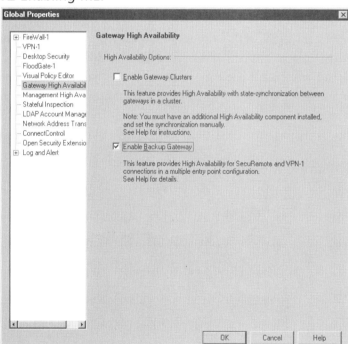

Overlapping VPN Domains

A VPN domain (a.k.a. an encryption domain) defines the entirety of the network residing behind the VPN-1/FireWall-1 device, and also includes the VPN-1/

FireWall-1 gateway(s). Recent versions of VPN-1 support the use of overlapping VPN domains. This inclusion is the key element that allows the implementation of High Availability for VPN connections. There are three methods of creating an overlapping VPN domain:

- Partial Overlap
- Full Overlap
- Proper Subset

Figure 12.13 shows you a graphical representation of these VPN domain types.

Figure 12.13 VPN Domain Types

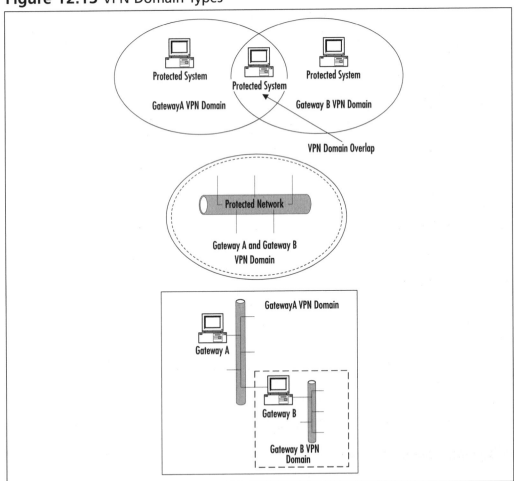

Check Point has included support for Full Overlap and Proper Subset VPN domains. Since it isn't a supported method, Partial Overlap is outside of the scope of this chapter. We'll look at the particulars of the two supported VPN domains in the next couple of paragraphs.

As I mentioned in the first paragraph of this section, a VPN domain consists of the network residing behind the gateway, including that gateway. What this means for you, as a firewall administrator, is that you define a network object consisting of the protected network and then point to that network object within the configuration of the workstation object that is the VPN gateway. Implementing a Fully Overlapping VPN domain isn't much more difficult. All you need to do is properly define the network object. Simply define a group of network objects containing all of the involved gateways and all of their protected networks, and then point to this new group object as the VPN domain for those gateways.

This type of VPN domain is very handy when dealing with critical connections. When a SecuRemote client attempts to communicate with a server residing within this overlapping domain, it will attempt to connect to all of the gateways, and will complete that connection with the first gateway to respond. This brings up a potential problem in that traffic that came in through one gateway could possibly be sent back out through a different gateway, which would result in that packet not being encrypted. To prevent this from happening, you have two choices.

- The use of Network Address Translation. Using NAT enables you to hide the connections passing through the gateway behind the gateway. This requires the use of a sensible hiding IP address (the hiding address, that is, for the SecuRemote client) that is routable to the issuing gateway.

- The use of IP pools. IP Pools enable you to assign an address to the SecuRemote client from a previously configured source. This source can be either a network object or an address range.

Note that State Synchronization cannot be considered a solution to asymmetric routing. There is no way that you could hope two firewalls could synchronize fast enough to avoid this problem.

My favorite solution to the problem of asymmetric routing by far is the use of IP pools. If you ever have to use a VPN solution that doesn't support pools, you'll quickly see why having them available is far superior to not having them. To enable pools, you need to modify the Global Properties to place a check in the field called **Enable IP Pool NAT for SecuRemote and VPN connections**. What to do when the pool evaporates is up to you. Figure 12.14 illustrates this panel.

Figure 12.14 Enabling IP Pool NAT

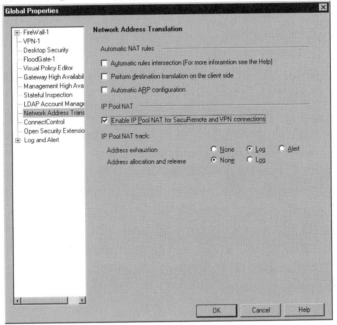

Address exhaustion, which has the familiar three options of None, Log, and Alert, defines what to do when the addresses allocated to your pool are all gone. I don't recommend selecting **None**. Address allocation and release is a must for logging. Equate this with DHCP lease information as far as function, and consider the gap in your security policy if you didn't have accountability here.

Gateway Configuration

The gateway configuration is much more simple than the SEP configuration. This is essentially because, as I mentioned, this is more of a failover solution as compared to a High Availability solution. The gateways aren't clustered and there's no way to synchronize. SecuRemote clients will connect to their primary gateway as normal. If that gateway fails, then the connections are reestablished with the backup gateway. This takes a few seconds, so there will be a momentary interruption in the user's connection. But momentary is sure a lot better than permanent, I think you'll agree. If, however, you don't want even a moment's interruption, SEP is the only real way to go.

Once you've enabled backup gateways in the Global Properties, you are able to define them within the Workstation object representing the gateways in your infrastructure. On the **VPN tab** of the **Workstation properties panel**, you'll see a new checkbox called **Use Backup Gateways:** and an associated pull-down menu. Place a checkmark in this box and select the desired backup gateway from the list, and you're off to the races. The results will resemble the panel as shown in Figure 12.15.

Figure 12.15 Configuring a Backup Gateway

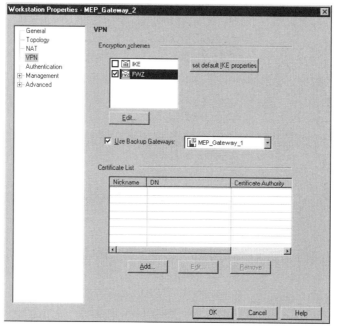

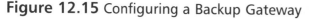

Designing & Planning…

Why Not Go All Out?

So, you aren't sure if either SEP or MEP is the solution for you. Say, for example, that you have a really mission-critical connection, one that just cannot be down. But you also have a requirement for redundant connections. These redundant connections have to be available even if an entire site goes down.

There's nothing that says you can't use both SEP and MEP in tandem. You could define a SEP group to handle the requirement for the highly available connection and then use MEP to define a redundant backup link!

The next step is to define the VPN domain for this gateway. There are really no special tricks involved here. All you need to do is define the proper VPN domain for this gateway, just as you would if you were using a single gateway solution. Figure 12.16 illustrates this panel.

Figure 12.16 Selecting the VPN Domain

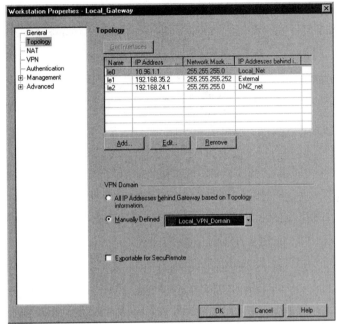

Overlapping VPN Domains

Establishing a MEP configuration using an overlapping VPN domain makes things about as easy as possible. In simple terms, an overlapping VPN domain makes the VPN domain of all participating gateways identical. While a VPN domain usually contains a single gateway and the network that resides behind it, when establishing an overlap, the domain contains all of the gateways and their respective protected networks. Configuring a MEP configuration for a fully overlapping encryption setup isn't all that hard. Let's take a look at the steps. For these examples, we'll assume a dual gateway architecture protecting the following networks:

- 10.1.1.0/24

- 10.1.2.0/24

Figure 12.17 shows you a MEP configuration using a fully overlapping VPN domain.

Figure 12.17 Fully Overlapping VPN Domain

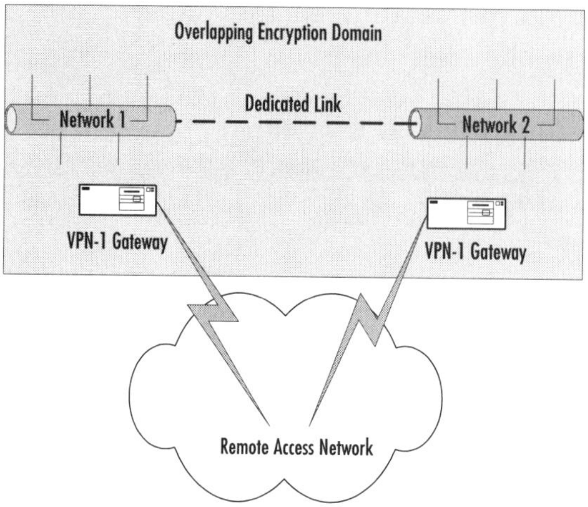

NOTE

Check Point Next Generation does not support partially overlapping VPNs. This situation should be avoided at all costs. A common real world example of this is configuring a gateway as an endpoint for a VPN, but failing to make the gateway a member of its own encryption domain. If the gateway has a DMZ interface it is very easy for the gateway itself to belong to two encryption domains that are then "partially overlapping". Ironically, it is the gateway itself that is causing the "partially overlapping" conflict.

The first step is to define these networks for use within your Rule Base. By selecting **Manage | Network Objects | New | Network** from your Policy Editor, you'll be able to create the networks representing your VPN domain. You'll also need to create the Workstation objects representing the gateways that you'll be using. After you have done that, you need to place them all into a group. Select **Manage | Network Objects | New | Group | Simple Group** from the Policy Manager menu, and create a group like you see in Figure 12.18.

Next, you have to configure this new VPN domain on all of the firewalls that are participating within the configuration, and that's it. Shown in Figure 12.19 is what your Topology panel will look like. Note the Manually Defined VPN domain.

Figure 12.18 Overlapping VPN Domain Group

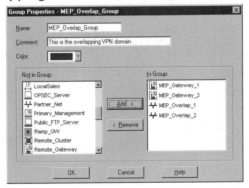

Figure 12.19 Overlapping VPN Domain

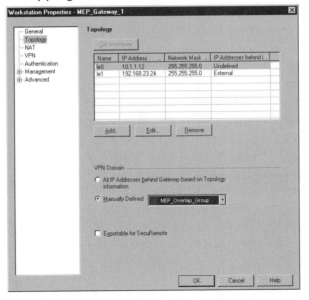

You also must use some means of avoiding the problem of asymmetric routing. This problem occurs when a SecuRemote Client connects in through a HA MEP gateway and reaches its internal target. The reply, however, might see two possible exit points, and the reply packet might get routed through a different gateway than the one providing the original entry point. The exit gateway knows nothing about any VPN encrypted connection, thus destroying the original client-to-site VPN. Again, my favorite solution is the use of IP pools. You'll also need to make sure that the routing within your network is properly configured to handle passing the traffic back to the network associated with the IP pool network. To associate an IP Pool with the gateway, you first must define an address range that will be used as the pool. After you do that, access the **Work-station properties** and select the **NAT panel**. Place a checkmark in the box marked **Use IP Pool NAT for SecuRemote and VPN connections**, select the previously defined address range object, and you're ready to go. Figure 12.20 shows you this final configuration panel.

Figure 12.20 Using IP Pools

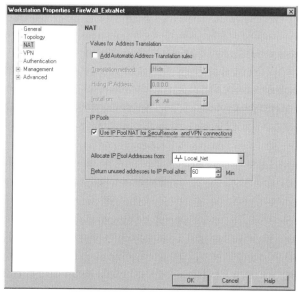

When your SecuRemote clients attempt to initiate a connection, the first gateway to respond will be selected. This is a pretty simple method and is one of the reasons that this configuration is so straightforward.

Other High Availability Methods

So far, we've been discussing some generic High Availability configurations, and we've only mentioned using the Check Point HA module. There are, however, other ways to accomplish the task of High Availability. Many vendors have developed HA solutions for Check Point VPN-1/FireWall-1, and some of them are very good. Stonesoft (http://www.stonesoft.com) is one of the more established players in this market with their StoneBeat FullCluster product, which provides both HA and load balancing. Another popular choice is RainWall from Rainfinity (http://www.rainfinity.com). You can see a full listing of Check Point OPSEC certified products at http://www.checkpoint.com/opsec/performance.html.

Discussion of the configuration for each of these products is beyond the scope of this book.

Routing Failover

Another failover method is to use a routing protocol to handle moving traffic around a downed firewall. The most popular method of implementing this is by using VRRP, or the Virtual Router Redundancy Protocol. I only know of one platform that currently supports VRRP, and that is the excellent Nokia appliance. The firewall software will have to take over the duties of synchronization, but that's not unusual to the HA solutions we've looked at.

Configuration of VRRP is outside the scope of this text, but we can discuss some of the more general points that you'll be dealing with. First, you need to decide which version of VRRP you want to implement. There are two versions in common use: VRRP v2 and VRRP Monitored Circuit. Unless you have a pressing need to use VRRP v2 (address-space exhaustion, backward compatibility, etc.), you should opt for Monitored Circuit. In either of these configurations, you may experience problems with asymmetric routing. One of the main differences in v2 and Monitored Circuit is the convergence time, that is, the time it takes for a failure to be detected and corrected. In earlier versions of IPSO, convergence time could be over eight seconds. Using Monitored Circuit, the convergence time is less than one second. VRRP uses HELO messages, sent at a default interval of one second, to a multicast destination (which must be allowed in the Rule Base) to announce their status. This HELO message includes a priority, which is used to determine which gateway should be the active member of the cluster. If the primary machine detects a failed interface, for example, it would decrement its priority, thus notifying the backup gateway to take over the cluster. Remember to include all of the firewall interfaces in the tracking list. It wouldn't do much good if the outside interface was down, but not tracked, and the inside interface was still taking traffic.

Hardware Options

A final method that I want to touch on briefly is the use of an external, hardware-based solution. Examples of these abound, and their usefulness varies… caveat emptor. My main gripe with a hardware-based load balancer or High Availability solution is that they generally introduce a single point of failure, which in essence is counter-productive. Generally, the meantime between failure (MTBF) of these units far exceeds that of the standard server machine, but I've rebooted far too many of these things to feel really comfortable with them. Also, most of these products don't really offer a true highly available solution. Load Balancing with a health-checking option (which will direct packets around a downed unit) is the best you can expect, which is still pretty good.

One notable exception is the Foundry ServerIron XL content switch. This product was the first to be OPSEC-certified to provide full failover support, including the failover of active VPN sessions. ServerIron also supports clustering and synchronization of its load balancers, so that they are not a single point of failure. Also, the configuration commands for this switch are nearly identical to those of the Cisco IOS, which makes the learning curve simpler. You can get more information at http://www.checkpoint.com/opsec/partners/foundry.html.

Summary

I hope you've gained as much from reading this chapter as I have from writing it. While you might not be using, or even considering, implementing a Highly Available solution within your network, it is a good idea to be aware of the capabilities that Check Point VPN-1/FireWall-1 offers you.

If you are currently using a Highly Available solution, I hope that the coverage of some of the finer details has given you food for thought and perhaps some new configuration techniques. While most of the focus was on the VPN aspects of HA solutions, keep in mind that HA is also a valuable solution for any mission-critical network boundary.

We also gave some attention to third-party solutions for HA, such as VRRP and hardware options for high availability. While we can't go into much detail on the vast amount of HA solutions out there (Windows 2000 clustering and IBM HACMP as two examples), I hope you have something new to chew on and research.

Solutions Fast Track

Check Point High Availability (CPHA)

- ☑ Remember that the Check Point High Availability module is a separately purchased product. Make sure that you have the proper license before using it.

- ☑ If using State Synchronization, don't be afraid to tailor the synchronized protocols.

- ☑ Be sure that you have properly defined the necessary components using the cphaprob command.

Single Entry Point VPN Configurations (SEP)

- ☑ Synchronization is a must with a SEP VPN.

- ☑ Before enabling a SEP gateway configuration, make sure that Clusters are enabled in the Global Properties and that HA has been turned on each enforcement module.

Multiple Entry Point VPN Configurations (MEP)

☑ Remember that a MEP solution is the most simple of failover solutions; synchronization of connections isn't available.

☑ Use IP Pools or NAT to circumvent problems associated with asymmetric routing.

Other High Availability Methods

☑ Remember to ensure that your hardware HA mechanism does not become a single point of failure.

☑ It may be wise to select an OPSEC certified hardware solution.

Frequently Asked Questions

The following Frequently Asked Questions, answered by the authors of this book, are designed to both measure your understanding of the concepts presented in this chapter and to assist you with real-life implementation of these concepts. To have your questions about this chapter answered by the author, browse to **www.syngress.com/solutions** and click on the **"Ask the Author"** form.

Q: Is it possible to change the defined MAC address for my gateway cluster?

A: Yes; it is actually pretty easy. On Solaris, for example, all you need to do is edit a file called /etc/etheraddr.[interface], where [interface] is the name of the desired interface: le0, for example. Put in the MAC address you want config-ured and reboot the machine. On Windows, you'll need to add a registry entry. This is actually pretty easy, too. Running Win2K, locate the key \HKEY_LOCAL_MACHINE\SYSTEM\CurrentControlSet\Control\ Class\{4D36E972-E325-11CE-BFC1-08002BE10318}. Under this entry, you'll find a bunch of four-digit number entries. One of these is your device driver for the specific adaptor, identified by the DriverDesc key. Add a key of type STRING to this, called NetworkAddress, containing the MAC address you desire.

Q: I've been told that State Synchronization uses authentication between cluster members. My machines are connected via crossover cable. Is there a way to disable authentication?

A: Indeed there is. You simply need to edit the $FWDIR/lib/control.map file and add the sync directive to the line that currently reads: "* : getkey,gettopo,gettopossl,certreq/none."

Q: In prior methods, I had to edit the sync.conf file and run the putkeys command in order to establish synchronization peers; is this no longer the case?

A: You are referring to what is called the Old Sync Method. FireWall-1 NG uses what is known as the New Sync Method, and this configuration is all GUI based. No need to meddle with the sync.conf file anymore. (Note that you still *can* use the old method, but then you *must* use the putkeys command.)

Q: With so many choices for HA solutions, is there a source I can go to to get an independent answer?

A: I haven't seen a definitive review of all HA solutions, but I have seen a comparison of two of the popular third-party solutions: StoneBeat and RainWall. It's located at http://www.allasso.co.uk/base/docs/1993037987.pdf and is worth a read. Even if it doesn't cover the specific solution you are considering, it may help you ask the right questions.

Appendix A

Class C Subnet Mask Cheat Sheet

This cheat sheet can come in handy when working with network addresses and subnet masks. A standard netmask is written 255.255.255.0 which is equivalent to the aggregate /24. Using aggregates has become popular because computer people tend to be lazy and it only requires three keystrokes.

Table A.1 Netmasks and Aggregates

Netmasks and Aggregates			
Subnet Mask	255.255.255.0	**Hex Mask**	0xffffff00
Subnet Bits/Aggregate	24	**Host Bits**	8
Number of Subnets	1	**Hosts per Subnet**	254
Network Address	**Host IP Range**	**Broadcast Addresses**	
.0	.1 - .254	.255	
Subnet Mask	255.255.255.128	**Hex Mask**	0xffffff80
Subnet Bits/Aggregate	25	**Host Bits**	7
Number of Subnets	2	**Hosts per Subnet**	126
Network Address	**Host IP Range**	**Broadcast Addresses**	
.0	.1 - .126	.127	
.128	.129 - .254	.255	
Subnet Mask	255.255.255.192	**Hex Mask**	0xffffffc0
Subnet Bits/Aggregate	26	**Host Bits**	6
Number of Subnets	4	**Hosts per Subnet**	62
Network Address	**Host IP Range**	**Broadcast Addresses**	
.0	.1 - .62	.63	
.64	.65 - .126	.127	
.128	.129 - .190	.191	
.192	.193 - .254	.255	
Subnet Mask	255.255.255.224	**Hex Mask**	0xffffffe0
Subnet Bits/Aggregate	27	**Host Bits**	5
Number of Subnets	8	**Hosts per Subnet**	30
Network Address	**Host IP Range**	**Broadcast Addresses**	
.0	.1 - .30	.31	
.32	.33 - .62	.63	
.64	.65 - .94	.95	
.96	.97 - .126	.127	

Continued

Table A.1 Continued

Network Address	Host IP Range	Broadcast Addresses	
.128	.129 - .158	.159	
.160	.161 - .190	.191	
.192	.193 - .222	.223	
.224	.225 - .254	.255	
Subnet Mask	255.255.255.240	**Hex Mask**	0xfffffff0
Subnet Bits/Aggregate	28	**Host Bits**	4
Number of Subnets	16	**Hosts per Subnet**	14
Network Address	**Host IP Range**	**Broadcast Addresses**	
.0	.1 – .14	.15	
.16	.17 - .30	.31	
.32	.33 - .46	.47	
.48	.49 - .62	.63	
.64	.65 - .94	.79	
.80	.81 - .94	.95	
.96	.97 - .110	.111	
.112	.113 - .126	.127	
.128	.129 - .142	.143	
.144	.145 - .158	.159	
.160	.161 - .174	.175	
.176	.177 - .190	.191	
.192	.193 - .206	.207	
.208	.209 - .222	.223	
.224	.225 - .238	.239	
.240	.241 - .254	.255	
Subnet Mask	255.255.255.248	**Hex Mask**	0xfffffff8
Subnet Bits/Aggregate	29	**Host Bits**	3
Number of Subnets	32	**Hosts per Subnet**	6
Network Address	**Host IP Range**	**Broadcast Addresses**	
.0	.1 – .6	.7	
.8	.9 - .14	.15	
.16	.17 - .22	.23	

Continued

Table A.1 Continued

Network Address	Host IP Range	Broadcast Addresses
.24	.25 - .30	.31
.32	.33 - .38	.39
.40	.41 - .46	.47
.48	.49 - .54	.55
.56	.57 - .62	.63
.64	.65 - .70	.71
.72	.73 - .78	.79
.80	.81 - .86	.87
.88	.89 - .94	.95
.96	.97 - .102	.103
.104	.105 - .110	.111
.112	.113 - .118	.119
.120	.121 - .126	.127
.128	.129 - .134	.135
.136	.137 - .142	.143
.144	.145 - .150	.151
.152	.153 - .158	.159
.160	.161 - .166	.167
.168	.169 - .174	.175
.176	.177 - .182	.183
.184	.185 - .190	.191
.192	.193 - .198	.199
.200	.201 - .206	.207
.208	.209 - .214	.215
.216	.217 - .222	.223
.224	.225 - .230	.231
.232	.233 - .238	.239
.240	.241 - .246	.247
.248	.249 - .254	.255

Continued

Table A.1 Continued

Subnet Mask	255.255.255.252	Hex Mask	0xfffffffc
Subnet Bits/Aggregate	30	**Host Bits**	2
Number of Subnets	64	**Hosts per Subnet**	2
Network Address	**Host IP Range**	**Broadcast Addresses**	
.0	.1 – .2	.3	
.4	.5 - .6	.7	
.8	.9 - .10	.11	
.12	.13 - .14	.15	
.16	.17 - .18	.19	
.20	.21 - .22	.23	
.24	.25 - .26	.27	
.28	.29 - .30	.31	
.32	.33 - .34	.35	
.36	.37 - .38	.39	
.40	.41 - .42	.43	
.44	.45 - .46	.47	
.48	.49 - .50	.51	
.52	.53 - .54	.55	
.56	.57 - .58	.59	
.60	.61 - .62	.63	
.64	.65 - .66	.67	
.68	.69 - .70	.71	
.72	.73 - .74	.75	
.76	.77 - .78	.79	
.80	.81 - .82	.83	
.84	.85 - .86	.87	
.88	.89 - .90	.91	
.92	.93 - .94	.95	
.96	.97 - .98	.99	
.100	.101 - .102	.103	
.104	.105 - .106	.107	
.108	.109 - .110	.111	
.112	.113 - .114	.115	

Continued

Table A.1 Continued

Network Address	Host IP Range	Broadcast Addresses
.116	.117 - .118	.119
.120	.121 - .122	.123
.124	.125 - .126	.127
.128	.129 - .130	.131
.132	.133 - .134	.135
.136	.137 - .138	.139
.140	.141 - .142	.143
.144	.145 - .146	.147
.148	.149 - .150	.151
.152	.153 - .154	.155
.156	.157 - .158	.159
.160	.161 - .162	.163
.164	.165 - .166	.167
.168	.169 - .170	.171
.172	.173 - .174	.175
.176	.177 - .178	.179
.180	.181 - .182	.183
.184	.185 - .186	.187
.188	.189 - .190	.191
.192	.193 - .192	.195
.196	.197 - .198	.199
.200	.201 - .202	.203
.204	.205 - .206	.207
.208	.209 - .210	.211
.212	.213 - .214	.215
.216	.217 - .218	.219
.220	.221 - .222	.223
.224	.225 - .226	.227
.228	.229 - .230	.231
.232	.233 - .234	.235
.236	.237 - .238	.239

Continued

Table A.1 Continued

Network Address	Host IP Range	Broadcast Addresses	
.240	.241 - .242	.243	
.244	.245 - .246	.247	
.248	.249 - .250	.251	
.252	.253 - .254	.255	
Subnet Mask	255.255.255.255	**Hex Mask**	0xffffffff
Subnet Bits/Aggregate	32	**Host Bits**	0
Number of Subnets	255	**Hosts per Subnet**	1

Spoofing: Attacks on Trusted Identity

In this Appendix, we will make a slight departure from focusing on securing your network using Check Point products, and instead focus on the theories and methodologies behind spoofing attacks. To successfully secure your systems, you must understand the motives and the means of those who intend to launch a malicious attack against your network. In this Appendix Dan "Effugas" Kaminsky, world-renowned cryptography expert and frequent speaker at the Black Hat Briefings and DEF CON, provides invaluable insight to the inner workings of a spoof attack. Look for the Syngress icon in the margin to find utilities and code samples, which are available for download from www.syngress.com/solutions.

SYNGRESS
syngress.com

Introduction

> I shall suppose, therefore, that there is, not a true Network, which is the sovereign source of trust, but some Evil Daemon, no less cunning and deceiving than powerful, which has deployed all of its protocol knowledge to deceive me. I will suppose that the switches, the admins, the users, headers, commands, responses and all friendly networked communications that we receive, are only illusory identities which it uses to take me in. I will consider myself as having no source addresses, obfuscated protocols, trusted third parties, operational client code, nor established state, but as believing wrongly that I have all such credentials.
> —Dan "Effugas" Kaminsky

What It Means to Spoof

Merike Keao, in *Designing Network Security*, defines *spoofing attacks* as "providing false information about a principal's identity to obtain unauthorized access to systems and their services." She goes on to provide the example of a *replay attack*, which occurs when authentication protocols are weak enough to allow a simple playback of sniffed packets to provide an untrusted user with trusted access. Merike's definition is accurate, but certain clarifications should be made to accurately separate spoofing attacks from other, network-based methods of attack.

Spoofing Is Identity Forgery

The concept of assuming the identity of another is central to the nature of the spoof. The canonical example of spoofing is the Internet Protocol (IP) spoofing attack. Essentially, Transmission Control Protocol/IP (TCP/IP) and the Internet trusts users to specify their own source address when communicating with other hosts. But, much like the return addresses we place on letters we mail out using the U.S. Postal Service, it's up to the sender of any given message to determine the source address to preface it with. Should the sender use a falsified source address, no reply will be received. As we will see in this chapter, this is often not a problem.

Spoofing Is an Active Attack against Identity Checking Procedures

Spoofing at its core involves sending a message that is not what it claims to be. Take the example of an IP spoofed packet that takes down a network. Now, this message may appear to have been sent by a different, more trusted individual than the one actually sending it, or it may appear to have been sent by nobody that could have ever existed (thus ensuring the anonymity of the attacker). This spoof was not in the content of the message (though one could certainly claim that the engineers of a TCP/IP stack never intended for packets to be received that consisted of an oversized ping request). With the sender of the Ping of Death concealed by a forged source address, though, the identity of the sender was left recorded in error and thus spoofed.

Spoofing Is Possible at All Layers of Communication

One of the more interesting and unrecognized aspects of spoofing is that, as a methodology of attack, it can and will operate at all layers in-between the client and the server. For example, the simplest level of spoof involves physically overpowering or intercepting trusted communications. Splicing into a trusted fiberoptic link and inserting malicious streams of data is a definite spoof, as long as that data is presumed to be coming from the router at the other end of the fiberoptic link. Similarly, locally overpowering the radio signal of a popular station with one's own pirate radio signal also qualifies as a spoof; again, provided the identity of the faux station is not disclosed. What's critical to the implementation of a spoof is the misappropriation of identity, not the specific methodology used to implement the attack.

What's less commonly recognized as spoofing is when the content itself is spoofed. Packets that directly exploit weaknesses in online protocols have no valid "message" to them, but are (when possible) delivered with their source address randomized or false-sourced in an attempt to redirect blame for the packet. Such packets are spoofs, but they merely misappropriate identity at the layer of the network—an administrator, examining the packets directly in terms of the content they represent, would clearly detect an attempt to overflow a buffer, or request excessive permissions in an attempt to damage a network. The packet itself is exactly what it appears to be, and is being sent by somebody who is obviously intending to damage a network. No content-level spoofing is taking place, although the falsified headers are clearly representing a spoof of their own.

However, it is truly the *content-level* spoof that is the most devious, for it focuses on the intent of code itself, rather than the mere mechanics of whether a failure exists. The issue of intent in code is so critical to understand that it earns a rule of its own. Suffice it to say, however, that packets, software packages, and even entire systems may constitute a spoofing attack if they possess a hidden identity other than the one they're trusted to maintain.

Spoofing Is Always Intentional

This is a strange trait, because two absolutely identical packets may be generated from the same host within two minutes of each other, and one may be spoofed while the other wouldn't be. But bear with me.

Spoofing involves the assumption of an online identity other than my own, but as an administrator, I cannot (sadly enough) plug myself directly into an Ethernet network. Instead, I connect a computer to the network and interface with it through that. The computer is essentially a proxy for me, and it grants me a window into the world of networks.

If I tell my proxy to lie about who I am, my proxy is still representing my identity; it is just misrepresenting it publicly. It is spoofing my identity with my consent and my intent.

If my proxy, however, breaks down and sends garbled information about who I am, without me telling it to, it is no longer representing my identity. Rather, it is executing the "will" of its own code, and of course presumably *having no will*, it cannot be representing anything other than what it actually is: a malfunctioning noisemaker.

This is relevant specifically because of Keao's analysis of accidental routing updates; essentially, Sun workstations with multiple network ports will advertise that fact using the older routing protocol Routing Information Protocol version 1 (RIPv1). Because all that's needed to update the public routes with RIPv1 is a public announcement that one is available, entire networks could be rendered unstable by an overactive engineering lab.

Now, you can do some very powerful things by spoofing RIPv1 messages. You can redirect traffic through a subnet you're able to sniff the traffic of. You can make necessary servers unreachable. In summary, you can generally cause havoc with little more than the knowledge of how to send a RIPv1 message, the capability to actually transmit that message, and the intent to do so.

Set a station to take down a network with invalid routes, and you've just established a human identity for a noisy computer to misrepresent online. After all, maybe you're the disgruntled administrator of a network, or maybe you're somebody who's penetrated it late at night, but either way, your intent to create an unstable network has been masked by the operating system's "unlucky propensity" to accidentally do just that.

Then again, as much as such an "unlucky propensity" could theoretically be abused as an excuse for network downtime, mistakes *do* happen. Blaming administrators for each and every fault that may occur exposes as much blindness to the true source of problems as exclusively blaming vendors, hackers (crackers, more accurately), or anyone else. It really *was* the operating system's "unlucky propensity" at fault; the identity of the attacker was ascertained correctly.

Three corollaries flow from this: First, intentionally taking down a network and then blaming it on someone else's broken defaults shifts the blame from you to whoever installed or even built those workstations. *Plausible deniability* equivocates to having the ability to reasonably *spoof yourself as an innocent person* at all times.

Second, if those workstations were *intentionally* configured to "accidentally" take down networks at the factory, it'd still be a spoofing attack. The difference is that you'd be the victim, instead of the attacker.

Third, don't make it easy to take down your network.

Spoofing May Be Blind or Informed, but Usually Involves Only Partial Credentials

Blind spoofing involves submitting identifying information without the full breadth of knowledge that the legitimate user has access to. *Informed spoofing* is generally much more effective, and it defeats protections that check for a bidirectional path between the client and the server (generally, by the server sending the client a request, and assuming a connection exists if the client can echo back a response).

However, although spoofing does scale up to encompass most *identity forging attacks*, a flat-out improper login with a stolen password is not generally considered to be a spoof. The line is somewhat blurry, but spoofing generally does not involve supplying the exact credentials of the legitimate identity. Presuming the existence of credentials that are uniquely assigned to individual users, theft of those credentials isn't generally considered a spoofing attack, though it does provide the ability to impersonate a user. The problem is, technically, individually unique material essentially represents a user's online identity. Failures by the user to keep that data secret are absolutely failures, but of a somewhat different type.

Of course, an informed spoof that involves stealing or co-opting a user's identity in transit is most assuredly fair game, as are attacks that take advantage of redundancies between multiple users' identities. But *spoofing* is a term rarely applied to simply connecting as root and typing the password.

Spoofing Is Not the Same Thing as Betrayal

A system that trusts its users can be betrayed, sometimes brutally. That's one of the risks of having trusted users; ideally, the risk is calculated to be worth the benefits of that trust. If users abuse their powers and cause a security breach, they've not spoofed anything; they were granted powers and the freedom to use them. That they abused that power meant they were given either too much power or trust. At best, they may have spoofed themselves as someone worthy of that power; but the moment they used it, as themselves, without an attempt to frame another, no spoof was in place.

Spoofing Is Not Necessarily Malicious

One important thing to realize about spoofing is that it's not always an attack. Redundancy systems, such as Hot Swappable Router Protocol (HSRP) and Linux's Fake project (www.au.vergenet.net/linux/fake) maximize uptime by removing single-point-of-failure characteristics from server farms. The problem is, IP and Ethernet are designed to have but one host per address; if the host is down, so be it. Without address spoofing, connections would be lost and reliability would suffer as users switched servers. With it, downtime can be made nearly invisible.

IBM's Systems Network Architecture (SNA) protocol for mainframes is also one that benefits strongly from spoofed content on the wire. The standard essentially calls for keepalive packets over a dedicated line to be repeated every second. If one keepalive is missed, the connection is dropped. This works acceptably over dedicated lines where bandwidth is predictable, but tunneling SNA over the Internet introduces intermittent lags that often delay keepalives past the short timeout periods. Connections then must be torn down and reestablished—itself an expensive process over standard SNA. Numerous systems have been built to spoof both the keepalives and the mainframe path discovery process of SNA locally.

The question is, if these systems are all receiving the messages their users want them to be receiving, why is this spoofing? The answer is that systems have design assumptions built into them regarding the identities of certain streams of data; in the SNA case, the terminal presumes the keepalives are coming from the mainframe. If keepalives are sent to that terminal whether or not the mainframe is sending keepalives, the original design assumption has been spoofed.

Sometimes, spoofing on one layer is simply a reference to addressing at another. For example, many Web servers with independent names may be virtually hosted behind a single installation of Apache. Even though each Domain Name System (DNS) name for each of the virtual hosts resolves to the same IP address, Apache knows which Web site to serve because the Hypertext Transfer Protocol (HTTP) application-layer protocol re-reveals the DNS address expected by the user. Lower-layer protocols expect such information to be lost in the DNS name resolution process; because HTTP reintroduced this information, it provided a means for a server to spoof virtual hosts as the "one true server" addressable at a given IP.

Spoofing Is Nothing New

There is a troubling tendency among some to believe that, "If it's Net, it's new." Attacks against identity are nothing new in human existence; they strike to the core of what we experience and who we allow ourselves to depend upon.

Background Theory

> I shall suppose, therefore, that there is, not a true God, who is the sovereign source of truth, but some evil demon, no less cunning and deceiving than powerful, who has used all his artifice to deceive me. I will suppose that the heavens, the air, the earth, colors, shapes, sounds and all external things that we see, are only illusions and deceptions which he uses to take me in. I will consider myself as having no hands, eyes, flesh, blood or senses, but as believing wrongly that I have all these things."
> —Rene Descartes, "First Meditation about the Things We May Doubt"

It was 1641 when Rene Descartes released his meditations about the untrustworthiness of human existence. Because everything that we've sensed and all that we've ever been taught could have been explicitly generated and displayed to us by a so-called "Evil Demon" to trick and confuse us, there was indeed little we could depend on truly reflecting the core nature of reality around us. Just as we lie dormant at night believing wholeheartedly in the truth of our dreams, so too do we arbitrarily (and possibly incorrectly) trust that the world around us is indeed what we perceive it to be.

The more we trust the world around us, the more we allow it to guide our own actions and opinions—for example, those who talk in their sleep are simply responding to the environment in which they are immersed. Ironically, excess distrust of the world around us ends up exerting just as much influence over us. Once we feel we're unfree to trust *anything*, we either refuse to trust at all, or (more realistically) we use superstition, emotions, and inconsistent logic to determine whether we will trust potential suppliers for our various needs that must get met, securely or not.

If we cannot trust everything but we must trust something, one major task of life becomes to isolate the trustworthy from the shady; the knowledgeable from the posers. Such decisions are reached based upon the risk of choosing wrong, the benefit of choosing correctly, and the experience of choosing at all—this isn't all that surprising.

The Importance of Identity

What is surprising is the degree to which *whom* we trust is so much more important, natural, and common than *what* we trust. Advertisers "build a brand" with the knowledge that, despite objective analysis or even subjective experiences, people trust less the objects and more the people who "stand behind" those objects. (Though I'm getting ahead of myself, what else can advertising be called *but* social engineering?) Even those who reject or don't outright accept the claims of another person's advertising are still referring to the personal judgment and quality analysis skills of another: themselves! Even those who devote themselves to their own evaluations still increase the pool of experts available to provide informed opinions; a cadre of trusted third parties eventually sprouts up to provide information without the financial conflict of interest that can color or suppress truth—and thus trustworthiness.

Philosophy, psychology, epistemology, and even a bit of marketing theory—what place does all this have in a computer security text? The answer is simple: *Just because something's Internet-related doesn't mean it's necessarily new.* Teenagers didn't discover that they could forge their identities online by reading the latest issue of *Phrack*; beer and cigarettes have taught more people about spoofing their identity than this book ever will. The question of who, how, and exactly what it means to trust (in the beer and cigarettes case, "who can be trusted with such powerful chemical substances") is ancient; far more ancient than even Descartes.

But the paranoid French philosopher deserves mention, if only because even he could not have imagined how accurately computer networks would fit his model of the universe.

The Evolution of Trust

One of the more powerful forces that guides technology is what is known as *network effects*, which state that the value of a system grows exponentially with the number of people using it. The classic example of the power of network effects is the telephone: one single person being able to remotely contact another is good. However, if five people have a telephone, each of those five can call any of the other four. If 50 have a telephone, each of those 50 can easily call upon any of the other 49.

Let the number of telephones grow past 100 million. Indeed, it would appear that the value of the system has jumped dramatically, if you measure value in terms of "how many people I can remotely contact." But, to state the obvious question: How many of those newly accessible people will you want to remotely contact? Now, how many of them would you rather not remotely contact *you*?

Asymmetric Signatures between Human Beings

At least with voice, the worst you can get is an annoying call on a traceable line from disturbed telemarketers. Better yet, even if they've disabled CallerID, their actual voice will be recognizable as distinctly different from that of your friends, family, and coworkers. As a human being, you possess an extraordinarily fine-grained recognition system capable of extracting intelligible and identifying content from extraordinarily garbled text. There turns out to be enough redundancy in average speech that even when vast frequency bands are removed, or if half of every second of speech is rendered silent, we still can understand most of what we hear.

Speech, of course, isn't perfect. *Collisions*, or cases where multiple individuals share some signature element that cannot be easily differentiated from person to person (in this case, vocal pattern), aren't unheard of. But it's a system that's universally deployed with "signature content" contained within every spoken word, and it gives us a classical example of a key property that, among other things, makes after-the-fact investigations much, much simpler in the real world: Accidental release of identifying information is normally *common*. When we open our mouths, we tie our own words to our voice. When we touch a desk, or a keyboard, or a remote control, we leave oils and an imprint of our unique fingerprints. When we leave to shop, we are seen by fellow shoppers and possibly even recognized by those we've met before. We don't choose this—it just is. However, my fellow shoppers cannot mold their faces to match mine, nor slip on a new pair of fingerprints to match my latest style. The information we leave behind regarding our human identities is substantial, to be sure, but it's also asymmetric. Traits that another individual can mimic successfully by simply observing our behavior, such as usage of a "catch phrase" or possession of an article of clothing, are simply given far less weight in terms of identifying who we are to others. Finally, human trust is based on traits that are universal, or nearly so: It is nearly unimaginable to conjure up the thought of a person without a face, and those that hide their faces evoke fear and terror. While an individual may choose not to speak, we have a surprising amount of awareness for what somebody ought to sound like—thus the shock when a large boxer's voice ends up being squeaky and strained. Unique fingerprints are especially distributed, with even more variation between fingers than exists between faces or voices.

> **NOTE**
>
> We can generally recognize the "voiceprint" of the person we're speaking to, despite large quantities of random and nonrandom noise. In technical terminology, we're capable of learning and subsequently matching the complex nonlinear spoken audio characteristics of timbre and style emitted from a single person's larynx and vocal constructs across time and a reasonably decent range of sample speakers, provided enough time and motivation to absorb voices. The process is pointedly asymmetric; being able to recognize a voice does not generally impart the ability to express that voice (though some degree of mimicry is possible).

Deciding who and who not to trust can be a life or death judgment call—it is not surprising that humans, as social creatures, have surprisingly complex systems to determine, remember, and rate various other individuals in terms of the power we grant them. Specifically, the facial recognition capabilities of infant children have long been recognized as extraordinary. However, we have limits to our capabilities; our memories simply do not scale, and our time and energy are limited. As with most situations when a core human task can be simplified down to a rote procedure, technology has been called upon to represent, transport, and establish identity over time and space.

That it's been called upon to do this for us, of course, says nothing about its ability to do so correctly, particularly under the hostile conditions that this book describes. Programmers generally program for what's known as Murphy's Computer, which presumes that everything that can go wrong, will, at once. This seems appropriately pessimistic, but it's the core seed of mistaken identity from which all security holes flow. Ross Anderson and Roger Needham instead suggest systems be designed not for Murphy's Computer but, well, Satan's. Satan's Computer only *appears* to work correctly. Everything's still going wrong.

Establishing Identity within Computer Networks

The problem with electronic identities is that, while humans are very accustomed to trusting one another based on accidental disclosure (how we look, the prints we leave behind, and so on), *all bits transmitted throughout computer networks are explicitly chosen and equally visible, recordable, and repeatable, with perfect accuracy.* This portability of bits is a central tenet of the digital mindset; the intolerance for even the smallest amount of signal degradation is a proud stand against the vagaries of the analog world, with its human existence and moving parts. By making all signal components explicit and digital, signals can be amplified and retransmitted ad infinitum, much unlike the analog world where excess amplification eventually drowns whatever's being spoken underneath the rising din of thermal noise. But if everything can be stored, copied, repeated, or destroyed, with the recipients of those bits none the wiser to the path they may or may not have taken...

Suddenly, the seemingly miraculous fact that data can travel halfway around the world in milliseconds becomes tempered by the fact that *only the data itself has made that trip.* Any ancillary signal data that would have uniquely identified the originating host—and, by extension, the trusted identity of the person operating that host—must either have been included within that data, or lost at the point of the first digital duplicator (be it a router, a switch, or even an actual repeater).

If accidental transmission is critical to human trust—it's lost on computer networks, because nothing is accidental. If asymmetric traits are critical—every bit is equally copyable, so what now? If universal traits are sought, the infinitely variable or completely standardized nature of any given packet is the downfall of trust.

This doesn't mean that identity cannot be transmitted or represented online, but it does mean that unless active measures are taken to establish and safeguard identity *within the data itself,* the recipient of any given message has no way to identify the source of a received request. Accidents are mostly untrustable, though an entire class of vulnerability analysis centers on using accidental variations in TCP/IP behavior along undefined lines to determine whether a remote host is of one operating system or another. But there is one universal trait to be found— legitimate remote hosts that wish to communicate either send or are willing to receive data. Within this data, we can embed asymmetries. Perhaps we can asymmetrically make it easier for the legitimate host to receive our data, because the network will usually route data directly rather than be misdirected. Perhaps we can add something to be returned, or demand a password that the other side is asymmetrically more likely to possess than an untrusted attacker. There's even a branch of cryptography that's internally asymmetrical, and we can use it to represent trust relationships quite well. There are many methods, and we will go over them.

NOTE

Residual analog information that exists before the digital repeaters go to work is not always lost. The cellular phone industry is known to monitor the transmission characteristics of their client's hardware, looking for instances where one cellular phone clones the abstract *data* but not the radio frequency fingerprint of the phone authorized to use that data. The separation between the easy-to-copy programmable characteristics and the impossible-to-copy physical characteristics makes monitoring the analog signal a good method for verifying otherwise cloneable cell phone data. But this is only feasible because the cellular provider is always the sole provider of phone service for any given phone, and a given phone will only be used for one and only one cell phone number at a time. Without much legitimate reason for transmission characteristics on a given line changing, fraud can be deduced from analog variation.

Return to Sender

Data packets on the Internet *do* have return addresses, as well as source ports that are expecting a response back from a server. It says so in the Request for Comments (RFCs), and shows up in packet traces. Clients provide their source address and port to send replies to, and they send that packet to the server. This works perfectly for trusted clients, but if all clients were trusted, there'd be no need to implement security systems. You'd merely ask the clients whether they think they're authorized to view some piece of data, and trust their judgment on that matter.

Because the client specifies his own source, and networks require only a destination to get a packet from point *Anywhere* to point B, source information must be suspect unless every network domain through which the data traveled is established as trusted. With the global nature of the Internet, such judgments cannot be made with significant accuracy.

The less the administrator is aware of, though, the more the administrator should be aware *of what* he or she has understanding of. It's at this point—the lack of understanding phase—that an admin must make the decision of whether to allow *any* users networked access to a service at all. This isn't about selective access; this is about total denial to all users, even those who would be authorized if the system could (a) be built at all, and (b) be secure to a reasonable degree. Administrators who are still struggling with the first phase should generally not assume they've achieved the second unless they've isolated their test lab substantially, *because security and stability are two halves of the same coin.* Most security failures are little more than controlled failures that result in a penetration, and identity verification systems are certainly not immune to this pattern.

Having determined, rightly or wrongly, that a specific system should be made remotely accessible to users, and that a specific service may be trusted to identify whether a client should be able to retrieve specific content back from a server, two independent mechanisms are (always) deployed to implement access controls.

In the Beginning, There Was…a Transmission

At its simplest level, all systems—biological or technological—can be thought of as determining the identities of their peers through a process I refer to as a *capability challenge.* The basic concept is quite simple: There are those whom you trust, and there are those whom you do not. Those whom you do trust have specific abilities that those whom you do not trust, lack. Identifying those differences leaves you with a *trusted capabilities index.* Almost anything may be used as a basis for separating trustworthy users from the untrusted masses—provided its existence can be and is transmitted from the user to the authenticating server.

In terms of spoofing, this essentially means that the goal is to transmit, as an untrusted user, what the authenticating agent believes only a trusted user should be able to send. Should that fail, a compromise against the trusted capabilities index itself will have devastating effects on any cryptosystem. I will be discussing the weaknesses in each authentication model.

There are six major classifications into which one can classify almost all authentication systems. They range from weakest to strongest in terms of proof of identity, and simplest to most complicated in terms of simplicity to implement. None of these abilities occur in isolation—indeed, it's rather useless to be able to encode a response but not be able to complete transmission of it, and that's no accident—and in fact, it turns out that the more complicated layers almost always depend on the simpler layers for services. That being said, I offer in Tables B.1 and B.2 the architecture within which all proofs of identity *should* fit.

Table B.1 Classifications in an Authentication System

Ability	English	Examples
Transmit	"Can it talk to me?"	Firewall Access Control Lists (ACLs), Physical Connectivity
Respond	"Can it respond to me?"	TCP Headers, DNS Request IDs
Encode	"Can it speak my language?"	NT/Novell Login Script Initialization, "Security through Obscurity"
Prove shared secret	"Does it share a secret with me?"	Passwords, Terminal Access Controller Access Control System (TACACS+) Keys
Prove private keypair	"Does it match my public keypair?"	Pretty Good Privacy (PGP), Secure Multipurpose Internet Mail Extensions (S/MIME), Secure Sockets Layer (SSL) through Certificate Authority (CA)
Prove identity key	"Is its identity independently represented in my keypair?"	Secure Shell (SSH), Dynamically Rekeyed OpenPGP

This, of course, is no different than interpersonal communication (see Table B.2)—no different at all!

Table B.2 Classifications in a Human Authentication System

Ability	Human "Capability Challenge"	Human "Trusted Capability Index"
Transmit	Can I hear you?	Do I care if I can hear you?
Respond	Can you hear me?	Do I care if you can hear me?
Encode	Do I know what you just said?	What am I waiting for somebody to say?
Prove shared secret	Do I recognize your password?	What kind of passwords do I care about?
Prove private keypair	Can I recognize your voice?	What exactly does this "chosen one" sound like?
Prove identity key	Is your tattoo still there?	Do I have to look?

Capability Challenges

The following details can be used to understand the six methods listed in Tables B.1 and B.2.

Ability to Transmit: "Can It Talk to Me?"

At the core of all trust, all networks, all interpersonal, and indeed all *intra*personal communication itself, can be found but one, solitary concept: Transmission of information—sending something that could represent anything somewhere.

This does *not* in any way mean that all transmission is perfect.

The U.S. Department of Defense, in a superb (as in, must-read, run, don't walk, bookmark, and highlight the URL for this now) report entitled "Realizing the Potential of C4I," notes the following:

> "The maximum benefit of C4I [command, control, communications, computers, and intelligence] systems is derived from their interoperability and integration. That is, to operate effectively, C4I systems must be interconnected so that they can function as part of a larger "system of systems." *These electronic interconnections multiply many-fold the opportunities for an adversary to attack them.*"
> —Realizing the Potential of C4I www.nap.edu/html/C4I

> "The only way to secure a system is not to plug it in."
> —Unknown

A system entirely disconnected from any network won't be hacked (at least, not by anyone without local console access), but it won't be used much either. Statistically, a certain percentage of the untrusted population will attempt to access a resource they're not authorized to use, a certain smaller percentage will attempt to spoof their identity. Of those who attempt, an even smaller *but nonzero* percentage will actually have the skills and motivation necessary to defeat whatever protection systems have been put in place. Such is the environment as it stands, and thus the only way to absolutely prevent data from ever falling into untrusted hands is to fail to distribute it at all.

It's a simple formula—if you want to prevent remote compromise, just remove all remote access—but also statistically, only a certain amount of trusted users may be refused access to data that they're authorized to see before security systems are rejected as too bulky and inconvenient. *Never forget the bottom line when designing a security system; your security system is much more likely to be forgotten than the bottom line is.* Being immune from an attack is invisible, being unable to make payroll isn't.

As I said earlier, you can't trust everybody, but you must trust somebody. If the people you do trust all tend to congregate within a given network that you control, then controlling the entrance (ingress) and exit (egress) points of your network allows you, as a security administrator, to determine what services, if any, users outside your network are allowed to transmit packets to. *Firewalls*, the well-known first line of defense against attackers, *strip the ability to transmit from those identities communicating from untrusted domains.* Although a firewall cannot intrinsically trust anything in the data itself, because that data could have been forged by upstream domains or even the actual source, it has one piece of data that's all its own: It knows which side the data came in from. This small piece of information is actually enough of a "network fingerprint" to prevent, among (many) other things, untrusted users outside your network from transmitting packets to your network that appear to be from inside of it, and even trusted users (who may actually be untrustable) from transmitting packets outside of your network that do not appear to be from inside of it.

It is the latter form of filtering—*egress filtering*—that is most critical for preventing the spread of distributed denial of service (DDoS) attacks, because it prevents packets with spoofed IP source headers from entering the global Internet at the level of the contributing Internet service provider (ISP). Egress filtering may be implemented on Cisco devices by using the command *ip verify unicast reverse-path*; you can find further information on this topic at www.sans.org/y2k/egress.htm.

Ability to transmit ends up being the most basic level of security that gets implemented. Even the weakest, most wide-open remote access service cannot be attacked by an untrusted user if that user has no means to get a message to the vulnerable system. Unfortunately, depending upon a firewall to strip the ability to transmit messages from anyone who might threaten your network just isn't enough to really secure it. For one, unless you use a "military-style firewall" (read: *air firewall*, or a complete lack of connection between the local network and the global Internet), excess paths are always likely to exist. The Department of Defense continues:

> "The principle underlying response planning should be that of 'graceful degradation'; that is, the system or network should lose functionality gradually, as a function of the severity of the attack compared to its ability to defend against it."

Ability to Respond: "Can It Respond to Me?"

One level up from the ability to send a message is the ability to respond to one. Quite a few protocols involve some form of negotiation between sender and receiver, though some merely specify intermittent or on-demand proclamations from a host announcing something to whomever will listen. When negotiation is required, systems must have the capability to create response transmissions that relate to content transmitted by other hosts on the network. This is a capability above and beyond mere transmission, and is thus separated into the *ability to respond*.

Using the ability to respond as a method of the establishing the integrity of the source's network address is a common technique. As much as many might like source addresses to be kept sacrosanct by networks and for spoofing attacks the world over to be suppressed, there will always be a network that can *claim* to be passing an arbitrary packet while in fact it *generated* it instead.

To handle this, many protocols attempt to cancel source spoofing by transmitting a signal back to the supposed source. If a *response* transmission, containing "some aspect" of the original signal shows up, some form of interactive connectivity is generally presumed.

This level of protection is standard in the TCP protocol itself—the three-way handshake can essentially be thought of as, "Hi, I'm Bob." "I'm Alice. You say you're Bob?" "Yes, Alice, I'm Bob." If Bob tells Alice, "Yes, Alice, I'm Bob," and Alice hasn't recently spoken to Bob, then the protocol can determine that a *blind spoofing* attack is taking place. (In actuality, protocols rarely look for attacks; rather, they function only in the absence of attacks. This is because most protocols are built to establish connectivity, not fend off attackers. But it turns out that by failing to function, save for the presence of some moderately difficult to capture data values, protocols end up significantly increasing their security level simply by vastly reducing the set of hosts that could easily provide the necessary values to effect an attack. Simply reducing the set of hosts that can execute a direct attack from "any machine on the Internet" to "any machine on one of the ten subnets in between the server and the client" can often reduce the number of hosts able to mount an effective attack by many orders of magnitude!)

In terms of network-level spoofs against systems that challenge the ability to respond, there are two different attack modes: *blind spoofs*, where the attacker has little to no knowledge of the network activity going in or coming out of a host (specifically, not the thus-far unidentified variable that the protocol is challenging this source to respond with), and *active spoofs*, where the attacker has at least the full capability to sniff the traffic exiting a given host and possibly varying degrees of control over that stream of traffic. We discuss these two modes separately.

Blind Spoofing

From a purely theoretical point of view, the blind spoofer has one goal: Determine a method to predict changes in the variable (predictive), then provide as many possible transmissions as the protocol will withstand to hopefully hit the single correct one (probabilistic) and successfully respond to a transmission that was never received.

One of the more interesting results of developments in blind spoofing has been the discovery of methods that allow for blind *scanning* of remote hosts. It is, of course, impossible to test connectivity to a given host or port without sending a packet to it and monitoring the response (you can't know what *would* happen if you sent a packet without actually having a packet sent), but blind scanning allows for a probe to examine a subject without the subject being aware of the source of the probing. Connection attempts are sent as normal, but they are spoofed as if they came from some other machine, known as a *zombie host*. This zombie has Internet connectivity but barely uses it—a practically unused server, for instance. Because it's almost completely unused, the prober may presume that all traffic in and out of this "zombie" is the result of its action, either direct or indirect.

The indirect traffic, of course, is the result of packets returned to the zombie from the target host being probed.

For blind scanning, the probing host must somehow know that the zombie received positive responses from the target. Antirez discovered exactly such a technique, and it was eventually integrated into Fyodor's *nmap* as the *–sI* option. The technique employed the *IPID* field. Used to reference one packet to another on an IP level for fragmentation reference purposes, *IPID*s on many operating systems are simply incremented by one for each packet sent. (On Windows, this increment occurs in little-endian order, so the increments are generally by 256. But the core method remains the same.) Now, in TCP, when a host responds positively to a port connection request (a SYN), it returns a connection request acknowledged message (a SYN|ACK). But when the zombie receives the SYN|ACK, it never requested a connection, so it tells the target to go away and reset its connection. This is done with a RST|ACK, and no further traffic occurs for that attempt. This RST|ACK is also sent by the target to the zombie if a port is closed, and the zombie sends nothing in response.

What's significant is that the zombie is sending a packet out—the RST|ACK—every time the prober hits an open port on the target. This packet being sent increments the IPID counter on the zombie. So the prober can probe the zombie before and after each attempt on the target, and if the IPID field has incremented more times than the zombie has sent packets to the prober, the prober can assume the zombie received SYN|ACKs from the target and replied with RST|ACKs of its own.

And thus, a target can be probed without ever knowing who legitimately probed it, while the prober can use almost any arbitrary host on the Internet to hide its scans behind.

A blind scan is trivial in *nmap*; simply use *nmap –sI zombie_host:port target:port* and wait. For further information, read www.bursztein.net/secu/temoinus.html.

Active Spoofing

Most variable requests are trivially spoofable if you can sniff their release. You're just literally proving a medium incorrect when it assumes that only trusted hosts will be able to issue a reply. You're untrusted, you found a way to actively discover the request, and you'll be able to reply. You win—big deal.

What's moderately more interesting is the question of modulation of the existing datastream on the wire. The ability to transmit doesn't grant much control over what's on the wire—yes, you should be able to jam signals by overpowering them (specifically relevant for radio frequency–based media)—but generally transmission ability does not imply the capability to understand whatever anyone else is transmitting. Response spoofing is something more; if you're able to actively determine what to respond to, that implies some advanced ability to *read* the bits on the wire (as opposed to the mere control bits that describe when a transmission may take place).

This doesn't mean you can respond to everything on the wire—the ability to respond is generally tapped for anything but the bare minimum for transmission. Active bit-layer work in a data medium can include the following subcapabilities:

- **Ability to sniff some or all preexisting raw bits or packets** Essentially, you're not adding to the wire, but you're responding to transmissions upon it by storing locally or transmitting on another wire.

- **Ability to censor (corrupt) some or all preexisting raw bits or packets before they reach their destination** Your ability to transmit within a medium has increased—now, you can scrub individual bits or even entire packets if you so choose.

- **Ability to generate some or all raw bits or packets in response to sniffed packets** The obvious capability, but obviously not the only one.

- **Ability to modify some or all raw bits or packets in response to their contents** Sometimes, making noise and retransmitting is not an option. Consider live radio broadcasts. If you need to do modification on them based on their content, your best bet is to install a sufficient signal delay (or co-opt the existing delay hardware) *before* it leaves the tower. Modulation after it's in the air isn't inconceivable, but it's pretty close.

- **Ability to delete some or all raw bits or packets in response to their contents** Arbitrary deletion is harder than modification, because you lose sync with the original signal. Isochronous (uniform bitrate) streams *require* a delay to prevent the transmission of false nulls (you should be sending *something*, right? Dead air is something.).

It is *entirely conceivable* that any of these subcapabilities may be called upon to *legitimately* authenticate a user to a host. With the exception of packet corruption (which is essentially done only when deletion or elegant modification is unavailable and the packet absolutely must not reach its destination), these are all common operations on firewalls, virtual private networks' (VPNs) concentrators, and even local gateway routers.

What Is the Variable?

We've talked a lot about a variable that might need to be sniffed, or probabilistically generated, or any other of a host of options for forging the response ability of many protocols.

But what's the variable?

These two abilities—*transmission* and *response*—are little more than core concepts that represent the ability to place bits on a digital medium, or possibly to interpret them in one of several manners. *They do not represent any form of intelligence regarding what those bits mean in the context of identity management.* The remaining four layers handle this load, and are derived mostly from common cryptographic identity constructs.

Ability to Encode: "Can It Speak My Language?"

The ability to transmit meant the user could send bits, and the ability to respond meant that the user could listen to and reply to those bits if needed. But how to know what's needed in *either* direction? Thus enters the *ability to encode*, which means that a specific host/user has the capability to construct packets that meet the requirements of a specific protocol. If a protocol requires incoming packets to be decoded, so be it—the point is to support the protocol.

For all the talk of IP spoofing, TCP/IP is just a protocol stack, and IP is just another protocol to support. Protections against IP spoofing are enforced by using protocols (like TCP) that demand an ability to respond before initiating communications, and by stripping the ability to transmit (dropping unceremoniously in the bit bucket, thus preventing the packet from transmitting to protected networks) from incoming or outgoing packets that were obviously source-spoofed.

In other words, all the extensive protections of the last two layers may be *implemented* using the methods I described, but they are *controlled* by the *encoding authenticator* and above. (Not everything in TCP is mere encoding. The randomized sequence number that needs to be returned in any response is essentially a very short-lived "shared secret" unique to that connection. Shared secrets are discussed further in the next section.)

Now, although obviously encoding is necessary to interact with other hosts, this isn't a chapter about interaction—it's a chapter about authentication. Can the mere ability to understand and speak the protocol of another host be sufficient to authenticate one for access?

Such is the nature of public services.

Most of the Web serves entire streams of data without so much as a blink to clients whose only evidence of their identity can be reduced down to a single HTTP call: *GET /*. (That's a period to end the sentence, not an obligatory Slashdot reference. *This* is an obligatory Slashdot reference.)

The *GET* call is documented in RFCs (RFC1945) and is public knowledge. It is possible to have higher levels of authentication supported by the protocol, and the upgrade to those levels is reasonably smoothly handled. But the base public access system depends merely on one's knowledge of the HTTP protocol and the ability to make a successful TCP connection to port 80.

Not all protocols are as open, however. Through either underdocumentation or restriction of sample code, many protocols are entirely closed. The mere ability to speak the protocol authenticates one as worthy of what may very well represent a substantial amount of trust; the presumption is, if you can speak the language, you're skilled enough to use it.

That doesn't mean anyone wants you to, unfortunately.

The war between open source and closed source has been waged quite harshly in recent times and will continue to rage. There is much that is uncertain; however, there is one specific argument that can actually be won. In the war between open protocols versus closed protocols, the mere ability to speak to one or the other should *never, ever, ever* grant you enough trust to order workstations to execute arbitrary commands. Servers must be able to provide *something*— maybe even just a password—to be able to execute commands on client machines.

Unless this constraint is met, a deployment of a master server anywhere conceivably allows for control of hosts *everywhere*.

Who made this mistake?

Both Microsoft *and* Novell. Neither company's client software (with the possible exception of a Kerberized Windows 2000 network) does *any* authentication on the domains they are logging in to beyond verifying that, indeed, they know how to say "Welcome to my domain. Here is a script of commands for you to run upon login." The presumption behind the design was that nobody would ever be on a LAN (local area network) with computers they owned themselves; the physical security of an office (the only place where you find LANs, apparently) would prevent spoofed servers from popping up. As I wrote back in May of 1999:

> "A common aspect of most client-server network designs is the login script. A set of commands executed upon provision of correct

username and password, the login script provides the means for corporate system administrators to centrally manage their flock of clients. Unfortunately, what's seemingly good for the business turns out to be a disastrous security hole in the University environment, where students logging in to the network from their dorm rooms now find the network logging in to them. This hole provides a single, uniform point of access to any number of previously uncompromised clients, and is a severe liability that must be dealt with the highest urgency. Even those in the corporate environment should take note of their uncomfortable exposure and demand a number of security procedures described herein to protect their networks."
—Dan Kaminsky "Insecurity by Design: The Unforeseen
    Consequences of Login Scripts" www.doxpara.com/login.html

Ability to Prove a Shared Secret: "Does It Share a Secret with Me?"

This is the first *ability check* where a cryptographically secure identity begins to form. *Shared secrets* are essentially tokens that two hosts share with one another. They can be used to establish links that are:

- **Confidential** The communications appear as noise to any other hosts but the ones communicating.

- **Authenticated** Each side of the encrypted channel is assured of the trusted identity of the other.

- **Integrity Checked** Any communications that travel over the encrypted channel cannot be interrupted, hijacked, or inserted into.

Merely sharing a secret—a short word or phrase, generally—does not directly win all three, but it does enable the technologies to be deployed reasonably straightforwardly. This does not mean that such systems have been. The largest deployment of systems that depend upon this ability to authenticate their users is by far the password contingent. Unfortunately, Telnet is about the height of password-exchange technology at most sites, and even most Web sites don't use the Message Digest 5 (MD5) standard to exchange passwords.

It could be worse; passwords to every company could be printed in the classified section of the *New York Times*. That's a comforting thought. "If our firewall goes, every device around here is owned. But, at least my passwords aren't in the *New York Times*."

All joking aside, there are actually deployed cryptosystems that do grant cryptographic protections to the systems they protect. Almost always bolted onto decent protocols with good distributed functionality but very bad security (ex: RIPv2 from the original RIP, and TACACS+ from the original TACACS/XTACACS), they suffer from two major problems:

First, their cryptography isn't very good. Solar Designer, with an example of what every security advisory would ideally look like, talks about TACACS+ in "An Analysis of the TACACS+ Protocol and its Implementations." The paper is located at www.openwall.com/advisories/OW-001-tac_plus.txt. Spoofing packets such that it would appear that the secret was known would not be too difficult for a dedicated attacker with active sniffing capability.

Second, and much more importantly, *passwords lose much of their power once they're shared past two hosts!* Both TACACS+ and RIPv2 depend on a single, shared password throughout the entire usage infrastructure (TACACS+ actually could be rewritten not to have this dependency, but I don't believe RIPv2 could). When only two machines have a password, look closely at the implications:

- **Confidential?** The communications appear as noise to any other hosts but the ones communicating...but could appear as plaintext to any other host who shares the password.

- **Authenticated?** Each side of the encrypted channel is assured of the trusted identity of the other...assuming none of the other dozens, hundreds, or thousands of hosts with the same password have either had their passwords stolen or are actively spoofing the other end of the link themselves.

- **Integrity Checked?** Any communications that travel over the encrypted channel cannot be interrupted, hijacked, or inserted into, unless somebody leaked the key as above.

Use of a single, shared password between two hosts in a virtual point-to-point connection arrangement works, and works well. Even when this relationship is a client-to-server one (for example, with TACACS+, assume but a single client router authenticating an offered password against CiscoSecure, the backend Cisco password server), you're either the client asking for a password or the server offering one. If you're the server, the only other host with the key is a client. If you're the client, the only other host with the key is the server that you trust.

However, if there are multiple clients, every other client could conceivably become your server, and you'd never be the wiser. Shared passwords work great for point-to-point, but fail miserably for multiple clients to servers: "The other end of the link" is no longer necessarily trusted.

> **NOTE**
>
> Despite that, TACACS+ allows *so* much more flexibility for assigning access privileges and centralizing management that, in spite of its weaknesses, implementation and deployment of a TACACS+ server still remains one of the better things a company can do to increase security.

That's not to say that there aren't any good spoof-resistant systems that depend upon passwords. Cisco routers use SSH's password-exchange systems to allow an engineer to securely present his password to the router. The password is used only for authenticating the user to the router; all confidentiality, link integrity, and (because we don't want an engineer giving the wrong device a password!) router-to-engineer authentication is handled by the next layer up: the *private key*.

Ability to Prove a Private Keypair: "Can I Recognize Your Voice?"

Challenging the ability to prove a private keypair invokes a cryptographic entity known as an *asymmetric cipher*. Symmetric ciphers, such as Triple-DES, Blowfish, and Twofish, use a single key to both encrypt a message and decrypt it. If just two hosts share those keys, authentication is guaranteed—if you didn't send a message, the host with the other copy of your key did.

The problem is, even in an ideal world, such systems do not scale. Not only must every two machines that require a shared key have a single key for each host they intend to speak to—an exponential growth problem—but those keys must be transferred from one host to another in some trusted fashion over a network, floppy drive, or some data transference method. Plaintext is hard enough to transfer securely; critical key material is almost impossible. Simply by spoofing oneself as the destination for a key transaction, you get a key and can impersonate two people to each other.

Yes, more and more layers of symmetric keys can be (and in the military, are) used to insulate key transfers, but in the end, secret material has to move.

Asymmetric ciphers, such as RSA, Diffie-Helman/El Gamel, offer a better way. Asymmetric ciphers mix into the same key the ability to encrypt data, decrypt data, sign the data with your identity, and prove that you signed it. That's a lot of capabilities embedded into one key—the asymmetric ciphers split the key into two: one of which is kept secret, and can decrypt data or sign your independent identity—this is known as the private key. The other is publicized freely, and can encrypt data for your decrypting purposes or be used to verify your signature without imparting the ability to forge it. This is known as the *public key*.

More than anything else, the biggest advantage of private key cryptosystems is that key material never needs to move from one host to another. Two hosts can prove their identities to one another without having ever exchanged anything that can decrypt data or forge an identity. Such is the system used by PGP.

Ability to Prove an Identity Keypair: "Is Its Identity Independently Represented in My Keypair?"

The primary problem faced by systems such as PGP is: What happens when people know me by my ability to decrypt certain data? In other words, what happens when I can't change the keys I offer people to send me data with, because those same keys imply that "I" am no longer "me?"

Simple. The British Parliament starts trying to pass a law saying that, now that my keys can't change, I can be made to retroactively unveil every e-mail I have ever been sent, deleted by me (but not by a remote archive) or not, simply because a recent e-mail needs to be decrypted. Worse, once this identity key is released, they are now cryptographically me—in the name of requiring the ability to *decrypt* data, they now have full control of my *signing identity*.

The entire flow of these abilities has been to isolate out the abilities most focused on identity; the identity key is essentially an asymmetric keypair that is never used to directly encrypt data, only to authorize a key *for the usage of* encrypting data. SSH and a PGP variant I'm developing known as Dynamically Rekeyed OpenPGP (DROP) all implement this separation on identity and content, finally boiling down to a single cryptographic pair everything that humanity has developed in its pursuit of trust. The basic idea is simple: A keyserver is updated regularly with short-lifespan encryption/decryption keypairs, and the mail sender knows it is safe to accept the new key from the keyserver because even though the new material is unknown, it is signed by something long term that *is* known: The long-term key. In this way, we separate our short-term requirements to accept mail from our long-term requirements to retain our identity, and restrict our vulnerability to attack.

In technical terms, the trait that is being sought is that of Perfect Forward Secrecy (PFS). In a nutshell, this refers to the property of a cryptosystem to, in the face of a future compromise, to at least compromise no data sent in the past. For purely symmetric cryptography, PFS is nearly automatic—the key used today would have no relation to the key used yesterday, so even if there's a compromise today, an attacker can't use the key recovered to decrypt past data. All future data, of course, might be at risk—but at least the past is secure. Asymmetric ciphers scramble this slightly: Although it is true that every symmetric key is usually different, each individual symmetric key is decrypted using the same asymmetric private key. Therefore, being able to decrypt today's symmetric key also means being able to decrypt yesterday's. As mentioned, keeping the same decryption key is often necessary because we need to use it to validate our identity in the long term, but it has its disadvantages.

Tools & Traps...

Perfect Forward Secrecy: SSL's Dirty Little Secret

The dirty little secret of SSL is that, unlike SSH and unnecessarily like standard PGP, its standard modes are *not* perfectly forward secure. This means that an attacker can lie in wait, sniffing encrypted traffic at its leisure for as long as it desires, until one day it breaks in and steals the SSL private key used by the SSL engine (which is extractable from all but the most custom hardware). At that point, all the traffic sniffed becomes retroactively decryptable—all credit card numbers, all transactions, all data is exposed no matter the time that had elapsed. This could be prevented within the existing infrastructure if VeriSign or other Certificate Authorities made it convenient and inexpensive to cycle through externally-authenticated keypairs, or it could be addressed if browser makers mandated or even really supported the use of PFS-capable cipher sets. Because neither is the case, SSL is left significantly less secure than it otherwise should be.

To say this is a pity is an understatement. It's the dirtiest little secret in standard Internet cryptography.

Configuration Methodologies: Building a Trusted Capability Index

All systems have their weak points, as sooner or later, it's unavoidable that we arbitrarily trust somebody to teach us who or what to trust. Babies and 'Bases, Toddlers 'n TACACS+—even the best of security systems will fail if the initial configuration of their Trusted Capability Index fails.

As surprising as it may be, it's not unheard of for authentication databases that lock down entire networks to be themselves administered over unencrypted links. The chain of trust that a system undergoes when trusting outside communications is extensive and not altogether thought out; later in this chapter, an example is offered that should surprise you.

The question at hand, though, is quite serious: Assuming trust and identity is identified as something to lock down, where should this lockdown be centered, or should it be centered at all?

Local Configurations vs. Central Configurations

One of the primary questions that comes up when designing security infrastructures is whether a single management station, database, or so on should be entrusted with massive amounts of trust and heavily locked down, or whether each device should be responsible for its own security and configuration. The intention is to prevent any system from becoming a single point of failure.

The logic seems sound. The primary assumption to be made is that security considerations for a security management station are to be equivalent to the sum total of all paranoia that should be invested in each individual station. So, obviously, the amount of paranoia invested in each machine, router, and so on, which is obviously bearable if people are still using the machine, must be superior to the seemingly unbearable security nightmare that a centralized management database would be, right?

The problem is, companies don't exist to implement perfect security; rather, they exist to use their infrastructure to get work done. Systems that are being used rarely have as much security paranoia implemented as they need. By "offloading" the security paranoia and isolating it into a backend machine that *can* actually be made as secure as need be, an infrastructure can be deployed that's usable on the front end and secure in the back end.

The primary advantage of a centralized security database is that it models the genuine security infrastructure of your site—as an organization gets larger, blanket access to all resources should be rare, but access as a whole should be consistently distributed from the top down. This simply isn't possible when there's nobody in charge of the infrastructure as a whole; overly distributed controls mean access clusters to whomever happens to want that access.

Access at will never breeds a secure infrastructure.

The disadvantage, of course, is that the network becomes trusted to provide configurations. But with so many users willing to Telnet into a device to change passwords—which end up atrophying because nobody wants to change hundreds of passwords by hand—suddenly you're locked into an infrastructure that's dependent upon its firewall to protect it.

What's scary is, in the age of the hyperactive Net-connected desktop, firewalls are becoming less and less effective, simply because of the large number of opportunities for that desktop to be co-opted by an attacker.

Desktop Spoofs

Many spoofing attacks are aimed at the genuine owners of the resources being spoofed. The problem with that is, people generally notice when their own resources disappear. They rarely notice when someone else's does, unless they're no longer able to access something from somebody else.

The best of spoofs, then, are completely invisible. Vulnerability exploits break things; although it's not impossible to invisibly break things (the "slow corruption" attack), power is always more useful than destruction.

The advantage of the spoof is that it absorbs the power of whatever trust is embedded in the identities that become appropriated. That trust is maintained for as long as the identity is trusted, and can often long outlive any form of network-level spoof. The fact that an account is controlled by an attacker rather than by a genuine user does maintain the system's status as being *under spoof*.

The Plague of Auto-Updating Applications

Question: What do you get when you combine multimedia programmers, consent-free network access to a fixed host, and no concerns for security because "It's just an auto-updater?" Answer: Figure B.1.

What good firewalls do—and it's no small amount of good, let me tell you— is prevent all network access that users themselves don't explicitly request. Surprisingly enough, users are generally pretty good about the code they run to access the Net. Web browsers, for all the heat they take, are *probably* among the most fault-tolerant, bounds-checking, attacked pieces of code in modern network deployment. They may *fail* to catch everything, but you know there were at least teams *trying* to make it fail.

Figure B.1 What Winamp Might As Well Say

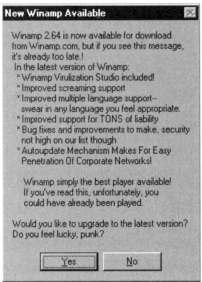

See the Winamp auto-update notification box in Figure B.1. Content comes from the network, authentication is nothing more than the ability to encode a response from www.winamp.com in the HTTP protocol GETting /update/ latest-version.jhtml?v=2.64 (Where 2.64 here is the version I had. It will report whatever version it is, so the site can report if there is a newer one.). It's not difficult to provide arbitrary content, and the buffer available to store that content overflows reasonably quickly (well, it will overflow when pointed at an 11MB file).

However many times Internet Explorer is loaded in a day, it generally asks you before accessing any given site save the homepage (which most corporations set). By the time Winamp asks you if you want to upgrade to the latest version, it's already made itself vulnerable to every spoofing attack that could possibly sit between it and its rightful destination.

If not Winamp, then Creative Labs' Sound Blaster Live!Ware. If not Live!Ware, then RealVideo, or Microsoft Media Player, or some other multimedia application straining to develop marketable information at the cost of their customers' network security.

Notes from the Underground…

Auto Update as Savior?

I'll be honest: Although it's quite dangerous that so many applications are taking it upon themselves to update themselves automatically, at least something is leading to making it easier to patch obscenely broken code. Centralization has its advantages: When a major hole was found in AOL Instant Messenger, which potentially exposed over fifty million hosts to complete takeover, the centralized architecture of AOL IM allowed them to completely filter their entire network of such packets, if not completely automatically patch all connecting clients against the vulnerability. So although automatic updates and centralization has significant power—this power can be used to great effect by legitimate providers. Unfortunately, the legitimate are rarely the only ones to partake in any given system. In short: It's messy.

Impacts of Spoofs

Spoofing attacks can be extremely damaging—and not just on computer networks. Doron Gellar writes:

> The Israeli breaking of the Egyptian military code enabled them to confuse the Egyptian army and air force with false orders. Israeli officers "ordered an Egyptian MiG pilot to release his bombs over the sea instead of carrying out an attack on Israeli positions." When the pilot questioned the veracity of the order, the Israeli intelligence officer gave the pilot details on his wife and family." The pilot indeed dropped his bombs over the Mediterranean and parachuted to safety.
> —Doron Gellar, Israeli Intelligence in the 1967 War

In this case, the pilot had a simple "trusted capabilities index": His legitimate superiors would know him in depth; they'd be aware of "personal entropy" that no outsider should know. He would challenge for this personal entropy—essentially, a shared key—as a prerequisite for behaving in a manner that obviously violated standard security procedure. (In general, the more damaging the request, the higher the authentication level should be—thus we allow anyone to ping us, but we demand higher proof to receive a root shell.) The pilot was tricked—

Israeli intelligence earned its pay for that day—but his methods were reasonably sound. What more could he have done? He might have demanded to hear the voice of his wife, but voices can be recorded. Were he sufficiently paranoid, he might have demanded his wife repeat some sentence back to him, or refer to something that only the two of them might have known in their confidence. Both would take advantage of the fact that it's easy to recognize a voice but hard to forge it, while the marriage-secret would have been something almost guaranteed not to have been shared, even accidentally.

In the end, of course, the spoof was quite effective, and it had significant effects. Faking identity is a powerful methodology, if for no other reason that we invest quite a bit of power in those that we trust and spoofing grants the untrusted access to that power. While brute force attacks might have been able to jam the pilot's radio to future legitimate orders, or the equivalent "buffer overflow" attacks might have (likely unsuccessfully) scared or seduced the pilot into defecting—with a likely chance of failure—it was the spoof that eliminated the threat.

Subtle Spoofs and Economic Sabotage

The core difference between a vulnerability exploit and a spoof is as follows: A vulnerability takes advantage of the difference between what something *is* and what something *appears to be*. A spoof, on the other hand, takes advantage of the difference between *who is sending something* and *who appears to have sent it*. The difference is critical, because at its core, the most brutal of spoofing attacks don't just mask the identity of an attacker; they mask the fact that an attack even took place.

If users don't know there's been an attack, they blame the administrators for their incompetence. If administrators don't know there's been an attack, they blame their vendors…and maybe eventually select new ones.

Flattery Will Get You Nowhere

This isn't just hypothetical discussion. In 1991, Microsoft was fending off the advances of DR DOS, an upstart clone of their operating system that was having a significant impact on Microsoft's bottom line. Graham Lea of the popular tech tabloid *The Register*, reported last year at www.theregister.co.uk/991105-000023.html (available in Google's cache; 1999 archives are presently unavailable from *The Register* itself on Microsoft's response to DR DOS's popularity:

"David Cole and Phil Barrett exchanged e-mails on 30 September 1991: "It's pretty clear we need to make sure Windows 3.1 only runs on top of MS DOS or an OEM version of it," and "The approach we will take is to detect dr 6 and refuse to load. The error message should be something like 'Invalid device driver interface.'" Microsoft had several methods of detecting and sabotaging the use of DR-DOS with Windows, one incorporated into "Bambi," the code name that Microsoft used for its disk cache utility (SMARTDRV) that detected DR-DOS and refused to load it for Windows 3.1. The AARD code trickery is well-known, but Caldera is now pursuing four other deliberate incompatibilities. One of them was a version check in XMS in the Windows 3.1 setup program which produced the message: "The XMS driver you have installed is not compatible with Windows. You must remove it before setup can successfully install Windows." Of course there was no reason for this."

It's possible there was a reason. Former Microsoft executive Brad Silverberg described this reasoning behind the move bluntly: "What the guy is supposed to do is feel uncomfortable, and when he has bugs, suspect that the problem is DR-DOS and then go out to buy MS-DOS. Or decide to not take the risk for the other machines he has to buy for in the office."

Microsoft could have been blatant, and publicized that it just wasn't going to let its graphical shell interoperate with DR-DOS (indeed, this has been the overall message from AOL regarding interoperability among Instant Messenger clients). But that might have led to large customers requesting they change their tactics. A finite amount of customer pressure would have forced Microsoft to drop its anti–DR-DOS policy, but no amount of pressure would have been enough to make DR-DOS work with Windows. Eventually, the vendor lost the faith of the marketplace, and faded away according to plan.

What made it work? More than anything else, the subtlety of the malicious content was effective. By appearing to make DR-DOS *not an outright failure*— which might have called into serious question how two systems as similar as DR-DOS and MS-DOS could end up so incompatible—but a *pale and untrustworthy imitation* of the real thing was brilliance. By doing so, Microsoft shifted the blame, the cost, and the profit *all* to its benefit, and had it not been for an extensive investigation by Caldera (who eventually bought DR-DOS), the information never would have seen the light of day. It would have been a perfect win.

Subtlety Will Get You Everywhere

The Microsoft case gives us excellent insight on the nature of what *economically motivated sabotage* can look like. Distributed applications and systems, such as help-desk ticketing systems, are extraordinarily difficult to engineer scalably. Often, stability suffers. Due to the extreme damage such systems can experience from invisible and unprovable attackers, specifically engineering both stability and security into systems we intend to use, sell, or administrate may end up just being good self-defense. Assuming you'll always know the difference between an active attack and an everyday system failure is a false assumption to say the least.

On the flipside, of course, one *can* be overly paranoid about attackers! There have been more than a few documented cases of large companies blaming embarrassing downtime on a mythical and convenient attacker. (Actual cause of failures? Lack of contingency plans if upgrades didn't go smoothly.)

In a sense, it's a problem of signal detection. Obvious attacks are easy to detect, but the threat of subtle corruption of data (which, of course, will generally be able to propagate itself across backups due to the time it takes to discover the threats) forces one's sensitivity level to be much higher; so much higher, in fact, that false positives become a real issue. Did "the computer" lose an appointment? Or was it never entered (user error), incorrectly submitted (client error), incorrectly recorded (server error), altered or mangled in traffic (network error, though reasonably rare), or was it actively and maliciously intercepted?

By attacking the trust built up in systems and the engineers who maintain them, rather than the systems themselves, attackers can cripple an infrastructure by rendering it unusable by those who would profit by it most. With the stock market giving a surprising number of people a stake in the new national lottery of their our own jobs and productivity, we've gotten off relatively lightly.

Selective Failure for Selecting Recovery

One of the more consistent aspects of computer networks is their actual consistency—they're highly deterministic, and problems generally occur either consistently or not at all. Thus, the infuriating nature of testing for a bug that occurs only intermittently—once every two weeks, every 50,000 +/–3,000 transactions, or so on. Such bugs can form the *gamma-ray bursts* of computer networks—supremely major events in the universe of the network, but they occur so rarely for so little time that it's difficult to get a kernel or debug trace at the moment of failure.

Given the forced acceptance of intermittent failures in advanced computer systems ("highly deterministic…more or less"), it's not surprising that spoofing intermittent failures as accidental—as if they were mere hiccups in the Net—leads to some extremely effective attacks.

The first I read of using directed failures as a tool of surgically influencing target behavior came from RProcess's discussion of Selective DoS in the document located at www.mail-archive.com/coderpunks%40toad.com/msg01885.html. RProcess noted the following extremely viable methodology for influencing user behavior, and the subsequent effect it had on crypto security:

> By selective denial of service, I refer to the ability to inhibit or stop some kinds or types of messages while allowing others. If done carefully, and perhaps in conjunction with compromised keys, this can be used to inhibit the use of some kinds of services while promoting the use of others.
>
> An example: User X attempts to create a nym [Ed: Anonymous Identity for Email Communication] account using remailers A and B. It doesn't work. He recreates his nym account using remailers A and C. This works, so he uses it. Thus he has chosen remailer C and avoided remailer B. If the attacker runs remailers A and C, or has the keys for these remailers, but is unable to compromise B, he can make it more likely that users will use A and C by sabotaging B's messages. He may do this by running remailer A and refusing certain kinds of messages chained to B, or he may do this externally by interrupting the connections to B.

By exploiting vulnerabilities in one aspect of a system, users flock to an apparently less vulnerable and more stable supplier. It's the ultimate spoof: Make people think they're doing something because *they* want to do it—like I said earlier, advertising is nothing but social engineering. But simply dropping every message of a given type would lead to both predictability and evidence. Reducing reliability, however, particularly in a "best effort" Internet, grants both plausible deniability to the network administrators and impetus for users to switch to an apparently more stable (but secretly compromised) server/service provider.

NOTE

RProcess did complete a reverse engineering of Traffic Analysis Capabilities of government agencies (located at http://cryptome.org/tac-rp.htm) based upon the presumption that the harder something was for agencies to crack, the less reliable they allowed the service to remain. The results should be taken with a grain of salt, but as with much of the material on Cryptome, is well worth the read.

Bait and Switch: Spoofing the Presence of SSL Itself

If you think about it, really sit down and consider—why does a given user believe they are connected to a Web site through SSL? This isn't an idle question; the significant majority of HTTP traffic is transmitted in the clear anyway; why should a user think one Web site out of a hundred is or isn't encrypted and authenticated via the SSL protocol? It's not like users generally watch a packet sniffer sending their data back and forth, take a protocol analyzer to it, and nod with approval the fact that "it looks like noise."

Generally, browsers inform users of the usage of SSL through the presence of a precious few pixels:

- A "lock" icon in the status bar

- An address bar that refers to the expected site *and* has an *s* after *http*.

- Occasionally, a pop-up dialog box informs the user they're entering or leaving a secure space.

There's a problem in this: We're trying to authenticate an array of pixels—coincidentally described through HTML, JPEG, and other presentation layer protocols—using SSL. But the user doesn't really know what's being sent on the network, instead the browser is trusted to provide a signal that cryptography is being employed. But how is this signal being provided? Through an array of pixels.

We're authenticating one set of images with another, assuming the former could never include the latter. The assumption is false, as Figure B.2 from www.doxpara.com/popup_ie.html shows.

X10, the infamous pseudo-porn window spammers, didn't actually host that page, let alone use SSL to authenticate it. But as far as the user knows, the page not only came from X10.Com, but it was authenticated to come from there. How'd we create this page? Let's start with the HTML:

```
[root@fire doxpara]# cat popup_ie.html
<HTML>
<HEAD>
<script type="text/javascript"><!--
function popup() {
window.open('http://www.doxpara.com/x10/webcache.html?site=https://www.x
10.com/hotnewsale/webaccessid=xyqx1412&netlocation=241&block=121&pid=811
22&&sid=1','','width=725,height=340,resizable=1,menubar=1,toolbar=1,stat
usbar=0,location=1,directories=1');
```

```
    }
//--></script>
</HEAD>
<BODY BGCOLOR="black" onLoad="popup()">
<FONT FACE="courier" COLOR="white">
<CENTER>
<IMG SRC="doxpara_bw_rs.gif">
<BR><BR>
Please Hold:   Spoofing SSL Takes A Moment.
Activating Spam Subversion System...
</BODY>
</HTML>
```

Figure B.2 An SSL Authenticated Popup Ad?

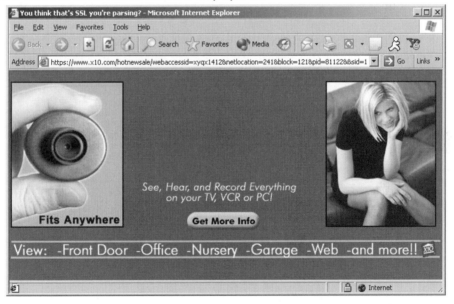

We start by defining a JavaScript function called *popup()*. This function first pops up a new window using some basic JavaScript. Second, it removes the status bar from the new window, which is necessary because we're going to build our own. Finally, it specifies a fixed size for the window and uses a truly horrific hack to fill the address bar with whatever content we feel like. This function is executed immediately when the page is loaded, and various random fluff follows. In the next section, you'll see what's so effective about this function.

Notes from the Underground...

The Joys of Monoculture: Downsides of the IE Web

Most of these techniques would port to the document models included in other browsers, but why bother when IE has taken over 90 percent of the Web? Variability is actually one of the major defenses against these attacks. The idea is that because we can so easily predict what the user is used to seeing, we have a straightforward way of faking out their expectations. Interestingly enough, the skin support of Windows XP is actually a very positive step towards defending against this style of attacks; if you can't remotely query what skin a user is using, you can't remotely spoof their "window dressing."

On the flip side, Internet Explorer 6's mysterious trait of "forgetting" to keep the status bar active does tend to make the task of spoofing it moderately unnecessary (though an attacker still needs to guess whether or not to spoof something).

For once, the classic rejoinder is almost accurate: "It's not a bug, it's a feature."

Lock On: Spoofing a Status Bar in HTML

The most notable sign of SSL security is the lock in the lower right-hand corner of the window. The expected challenge is for an attacker to acquire a fake SSL key, go through the entire process of authenticating against the browser, and only then be able to illegitimately achieve the secure notification to the user. Because it's cryptographically infeasible to generate such a key, it's supposed to be infeasible to fake the lock. But we can do something much simpler: Disable the user's status bar, and manually re-create it using the much simpler process of dropping pixels in the right places. Disabling the status bar wasn't considered a threat originally, perhaps because Web pages are prevented from modifying their own status bar setting. But kowtowing to advertising designers created a new class of entity—the pop-up window—with an entirely new set of capabilities. If you notice, the *popup()* function includes not only an address, but the ability to specify height, width, and innumerable properties, including the capability to set *statusbar=0*. We're using that capability to defeat SSL.

Once the window is opened up, free of the status bar, we need to put something in to replace it. This is done using a frame that attaches itself to the bottom of the pop-up, like so:

```
[root@fire x10]# cat webcache.html
<html>
<head>
<title>You think that's SSL you're parsing?</title>
</head>
<frameset rows="*,20" frameborder="0" framespacing="0" topmargin="0"
leftmargin="0" rightmargin="0" marginwidth="0" marginheight="0"
framespacing="0">
<frame src="encap.html">
<frame src="bottom.html" height=20 scrolling="no" frameborder="0"
marginwidth="0" marginheight="0" noresize="yes">
</frameset>
<body>
</body>
</html>
```

The height of the status bar is exactly 20 pixels, and there's none of the standard quirks of the frame attached, so we just disable all of them. Now, the contents of bottom.html will be rendered in the exact position of the original status bar. Let's see what bottom.html looks like:

```
[root@fire x10]# cat bottom.html
<HTML>
<body bgcolor=#3267CD topmargin="0" leftmargin="0">
<TABLE CELLSPACING="0" CELLPADDING="0" VALIGN="bottom">
<TR ALIGN=center>
<TD><IMG hspace="0" vspace="0" ALIGN="left" SRC="left.gif"></TD>
<TD WIDTH=90%><IMG hspace="0" vspace="0" VALIGN="bottom" WIDTH=500
HEIGHT=20 SRC="midsmall.gif"></TD>
<TD><IMG hspace="0" vspace="0" ALIGN="right" SRC="right.gif"></TD>
</TR>
</TABLE>
</BODY>
</HTML>
```

If you think of a status bar, at least under Internet Explorer, here's about what it's composed of: A unique little page on the left, a mostly blank space in the middle, and some fields on the right. So we copy the necessary patterns of pixels and spit it back out as needed. (The middle field is stretched a fixed amount—there are methods in HTML to make the bar stretch left and right with the window itself, but they're unneeded in this case.) By mimicking the surrounding environment, we spoof user expectations for who is providing the status bar—the user expects the system to be providing those pixels, but it's just another part of the Web page.

A Whole New Kind of Buffer Overflow: Risks of Right-Justification

This is just painfully bad. You may have noted an extraordinary amount of random variables in the URL that *popup_ie.html* calls. We're not just going to do *http://www.doxpara.com/x10/webcache.html*, we're going to do *http://www.doxpara.com/x10/webcache.html?site=https://www.x10.com/hotnewsale/webaccessid=xyqx1412&netlocation=241&block=121&pid=81122&&sid=1.* The extra material is ignored by the browser and is merely sent to the Web server as ancillary information for its logs. No ancillary information is really needed—it's a static Web page, for crying out loud—but the client doesn't know that we have a much different purpose for it. Because for each character you toss on past what the window can contain, the text field containing the address loses characters on the left side. Because we set the size of the address bar indirectly when we specified a window size in *popup_ie.html*, and because the font used for the address bar is virtually fixed (except on strange browsers that can be filtered out by their uniformly polluted outgoing HTTP headers), it's a reasonably straightforward matter of trial and error to specify the exact number and style of character to delete the actual source of the Web page—in this case: *http://www.doxpara.com/x10?.* We just put on enough garbage variables and—poof—it just looks like yet another page with too many variables exposed to the outside world.

Individually, each of these problems is just a small contributor. But when combined, they're deadly. Figure B.2 illustrates what the user sees; Figure B.3 illustrates what's really happening.

Total Control: Spoofing Entire Windows

One of the interesting security features built into early, non–MS Java Virtual Machines was a specification that all untrusted windows had to have a status bar notifying the user that a given dialog box was actually being run by a remote server and wasn't in fact reflecting the local system.

Figure B.3 The Faked Pop-Up Ad Revealed

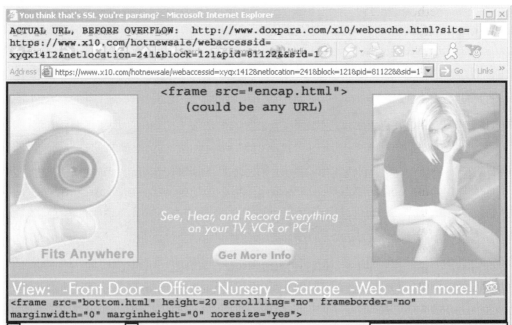

The lack of this security feature was one of the more noticeable omissions for Microsoft Java environments.

Some systems remain configured to display a quick notification dialog box when transitioning to a secure site. This notification looks something like Figure B.4.

Figure B.4 Explicit SSL Notification Dialog Box

Unfortunately, this is just another array of pixels, and using the "chromeless pop-up" features of Internet Explorer, such pixels can be spoofed with ease, such as the pop-up ad shown in Figure B.5.

Figure B.5 Arbitrary Web-Supplied Notification Dialog Box

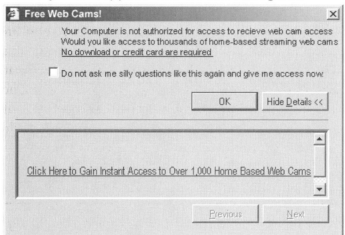

That's not an actual window, and small signs give it away—the antialiased text in the title bar, for example. But it's enough. This version is merely a graphic, but HTML, Java, and especially Flash are rich enough tools to spoof an entire GUI—or at least one window at a time. You trust pixels; the Web gives pixels. In this case, you expect extra pixels to differentiate the Web's content from your system's; by bug or design there are methods of removing your system's pixels leaving the Web to do what it will. (In this case, all that was needed was to set two options against each other: First, the *fullscreen=1* variable was set in the *popup* function, increasing the size of the window and removing the borders. But then a second, contradictory set of options was added—*resizable=0*, and an explicitly enumerated height and width. So the resizing of fullscreen mode got cancelled, but the borders were already stripped—by bug or design, the result was chromeless windows all ready for fake chrome to be slathered on.)

Attacking SSL through Intermittent Failures

Occasionally, we end up overthinking a problem—yes, it's possible to trick a user into thinking they're in a secure site. But you don't always need to work so hard. What if, 1 out of every 1,000 times somebody tried to log in to his bank or stockbroker through their Web page, the login screen was not routed through SSL?

Would there be an error? In a sense. The address bar would definitely be missing the *s* in https, and the 16×16 pixel lock would be gone. But that's it, just that once; a single reload would redirect back to https.

Would anybody ever catch this error?

Might somebody call up tech support and complain, and be told anything other than "reload the page and see if the problem goes away?"

The problem stems from the fact that not all traffic is able to be either encrypted or authenticated. There's no way for a page itself to securely load, saying "If I'm not encrypted, scream to the user not to give me his secret information." (Even if there was, the fact that the page was unauthenticated would mean an attacker could easily strip this flag off.) The user's willingness to read unencrypted and unauthenticated traffic means that anyone who's able to capture his connection and spoof content from his bank or brokerage would be able to prevent the page delivered from mentioning its insecure status anyway.

NOTE

The best solution will probably end up involving the adding of a lock under and/or to the right of the mouse pointer whenever navigating a secure page. It's small enough to be moderately unobtrusive, doesn't interrupt the data flow, communicates important information, and (most importantly) is directly in the field of view at the moment a secured link receives information from the browser. Of course, we'd have to worry about things like Comet Cursor allowing even the mouse cursor to be spoofed...so the arms race would continue.

In Pixels We Trust: The Honest Truth

"Veblen proposed that the psychology of prestige was driven by three "pecuniary canons of taste": conspicuous leisure, conspicuous consumption, and conspicuous waste. Status symbols are flaunted and coveted not necessarily because they are useful or attractive (pebbles, daisies, and pigeons are quite beautiful, as we rediscover when they delight young children), but often because they are so rare, wasteful, or pointless that only the wealthy can afford them. They include clothing that is too delicate, bulky, constricting, or stain-prone to work in, objects too fragile for casual use or made from unobtainable materials, functionless objects made with prodigious labor, decorations that consume energy, and pale skin in lands where the plebeians work the fields and suntans in lands where they work indoors. The logic is: You can't see all my wealth and earning power (my bank account, my lands, all my allies and

flunkeys), but you can see my gold bathroom fixtures. No one could afford them without wealth to spare, therefore you know I am wealthy."
—Steven Pinker, "How The Mind Works"

Let's be honest: It isn't the tiny locks and the little characters in the right places we trust. There are sites that appear professional, and there are sites that look like they were made by a 13-year old with a pirated copy of Photoshop and a very special problem with Ritalin. Complaining about the presumptions that people might come to based on appearances only does tend to ignore the semicryptographic validity in those presumptions—there's a undeniable asymmetry to elegance and class. It's much easier to recognize than it is to generate. But the analogy to the real world does break down: Although it is indeed difficult to create an elegant site, especially one with a significant amount of backend dynamic programming evident (yes, that's why dynamic content impresses), it's trivial to copy any limited amount of functionality and appearances. We don't actually trust the pixels along the borders telling us whether a site is secure or not. We're really looking at the design itself—even though just about anyone can rip off any design he or she likes and slap it onto any domain he gets access to. (Of course, the access to domains is an issue—note the wars for domain names.)

Down and Dirty: Engineering Spoofing Systems

We've discussed antispoofing measures from trivial to extensive, but a simple question remains: How do we actually build a system to execute spoofs? Often, the answer is to study the network traffic, re-implement protocol messengers with far simpler and more flexible code, and send traffic outside the expectations of those who will be receiving it.

Spitting into the Wind: Building a Skeleton Router in Userspace

For ultimate flexibility, merely relying on command-level tools is ultimately an untenable constraint: Actual code is needed. However, too much code can be a hindrance—the amount of functionality never employed because it was embedded deep within some specific kernel is vast, and the amount of functionality never built because it wouldn't elegantly fit within some kernel interface is even greater. Particularly when it comes to highly flexible network solutions, the highly tuned network implementations built into modern kernels are inappropriate for our uses. We're looking for systems that *break* the rules, not necessarily that follow them.

It's robustness in reverse.

What we need is a simple infrastructure within which we can gain access to arbitrary packets, possibly with, but just as well without, kernel filtering, operate on them efficiently but easily, and then send them back out as needed. DoxRoute 0.1, available at www.doxpara.com/tradecraft/doxroute and documented (for the first time) here, is a possible solution to this problem.

Designing the Nonexistent: The Network Card That Didn't Exist but Responded Anyway

As far as a network is concerned, routers inherently do three things:

- Respond to ARP packets looking for a specific MAC address

- Respond to Ping requests looking for a specific IP address

- Forward packets "upstream," possibly requesting information about where upstream is

Traditionally, these duties have been handled by the kernels of operating systems—big, hulking complex beasts at worst, fast and elegant black boxes at best—with some addressing and filtering provided by the network card itself. More dedicated systems from Cisco and other vendors move more of routing into hardware itself; specialized ASICs are fabbed for maximum performance. But the network doesn't care how the job is done—it doesn't care if the work is done in hardware, by kernel…or in this case, by a couple hundred lines of cross-platform C code.

DoxRoute is an interesting solution. It was an experiment to see if simple software, linked through *libnet* and *libpcap*, could reasonably spoof actually machinery on a network, as well as the basic functionality usually expected to be accomplished through complex kernel code. The answer is that it can, with a surprising amount of elegant simplicity and completely unexpected levels of performance. Probably because of the zero-copy nature of *libpcap*-to-*libnet* in-situ packet mangling, extraordinary levels of performance have been witnessed: A 12mbit stream took up about 2 percent CPU on a P3-800, and latency was seen to drop as low a 230us(.23ms) for an ICMP echo. Both figures could probably be improved with a slight amount of code simplification, too.

> **NOTE**
>
> By far, this isn't the first attempt to talk "directly to the wire" to implement a basic network stack. It's not even the most "complete"—Miniweb, at www.dunkels.com/adam/miniweb, compiles down to a IP-level Web server with a reasonably workable TCP implementation in about thirty compiled bytes. There are systems that simulate entire server farms from a single machine. What DoxRoute has is that it's simple, stateless, reasonably cross-platform, and decently straightforward. It has been designed for extraordinary, hopefully excessive simplicity.

Implementation: DoxRoute, Section by Section

Execution of DoxRoute is pretty trivial:

```
[root@localhost effugas]# ./doxroute -r 10.0.1.254 -c -v 10.0.1.170
ARP REQUEST: Wrote 42 bytes looking for 10.0.1.254
Router Found: 10.0.1.254 at 0:3:E3:0:4E:6B
DATA: Sent 74 bytes to 171.68.10.70
DATA: Sent 62 bytes to 216.239.35.101
DATA: Sent 60 bytes to 216.239.35.101
DATA: Sent 406 bytes to 216.239.35.101
DATA: Sent 60 bytes to 216.239.35.101
DATA: Sent 60 bytes to 216.239.35.101
```

Because this implementation is so incomplete, there's actually no state being maintained on the router (so don't go replacing all those 7200s). So it's actually possible to kill the routing process on one machine and restart it on another without any endpoints noticing the switchover.

Plenty of complete systems of active network spoofing tools are out there; for example, Ettercap (at http://ettercap.sourceforge.net) is one of the more interesting packages for using spoofs to execute man-in-the-middle (MITM) attacks against sessions on your network, with extensive support for a wide range of protocols. Good luck building your specific spoof into this. DoxRoute provides the infrastructure for answering the question "What if we could put a machine on the network that did…"? Well, if we can spoof an entire router in a few lines of code, spoofing whatever else is a bit less daunting.

Tools & Traps...

Flexible Routing in UNIX: On the Horizon?

UNIX routing may be fast, but it's ridiculously inflexible. Want to route traffic by port? You can't. Want to route traffic by source host? Nope. Want to restrict bandwidth along a very tightly defined set of network activities? Good luck. DoxRoute's major goal, of which only glimmers shine through now, is to provide a decent method for programming really interesting filters and rulesets for network traffic. The reality is that kernel programming is too dangerous, too difficult, and too not portable for most people to work with; DoxRoute by contrast fits in a couple pages of annotated text. The goal: "If you want to route all packets sent on the third Sunday of every month with an odd number of bytes containing the word *ziggy-bop* through cable modem instead of DSL...OK."

What we're going to do for this implementation really isn't too complicated. After reading a few options from the user, we're going to initialize our packet capture and packet generation engines, compare each incoming packet we receive to a short list of rules, and possibly emit some form of response. With some more detail, here's the plan:

1. Establish configuration

    a. Set static variables

    b. Set defaults

    c. Parse command line

2. Begin sniffing

    a. Open listening device at maximum performance level

    b. Apply kernel filtering to soon-to-be-active datastream

    c. Activate stream

3. Begin spoofing

    a. Open sending device at maximum performance level

    b. Send an ARP request seeking the MAC address of the router

4. Parse sniffed packets (infinite loop, triggered by packet reception)

   a. Apply parsing structures

   b. Claim userspace IP and MAC address

      i. Look for ARP requests for our IP address

      ii. Destructively mangle ARP request into ARP reply with our userspace IP attached to our userspace MAC address

      iii. Send mangled packet

   c. Look for ARP replies providing the MAC address of the router

      i. Cache for future routing purposes

   d. Look for PING (ICMP Echo) requests to our IP and MAC address

      i. Destructively mangle ICMP ECHO into ICMP echo reply

      ii. Reduce TTL of packet

      iii. Re-checksum packet

      iv. Send mangled packet

   e. Route any other packet to our MAC address

      i. Possibly check that this is an IP packet

      ii. Destructively reroute Ethernet destination to upstream and Ethernet source to local

      iii. If checksumming is enabled, decrement TTL and recalculate packet checksum

      iv. Send mangled packet

Starting Off: Preprocessor Directives and Function Declarations

The following is the entirety of the code for DoxRoute. It is heavily commented, and indentation has been stripped for discussion purposes. Let's begin!

```
#define TITLE     "DoxRoute: Userspace IP Router"
#define VERSION   "0.1"
#define CODERS    "Copyright (C) 2001 Dan Kaminsky (dan@doxpara.com)"
#define CODENAME  "Bender"
#define GIANT     "Mark Grimes(obecian@packetninja.net)"
```

Of course, we have to give credit where credit is due. This entire piece of code is, amazingly enough, built from Grimes' brilliant *nemesis* package, although by now it bears little to no resemblance.

```
#include <stdio.h>

#include <stdlib.h>

#include <unistd.h>

#include <libnet.h>

#include <pcap.h>


#ifndef IPV4_ADDR_LEN

#define IPV4_ADDR_LEN 4

#endif
```

The first thing is to define the libraries this application is going to use. We need three sets to make DoxRoute work: The "standard libraries," generic to almost any C application, are pulled in through *stdio.h*, *stdlib.h*, and *unistd*. We then need a system for sending spoofed packets; this is encapsulated within *libnet.h*, obviously *libnet*. Finally, we need a system for listening on the wire for whatever packets might come in; this is done with *pcap.h*, for *libpcap*.

And that's it.

What's more important than what *is* here is what *isn't*. Usually, any networking code—especially low-level packet mangling—involves innumerable OS-dependent system libraries and header *includes* that vary just enough from platform to platform so as to cause unimaginable amounts of pain from platform to platform and even from kernel revision to kernel revision. You end up with hordes of preprocessor directives ("with enough *#ifdef*'s, all things are possible") specifying exactly how to act on which system, and your code is complete spaghetti.

Libpcap and *libnet* change that. Packets come in, packets go out, and there's some base structs we can use to understand what's going on. All the normal OS-dependent rigmarole is completely bypassed:

```
void              usage();

void              print_ip(FILE * stream, u_char * ip);

void              print_mac(FILE * stream, u_char * mac);


int

main(int argc, char **argv)

{
```

Variable Declarations

These are the basic variables for *getopt*, the generic command-line option parser:

```
int              opt;
extern char      *optarg;
extern int       opterr;
```

By now, you've probably noticed that almost all command-line apps on UNIX share a similar syntax—something like *foo -X −y argument*. This syntax for accepting options is standardized and handled by the *getopt* library. Very old platforms require you to add *#include <getopt.h>* to the beginning of your code to parse your options successfully. More modern standards put *getopt* as part of *unistd.h*:

```
pcap_t           *pcap;        /* PCAP file descriptor */
u_char           *packet;      /* Our newly captured packet */
struct pcap_pkthdr pkthdr;     /* Packet metadata--time received, size */
struct bpf_program fp;         /* Structure to hold kernel packet-filter */
char             pfprogram[255];  /* Buffer for uncompiled packet filter */
char             dev[255];     /* Name of device to use */
int              immediate = 1; /* Flag to suck packets at max speed */
int              promisc = 1;  /* Flag to grab all packets visible  */
```

Of special note is the *pfprogram* buffer—the same expressions we can use to program *tcpdump* or *tethereal*, such as *port 22* or *host 1.2.3.4* and *udp*, are actually the exact input specified into *libpcap* for filter design. *Libpcap* itself does the translation—you just pass a human-parseable phrase and it does the rest. That's pretty impressive:

```
struct libnet_ethernet_hdr *eth = NULL;
struct libnet_ip_hdr *ip = NULL;
struct libnet_tcp_hdr *tcp = NULL;
struct libnet_arp_hdr *arp = NULL;
struct libnet_icmp_hdr *icmp = NULL;
struct libnet_udp_hdr *udp = NULL;
```

These are basic packet types from *libnet*, all defined in *include/libnet/libnet-headers.h*. It cannot be put into words how time-saving these standardized structs are, at least when it comes to creating portable network tools:

```
struct libnet_link_int *l;
u_char       *newpacket;

u_char user_ip[IPV4_ADDR_LEN+1];
u_char upstream_ip[IPV4_ADDR_LEN+1];
u_char test_ip[IPV4_ADDR_LEN+1];
struct in_addr  test_ipa;

/* MAC addresses = Local Link-Level Hardware Addresses On The Network */
u_char user_mac[ETHER_ADDR_LEN+1];       /* MAC to receive packets on */
u_char upstream_mac[ETHER_ADDR_LEN+1]; /* MAC to forward packets to */
u_char bcast_mac[ETHER_ADDR_LEN+1];      /* Forward addr for all MACs */
u_char test_mac[ETHER_ADDR_LEN+1];       /* A buffer to test against */
```

An embarrassing and probably unnecessary hack lives here. Essentially, we create static arrays to store various addresses—our IP address, the upstream router's MAC address, and so on. But because of strangeness in *sscanf* and the fact that we're playing fast and loose with type safety, buffers are getting overwritten in strange and ill-defined ways. We clean this up by creating buffers one unit larger than they need to be—it's ugly and inelegant, but oh, well.

The correct solution is to write our own *sscanf* variant for parsing out MAC and IP addresses correctly—but I'm trying to keep this code reasonably straightforward:

```
char            errbuf[255];
int             do_checksum = 0;
int             verbose = 0;
int             i = 0;
```

Setting Important Defaults

One thing that's important for any tool is to have default behavior, minimizing the amount of knowledge somebody needs to have when they first run your system. For example, Web servers don't need to be told the index page to load whenever someone connects to http://www.host.com—the default, if nothing else is specified, is for a connection to that address to be responded to as if the user requested http://www.host.com/index.html. Similarly, we need defaults for routing packets:

```
/* Set Broadcast MAC to FF:FF:FF:FF:FF:FF*/
bcast_mac[0] = 0xFF;
bcast_mac[1] = 0xFF;
bcast_mac[2] = 0xFF;
bcast_mac[3] = 0xFF;
bcast_mac[4] = 0xFF;
bcast_mac[5] = 0xFF;
```

Sometimes default selection is easy—basic Ethernet standards specify that all packets delivered to the destination MAC address FF:FF:FF:FF:FF:FF should be received by all hosts on a given subnet. Ethernet only recently became a switched medium, so this used to be more of an "advisory" message to network cards that they should pass a packet up to the operating system even though it wasn't addressed specifically to that host. Now, traffic isn't even seen by a host's network card unless the switch deems it destined to them. Broadcast MACs render this so.

Many protocols make requests of all hosts on the local subnet—ARP is going to be the most relevant for our purposes:

```
/* Set Default Userspace MAC Address to 00:E0:B0:B0:D0:D0 */
user_mac[0] = 0x00;
user_mac[1] = 0xE0;
user_mac[2] = 0xB0;
user_mac[3] = 0xB0;
user_mac[4] = 0xD0;
user_mac[5] = 0xD0;
```

We're going to be creating a virtual network card on the network, and this is the default address we ship with. We could use any value—indeed, it'd be trivial and often good to randomize this value—but randomization would mean that we couldn't start and stop the router at will; each time it started back up, hosts would have to re-resolve the gateway IP they were looking for into the new MAC address we were serving. (If you do decide to implement randomization, take care that the low-order bit of the first byte, *user_mac[0]*, doesn't get set. If it does, then it would be a multicast MAC address, which will have interesting effects.)

```
/* Set Default Upstream IP */
upstream_ip[0] = 10;
upstream_ip[1] = 0;
```

```
upstream_ip[2] = 1;
upstream_ip[3] = 254;
```

DoxRoute is not a complete router implementation—it's barely even a skeleton. We just bounce packets to the real gateway. Based on experience, 10.0.1.254 is commonly used for gatewaying packets out of the private networks that DoxRoute really should only be run on.

We do *not*, incidentally, set a default *user_ip* to host our service. The reason is known as the Good Neighbor policy: When possible, don't break existing systems. Any IP we shipped with may very well be used on systems already deployed. Instead, let the user find us a free IP and listen there. A more complex implementation could actually DHCP for an address, but this would have rather serious implications for clients wishing to route through an apparently mobile router.

```
/* Set Default Interface */
snprintf(dev, sizeof(dev), "%s", pcap_lookupdev(NULL));
```

The man page says, "*pcap_lookupdev()* returns a pointer to a network device suitable for use with *pcap_open_live()* and *pcap_lookupnet()*. If there is an error, NULL is returned and *errbuf* is filled in with an appropriate error message." That's a bit unclear—it actually returns a pointer to a string containing the name of the device, which we dutifully store for future possible usage.

On the Line: Using Command-Line Options to Avoid Hard-Coded Dependencies

Ahhhh, *getopt*. It's a useful and standard function for parsing UNIX-style command lines, but it's not always so clear as to how to write software with it. Here is a decent summary usage:

```
/* Parse Options */
while ((opt = getopt(argc, argv, "i:r:R:m:cv")) != EOF) {
    switch (opt) {
    case 'i':        /* Interface */
        snprintf(dev, sizeof(dev), "%s", optarg);
        break;
    case 'v':
        verbose = 1;
        break;
```

A loop is established that will cycle through and eventually exhaust flag-bearing options existing upon the command line. This loop takes in and decrements the argument count and a pointer to the first argument found, and well as a string specifying how the flags are to be parsed.

There are primarily two kinds of options for any command-line tool—those that include an additional argument, as in *doxroute −i eth0*, and those that are complete in and of themselves, such as in *doxroute −v. getopt* would represent these two in its parsing string as *i:v*—the colon after the *i* means that there is an argument to parse, and the pointer *optarg* should be pointing there; the lack of the colon after the *v* means simple presence of the flag is enough complete the necessary work (in this case, setting the global variable to *1*, activating app-wide verbosity):

```
case 'r':        /* Router IP */
        sscanf(optarg, "%hu.%hu.%hu.%hu",
        &upstream_ip[0], &upstream_ip[1], &upstream_ip[2],
&upstream_ip[3]);
        break;
case 'R':        /* Router MAC */
        sscanf(optarg, "%X:%X:%X:%X:%X:%X",
        &upstream_mac[0], &upstream_mac[1], &upstream_mac[2],
                &upstream_mac[3], &upstream_mac[4],
&upstream_mac[5]);
        break;
case 'm':        /* Userspace MAC */
        sscanf(optarg, "%X:%X:%X:%X:%X:%X",
                &user_mac[0], &user_mac[1], &user_mac[2],
                &user_mac[3], &user_mac[4], &user_mac[5]);
        break;
```

Not the cleanest ways to parse addresses off the command line, but it works. It's for this that we had to do that horrific +1 hack due to bugs in type handling:

```
case 'c':        /* Checksum */
        do_checksum = 1;
        break;
default:
        usage();
```

```
        }
    }
    /* Retrieve Userspace IP Address */
    if (argv[optind] != NULL) {
            sscanf(argv[optind], "%hu.%hu.%hu.%hu",
                    &user_ip[0], &user_ip[1], &user_ip[2],
&user_ip[3]);
        } else
            usage();
```

Whatever *getopt* can't touch—in other words, whatever lacks a flag—we parse here. Now, we can demand the most important data for this software—the IP address it will soon be surreptitiously accepting. It should be noted that to function out to *usage()* is almost always to exit the program with an error flag; we're basically saying that the user did something wrong and they should RTFM that pops up to see what.

Starting Libpcap

Now, we need to prepare for actually monitoring our network for the "interesting traffic" we plan to respond to:

```
/* Begin sniffing */
pcap = pcap_open_live(dev, 65535, promisc, 5, NULL);
if (pcap == NULL) {
    perror("pcap_open_live");
    exit(EXIT_FAILURE);
}
```

Pop open the primary interface, with specifications to grab as much as possible, regardless of how large it was. Grab all packets visible to the interface, regardless of whether they're addressed to the kernel-sanctioned MAC address. Use a minimum delay for parsing packets, and just drop errors:

```
if (ioctl(pcap_fileno(pcap), BIOCIMMEDIATE, &immediate)) {
    /*perror("Couldn't set BPF to Immediate Mode."); */
}
```

We set a delay of 5ms before a packet in the queue is dumped for processing; this is to handle those platforms which might not do well with quick context switching. Performance-wise, however, we really want to deal with each packet the moment it comes in. Linux does this no matter what, but the BSDs and possibly some other platforms use an IO Control, or IOCTL, to specify what is known as Immediate Mode. This mode is somewhat of a very distant cousin to the *TCP_NODELAY* socket option that forces each data segment to be dealt with as quickly as possible, as opposed to when just the right amount of data is ripe to be passed to the next layer.

This IOCTL so significantly improves performance that's it's unimaginable to operate on some platforms without it. Overall, the flag tells *libpcap* to block on reads, buffer as little as possible, and grant the fastest possible turnaround times for our router. That's a good thing.

Some platforms may complain about sending this IOCTL; the commented section may be uncommented if you want to know whether problems are coming from this line:

```
/*
 * Create the filter to catch ARP requests, ICMP's, and routable
 * packets.
 */
snprintf(pfprogram, sizeof(pfprogram), "arp or icmp or ether dst
%hX:%hX:%hX:%hX:%hX:%hX", user_mac[0], user_mac[1], user_mac[2],
user_mac[3], user_mac[4], user_mac[5]);


/* Compile and set a kernel-based packet filter*/
if (pcap_compile(pcap, &fp, pfprogram, 1, 0x0) == -1) {
        pcap_perror(pcap, "pcap_compile");
        exit(EXIT_FAILURE);
}
if (pcap_setfilter(pcap, &fp) == -1) {
        pcap_perror(pcap, "pcap_setfilter");
        exit(EXIT_FAILURE);
}
```

Just because we can respond to all visible packets doesn't mean we want to—if nothing else, we don't want to see all the traffic genuinely being handled by the kernel! First, we configure the filter using an *snprintf*—we do this now, after the *getopt* is complete, so we can filter specifically for packets destined for our

MAC address, and we need to know our MAC before we can listen for it. From there, it's a simple matter to compile and activate the filter rule, as we see in the preceding code.

As much as the kernel can get in our way, the existence of efficient kernel code written by other people with an elegant and trivial interface accessible from userspace in a cross-platform manner is not something to take lightly. We'll be looking for specific packet types later, but any help we can get lightening our packet-parsing load is useful—don't look a gift horse in the mouth and all that.

From this point on, we're finally actually capturing packets.

Starting Libnet

```
/* Get Direct Connection To The Interface   */
if ((l = libnet_open_link_interface(dev, errbuf)) == NULL) {
        fprintf(stderr, "Libnet failure opening link interface: %s",
        errbuf);
}
```

The link interface essentially gives us a method to toss raw packets out on the wire, just as we received them. *Libpcap* gives us raw packets, *libnet* sends out raw packets. The symmetry between the two becomes extraordinarily useful later.

There is a cost, however. The ability to specify the exact hardware addresses we're sending data to means we get no help from the kernel determining which hardware address we're going to send to—we have to do everything ourselves. That gets annoying when trying to send packets to random hosts both on and off your subnet—you have to manually handle routing, ARP requests, and so on. An intermediate method of sending packets keeps the kernel in charge of Layer 2 local routing but still gives the application reasonably free reign at Layer 3 (IP) and above. This interface is known as the raw socket interface, and is accessed using a slightly different set of *libnet* calls. However, for the purposes of this routing software, the raw link interface is necessary—we don't necessarily want to route packets to the same place the system kernel normally would.

Packet Generation: Looking for the Next Hop

```
/* Lookup the router */
```

Remember, we've got no help from the kernel as to where the router is, and all we really want to ask of the user is an IP address. We've got a reasonably flex-ible network stack here—let's have it broadcast an ARP (Address Resolution

Protocol) request asking what hardware address matches the IP address we've been told to route through. Here, we see how to start a packet from scratch and send it off:

```
libnet_init_packet(LIBNET_ETH_H + LIBNET_ARP_H, &newpacket);
```

A simple *malloc* wrapper, *libnet_init_packet* initializes a given amount of memory (in this case, the amount required by both Ethernet and ARP headers) and makes *newpacket* point to the memory location thus allocated:

```
libnet_build_ethernet(bcast_mac,        /*eth->ether_dhost*/
                      user_mac,         /*eth->ether_shost*/
                      ETHERTYPE_ARP,    /*eth->ether_type*/
                      NULL,             /*extra crap to tack on*/
                      0,                /*how much crap*/
                      newpacket);
```

We need to define the complete basics of this packet—where it's going, where it's coming from, what kind of packet it is, and so on. In this case, it's a broadcasted ARP message from our userspace MAC address. So right at the memory location starting our *newpacket*, we throw in the Ethernet headers:

```
libnet_build_arp(ARPHRD_ETHER,
                 ETHERTYPE_IP,
                 ETHER_ADDR_LEN,
                 IPV4_ADDR_LEN,
                 ARPOP_REQUEST,
                 user_mac,
                 user_ip,
                 bcast_mac,
                 upstream_ip,
            NULL,
             0,
             newpacket + LIBNET_ETH_H);
```

Libnet provides pretty useful functions and defines– with almost all endian issues handled, no less—for filling in the fields of a given packet. This ARP packet is requesting, on behalf of the user's MAC and IP address, that the IP address listed in *upstream_ip* be accounted for by anyone who might care to listen.

Of note is that this pile of bytes is not added straight to the *newpacket* pointer; rather, it is tossed on following the fixed-size Ethernet header:

```
i = libnet_write_link_layer(l, dev, newpacket, LIBNET_ETH_H +
   LIBNET_ARP_H);
if (verbose){
      fprintf(stdout, "ARP REQUEST: Wrote %i bytes looking for " , i);
      print_ip(stdout, upstream_ip);
      }
```

And thus where the rubber hits the road—we spit out the Ethernet and ARP headers found at *newpacket*, and throw the number of bytes written up for verbose debugging. *Libnet_write_link_layer* takes in a *libnet* link number, its associated device, the memory address of the packet to be sent, and how large the packet is, then returns how many bytes were successfully shoved onto the network:

```
libnet_destroy_packet(&newpacket);
```

If *libnet_init_packet* was analogous to *malloc*, this is simply free with a better name.

Ta dah! You just sent a packet. Now what?

Packet Retrieval: Picking Up Return Traffic

```
/* Get the next packet from the queue, */
while (1) {
      packet = (u_char *) pcap_next(pcap, &pkthdr);
      if (packet) {
```

Note that *pcap_next* is a simple function: Given an active *libcpap* file descriptor and a place to put packet metadata, *pcap_next* returns the memory address of a captured packet. This memory is readable and writable, as we end up taking advantage of.

Of some note is that, either because of the immediate mode *ioctl*, or due to the platform you're running *libpcap* on, the *pcap_next* withdrawal will probably block until there's a packet to be read. If not, though, the *if* (packet) loop will just keep repeating until there's a packet to parse:

```
/*
 * Make packet parseable -- switching on
 * eth->ether_type and ip->ip_p is also a valid
```

```
 * strategy.  All structs are defined in
 * /usr/include/libnet/libnet-headers.h
 */


/* Layer 1: libnet_ethernet_hdr structs */
(char *)eth = (char *)packet;
/* Layer 2: libnet_arp_hdr / libnet_ip_hdr structs */
(char *)arp = (char *)ip = (char *)packet + LIBNET_ETH_H;


/*
 * Layer 3:  libnet_icmp_hdr / libnet_tcp_hdr /
 * libnet_udp_hdr structs
 */
(char *)icmp = (char *)tcp = (char *)udp = (char *)packet + LIBNET_ETH_H
+ LIBNET_IP_H;
```

The strategy here is simple: Align each struct with the memory location on the packet that would be accurate if this was a packet of this type. This is slightly naïve—we're "filling" structs with incorrect data, rather than only choosing via *eth->ether_type* (Layer 2) and *ip->ip_p* (Layer 3) which structures match which packets. Because of this, we lose *segfaults* when we misparse packets; for instance, if we attempt to get the TCP sequence number of a UDP packet that has no such value. But on the flip side, it's a matter of flexibility—just as kernels generally presume nobody would ever want to read data a certain way, it's not necessarily DoxRoute's place to presume how you will read a given packet.

One important caveat when parsing packets is that packets captured off the localhost interface have no Ethernet header to speak of—so don't offset *LIBNET_ETH_H* when reading off of localhost:

```
/* Handle ARPs: */
if (ntohs(eth->ether_type) == ETHERTYPE_ARP &&
    arp->ar_op == htons(ARPOP_REQUEST) &&
    !memcmp(arp->ar_tpa, user_ip, IPV4_ADDR_LEN)) {


    /*
     * IF: The ethernet header reports this as an
     * ARP packet, the ARP header shows it a
```

```
    * request for translation, and the address

    * being searched for corresponds to this

    * "stack"...

    *

    */
```

At this point, we're looking for ARP requests. The first thing to do is to make sure it's actually an ARP packet making a request of us. This necessitates a couple of things—first, as annoying as it is, we need to alter the endian-ness of the *eth->ether_type* datum, at least on little-endian systems. (This code most likely does not work well on big-endian systems.) This is done using an *ntohs* call, ordering a switch from network to host order. Then, we need to verify that the remote side is making a request—again, necessitating a byte-order switch, this time using *htons* to turn the host's conception of an ARP request into what we might have seen on the network. Finally, we're concerned about whether this request we've found actually corresponds to the IP address whose presence we seek to spoof on this network. This is done by inverting the results of a *memcmp*, which returns the first byte that differs between two buffers, so a "0" means there is no difference— exactly what we want, thus we flip it to a 1:

```
memcpy(eth->ether_dhost, eth->ether_shost, ETHER_ADDR_LEN);
memcpy(eth->ether_shost, user_mac, ETHER_ADDR_LEN);
```

One of the really cool things we can do because of the compatibility of *libpcap* and *libnet* buffers is to in-place permute a packet into what we wish it to be on the network, then send it back out the door without having to reinitialize memory or pass contents across various contexts or whatnot. (This ain't revolutionary—kernels have been doing this for years—but hey, we're in userspace, we're supposed to be running Netscape or mpg123 or something, not simulating a network card!) We're going to be responding to the source of this Ethernet packet, so we simply and destructively copy the data signifying the original source of the data into the destination field. Next, we copy over the MAC address we claim exists on this network into the "source host" field of the Ethernet packet:

```
memcpy(arp->ar_tha, arp->ar_sha, ETHER_ADDR_LEN);
memcpy(arp->ar_sha, user_mac, ETHER_ADDR_LEN);
```

Ahhh, acronyms. What a great way to start the day. ARP acronyms actually aren't too bad—*tha* and *sha* are nothing more than "target host address" and "source host address". More in-place copying, exactly equivalent to what we just did on the Ethernet level—"ARP Source user_mac informing ARP Target guy who last sent me an ARP request"). I hope you're not surprised by the protocol redundancy:

```
arp->ar_op = htons(ARPOP_REPLY);

memcpy(test_ip, arp->ar_spa, IPV4_ADDR_LEN);

memcpy(arp->ar_spa, arp->ar_tpa, IPV4_ADDR_LEN);

memcpy(arp->ar_tpa, test_ip, IPV4_ADDR_LEN);
```

Finally, after transforming this packet in-*situ* from a request to a reply, we swap the Protocol Addresses—IPs, in this case—using a cheap temp variable. (*XOR* would work, but I'm lazy and you have to understand this.) With this, we've got a reasonably complete and correct ARP reply going out with inverted IPs, completed ARP hardware addresses, and correct Ethernet characteristics. Boom, done:

```
i = libnet_write_link_layer(l, dev, packet, pkthdr.caplen);

if (verbose)
        fprintf(stdout, "ARP: Wrote %i bytes\n", i);
```

The *pkthdr* structure is useful—it's basically a small collection of metadata outlining when this data was captured and how much of it there was to play with. The *caplen* element refers to captured length, and is perfect for our link-writing function, which really needs a count of how many bytes it's supposed to send. Because in-*situ* packet modification won't generally modify the length of a given packet (though this could change), knowing the original length of a packet provides perfect knowledge of how much to send back out.

That we're dealing with a fixed-size protocol like FTP and not a variable-size protocol like DNS helps too:

```
/* Handle ARP replies (responding with upstream IP) */
} else if (eth->ether_type == ntohs(ETHERTYPE_ARP) &&
        arp->ar_op == htons(ARPOP_REPLY) &&
        !memcmp(arp->ar_spa, upstream_ip, IPV4_ADDR_LEN)){
```

This is the same process as listening for ARPOP_REQUESTs, only now we're checking for *ARPOP_REPLY*s:

```
memcpy(upstream_mac, arp->ar_sha, ETHER_ADDR_LEN);

if (verbose)
```

```
fprintf(stdout, "Router Found: %hu.%hu.%hu.%hu at %X:%X:%X:%X:%X:%X\n",

upstream_ip[0], upstream_ip[1], upstream_ip[2], upstream_ip[3],

upstream_mac[0], upstream_mac[1], upstream_mac[2], upstream_mac[3],

upstream_mac[4], upstream_mac[5]);
```

Remember way back when we sent that ARP request looking for our router?
Here's how we handle the reply. We take the MAC address we're offered, store it
in the *upstream_mac* buffer by copying it out of the data in the *arp->ar_sha* element, and poof. We're done.

Note that this approach—stateless to the hilt—is actually vulnerable to a
spoofing attack of its own. Anyone can gratuitously send at any time an unre-
quested ARP to us that we'll use to update our *upstream_mac* value. There are
decent solutions to this (use a trigger variable to prevent the link from being
updated, have a router monitor react to a downed site, and so on), but they're
outside the scope of this chapter:

```
/* Handle ICMP ECHO (Ping) */

} else if (!memcmp(eth->ether_dhost, user_mac, ETHER_ADDR_LEN) &&

      ntohs(eth->ether_type) == ETHERTYPE_IP &&

      memcmp((u_char *) & ip->ip_dst, user_ip, IPV4_ADDR_LEN) &&

      ip->ip_p == IPPROTO_ICMP &&

      icmp->icmp_type == ICMP_ECHO) {
```

Ah, Ping. How I've missed thee. The real measure of whether a host is online
or not is not whether it shows up in your ARP cache when you try to reach it—
it's whether it responds to pings. A ping is actually an Echo from the ICMP sub-
channel of the IP protocol, addressed to a given host with an IP *ethertype* and the
correct hardware address. We check all five of these conditions before treating this
as a ping packet.

A moderately strange method of casting is used to check the IP. It works:

```
/* Swap Source and Destination MAC addresses */

memcpy(test_mac, eth->ether_dhost, ETHER_ADDR_LEN);

memcpy(eth->ether_dhost, eth->ether_shost, ETHER_ADDR_LEN);

memcpy(eth->ether_shost, test_mac, ETHER_ADDR_LEN);
```

Alice sends a packet From Alice To Bob…Bob replies with a packet From
Bob To Alice—just the inverse. That's all we're doing here, then—inverting source
and destination to represent a response:

```
/* Swap Source and Destination IP addresses */
test_ipa = ip->ip_dst;
ip->ip_dst = ip->ip_src;
ip->ip_src = test_ipa;
```

Same thing as we did to MAC addresses, only now it's for Layer 3 Ips:

```
/*
 * Change the packet to a reply, and decrement time
 * to live
 */
icmp->icmp_type = ICMP_ECHOREPLY;
ip->ip_ttl--;
```

As a general rule, systems that have any risk of experiencing routing loops (almost all) really need to decrement the Time To Live (TTL) with each hop. The problem is this—if you don't decrement, and you're doing anything even remotely strange with your routing (like, say, doing it all in userspace), you run the risk of routing data in circles, forever. Decrementing TTL lets circles die out, instead of amplifying into a network-killing feedback loop.

This implementation does not drop packets with a zero TTL. I leave it as an exercise to the reader to figure out how:

```
/* Recalculate IP and TCP/UDP/ICMP checksums */
libnet_do_checksum(packet + LIBNET_ETH_H, IPPROTO_IP, LIBNET_IP_H);
libnet_do_checksum(packet + LIBNET_ETH_H, IPPROTO_ICMP,
pkthdr.caplen - LIBNET_ETH_H - LIBNET_IP_H);
```

Because we're modifying the packet data (through the TTL decrement), we need to update the checksums that ensure the validity of the packet through noise or corruption or whatnot. This method of doing the Layer 4 (TCP/UDP/ICMP) checksum usually works for ICMP but will fail on occasion for TCP and UDP, due to its inability to take into account IP. It is placed here for example purposes—but for actual deployment, the router method works far better. However, the router method, using *ip->ip_len* as a length field, is possibly vulnerable to certain forms of attack (because you're trusting a variable to represent the actual length of a total set of data). So be careful:

```
i = libnet_write_link_layer(1, dev, packet, pkthdr.caplen);
if (verbose)
```

```
        fprintf(stdout, "ICMP: Wrote %i bytes\n", i);


/* Route Packet */
} else if (!memcmp(eth->ether_dhost, user_mac, ETHER_ADDR_LEN)) {
        memcpy(eth->ether_dhost, upstream_mac, ETHER_ADDR_LEN);
        memcpy(eth->ether_shost, user_mac, ETHER_ADDR_LEN);
```

After all we went through for ICMP, routing itself isn't too hard. Just take any packet that was addressed to our fake hardware address and wasn't meant for us and send it off to some other MAC address. Maybe we'll get around to lowering the TTL too:

```
if (do_checksum == 1) {
        ip->ip_ttl--;
        libnet_do_checksum(packet + LIBNET_ETH_H, IPPROTO_IP,
LIBNET_IP_H);
        libnet_do_checksum(packet + LIBNET_ETH_H, ip->ip_p,
        ntohs(ip->ip_len) - LIBNET_IP_H);
}
```

Note that, because only hosts issuing IP ARP requests should care about our fake MAC address, we probably don't need to worry too much about strange and broken non-IP packets getting checksum noise. But, just in case, it's certainly fair game to add a check that we're trying to route an IP packet.

That we happen to be much freer than in the kernel-only days does mean that a lot of kernels will always expect that they're talking to a fellow TCP/IP stack. That's a treasure trove of spoofing possibilities—whatever assumptions it makes can almost always be re-analyzed and defeated in interesting ways. We could randomly insert noise, we could change specific strings, we could send packets on demand, we could do bandwidth limitation, we could even create new IPs for other hosts on our subnet—or even other subnets, if we got devious enough. This is but an infrastructure; the point is that you don't even need a real piece of hardware on a network to do really interesting work. Some decently elegant software will fake whatever you need, and the network can be none the wiser. All you have to do is send this:

```
i = libnet_write_link_layer(l, dev, packet, pkthdr.caplen);
if (verbose)
        fprintf(stdout, "DATA: Sent %i bytes to %s\n", i, inet_ntoa(ip-
```

```
>ip_dst));

}}}


/* Enough for now ... */

pcap_close(pcap);


return EXIT_SUCCESS;

}


void

print_ip(FILE * stream, u_char * ip)

{

        fprintf(stream, "%i.%i.%i.%i\n", ip[0], ip[1], ip[2], ip[3]);

}


void

print_mac(FILE * stream, u_char * mac)

{

        fprintf(stream, "%X:%X:%X:%X:%X:%X\n", mac[0], mac[1], mac[2],

mac[3], mac[4], mac[5]);

}
```

At this point, it's just a matter of cleaning up resources and providing ourselves with a few useful functions for parsing the arrays we've been working with. One note about cleaning up resources—most systems have a limited number of packet captures they can do simultaneously; it's a kernel limitation set at compile time. Though this implementation has its packet capture file descriptor closed anyway on death of the app (it's an infinite loop preceding the close—we never genuinely reach this code), your future code may need to cycle through several different packet captures before the app dies. Be sure to close 'em when you're done!

```
void usage()

{

fprintf(stderr, "DoxRoute 0.1: Userspace TCP/IP Router, by Dan Kaminsky
```

```
(dan@doxpara.com)\n");
      fprintf(stderr, "
      Usage: doxroute [-i interface] [-m userspace_mac]\n");
      fprintf(stderr, "
      [-r/R upstream_ip/mac] [-cv] userspace_ip\n\n");
      fprintf(stderr, "
      Example: doxroute  -r 10.0.1.254 10.0.1.169\n");
      fprintf(stderr, "
      Options: \n");
      fprintf(stderr, "
      -i [interface]    : Select the interface to be used.\n");
      fprintf(stderr, "
      -r [upstream_ip]  : MAC Address of upstream router\n");
      fprintf(stderr, "
      -R [upstream_mac] : MAC Address of upstream router/gateway.\n");
      fprintf(stderr, "
      -m [userspace_mac]: MAC Address for this software.\n");
      fprintf(stderr, "
      -c : Verify Checksums(and decrement IP TTL).\n");
      fprintf(stderr, "
      -v : Verbose Mode.\n");
      fprintf(stderr, "
      Notice:  This is just a proof of concept.  Useful stuff
      later.\n"); exit(1);
}
```

And that's DoxRoute, in its entirety. It's not suggested that you try to type the entire thing out; simply grab the source from www.doxpara.com/tradecraft/doxroute. If you do type it out, the following compilation command should build *doxroute*:

```
gcc `libnet-config --defines` -O3 -Wall -funroll-loops -fomit-frame-
pointer -pipe -I/usr/local/include -L/usr/local/lib -lpcap -o doxroute
doxroute.c /usr/local/lib/libnet.a
```

You can find copies of *libnet* and *libpcap* at their homes within www.packetfactory.net/Projects/Libnet and www.tcpdump.org respectively. Of particular note, when monitoring DoxRoute or simply trying to learn a new protocol, is Ethereal. Ethereal is probably the best sniffing system engineered for UNIX, and you can find it at www.ethereal.com.

Bring Out the Halon: Spoofing Connectivity Through Asymmetric Firewalls

In an ideal world, the network itself is a practically transparent abstraction—one system wants to talk to another, it just sends a packet to the address and "knows" that it will arrive. For various reasons, the Net has gotten significantly less transparent. More often than anything else, firewalls are deployed on the outside of each network to, if nothing else, prevent all but the most explicitly allowed incoming connections from being accepted. By contrast, outgoing connectivity is much more liberally allowed—it's very much a circumstance of asymmetric security, with incoming being banned unless explicitly allowed, and outgoing being allowed unless explicitly banned.

The presumption is that incoming connections come from the big bad outside world, where nothing can be trusted, but outgoing connections from the relatively small internal LAN, where most hosts are reasonably trusted. It's a valid presumption, for the most part, though it starts hitting problems when clients have been penetrated by various pieces of spyware (essentially, users are tricked into running software that opens network connections on their behalf—in a very real sense, the software spoofs being the user to the network).

Unfortunately, there's a pretty major problem that such firewalls hammer into: Although it's trivial for an outgoing-only network to connect to an unfirewalled host, or to one with a necessarily permissive incoming link allowance, the ability for two outgoing-only networks to communicate with one another is extraordinarily small. Even though *both* network firewalls trust their backend hosts to specify which remote hosts they wish to connect to, neither side can accept the connection from the other, so no communication can occur.

There is, however, another option. Given two hosts, both behind firewalls that allow only outgoing connectivity, and possibly a third host outside that may conspire to send a limited amount of network traffic for both, can we execute a spoof against the firewalls standing between our two networks such that each firewall thinks the other accepted the incoming connection?

Maybe. The firewalls are using connection asymmetries to differentiate between incoming and outgoing links. But most connections are inherently bidirectional—being the network manifestation of bidirectional UNIX sockets, this is unsurprising. It's only when a connection is initiated that real asymmetries exist—by spoofing the right initiation packets "from" the right hosts at the right times, it may very well be possible to reintroduce symmetry to the connection attempts and cause the two firewalled links to be able to communicate.

Symmetric Outgoing TCP: A Highly Experimental Framework for Handshake-Only TCP Connection Brokering

Suppose one were to consider, in extreme slow motion, the events that transpire if two hosts, both behind outgoing-only firewalls—especially address-translating NAT firewalls—were to attempt to establish outgoing TCP connections to one another. Alice would begin with a SYN packet, the opening shot in every TCP session initiation. This SYN packet would travel from Alice to her firewall, which would note in its "state table" that Alice attempted to contact Bob and that a suitably formatted response from Bob should be forwarded back to Alice. This packet would then be forwarded onto the Internet itself, perhaps with a return address pointing back to the firewall, and sent to who Alice saw as Bob.

Of course, it never reaches Bob, because "Bob" on the network is really Bob's firewall. Bob's firewall doesn't trust Alice any more than Alice's firewall trusts Bob, so Bob's firewall responds to Alice's call by essentially hanging up on her—it sends back a TCP Reset Connection, or RST|ACK packet to Alice. Of course, the moment Alice's firewall gets this reset response, it knows it's not going to receive a positive connection response, or SYN|ACK, from Bob. So it scratches out the entry in its state table, and Alice is left frustrated.

Bob, of course, has the same problem—he can't call upon Alice either; Alice's firewall will drop him just as quick as his firewall dropped her.

If you think about it, for a period of time things are looking good—each side can negotiate with their own firewall enough access to allow the other to send a response packet; the problem is that the responses that are coming are quite negative. This is by design—neither firewall wants the outside world coming in. But in this case, it's preventing the inside world from getting out. We want that state table entry, but we don't want that connection reset. Is there any way to get the former, but not the latter?

Yes, yes there is.

"I'm Going to Sing the Doom Song Now!" Using TTL-Doomed Packets for Local State Table Manipulation

IP can essentially be thought of as a "Lilypad Protocol" that allows packets to bounce from router to router along the way to their eventual destination. One very dangerous problem that can pop up in such hop (or graph, to be precise) networks is the infinite routing loop—for whatever reason, a sequence of routers can create a circular path that will never manage to get an individual packet to its final destination. It's like driving around in circles when lost out of town, while being too clueless to realize that it's the 30th time you've passed the very same Quicky-Mart.

In the real world, you can't drive around forever—eventually you run out of gas—but packets don't have gas tanks. Still, it's critical that packets not loop eternally, so each IP packet contains a TTL, or Time To Live value. We discussed these values back when we were building our userspace router—effectively, the client specifies a maximum number of hops a given packet may take en route to its destination (capped at 256), and each router the packet passes through en route to its final destination decrements the TTL count by one. If any router receives a packet with a null TTL—well, that packet is dropped on the floor, and maybe an ICMP time-exceeded message is sent. It's these messages that are used to implement route tracing—a packet is allowed to go one hop, then two, then three....

And that's where things start to get interesting. Firewalls are already allowing packets out with low TTLs; they even pass the ICMP responses back for evaluation by the client. These are packets that are legitimately addressed but are doomed to expire before reaching their destination. The packet is legitimately sent but never received—that's exactly what we're looking for! The legitimately sent packet opens up the entry in the state table, but because it never arrives at its destination, no RST response comes to close it.

At least, no response actually sent by Alice or Bob.

Network Egalitarianism: SYM|ACK Down

Although Alice and Bob can both initiate connections using SYN packets, and can even transmute the state-killing RST into an innocent ICMP time-exceeded message by sending a doomed SYN packet, that state table is still left waiting for a SYN|ACK to acknowledge the connection attempt. This is somewhat of a problem—there just doesn't appear to be any mechanism by which Alice or Bob could directly send that SYN|ACK; it's an inherent element of accepting an incoming connection, and the state machine that the firewall has implemented is only allowing outgoing connections.

Using the typology described earlier, the ability to respond has been blocked.

But just because Alice can't send a packet doesn't mean Bob can't receive one—it just means that someone else has to do the sending for Alice. This someone, known as a connection broker, would receive a message from Alice describing the SYN|ACK she would expect to receive from Bob, if his firewall would only let him (A similar message would be received from Bob, describing what he'd want from Alice.) The broker couldn't watch the initial SYN dying in the middle of the Net, but if both clients could provide sufficient information about the SYN they sent and the nature of the response they're expecting the other to provide, the connection broker could spoof Alice SYN|ACKing Bob and Bob SYN|ACKing Alice.

I've dubbed these packets SYM|ACKs, for they are **Ack**nowledgements both **Sym**metric and **Sim**ulated. The broker simulates the transmission of two near-identical but inversely routed packets onto the net. These specially formulated packets share more than their similar structure; they allow both firewalls to maintain symmetric states throughout the entire handshaking process. Both clients send a SYN, both firewalls await a SYN|ACK, both clients are forwarded that SYN|ACK and are simultaneously granted the capacity to send ACKs to one another. (Of course—because neither firewall expects to be receiving an ACK, we do need to Doom these packets, too.) With both sides satisfied with their handshake, we're left with a nice, bidirectionally capable, symmetric link between two hosts that couldn't talk to each other in the first place. At this point, there's no need for the broker to do anything, and indeed once the two sides exchange their first few packets, the broker couldn't intrude back into the session if he tried (though he could probably spoof an ICMP Host Unreachable message to both sides, disconnecting their link).

Perfect? No. No third host should be required for two systems to talk to each other—this is a pretty awful hack, made necessary by incomplete firewall engineering. There are also various issues that stand in the way of this working at all.

The Mechanics of Numbers: Semiblind Spoofing of SYN|ACK Packets

Although the connection broker is indeed informed of both when and mostly where it is supposed to spoof, there are nontrivial issues surrounding the bloody details of exactly what gets sent. Beyond the timing and the location of a packet, an actual SYN connection initiation packet contains two chunks of random data that must be matched perfectly for a firewall to accept a given response: The source port number and the Initial Sequence Number (ISN).

First, the source port number. Ranging from 0 to 65535, this port number is used by the client to differentiate between any number of possible connections to the same service on the same host. Normal firewalls simply pass this port number along, meaning that Alice can simply select a port in advance and know, when it dies in transit, what port number it carried through the firewall. Firewalls implementing Network Address Translation are trickier: They're multiplexing entire networks behind a single IP address, using local port numbers to differentiate between a whole set of backend connections. Because those connections theoretically chose their local port numbers randomly, it doesn't (normally) matter if the outside world sees a different port, as long as the NAT process translates the external value back to the internal one during the translation process.

For our purposes, this means that Alice doesn't necessarily know the port number that the SYN|ACK is supposed to be sent to; while normally it would come from what she set as her destination port and go to what she set as her source port, now it has to go to some other source port that only the firewall and the Internet's routers have seen. What can she do?

Luckily, many NAT implementations will attempt to match local port numbers; she may not have to do anything at all unless she's collided with an existing local port being used. Those that do vary port numbers almost always increment them on a per-connection basis; this allows for a trivial method for Alice to indirectly inform the broker of the port that will be used by her firewall. Right before sending her Doomed SYN, Alice starts up a session with the broker. This informs the broker of two things: First, it implicitly provides the globally routable address of Alice's firewall, absolving her of the duty to find out herself. Second, it provides the source port number, minus one, of the SYN that Alice's firewall will translate on her behalf. Because we presume sequential port numbers for sequential connections, and we assume that no other connections will be opened by anyone else in the small period of time we'll allow between the broker link and the SYN, the broker can deduce the port number pretty easily.

Of course, neither presumption is guaranteed to be valid, but we can check for this. By quickly opening multiple connections to the broker and monitoring what port numbers the NAT selects, the broker can determine whether the NAT's source ports are completely random, sequential, or predictable to a fault. Responding to completely random ports is…well, it's not impossible, but it's embarrassingly ugly. Source port numbers, as said earlier, have a range of 0 to 65535—16 bits of entropy. With no hints as to which number to choose, we could just keep sending SYM|ACKs with random port numbers until we found one that worked—but then we'd be sending an average of 32,000 packets for every successful guess (we're likely to get our answer after searching about half the sample set). This is completely infeasible. However, if we also send a decent number of Doomed SYN packets, they'll each occupy a different source port number on the NAT's unified IP and will each qualify as a successful match for our SYM|ACKs to mesh with.

How many packets would be necessary? Surprisingly few. We're looking for a collision among 65,000 possibilities; according to cryptographic theory, we only need to search through the square root of all possible options before we have a greater than 50 percent chance of coming across a matching pair. (This is known as the Birthday Paradox, so named because it means that a room with twenty people has a greater than fifty percent chance of having two people with the same birthday. This violates expectations—those we meet have a 1/365 chance of sharing our birthday—but is reasonably logical, because the more people are in a room, the more birthdays there are to match.) So, with Alice dooming 256 SYNs and the broker spoofing 256 SYN|ACKs from Bob, there's a greater than 50 percent chance that Alice will receive a valid SYN|ACK appearing to come from Bob. (Bob will have to suffer through a storm of 255 TCP RSTs, however.)

Of some note is that while the number of packets are large, the size of these packets is absolutely miniscule. With zero payload, a TCP packet is little more than (in *libnet* terms) LIBNET_ETH_H(Ethernet) + LIBNET_IP_H(IP) + LIBNET_TCP_H(TCP) bytes long. That's 14+20+20, or 54 bytes. 256×54 is almost 14K—certainly enormous by handshake standards, but that's smaller than your average image file and it's facilitating an otherwise impossible link. On some Layer-2 networks, such as Ethernet, frames may be padded out to 64 bytes, but the amount is still pretty small.

One very real problem is that we need to be able to know which of the many connections attempted actually resulted in a successful connection. Remember, a NATing firewall will translate back from what the outside world saw into what the private network needs to see—its own private IP, and its own chosen local port number in this case. That means Alice can't just look at the local port number to see which packet made it through. Alice also can't particularly ask the broker—it doesn't know, it sent out a couple hundred packets, how should it know what her firewall liked? The answer must be embedded somewhere in the packet. But where? I nominate the IP ID. A little-used field used to differentiate one IP packet from the next independently of higher layer protocols, it too can range from 0 to 65535. Being little used, it's likely left unmolested by most firewalls, unlike the local port numbers that are getting translated away. So if the IPID is set to the value of the destination port in the SYM|ACK, whichever SYM|ACK gets through will retain the mark that allowed it to pass inside the IP header.

But why do we need to pay so much attention to port numbers? Because unless we can achieve symmetry in port numbers, we're not going to be able to establish a connection. In a normal TCP handshake, the host initiating a connection uses some random source port to connect to a well known destination port, while the host receiving the connection inverts those ports; responses go from well known to random.

Assuming that there was a town in the Midwest called "Normal TCP Handshaking," well, we wouldn't be in Kansas anymore.

Post-handshake, we are absolutely required to achieve mirror symmetry in our port numberings—one host's destination port must be another's source, and vice versa. But past that, things get blurry. We always know what ports we're sending data to, but we don't necessarily know who's listening on them. We're eventually getting handshake data back from a spoofing server, but we're barely able to figure out which of many possible ports we're listening on ourselves—at least from the perspective of the rest of the Net. Choice isn't even an option here; we're lucky to have a link at all. Most problematically, the harder we have to fight to receive a successful SYM|ACK to our source port, the more important it is that the destination port we chose originally matches a source port the other side was able to acquire on their firewall. If they have as much trouble gaining access to a specific source port on the firewall as we do, the number of attempts required to achieve a connection will quickly obviate any chance of a TCP session leaking through. It's all possible, of course—just the odds become astronomically low that the stars and ports will align into a mirror formation. It's a bit like our original circumstance—limited control over our connective domain—down to the more restricted site connecting to the more liberal one.

And the worst part is—if you've got a Cisco PIX firewall without the *norandomseq* option enabled, the sequence numbers that every TCP packet needs to respond to become unpredictable from one session to the next. Because sequence numbers are 32 bits in length, it would require 16 bits of entropy—65,000 attempts—to beat a 50 percent chance at getting that SYM|ACK through. Good luck with that.

One of the biggest questions, of course, remains how these systems might get deployed. Most likely the reason doomed handshaking wasn't developed earlier was, well, it wasn't possible. There are no socket options that let you specify when a packet should expire, let alone ones that specify which exact components of the handshaking to execute as if they were from another host entirely. It wasn't until the mid-to-late 1990s that it became evident that simply hitting a site with a vast number of connection requests (a SYN flood) from non-existent hosts (which don't reply with a RST|ACK) caused most network stacks to completely freeze up. The tools available define the technology. Even though raw packet tools are old hat by now, I still know of no systems that provide a userspace alternative to the kernel for network services. DoxRoute is a start—and indeed, was responsible for realizing the possibilities of highly customizable network traffic. Most likely, the first major systems for doing the kinds of methods discussed in this section will be built with a DoxRoute style *libnet/libpcap* solution, either re-implementing socket calls themselves in userspace or, possibly, ordering the kernel to route some or all traffic into the loopback interface with a userspace shim picking traffic back out, mangling (or encrypting) it, and dumping it manually onto the actual network interface.

As they say, the only constant is change.

Summary

Spoofing is providing false information about your identity in order to gain unauthorized access to systems. The classic example of spoofing is IP spoofing. TCP/IP requires that every host fills in its own source address on packets, and there are almost no measures in place to stop hosts from lying. Spoofing is always intentional. However, the fact that some malfunctions and misconfigurations can cause the exact same effect as an intentional spoof causes difficulty in determining intent. Often, should the rightful administrator of a network or system want to intentionally cause trouble, he usually has a reasonable way to explain it away.

There are *blind spoofing attacks* in which the attacker can only send and has to make assumptions or guesses about replies, and *informed attacks* in which the attacker can monitor, and therefore participate in, bidirectional communications. Theft of all the credentials of a victim (that is, username and password) is not usually considered spoofing, but gives much of the same power.

Spoofing is not always malicious. Some network redundancy schemes rely on automated spoofing in order to take over the identity of a downed server. This is due to the fact that the networking technologies never accounted for the need, and so have a hard-coded idea of one address, one host.

Unlike the human characteristics we use to recognize each other, which we find easy to use, and hard to mimic, computer information is easy to spoof. It can be stored, categorized, copied, and replayed, all perfectly. All systems, whether people or machines interacting, use a capability challenge to determine identity. These capabilities range from simple to complex, and correspondingly from less secure to more secure.

Technologies exist that can help safeguard against spoofing of these capability challenges. These include firewalls to guard against unauthorized transmission, nonreliance on undocumented protocols as a security mechanism (no security through obscurity), and various crypto types to guard to provide differing levels of authentication.

Subtle attacks are far more effective than obvious ones. Spoofing has an advantage in this respect over a straight vulnerability. The concept of spoofing includes pretending to be a trusted source, thereby increasing chances that the attack will go unnoticed.

If the attacks use just occasional induced failures as part of their subtlety, users will often chalk it up to normal problems that occur all the time. By careful application of this technique over time, users' behavior can often be manipulated.

One major class of spoofing attacks disable security, then spoof the channel that informs the user that security has been enabled. By simply drawing the right pixels in the right places, we can make it appear that SSL has been activated. But then, the SSL pixels aren't what really matters—a site just needs to look good. People don't necessarily know that a well designed site could be ripped off by just anyone; most expensive looking things are inherently difficult to duplicate.

When implementing spoofing systems, it's often useful to actually sit down and directly re-implement whatever it is you seek in as simple and straightforward a method as possible, deliberately avoiding much of the excess complexities of the real thing. This way, you may very well achieve capabilities ruled out by the constraints of the legitimate system.

One major capability opened up by a manual approach to packet-based networking is the tantalizing possibility of bridging connections between two hosts that can only initiate connections, never receive them. By dooming outgoing connection initiation attempts to TTL expiration in the middle of the network, and then having a connection broker exploit the surviving entry in the state table, it might be possible to symmetricize two outgoing links. Serious problems arise when NAT comes into the picture and source port selection becomes progressively uncontrollable, though—much more research will be required to determine the best use for the newly discovered techniques.

Identity, intriguingly enough, is both center stage and off in the wings; the single most important standard and the most unrecognized and unappreciated need. It's difficult to find, easy to claim, impossible to prove, but inevitable to believe. You will make mistakes; the question is, will you engineer your systems to survive those mistakes?

I wish you the best of luck with your systems.

Solution Fast Track

What It Means to Spoof

- ☑ Merike Keao: Spoofing attacks are "providing false information about a principal's identity to obtain unauthorized access to a system."

- ☑ Spoofing attacks are active attacks that forge identity; are possible at all layers of communication; possess intent, possibly partial credentials, but not generally full or legitimate access. Spoofing is not betrayal, and it is certainly nothing new.

☑ Spoofing is not always, or even usually, malicious. Several critical network techniques, such as Mainframe/Internet access and the vast majority of Web sites depend on something that in some contexts qualify as spoofing.

Background Theory

☑ Trust is inherent to the human condition, and awareness of the weakness of trust is an ancient discovery dating to the time of Descartes and far beyond.

☑ Trust is necessary and unavoidable—we cannot trust anything, but we cannot trust nothing; we just end up falling back on superstition and convenience. We can't trust everything but we must trust something, so life becomes choosing what to trust.

The Evolution of Trust

☑ Human trust is accidental.

- Speaking accidentally ties our own voice to the words we speak.

- Touch accidentally ties our own fingerprints to the surfaces we touch.

- Travel accidentally ties our appearance to anybody who happens to see us.

☑ Human trust is asymmetric.

- Being able to recognize my voice doesn't mean you can speak with it.

- Being able to recognize my print doesn't mean you can swap fingers.

- Being able to recognize my face doesn't mean you can wear it.

☑ Human trust is universal.

- We don't choose to have a voice, a fingerprint, or a particularly unique face.

☑ We distrust easy-to-copy things, such as catchphrases and clothing.

Establishing Identity within Computer Networking

☑ All bits transmitted throughout computer networks are explicitly chosen and equally visible, recordable, and repeatable, with perfect accuracy.

☑ No accidental transmissions can be trusted, though we can use accidental behavior to surreptitiously discover a remote host's operating environment.

☑ Universal data exchange capacity of legitimate hosts means that we can use asymmetries in our data itself to establish trust with a remote host.

Capability Challenges

☑ **Ability to transmit: "Can it talk to me?"** The domain of firewalls, the concept is untrusted hosts don't even have the ability to transmit data to hosts down the line.

☑ **Ability to respond: "Can it respond to me?"** The first line of defense within many protocols, the concept is untrusted hosts don't receive a token that allows a response from the trusted host.

☑ **Ability to encode: "Can it speak my language?"** The most dangerous line of defense, in that it fails catastrophically when depended upon, the concept is that untrusted hosts don't know how to speak the protocol itself (though there's nothing particularly secret about what is being said).

☑ **Ability to prove a shared secret: "Does it share a secret with me?"** A very common line of defense, passwords fall within this category. Unfortunately, this collapses quickly once the passwords are shared.

☑ **Ability to prove a private keypair: "Can I recognize your voice?"** Used by PGP and SSL, this layer allows public key material to be shared while the private and security critical operations of decryption and signing may stay safely archived.

☑ **Ability to prove an identity keypair: "Is its identity independently represented in my keypair?"** Used by SSH and DROP, this prevents future compromises from leaving vulnerable present data—the only thing kept around for long periods of time is a key representing identity; everything else—including the key used to encrypt the symmetric keys—is shuffled.

Desktop Spoofs

☑ Auto-updating apps puncture holes in firewalls and run code from untrusted hosts, often without any verification at all.

☑ The alternative can be no patches and permanent vulnerability of client systems.

Impacts of Spoofs

☑ A vulnerability takes advantage of the difference between what something *is* and what something *appears to be.* A spoof, on the other hand, takes advantage of the difference between *who is sending something* and *who appears to have sent it.* The difference is critical, because at its core, the most brutal of spoofing attacks don't just mask the identity of an attacker; they mask the fact that an attack even took place.

☑ By causing intermittent failures in non-compromised systems, users can be redirected towards systems that are compromised. The spoof is that they believe the instabilities are inherent in the system, and the choice to switch is their own.

☑ SSL may be spoofed quite effectively through a three-part process: Expanding the URL to obfuscate the actual address in a pop-up dialog box, manually creating a status bar with the "SSL Lock" enabled, and encapsulating arbitrary but graphically trustworthy content in a top frame. Further damage may be done by specifying a size for a full-screen pop-up box, which will then be rendered without any operating system supplied borders or "chrome." This chrome may then be re-added according to the whim of the remote server.

Down and Dirty: Engineering Spoofing Systems

☑ Raw access to network resources, with minimal restrictions on what may be placed on the wire, can often yield surprisingly effective results when trying to design systems that break rules rather than follow them excessively.

☑ Libnet proves an effective, cross-platform means of generating and sending arbitrary (*spoofed*) packets onto the wire, while libpcap provides the opposite functionality of receiving those packets off the wire. The combination works quite well.

☑ A basic router can be projected onto the network from userspace by answering ARP requests for a "nonexistent" IP with an ARP reply serving a "nonexistent" MAC address, which is then sniffed for incoming packets. Ping packets addressed to the router may be shuffled in place and sent back out to the pinger, and anything else addressed to the proper MAC address may be considered destined for an alternate network. This is, of course, a gross oversimplification, but it's an infrastructure that may be built upon.

Frequently Asked Questions

The following Frequently Asked Questions, answered by the authors of this book, are designed to both measure your understanding of the concepts presented in this appendix and to assist you with real-life implementation of these concepts. To have your questions about this appendix answered by the author, browse to **www.syngress.com/solutions** and click on the **"Ask the Author"** form.

Q: Are there any good solutions that can be used to prevent spoofing?

A: There are solutions that can go a long way toward preventing specific types of spoofing. For example, implemented properly, SSH is a good remote-terminal solution. However, nothing is perfect. SSH is susceptible to a MITM attack when first exchanging keys, for example. If you get your keys safely the first time, it will warn after that if the keys change. The other big problem with using cryptographic solutions is centralized key management or control, as discussed in the chapter.

Q: Is there any way to check whether I'm receiving spoofed packets?

A: Generally, spoofed packets are being sent blindly, so the "source host" will suspiciously act like it isn't actually receiving any replies. (Funny that—it isn't!) But a brilliant method was discovered a while ago for determining, simply and reasonably reliably, whether a received packet was spoofed from another sender. Despoof, developed by the infamous Simple Nomad, operates on the simple presumption that an attacker doesn't know the legitimate number of network hops the actual host would need to traverse in order to actually send you packets. Because most routing on the Internet is reasonably symmetrical, measuring the number of hops to a given host will given an adequate measure of how many hops are required for a response. (Failing that, simply pinging a host and monitoring the amount the TTL was decremented on the packet's return trip will result in a value of the number of hops away some "source" might be.) Now, here's what's interesting. The spoofer can't test the network in-between you and the host he is spoofing as. By comparing a test packet's hops traveled (*ORIGINAL_TTL-TTL_OF_PACKET*, usually some offset from a power of two minus a number between one and twelve) to the established number of hops that actually should have been traveled, it's possible to detect that a packet took the wrong route from source to destination and was thus possibly spoofed. Interestingly enough, it's possible to get some knowledge of who the spoofer is, because the number of hops traveled will reflect *his* network path. Of course, it's more than possible for the spoofer to falsify his original TTL value so as to throw off your network monitors—but unless the attacker knows specifically to do so, he most likely won't (if for no other reason, his traffic then becomes obvious in midroute as being a network attack; it's a matter of choosing your risks, of course). You can find Despoof at http://razor.bindview.com/tools/desc/despoof_readme.html ; it's truly an interesting tool.

Q: How can attackers redirect my network traffic, so as to "seem" to be other hosts?

A: The easiest and most powerful methods involve taking over a host on the same physical subnet. Outside of subnets, some rare cases of network hijacking are possible by compromising intermediary routers—but most often, what is done centers on DNS servers. David Uelevich, founder of Everydns.Net, writes: "When looking up a record for a domain on a nameserver, it is usually the nameserver on the client's network which does the lookup and in turn passes the response to the client. The problem with DNS poisoning occurs when the clients nameserver accepts incorrect information from a remote server which is either deliberately or accidentally handing out responses which alter the client nameserver's behavior." Remember—IPs aren't usually directly addressed (indeed, with IPV6 they're almost impossible to be addressed at all directly; IPV6 addresses are four times longer than IPV4 IPs!). Usually they're referred to by DNS name. A compromise of the mapping between DNS name and IP address would have the same effect of breaking the mapping between your friend and his phone number—but while you're smart enough to realize the person on the other end of the line isn't your friend, your computer usually wouldn't be, unless perhaps SSL was being used for that specific connection attempt—in which case, the attacker could legitimately reroute you to your actual destination as a broker.

Q: Is SSL itself spoof-proof?

A: As far as it is implemented correctly, it's a sound protocol (at least we think so right now). However, that's not where you would attack. SSL is based on the Public Key Infrastructure (PKI) signing chain. If you were able to slip your special copy of Netscape in when someone was auto-updating, you could include your own signing key for "VeriSign," and pretend to be just about any HTTPS Web server in the world. Alternatively, a wide range of international and mostly unknown companies are trusted just as much as VeriSign to keep their signing keys secure; it is questionable whether so many provides are as protective as VeriSign claims to be about their private keys. A compromise of any of these international providers would be as equally damaging as a compromise of VeriSign's key; anyone could spoof being anyone. Also troubling, of course, is that SSL completely fails to be forward secret. A future compromise of a key that's highly secure today would immediately rend today's traffic public tomorrow. This is a ridiculous weakness that has no place in a major cryptographic standard.

Index

SYNGRESS SOLUTIONS...